STALIN AS WARLORD

STALIN AS WARLORD

ALFRED J. RIEBER

YALE UNIVERSITY PRESS
NEW HAVEN AND LONDON

For information about this and other Yale University Press publications, please contact:
U.S. Office: sales.press@yale.edu   yalebooks.com
Europe Office: sales@yaleup.co.uk   yalebooks.co.uk

Set in Minion Pro by IDSUK (DataConnection) Ltd
Printed in Great Britain by TJ Books, Padstow, Cornwall

Library of Congress Control Number: 2022939648

ISBN 978-0-300-26461-6

A catalogue record for this book is available from the British Library.

10 9 8 7 6 5 4 3 2 1

For Marsha, toujours

There can be no revolutionary action without revolutionary theory.
Lenin, *What Is to Be Done?*

Grey is theory, my friend; but green is the tree of life.
Lenin, quoting Goethe's *Faust*

You have to take Stalin according to periods of time; he was different. After the war you have one Stalin – before the war another. Between nineteen thirty-two and the forties still another. Before 1932 he was completely different. He changed. I saw no fewer than five or six Stalins.
Kaganovich, interviewed by Feliks Chuev

CONTENTS

ILLUSTRATIONS

PLATES

ACKNOWLEDGEMENTS

The sources for this book were gathered over many years, often for other projects and purposes. My initial interest in the war on the eastern front stemmed from the suggestion of my beloved fifth-grade teacher, Mrs Fass, to start a scrapbook on the conflict. Over the next four years I filled twenty-seven such books with clippings from newspapers and illustrated magazines of texts, maps and images, many related to the Russian experience in the war. I continued this interest throughout college and graduate school, making my first visit in January 1956 to the Soviet Union, where I encountered first-hand the devasting consequences of the conflict on ordinary people's lives. As a participant in the first year of the US–Soviet cultural exchange in 1958–59, these impressions were deepened by personal contacts and lasting friendships with Soviet citizens of several generations and different ethnic origins who had survived the war. I am very much indebted to them for sharing their experiences and memories, however painful they were. In the absence of access to archives, I sought to shed light indirectly on Stalin's role in my doctoral dissertation, revised as a monograph, *Stalin and the French Communist Party, 1941–1947* (Columbia University Press, 1962). It was only after the opening of the archives in 1991 that I was able to return to the subject that has preoccupied me ever since.

My appreciation for research support extends, therefore, to a large number of sponsors, including IREX, the American Council of Learned Societies, the Ford Foundation, the Collegium Budapest, St Antony's

College, Oxford, and several research grants from the Central European University in Budapest. My thanks go to Ulf Brunnbauer, Oleg Budnitskii and Silvio Pons for invitations to deliver papers at the Leibniz Institute for East and Southeast European Studies at the University of Regensburg, on Stalinism and War at the Higher School of Economics in Moscow, and the Conference on Rethinking Communist History at the Fondazione Gramsci in Rome. I am especially grateful to the staff of the Central European University Library, in particular to Vit Lucas, who tracked down with great energy and ingenuity numerous articles and collections that otherwise would have been unavailable to me. In Russia, I benefited from the assistance of archivists at the Gosudarstvennyi arkhiv rossiiskoi federatsii, Arkhiv vneshnei politiki rossiiskoi federatsii and Rossiiskii gosudarstvennyi arkhiv sotsial'no-politicheskoi istorii. I am indebted to Geoffrey Roberts, who encouraged me at an early stage in the writing and suggested the title; to Mark Harrison who answered questions and helped further my research into the career of Nikolai Voznesensky; to Giovanni Cadioli for sharing with me his research on Voznesensky; to Loren Graham who read and commented on an early draft of the chapter on the scientific and technical intelligentsia; to David Holloway for insights into Soviet intelligence and recent references to the atomic bomb project; to James Heinzen for references; to Marsha Siefert for her insights into Soviet cultural affairs, her unfailing tolerance with my long preoccupation with Stalin, her rapid response to my frantic calls for computer first aid, and her abiding love. The two anonymous reviewers for Yale University Press offered stimulating suggestions. My editor Joanna Godfrey was supportive at all stages, providing a critical assessment of the entire manuscript. The entire production staff of Yale University Press contributed in many ways to improving the quality of the book, with special thanks to Jacob Blandy for his meticulous copy-editing. For the errors which may remain, I alone am responsible.

PREFACE

It happens, on occasion, that a historian accustomed to toiling in the archives will be struck by a small incident that sheds more light on the murky world of politics than any single document. In my case such an incident occurred many years ago at an intimate dinner party in Moscow where the guest of honour was Ivy Litvinov, the English-born author and wife of the former commissar of foreign affairs, Maksim Litvinov. I had brought her as a gift a few novels by contemporary American writers. Her first words to me were: 'I hope you are not one of those who are fooled by this place.' Then she examined the books, carefully reading the first page of each one before setting it aside. 'Oh,' she said, 'these are not for me. Let's talk about Jane Austen.' In the course of a rather one-sided conversation, she mentioned that she used to read Austen during bridge games when she ended up, more often than not, as 'the dummy partner'. The other three habitual players were her husband Maksim, Petr Kapitsa and 'Jenő' Varga. She did not say, but I wondered what these friends had in common besides being devotees of an English card game. Upon reflection, it became clear. They had all spent years of their life abroad: Litvinov before the First World War as a self-imposed revolutionary exile in England (where he had met and married Ivy); Kapitsa, another exile in England, where he spent seven years at Rutherford's laboratory at Cambridge between the wars; Varga another exile, but from Hungary, where he had been a leading figure in the abortive revolution of 1919 before fleeing to the Soviet Union. In the course of their careers, they had all served Stalin loyally, Litvinov as a diplomat, Kapitsa as a scientist and Varga as an economist. But they were also from time to time forthright critics of his policies. In the end, they had all suffered demotion; Litvinov fired as foreign commissar, Kapitsa dismissed as head of the Institute of Physics and Varga removed as head of the Institute of World Politics and World Economics, which was then abolished after the war. They had all come under heavy attack on ideological grounds from their opponents in the Communist Party. Yet they were never arrested; they all survived. As I stepped out into that cold winter night in Moscow, I thought 'How extraordinary!' The diplomat, the scientist and the economist, all loyal to Stalin, but critical of policies he adopted, belonging to categories most distrusted by Stalin: Litvinov Jewish and married to a foreigner, Varga Jewish and a foreigner, and Kapitsa a longtime resident abroad and admirer of Great Britain. All of them demoted from their honoured positions yet survivors to the natural end of their lives. How could these apparent contradictions and inconsistencies be resolved? The search for answers led me to the idea of the paradox of Stalin's power.

INTRODUCTION
THE PARADOX OF POWER

Stalin remains one of the most divisive and controversial figures of modern history among both scholars and the general public in today's Russia and throughout the rest of the world. By a majority in the Western world he is condemned as a brutal dictator responsible for the enslavement and death of millions of people. But there are others who celebrate his role as the great modernizer of Russia and as the triumphal leader in the Soviet victory over fascism in the Second World War.[1] The central argument of this book attributes this divergence of opinion to the deep contradictions between Stalin's creative and destructive impulses, which combined to produce a paradox of power.[2]

In this he resembled two of his tsarist predecessors whom he most admired, Ivan the Terrible and Peter the Great. In portraying Peter, the great pre-revolutionary Russian historian Vasily Kliuchevsky compared the tsar to the captain of a ship-of-state who sought to rebuild it entirely even as he sailed it into the storm. Moshe Lewin put it more succinctly when he wrote that Stalin engaged in pulling down the old edifice of the state while simultaneously erecting a new one. The focus of this book is the period when the paradoxical character of his state-building met its greatest challenge during the years of preparing for war, fighting it and winning the peace.

The contradictions that helped shape Stalin's dualist worldview as creator and destroyer owed much to his experiences in the revolutionary underground of Georgia under tsarist rule and his active participation in the revolution of 1917, the civil war and creation of the Soviet state. He built his reputation as a youthful revolutionary on his skills as an organizer, propagandist and agitator within a disciplined party committed to a rational transformation of the world guided by Marxist theory. At the same time, his daily immersion in a secretive, conspiratorial world, his suffering in prisons and many years in lonely exile under harsh conditions turned a lively and convivial youth into a suspicious, devious, deceptive and tough-minded man.[3] These contradictory elements showed up in his paradoxical style of governance, which set irrational distrust against rational decision-making, leading to the purges of comrades also committed to building socialism. In his revolutionary years, Stalin had also developed a dual cultural identity between his native Georgia and his adopted Russia, which again gave him an appreciation – unlike his fellow Bolsheviks – of the importance of maintaining a creative tension in a multi-national state under Russian political hegemony. As the following chapters show, once in power, he often sacrificed the creative part of the tension – the cultural autonomy of the non-Russian nationalities – to the security interests of the state in conducting foreign policy and imposing political and ideological uniformity in domestic policy.[4] These were the contradictions that contributed to the paradoxical character of his rule.

From his experiences as a political commissar during the civil war and intervention (1918–21), Stalin became convinced of the close interaction of foreign and domestic policies based on his perception of the links between class enemies at home and hostile capitalist powers encircling the fledgling Soviet state. In his view, war together with the class struggle had become the twin engines of revolution. During the civil war, he already began to express doubts in the abilities of foreign communists to carry out their revolutions without the assistance of the Red Army. With the establishment of the Soviet Union, he declared that world revolution depended upon the building of socialism in Russia, and not the reverse, as had been accepted dogma.[5] Classical Marxism had portrayed the revolution as proceeding first in advanced capitalist countries where a skilled and literate working class had become the majority of the population and the social foundation for building socialism. But Russia in the 1920s was still an agrarian society where the proletariat, a small minority even before the revolution, had been further reduced by civil war. Thus, Stalin was forced to mobilize and transform peasants, the most backward social class in the population, to become in one generation the standard-bearers of socialist construction and the commanders of his armies. This paradoxical situation between what was modern and what remained archaic in the economy created many anomalies.[6] By standing Marx on his head, Stalin remained largely indifferent to – and often disdainful of – the activities of the Comintern. Paradoxically, as we shall see, he sacrificed foreign communists to Soviet interests in the name of pursuing the triumph of the socialist revolution.

Up to the Second World War, when he assumed the title of marshal and donned a suitable military uniform for his meetings with Churchill and Roosevelt, he represented himself in speech and dress – again uniquely among his Bolshevik colleagues – as a man of the people; he carried a peasant passport before the revolution. Yet he arbitrarily and ruthlessly imposed collectivization on the peasantry, dooming hundreds of thousands to deportation or death.[7] Collectivization was designed to secure state control over the production of grain and other agricultural products for the purposes of feeding the growing urban population of workers and providing a surplus for export. But the hasty and badly prepared implementation contributed to the famine of 1931–33 and the loss of the most enterprising and productive elements in the countryside.[8]

As the underlying theme of Part I, 'Preparing for War', I stress the paradoxical character of Stalin's actions in building and dismantling the basic components of a new state order. Once he had achieved his consolidation of power, Stalin's main goal was to launch the Soviet Union on the path of industrialization through planning, which in his hands was beset by chaos. The first two five-year plans (1929–32 and 1933–37) concentrated on building a heavy industrial base necessary to develop a modern armaments industry in anticipation of war. The third five-year plan (1938–41) began the completion of the shift but was interrupted by the war.[9] The rational allocation of resources, setting of production targets, fixing prices and wages were, however, from the beginning overly centralized and bureaucratized.[10] It was further undercut by Stalin's arbitrary interference in demanding accelerated tempos that were responsible for shoddy products, mistakes leading to serious damages and accidents which were then blamed on sabotage. The model for subsequent show trials was first applied in 1928 in the Shakhty mining region of the Donbas, where accusations of 'wrecking' were levelled against the internal class enemy, the 'bourgeois engineers', and the external enemy of the capitalist world, in this case German intelligence.[11] A similar case was fabricated to blame the engineers for failures on the Turkestan–Siberia Railway project in Central Asia.[12]

These themes served Stalin as the leitmotif of the Great Terror which he launched in 1934, following the assassination of Sergei Kirov, his close associate and member of the Politburo. Even as he assumed the pose of an intellectual with aspirations and claims as a Marxist theorist, he expressed contempt for intellectuals and inflicted severe punishments up to and including executions for the expression of opinions contrary to what he euphemistically called the 'Bolshevik spirit' (meaning, of course, his own). The victims of the purges included leading members of the Communist Party intelligentsia, who like him had been devoted disciples of Lenin, committed to the same goals of building socialism.[13] At the same time that he was constructing the foundations of socialism and a great power capable of fighting the war he assumed must come, Stalin paradoxically weakened the forces necessary to fight it to the point where enormous sacrifices and terrible losses – a tragic-heroic effort – were necessary to expel the aggressor, drive him back to his lair and destroy him.

The invasion of the Soviet Union in June 1941 by Nazi Germany and its allies posed the most serious challenge to Stalin's policies of state-building and exposed the flaws in his system engendered by their deep contradictions. Although he had long anticipated war, he was taken by surprise by the timing of the attack. A series of disasters followed. By the late autumn of 1941, Kiev had fallen, Leningrad was invested and Moscow under attack. The magnitude of these disasters was unprecedented. Of the standing army that numbered on the eve of the war 5 million men, almost 4 million were killed, missing or in German captivity by the end of the year.[14] Russia had never before lost so many men and surrendered so much territory in one year during the course of any war it had fought in the previous 300 years.

Yet these disasters did not lead to a complete collapse and surrender. Under Stalin's leadership the Soviet Union overcame the initial surprise, confusion and losses. Four years after the terrible defeats of 1941, a wholly new Red Army, completely re-equipped under an almost entirely different military command, destroyed the last elements of the German army, seized Hitler's capital and forced the Führer's suicide. The battle of Berlin dwarfed any other land battle ever fought, except for Stalingrad. Two months later, the Far Eastern Front of the Red Army cut through the Imperial Japanese Kwantung Army like butter, swiftly occupying all of Manchuria. The Soviet Union emerged from the long ordeal as the only great power on the Eurasian continent. Germany and Japan, its longtime rivals for control over its European and Asian borderlands, were utterly defeated. Tempered by four years of continuous fighting, the Red Army had developed into the world's largest army, equipped with the most numerous artillery and tank forces. Its victorious banners fluttered over Berlin, Vienna, Tehran and Port Arthur. Soviet international prestige had soared to its greatest heights. The communist parties of Europe and East Asia had grown from isolated, often illegal and demoralized sects into major contenders for political power not only in the territories occupied by the Red Army but in France, Italy, China and Southeast Asia as well. To all appearances it was a great, almost miraculous recovery. How can it be explained?

Most accounts fasten on Stalin as the key. Glorified in the postwar decade, his reputation suffered an eclipse under Khrushchev and then enjoyed a partial revival under Brezhnev, plummeted to new depths in the era of perestroika only to enjoy another resurrection under Vladimir Putin.[15] Stripped of the polemical verbiage, his role as a wartime leader still remains ambiguous and controversial. Much of the problem in evaluating his contribution lies in the contrast between the magnitude of his errors and the steadying power of his will, between the role of coercion and the spontaneous upsurge of patriotism in mobilizing the population. Finally, the difficulty remains of separating his accomplishments from those of his subordinates down the long chain of command to the people at the front, in the factories, on the kolkhozes.

The responses of Stalin, his lieutenants and the mass of the population to the many challenges of waging modern warfare were deeply shot through with contradictions. More than anyone else, Stalin personified the paradox of power that characterized Soviet society during the entire wartime experience. His miscalculations were largely to blame for the initial defeats and retreats that required three years to recoup. Among the population exposed to the brunt of the fighting, there were large-scale defections and desertions, especially in the early months of the war, and anti-Soviet movements lasting throughout the conflict and into the postwar era. But Stalin was able, perhaps by a narrow margin, to maintain control over the administrative and military levers of command and gradually to mobilize most of the country behind him.

The following account sheds new light on the contributions of the elements in Soviet society that he had sought to mobilize in the prewar era to build the socialist state and prepare the country for war. The psychology of politics in his new order combined direction and guidance from above with initiatives from below that matched the expectations of the leadership in what one Soviet historian has called the 'shock-brigade' response.[16] The outbreak of war triggered creative responses in the working class, among the military High Command, the institutes of the Academy of Sciences, the unions of writers, musicians and architects, the church, the Komsomol and the partisan movement in its early stage. Triumphant, Stalin paid a brief tribute to their contribution and then turned against many of those who by their actions had exhibited a measure of independent thinking or who threatened in his mind to overshadow his leadership as supreme warlord. Yet, as the final chapter shows, even during his declining years, when the morbid-pathological impulses appeared to dominate, he retained sufficient insight into the need to retain or recruit individuals with special talents who had proved their worth in the furnace of war to pursue his efforts to rebuild the edifice of the state and defend it against what he believed to be a new set of enemies.

Part II analyzes Stalin's reaction to the German invasion as he moved swiftly on two levels. At the apex of power, he ordered a drastic centralization while maintaining his full control over decision-making in the military as well as in the civilian sphere. At the same time, he sought to mobilize all elements of the population by orchestrating a mixture of familiar and new themes in Soviet propaganda and expanding the system of material rewards. He welcomed the creative responses to his appeals from the leaders and rank and file of the army, defence industries, the scientific and technical intelligentsia and the world of culture. But he set limits to their freedom of action and was quick to employ the well-honed instruments of repression when he believed these limits had been exceeded or scapegoats had to be found for his own mistakes or those of others. Mass mobilization of people and resources plus draconian measures and self-sacrifice had won the war, but was it a Pyrrhic victory?

Part III portrays Stalin's renewed mobilization policies in order to resume the march to socialism, rebuild the shattered economy, regain control over the intelligentsia, reorganize the international communist movement and consolidate his claim to be the leader of an emerging world power. It seeks to demonstrate how, once again, Stalin resorted to policies that were deeply paradoxical. Even before the fighting had ended, he began to turn against some of the architects of victory. Constructive and destructive impulses continued to coexist in winning the peace.

PART I

PREPARING FOR WAR

CHAPTER 1

MOBILIZATION AND REPRESSION AT THE CENTRE

By mid-1940 the apparent external successes of Stalin's foreign policy rested upon the uncertain foundations of a political system in turmoil. Stalin had kept the Soviet Union out of the war. When the policy of collective security appeared to falter, running the risk of exposing the country to the brunt of the war against the Axis powers, he had switched to a policy of accommodation with Germany and Japan. The Molotov-Ribbentrop Non-Aggression Pact in 1939 provided for spheres of influence between the Soviet Union and Nazi Germany. The Soviet-Japanese Neutrality Pact in 1941 accomplished the same end in East Asia for the Soviet Union and Japan. As a result he had gained valuable time and space with which to strengthen the country's defences, and had evaded an open conflict with Britain. At home, Stalin had eliminated every challenge to his personal dictatorship and had secured exclusive control over the conduct of foreign policy; he had tamed the Comintern. The danger no longer existed that foreign communist parties might, through a policy of revolutionary adventurism, drag the Soviet Union into an international conflict. Stalin had also undertaken a massive industrialization of the country that laid the foundations for a modern armaments industry. These were all extraordinary achievements. Yet the means he had chosen to obtain his ends threatened to undermine the very security of the state that he sought to guarantee.

The emerging Stalinist system of the thirties was rent by severe internal contradictions. Stalin had imposed political unity on the Communist Party by tearing it apart, first eliminating his rivals and then turning against many who had supported him in his struggle for power. Simultaneously, he launched a revolution from above, aiming to transform agriculture, industry and cultural life by a series of arbitrary acts accompanied by large-scale coercion. It was a leap in the dark taken without a clear understanding of its fearful consequences for the stability of society and the institutions of state power. From the outset it bore the imprint of Stalin's dark personality imposed upon the unfinished blueprint of a modernizing society.[1] As Stalin and his lieutenants demolished the old institutions, they strove simultaneously to construct a new order even before the ground had been cleared. This was not anything as simple as a Thermidorian Reaction against the excesses of the revolution: nor was it a case of the outsider become insider or the rebel tamed by the responsibilities of power. Rather, the revolutionaries themselves were tearing down a system, under the banner of the New Economic Policy that they themselves had helped to create, in the name of building socialism. Through means of mass mobilization, they involved in the process large numbers of people outside the power structure. This dual revolution from above and below had no precedent in modern Europe. Never before had a ruling elite undertaken to remake the social institutions through which they ruled and replace them with something different; never before had a regime in power unleashed a civil war against elements of its own population and then invited the population to participate in the struggle by denouncing their fellow citizens. The pace – indeed the fury – of the process reflected in part the demonic personality of its leader. The unpredictable, often irrational demands that Stalin imposed upon his subordinates as well as the population at large ran counter to the practice and theory of orderly planning upon which the whole tradition of European social democracy rested.

Yet, as scholars have recently pointed out, not all his policies struck a new note. There were elements of continuity linking aspects of Stalin's state terrorism to earlier European and Russian population policies emerging in the late nineteenth century and intensifying during the 'epoch of violence' from 1905 to 1920.[2] There was even a rough parallel between the military buildup by the tsarist government and its anticipation of a war in the years before 1914 and similar phenomena in the Soviet Union in the years before 1941. But the differences in the pursuit of these policies were also striking.

'The Soviet preoccupation with war', in the words of John Erickson, engendered a unique response.[3] The other was to create the organizations to give this propaganda institutional form.[4]

MOBILIZATION AS A TECHNIQUE OF GOVERNANCE

Robert Tucker provided a valuable insight into the Soviet system by describing it as 'a revolutionary mass movement regime under single party auspices'.[5] As a technique of governance, mass mobilization developed as a response to a fundamental dilemma facing the Bolshevik Party once it had taken power and emerged triumphant from the civil war of 1918–20. The party represented a minority of the population in 1917 and lost part of its proletarian base and many of its leading cadres in the struggle to retain power. With diminished forces, it faced the necessity of resolving two interconnected problems basic to its continued existence as a revolutionary party. The first was the task of building socialism in a poor, agrarian country with the majority of the predominantly peasant population opposed to this aim, hence to be regarded as an internal enemy. Second, revolution having failed elsewhere in Europe, the new state was isolated in the international community. It was encircled by capitalist powers, many of which had participated in the intervention to overthrow the Bolshevik regime, hence to be regarded as an external enemy. Although disparate in their aims, the internal and external enemies had been linked in their common opposition to Bolshevism. This linkage continued to exist in the minds of the Bolshevik leadership. The problems then were: how to win over the population to the goals of building socialism; how to defend against the threat posed by the outside powers; and how to break the connection between them.

The Bolsheviks were largely responsible for creating the dilemmas facing them. To justify the deviation from Marx's theory of revolution, Lenin had developed his own theory of revolution which proposed that backward agrarian Russia was the weakest link in the capitalist chain and thus ripest for revolution, particularly under the strain of modern war. Together with Trotsky he further argued that, once the revolution had broken out in Russia, it would trigger revolution in the advanced capitalist countries where a highly conscious, numerous and well-organized proletariat would come to the aid of embattled revolutionary forces in Russia and complete the socialist revolution. Once these speculations had failed to yield practical results, there was no question of renouncing power; there remained the burning question of how to construct a different road to socialism relying heavily on the resources of the Soviet state and society.

The internal party debates on this issue drew upon two earlier approaches to revolutionary tactics that had split the Russian Social Democratic Labour Party into two main factions (the Bolsheviks and Mensheviks) in the years before the revolution of 1917 and continued to divide the Bolsheviks – albeit less sharply – along factional lines. To reduce them to their most essential elements, these approaches have been defined as consciousness and spontaneity. In the Bolshevik debates, consciousness referred to the active intervention of the party in instilling the masses both with socialist values and a purposeful drive to achieve them – the Leninist concept of the party as the vanguard of the proletariat transposed to the entire population through mass mobilization. Spontaneity implied employing economic incentives and spreading literacy and specialized education to advance the socialist agenda and welcoming initiatives from below by the creative forces in the population embracing the same goals.

The two approaches were by no means exclusive. They were, in fact, combined in different proportions at different times. Instilling consciousness from above had a coercive side to it and a tendency to accelerate tempos of development. After 1929 Stalin resorted more and more to coercive measures of mass mobilization, launching simultaneously forced collectivization and rapid industrialization.

Collectivization involved forcing the peasants into collective farms (kolkhozes) by depriving them of their private holdings and livestock, which were placed under centralized management, and imposing annual production quotas of grain for deliveries to the state. More well-to-do peasants (those owning a few more acres of land and some livestock) were denounced as kulaks (literally 'tight-fisted ones'), an old term resurrected and applied in an arbitrary and indiscriminate way to identify alleged opponents of collectivization. The kolkhozes were required to hire agricultural machinery from machine-tractor stations run by urban workers. In addition, state-owned farms (sovkhozes), run on the lines of factories, a few of which had been established after the revolution, were expanded. They were to serve as the final form of agriculture in a communist society.

Together with coercion from above, Stalin and the Soviet leadership sought to guide the spontaneous responses to socialist goals from below. They undertook a programme of mobilizing the entire population through organizing 'campaigns' around well-defined themes promoting socialism, conducted through the press, by wall posters, on the radio, and in the cinema. To extol the values of discipline and self-sacrifice, mass demonstrations were organized on holidays, paramilitary organizations of youth were created, most notably the Communist Youth League (Komsomol), and schools where practical knowledge and patriotic values were taught were opened on a co-educational basis. The totality of these efforts has deservedly earned for Stalinist Russia the sobriquet 'the propaganda state'.[6]

Shortly after the Bolsheviks took power in November 1917, they confronted a problem they had not anticipated in their zeal to launch agrarian Russia on the path to socialism, a problem that immensely complicated the task and influenced – not to say distorted – the trajectory of their politics. Their revolution almost immediately met with a formidable array of domestic and foreign enemies. They were obliged then to combine mobilization with militarization. Under Stalin, this combination was to become a permanent feature of Soviet society. The first attempt to link a military command policy with the nationalization of industry, together with forcible requisition of grain from the peasantry to guarantee a reliable source of bread for the burgeoning working class, was undertaken under conditions of conflict and foreign intervention during the civil war from 1918 to 1920. This was aptly called War Communism. The connection between the external threat and resistance in the countryside, particularly in the borderlands, was to remain a constant source of grave anxiety among the leadership. The attempt to break the link under War Communism failed; a renewed assault during the war against the peasantry during collectivization from 1929 to 1932 was only partially successful.[7] The connection revived under the extraordinary conditions in the occupied territories during the Second World War.

The critical years 1926–27 witnessed a dramatic transformation in the campaign by the party leadership to combine several techniques of mobilization relating to preparations for war. The impetus came from the shock of a real war scare.[8] Ever sensitive to indications of Western machinations to weaken or threaten the fledgling Soviet state, at the Fifteenth Party Congress in December 1927 Soviet leaders expressed serious concern about the dangers arising from the activities of the French and British governments in organizing an anti-Soviet bloc in Eastern Europe. The Comintern picked up the issue. Politburo member and General Secretary of the Comintern Executive Nikolai Bukharin sought to exploit the war scare as a means of restoring the Comintern's position as a major instrument of Soviet foreign policy. He argued that the international communist movement could best defend the Soviet Union against the threat of war by intensifying the class struggle, strikes, intensive agitation and propaganda in the imperialist countries.[9] *Pravda* printed inflammatory articles, predicting the imminence of an attack from abroad, and a wave of panic hit the Soviet public. At first Stalin reassured the country (the first of the many poses he adopted to enhance his statesmanlike status). Already in May 1927 a series of unco-ordinated anti-Soviet provocations set alarm bells ringing. The British broke off diplomatic relations, the French terminated negotiations over debt repayment and the Chinese Nationalists attacked the Chinese Communist Party. The Soviet leadership seized the opportunity to exploit the charged atmosphere by associating the danger of war with the policies of the Left Opposition faction of the party, which continued to agitate for immediate international revolution A rising tide of xenophobia was set in motion, coupled with renewed fears that the deterioration of relations with the West jeopardized any hopes of obtaining the credits from abroad to finance industrialization.[10] Stalin now shifted his position to embrace the idea of autarchy. The completion of the big metallurgical plants in the newly constructed industrial towns of Magnitogorsk, Kuznetsk, Zaporozhe and others, plus advances in the production of machines and metalworking plants, contributed to a sharp decrease in the dependence of the economy on the importation of capital goods. By 1937, just a decade later, the basic tools for the defence industry, if not all the most specialized equipment, was produced in the Soviet Union.[11] (A notable example of the ability of Soviet designers to convert and improve the weapons design of foreign models was the purchase of the tank invented by the American J. Walter Christie and its subsequent modification providing the chassis for the famous T-34 tank.)[12] However, the large budgetary allocations for weapons do not give a full picture of actual implementation of the spending targets. The second five-year plan (1933–37), according to Lennart Samuelson, 'did not include rearmament, in the sense of massive equipping of the army with modern weapons'. But the basic heavy industries in mining, iron, steel and light metals had been established. By 1938, under another cloud of gathering war, the third five-year plan repaired that shortcoming, taking into account the likelihood of a war against either Germany or Japan – or both in the worst-case scenario.[13] The leap forward in mobilizing industry for war ran parallel to the mobilization of human resources for defence.

Such efforts were already under way in the mid-1920s, led by the commissar of war Mikhail Frunze and the deputy chief of staff Mikhail Tukhachevsky, to instil military values in the population and support economic sectors with military potential. They promoted a network of voluntary associations that popularized aviation and gave instructions on chemical warfare among civilians.[14] As the imagined war clouds gathered in January 1927, these organizations were unified for 'civil defence' under the Society for the Promotion of Defence, Aviation and Chemical Engineering (Osoaviakhim), which numbered 5 million people within a few years. The mobilization campaign reached its climax in July 1927 during 'Defence Week' with a massive effort to involve the civilian population in military exercises and to spread Bolshevik propaganda, especially in rural areas. The results were not encouraging; instead of being enlightened and aroused by patriotic sentiments, a wave of panic swept through the population, according to reports by the secret police and the Political Administration of the Red Army.[15]

At the height of the second wave of the war scare in April 1927, the Presidium of the Supreme Soviet of the National Economy declared: 'The production capacity which the military industry plants have at present does not match the volume of current mobilization requirements of the military department at all. For the majority of basic items of armaments, the military industry plants, at full stretch, can cover only a certain portion of the requirements declared by the military department. In some cases, this proportion is very low and amounts to only 10–15 per cent. For more than half of the items, the figure is not over 50 per cent.' The problem of military preparedness had been identified; it was then necessary to solve it. It is hard to disagree with the view that: 'There is every reason to maintain that, in fact, from 1928 the party and government led the country into a "period of preparation for war".'[16] To be sure, these preparations had to be fitted into the larger context of collectivization and industrialization as the basis for building 'socialism in one country'. But they were all of a piece.

The coincidence in late 1927 of the mounting crisis over the procurement of grain and the war scare increased pressure on the leadership to undertake radical measures. Lacking a concrete plan, Stalin was groping his way towards a solution that would base the country's economic and military development solely on the foundations of domestic industry. But the cost to internal stability quickly exceeded all expectations. With the implementation of full-scale collectivization in the winter of 1929/30 the leadership faced a groundswell of peasant resistance to forced deliveries; by the spring of 1930, the leadership faced another – this time hidden – war scare which may well have contributed to the decision to call a temporary halt to collectivization.[17] The disturbances were reportedly serious in the Polish settlements in Western Ukraine and Western Belarus. Together with information on the formation of the Organization of Ukrainian Nationalists (OUN), crises in the Communist Party of Western Ukraine, and the revival of a plan by Marshal Piłsudski to detach Ukraine from the Soviet Union, the party was revisited by memories of the civil war and intervention.[18] It was under these conditions that Stalin made his famous 'dizzy with success' speech, once again giving voice to his role as the reasonable moderator occupying the centre in times of crisis (a crisis for which of course he was responsible).[19] At the same time, his loyal ally and friend among the military leadership Kliment Voroshilov was demanding that the army be brought up to a state of full readiness and that 'the whole of political-educational work' be reorganized to 'guarantee the maximum operational vigilance of the military units'.[20] The entire bureaucracy now geared up to implement the 'preparatory period of war' law which had been drafted two years earlier.

Under heavy pressure, the commissariats and the State Planning Committee (Gosplan) hastily patched together a five-year programme. The estimates quickly proved unrealistic and production levels fell far short of the projected goals. In the rush to complete the draft, departmental competition and imbalances between the indicators relating to military industry and the totals for all Soviet industry contributed to the setback. In its criticism of the plans, the Politburo noted that 'these negative phenomena in military industry over the past period have been aggravated by long-term and systematic wrecking on the part of old specialists'.[21] These proved to be ominous words.

Over the next two years (1928–30), Stalin, in collaboration with the secret police, orchestrated a campaign accusing these 'old specialists' (the engineers, experts and scientists of the pre-revolutionary era, who had contributed to the Soviet economy under the New Economic Policy) of sabotage and wrecking linked to the machinations of anti-Soviet émigrés and the French and British governments. The accusations were orchestrated into a series of show trials aimed at galvanizing the party and economic bureaucracy. Material prepared for three successive trials from 1928 to 1930 – the Shakhty Trial of mining engineers in 1928, the so-called Industrial Party and the Toiling Peasants Party (invented by the secret police, both in 1930) – claimed to have exposed an extensive network of wreckers responsible for the major shortcomings in collectivization and the first five-year plan and even of plotting to overthrow the government.[22] Their alleged conspiracies were then used by Stalin and his associates to undermine the Right Opposition in the party and complete the process of destroying any potential internal challenge to the Stalinist cohort.

The purges not only spread fear among the specialists but confronted the party with the need to find replacements for the victims of the purge trials. In the scramble to find solutions, the party leaders divided over a number of issues relating to recruitment, level of previous training for technical schools and rigour of the curriculum. Stalin, always suspicious of engineers in general and sceptical of a broader curriculum, was less active and less decisive than might have been expected. His preference for training 'simple, practical people' drawn from the proletariat and his suspicion of the type of higher education reminiscent of the pre-revolutionary intelligentsia did not in this case win out all along the line. The new generation of younger specialists who began to enter the workforce after 1933 came mainly from intelligentsia backgrounds, and the curriculum, although narrow, included mathematics and science in addition to technical subjects. By the eve of the Second World War, the technical level of graduating engineers was superior to that of the early thirties.[23]

As the new approach to technical training gained ground, the party responded to the Japanese occupation of Manchuria by pressing for more investment in the defence industry and drafting plans for the adaptation of civilian factories to military production. Special attention was paid to tanks and aircraft; Tukhachevsky was already agitating for new allocations for rocket warfare. Although military production in the first five-year plan still amounted to a small share of the total allocated to heavy industry, during the first six months of 1932, according to R.W. Davies, it 'called upon the most skilled labour and the most complex materials and machines'.[24] By 1934 Voroshilov could boast to the Seventeenth Party Congress that since 1930 'the army has become as it were a different army in principle, in relation to the quantity and quality of its armaments, its organizational structure and the military preparedness of its cadres'.[25]

The place of general education in the process of mobilizing the population for the purpose of constructing socialism and defending the country was also undergoing a transition from 1938 to 1940. The central question was whether schools and classes should continue to be organized, as the revolution had established, on the principle of gender equality or, as in the pre-revolutionary era, on the separation of the sexes. The debate within the party and among professional educators and teachers focused on the issues of discipline, social roles and intellectual capacities. Andrei Zhdanov was put in charge of supervising the revision of the Rules of Conduct. He favoured the incorporation into the rules for gymnasium students of many ideas approved in 1877 by the tsarist government which consecrated the separation of girls and boys. While accepting Zhdanov's recommendation to cast the revised rules in Soviet terminology, the commissar of education and former diplomat Vladimir Potemkin elected to conserve the pre-revolutionary term 'gymnasium'. In the discussions, which dragged into the war and were finally concluded in 1943, a great deal of emphasis was placed on increased discipline to curb the hooliganism that had all too often disrupted mixed classes in the thirties.[26] The reforms encountered strong resistance and criticism from the population, reflecting the inherent contradiction between two fundamental principles of the Soviet system at war. The first was the hallowed ideal of gender equality that gained support during the war, with its glorification of heroic female warriors and civilian martyrs; the second was the emphasis on the specific physical and mental capabilities of men as fighters and women as agents of reproduction as essential to the war effort.[27]

Related to the issue of separating the sexes, the militarization of the curriculum was already under way before the war, but after the German attack in 1941 it became omnipresent. In addition to greater discipline, military terms and problems were introduced in subjects not normally taught in those terms, such as mathematics. Chemistry emphasized protection against toxic substances. Geography classes took up field sketching and language teaching introduced military vocabulary.[28]

PURGES AND PREPARATIONS FOR WAR

Since the 1990s, historians have benefited from the opening of the Soviet archives to cast fresh light on the complex origins of the terror and the linkage between the domestic, foreign and defence policy of the Soviet Union. During the Great Terror from 1936 to 1938, Stalin continued to be obsessed by the danger to his personal rule and the security of the Soviet Union, which he equated to an alliance between internal and external enemies, counter-revolution at home and capitalist intervention from abroad. In explaining the purges to Georgi Dimitrov in 1937, he linked the causes of the terror to a series of events that exemplified that dangerous combination: 1905, 1917, Brest-Litovsk and the civil war, but 'particularly collectivization'. That was when 'weak elements in the party fell away, went underground', he continued. 'Being powerless themselves, they linked up with our external enemies, promising the Germans Ukraine, the Poles Belarus, and the Japanese our Far East. They were waiting for a war.'[29]

Following hard on the heels of the official show trials of 1936–38, Stalin's *The History of the Communist Party of the Soviet Union*, known familiarly as *The Short Course* and published in 1938, embellished the role of foreign spying, terror and dismemberment that had been foreshadowed in the second show trial and played out prominently in the third. The dangers facing the Soviet Union were summarized in Stalin's clarion call: 'The second imperialist war has begun.'[30] It seems likely, as Oleg Khlevniuk has argued, that the mass operations in 1937 were connected to Stalin's interpretation of the subversive activities of the 'fifth column' of fascist spies and saboteurs behind the lines of Republican Spain as a likely scenario in the event of a war against the Soviet Union.[31]

Before proceeding to the impact of the purges on the key institutions of the preparations for war – the army, defence industry, the Foreign Commissariat and the Comintern – its generalizing effect should be considered. What emerges from the extensive literature on this phenomenon is the extent of the poisonous atmosphere which enveloped society as a whole. The increasingly arbitrary and irrational spread of the purges overwhelmed any attempts to identify specific individuals guilty of incompetence or corruption within the institutions that provided the sinews of war.

Without diminishing the personal equation of Stalin – his pathological distrust and suspicion – in unleashing the great purges, the extreme instability of the country must be considered as a major factor in the spread and vicious character of the trauma. The Soviet Union in the 1930s was an increasingly complex society undergoing a series of massive internal upheavals, sharpening social divisions that shattered the remnants of pre-revolutionary public morality and undermining the fragile structure of a new socialist value system. The Bolsheviks and other left-wing revolutionaries had nourished a parallel political culture in a pre-revolutionary Russia flush with conspiracy theories.[32] Coming to power through revolution and civil war as a distinct minority, they confronted a politically active, hostile emigration and a much larger potential opposition in the peasantry. Throughout the twenties their own ranks were riven with factions that often resorted to acting clandestinely. It is often forgotten that many members of the Socialist Revolutionary Party, Ukrainian Communist Party (Borotbisty) and Menshevik faction had joined the Bolshevik Party after 1920. How reliable were they? Stalin and his associates could hardly have forgotten that in the elections to the Constituent Assembly in late 1917 only a quarter of the population had voted for the Bolsheviks. How many of the remainder had since been converted to accept Bolshevik rule?

Purges through verification of documents were a way of life, although in the twenties dismissal from the party was not automatically followed by arrest as became the case later on. Scattered through the country were over 1.5 million former members of the party who had been excluded from its ranks between 1922 and 1937. They were an easy mark for denunciation when things went wrong. But they were also a source of denunciation among those seeking revenge. There was plenty of corruption and inefficiency in the system that the public was willing to blame on the brutal practice of ridding the country of kulaks and the irresponsible enthusiasts of the first five-year plan. Fear of and uncritical faith in the leaders, lies and real abuses were mixed up in a terrible 'kasha' of accusations. Whatever rational calculations may have entered into the initial decisions from above to select targets of destruction, a frenzy of denunciation soon threatened to endanger the stability of the entire system.[33] The governing body of Lenin's followers, constituting what Oleg Khlevniuk has called an 'unstable oligarchy', was decimated during the Great Terror by Stalin, who then instituted in its place a system of one-man rule.[34] By 1937 the war against society had entered a new stage of mass repressions.[35] At its most irrational, the killings under Stalin's direct orders were justified as a necessary measure to guarantee national security. His heavy reliance on the repressive organs of the secret police to carry out this task was brief and tapered off, without disappearing completely, when the police appeared to have acquired an institutional power that could potentially rival his own. He then turned against it. By the end of the decade the effects of the terror had a devastating effect on the capacity of the system to utilize the time and space brought by the Nazi-Soviet Pact to prepare the country for an external attack.

Despite the extensive research into the question of the purges, a key question remains unanswered. Did Stalin and his close associates, Vyacheslav Molotov, Lazar Kaganovich, Anastas Mikoian, Sergo Ordzhonikidze and the heads of the Commissariat of Internal Affairs (NKVD), really believe what some historians have called the fantastic stories of spying, sabotage and conspiracy? Or should the question be put somewhat differently? Did the leadership, shaped by its own revolutionary and conspiratorial past and intimidated and infected by Stalin's own morbid suspicions, accept along with him the idea that a vast potential for opposition existed within Soviet society that could in the event of war sap the will and undermine the unity of the country?[36] How could that danger best be anticipated? One line of attack was to accuse the potential oppositionists of harbouring thoughts of wrecking and sabotage, by the very fact of thinking them making themselves guilty of committing such acts.

Stalin must have often reflected on Trotsky's 'Clemenceau thesis'. During the height of the struggle for power and the war scare in July 1927, Trotsky had written to Ordzhonikidze that if in the event of war the ruling faction should prove incompetent in leading the country, then the opposition would seek to take over the direction of the war. He illustrated his intentions by citing the case of the French statesman Georges Clemenceau, who had waged a furious struggle in 1917 to replace the existing leadership with a more vigorous and determined one during the critical days when the

Germans were at the gates of Paris. Stalin and Molotov then presented Trotsky's views to the Central Committee as an endorsement of an insurrectionist policy. They continued to repeat the accusation every time they needed to impugn Trotsky's motives. At about the same time as the Clemenceau letter, a group of army leaders secretly notified the Politburo of their solidarity with the opposition. Among them were several generals who were executed during the purge of the Red Army ten years later.[37]

THE RED ARMY

The thirties were, on the one hand, a period of enormous growth in the defence industries and the modernization of the armed forces. On the other hand, by the end of the decade, the main architects of these powerful defences – weapons designers, the Red Army officer corps – were being arrested, imprisoned and often shot. The contradictions in war preparedness were most dramatically and tragically illustrated in the fate of the Red Army. By 1936 the army was well on its way to becoming the premier fighting force in Europe; it was led by a group of brilliant and innovative commanders, equipped with modern weapons and endowed with a strategic doctrine and tactical approach that foreshadowed total war. Within two years, however, its leading members had been repressed, their innovative thinking jettisoned, the country's defences severely weakened. This was Stalin's work. The shocking defeats in 1941–42 forced a return to the pre-purge military doctrine and a restoration of greater authority to commanders at the operational level that finally stabilized the front and permitted the great offensives of 1943–44.

In the intense military debates of the twenties the Frunze School, supported by Stalin, had emerged triumphant over Trotsky's concepts. A professional army, a unified one-man command and revolutionary class war were the salient features of the school, as opposed to Trotsky's preference for a militia army and his rejection of the army as the standard-bearer of the international proletarian revolution.[38] But differences soon emerged among the victors. The civil war had produced a whole group of talented young Red Army commanders with fresh ideas on the nature of warfare. They were for the most part products of pre-revolutionary training. The tsarist military academies, which had ceased to be the preserve of aristocrats, attracted larger numbers of impoverished nobles and non-nobles. The gradual democratization of the officer corps was particularly marked in the artillery and engineering branches. The new breed was thoroughly professional, scornful of the traditional branches like cavalry, and fascinated by technical innovations and new tactics.[39] None of them could match the imagination, breadth of vision and personal magnetism of Mikhail Tukhachevsky. By virtue of his bold theories and leadership qualities, he stood at the head of a group of senior officers – including Ieronim Uborevich, Iona Iakir and Iakov Alksnis – who were largely responsible for remoulding the Red Army and the air force. They encountered strong resistance from the old-fashioned cavalry leaders Voroshilov and Semeon Budenny, who had been Stalin's comrades in arms in the southwestern command during the civil war. The dispute was fundamental and bitter. The innovators stressed the vital importance of harnessing modern technology to new tactics. The veterans of the First Cavalry Army, meanwhile, were loath to surrender their horses.[40]

Stalin had a personal stake in the outcome of the technical disputes between the Tukhachevsky and Voroshilov groups. Twice during the civil war, in the North Caucasus campaign and during the advance on Moscow, Stalin deliberately refused or evaded orders to place the forces under his command at the disposal of Tukhachevsky. In the former case no great harm was done. But Stalin's irresolute decisions in the last stages of the Russo-Polish War were blamed for contributing to the defeat of the Red Army at the battle of Warsaw and gave rise to the persistent 'Vistula complex' within the army.

In the great debate during the twenties over the responsibility for the defeat, Tukhachevsky steadfastly maintained that Stalin and Budenny had disregarded the unity of command, but his criticism vanished from the pages of the professional journals and history books between 1931 and 1956. The only professional soldier not identified with the Southwest Army who supported Stalin was Boris Shaposhnikov who was also, not by accident, one of the very few top commanders to survive the purges of the thirties; Stalin appointed him in 1937 chief of staff of the Red Army.[41]

Beyond the personal resentment and jealousy Stalin felt for Tukhachevsky, the issue of revolutionary war divided them. The son of a nobleman, graduate of the elite cadet corps, Tukhachevsky embraced Marxism with the passion of the newly converted. He wedded his study of the science of warfare with Marx's theory of revolution to produce a 'strategy of civil war' that he believed should form the basis for Soviet foreign policy. He envisaged that the next war would be fought on two fronts, the external and internal. 'The Comintern', he wrote to Grigory Zinoviev in 1920, 'must prepare the proletariat with a military point of view for the advent of civil war, for the moment when the proletariat with all its armed forces would launch the attack on the armed forces of world capitalism.' The class analysis of war lent his strategic thinking an extraordinary breadth which encompassed the entire economic structure of the country.[42] He subsequently modified his views to the extent of admitting the value of a coalition with capitalist powers, but he remained attached to the idea of an international civil war with the proletariat and the Red Army combining their strength to overthrow capitalism. Stalin was to detect elements of Bonapartism in Tukhachevsky's emphasis on the leadership of the Red Army as the locus of command in guiding the international revolution.

During his meteoric career, Tukhachevsky pursued his innovative strategic ideas uncompromisingly, not hesitating to offend Voroshilov, his nominal chief, and repeatedly confronting Stalin. His main contributions to Soviet military doctrine and the preparedness of the Red Army lasted well into the Second World War and in some cases even beyond. Although his views underwent constant revision in response to study and the experience of military exercises, they can be summarized under six major rubrics: the mechanized army, the organization of weapons design and procurement, combined operations, deep penetration and non-stop offensive, the early period of war and the nature of total war.[43] Tukhachevsky was both a military intellectual and an active commander. As chief of staff of the Red Army and instructor at the Frunze Military Academy he insisted upon the close study of the First World War and the civil war as the source of insights for wars of the future. Yet he was not hidebound by lessons of the past. He sketched in the main outlines of a mechanized army even before the Soviet Union possessed the industrial base to create it.[44] He was thoroughly prepared in 1928 when the leadership authorized him to draft a five-year plan for the reconstruction of the armed forces. His ambitious proposals aimed to create a modern army with large tank forces, a powerful long-range air force and a new radio communications system. Voroshilov came out strongly against the plan, and Tukhachevsky submitted his resignation. Appointed commander of the Leningrad military district, he found a surprisingly broad scope for his talents under the protection of his admirer and friend Sergei Kirov.

From his Leningrad base, Tukhachevsky continued – with Kirov's help – to press for acceptance of his ideas. He was the key figure in drafting the new field regulations of 1929, which incorporated most of his ideas. He wrote several of the chapters and edited others.[45] The Central Committee accepted the regulations as the basis for its major policy statement, 'The State of Defence of the USSR', which incorporated the ideas of Tukhachevsky and his colleagues. He followed this up with another detailed plan submitted to Voroshilov in January 1930, 'On the basis of taking into account the latest factors of technology and the possibilities of mass military-technical production'. It amounted to nothing less than a massive rearmament of all the Soviet armed forces, but based on a new concept of modifying the design of machine-building factories to allow rapid conversions to military needs. Voroshilov distorted the plan in presenting it to Stalin, who reacted hostilely.[46]

Stalin announced that acceptance of the proposals 'would lead to the liquidation of socialist construction and its replacement by some kind of peculiar system of red militarism'. Undaunted, Tukhachevsky bombarded Stalin with letters and memos. Stalin did not answer – an ominous sign. Yet within six months, Stalin appointed Tukhachevsky deputy president of the Military Revolutionary Council, deputy commissar of defence for army and navy affairs and chief of armaments of the Red Army. A year later Stalin wrote to Tukhachevsky apologizing for his sharp and incorrect criticisms.[47] This extraordinary and possibly unique act of contrition must have cost Stalin dearly. But this was an extremely difficult period for Stalin politically: Kirov was in the ascendant, and there was clearly no figure of Tukhachevsky's stature to carry out the modernization – certainly not Voroshilov who, as Zhukov pointed out, 'was a dilettante in military questions and never understood them deeply or seriously'.[48]

Tukhachevsky was one of the first military leaders in the twentieth century to grasp the revolutionary implications of applying the systems approach in industrial organization. In an unpublished memo of 1931 he stressed the necessity of emulating industry in putting an end to the separation and isolation of different elements or processes and integrating them in a total concept of military training and administration. In his view, industrial methods dealing with the organization of labour, for example, could be fruitfully applied to common problems in branches of the military dealing with supply, such as railway units, sappers and mechanics. In the high-technology wars of the future, he insisted the need for repairs of military hardware and the general demand for specialized knowledge could best be met by those who understood the entire industrial process.[49]

Industry could also teach valuable lessons on the need to apply rapid and flexible methods of retraining and improved training on the job. 'A command staff not capable of such vital practical methods will turn out to be incapable of conducting a war successfully', Tukhachevsky argued. He was convinced that the Red Army possessed a great advantage over its potential opponents in the ability of its party and political cadres to match technical advances with military needs, to bridge the gap between the industry and army. Finally, Tukhachevsky concluded that ideological training of recruits to take creative initiatives inspired by the Bolshevik spirit like those in industry would enable the army to discard the old traditions and to promote the 'independence of the soldier and the small unit'. In a striking phrase, he summarized his aim: 'to make the formula "I await orders" unacceptable and incompatible with military shock-work [udarnichestvom]', meaning seizing the initiative from below.[50] This approach drew Tukhachevsky closer to the rational industrializers like Kuibyshev and Ordzhonikidze, but the idea of autonomy and initiative of the small units was completely lost on Stalin.

Once in place as chief of armaments, Tukhachevsky could put into practice on a national scale his experiments in weapons design supported by Kirov in the Leningrad district. In the early thirties, Tukhachevsky brought together an extraordinarily talented group of engineers and technicians who developed the prototypes for many of the major innovative weapons and models that were later put into large-scale production before and during the Second World War. Under his leadership, a number of weapons design offices were organized and funded. The roster of its members reads like a who's who of the leading figures in weapons design in the middle decades of the twentieth century: Vasily Degtiarev and Fedor Tokarev in small arms, Semeon Ginzburg in tank prototypes, to mention only the most prominent figures, as well as a younger group including Aleksandr Morozov, Vasily Grebin and Fedor Petrov, who designed the outstanding wartime models of tanks; and Andrei Tupolev, Nikolai Polikarpov, Dmitry Grigorovich and Aleksandr Mikulin in aircraft design. Almost all these men had already achieved worldwide recognition in the thirties as weapons innovators.

Tukhachevsky not only closely supervised their activities but insisted upon a strict regime of weapons testing.

It is difficult to single out any one of his achievements in weapons procurement. But it is fair to say that his initiative in reorganizing Soviet artillery through the production of new models and the simplification of types of weapons and the integration of artillery into battlefield tactics was largely responsible for the outstanding role played by this branch in winning the big tank battles on the eastern front in 1943. His views on airborne armies and rocketry were nothing less than visionary. As early as 1932 he organized military exercises that proved the feasibility of mass parachute landings with heavy equipment. With the backing of the commissar of heavy industry, Sergo Ordzhonikidze (another of his enthusiastic supporters), an experimental institute for airborne-landing research was created. Four years later, during manoeuvres in the Ukraine and Belarus, airborne forces gave a stunning demonstration of the ability to land up to 11,000 men with artillery and light tanks. Tukhachevsky was the first to propose the installation of rapid firing cannon in attack planes, and worked with Polikarpov to design the prototype of the flying tank destroyer that would mature in the famous Stormovik. Under his direction the first experiments with rocket weapons were carried out. He took personal control over the Hydrodynamics Laboratory in Leningrad, where several of the leading Soviet rocket experts of the interwar period carried out their earliest designs. In an era when research and development tended to be what Kenneth Bailes has called 'a series of fragmented pieces', Tukhachevsky brought together the two leading groups from the Leningrad Hydrodynamics Laboratory and the Moscow Group for the Study of Rocketry in 1933 to form the Reactive Research Institute, a unified centre for developing rocket technology. Experiments with liquid and solid fuels for artillery shells laid the groundwork for the creation of rocket artillery at the end of the thirties, evolving into the famous Katiusha multiple rocket launcher.[51] The special experimental Bureau No. 7 produced experimental models of long-range liquid-fuel rockets, but this work was allowed to lapse following Tukhachevsky's arrest in 1937.[52]

As a military theorist, Tukhachevsky deserves his reputation as the founder of modern Soviet strategic thinking. Despite his setback in the battle of Warsaw in 1920, he staunchly advocated the primacy of the offensive on both military and political grounds. To his way of thinking, technological advances would give primacy to attack over defence, reversing the pattern of the First World War but confirming the experience of the Russian Civil War. Long after it was unfashionable in Stalinist Russia to envisage warfare in class terms, he was convinced that a Red Army on the offensive would be able to bolster its strategic reserves from the liberated proletariat of the countries into which it was advancing. It was one of the few major articles of his strategic thinking that Stalin did not later incorporate into his own view. Tukhachevsky's concept of the 'non-stop offensive' required two basic conditions: an army that combined mass with mobility, and close co-operation between the various branches of the fighting services. Although he accepted the most advanced Western thinking on tanks, he rejected Western theories of the small elite army. He also refuted his Soviet colleagues who advocated a war of attrition. He fully grasped the importance of tanks organized into armoured divisions and providing both the mobility and fire power to effect the breakthrough. But he also stressed what had been overlooked by Western tank theorists like B.H. Liddell Hart and J.F.C. Fuller, namely the crucial supplementary role of heavy artillery and tactical aircraft. Tukhachevsky's thinking kept pace with the development of new technologies. In the field regulations of 1936, he admitted that the development of firepower had strengthened the role of defence, but he steadfastly opposed the idea that positional warfare was either inevitable or necessary. Instead, he restated his doctrine of the offensive, displaying a more sophisticated understanding of the operational details. He spelled out precisely the employment of artillery and aircraft to blast openings for tanks clearing the way for motorized infantry. He developed the concept of 'deep penetration' as the most effective tactic to disrupt lines of communication and supply, and inflict mortal damage on the enemy's rear as the prelude to completely annihilating his forces. He insisted that the offensive, combined operations of a mechanized army could only be carried out under three conditions: speed and suddenness of attack; centralization of command balanced by large initiatives for local unit commanders; and co-ordination of all branches of the armed forces.[53]

Early in his career, Tukhachevsky became convinced that the dimensions of the future war would extend far beyond anything that had been witnessed in the past. In 1926, in his work 'Questions of Contemporary Strategy', he argued that 'the basic feature of contemporary war is the grandiose scale in terms of economic and human resources that will be employed, the space occupied by the combatants and finally the protracted duration of the fighting'. He repeatedly pointed out that the future war would be conducted not only by the armed forces but also by the entire country. It was necessary to strengthen the war-making potential of the economy and the organizational infrastructure in order to mobilize all the human and natural resources of the country.[54]

Tukhachevsky devoted special attention to the early or frontier phase of this 'total war', and his analysis reads like an eyewitness description of the German blitzkrieg against the Soviet Union. He was utterly and unshakeably convinced that the war would be fought against Germany. He consistently argued that France was just as threatened as Soviet Russia and that Hitler's diplomatic strategy was to split these natural allies.[55] Tukhachevsky believed that the key to initial success rested with the army that could rapidly mobilize in the frontier zone and concentrate a series of rapid blows by aircraft, airborne troops and armour to achieve a breakthrough while at the same time disrupting the enemy's ability to do the same.[56]

With the growing threat of Nazi Germany and the uncertain political situation in the borderlands of the Soviet Union in Eastern Europe, Tukhachevsky modified his thinking on the early phase. Given the fact that the German forces would be in a better military and political position to launch a first strike, Tukhachevsky introduced in 1937 the idea of the 'covering force'. Powerful elements of the army would be deployed on the outer flanks of the fortified frontier zone. The Soviet mobile defence would take the full brunt of the enemy's mechanized onslaught. In contrast to the First World War, the frontier battles would be protracted. Then the covering Soviet forces would deliver the counterblows from the flanks. This idea was expanded by Aleksandr Svechin, professor of the Frunze Academy general staff, in his theory of 'peripheral strategy'. These views were opposed by Shaposhnikov and Aleksandr Egorov. But what remained essential in all these plans was the concept of a flexible operational defence. This presupposed an enemy attack, most probably German, which would be contained by the defensive forces until full mobilization and deployment of the Red Army would permit powerful counter-offensives to carry the fight to foreign soil.

Tukhachevsky put his ideas to the test in the field manoeuvres of 1936. His closest associates, Uborevich and Iakir, who were to perish with him within two years, took leading roles in their capacities as commanders of the Belarus and Kiev military districts, forming the outer flanks of the frontier zones. He correctly predicted that the combined enemy (German) forces would number 200 divisions (the actual number in 1941 was 190), that the core of the attacking force would be eighty divisions (the actual number was seventy-nine), that the Germans would enjoy local numerical superiority, and that the attack would come suddenly in line with the major military doctrines held by the Wehrmacht commanders. But the Soviet High Command refused to accept either the idea of German numerical superiority or the idea of a surprise attack. The actual exercises, worked out against Tukhachevsky's views, ended indecisively.[57]

Political opposition to Tukhachevsky increased with his growing reputation and influence over the modernization of the army. He had always been at odds with Voroshilov, whom he did not hesitate to criticize in private and in public.[58] During a discussion of the field regulations of 1936, Voroshilov raised an objection to one of the statutes. Zhukov, who was present, recalled that Tukhachevsky politely announced that the commission could not accept the commissar's correction. When Voroshilov asked why not, Tukhachevsky calmly replied, 'Because your corrections are incompetent, Comrade Commissar.'[59] For his part, Voroshilov rebuked Tukhachevsky in language characteristic of the Stalinist school of favouring *praktiki*, men who addressed industrial problems from a practical rather than theoretical perspective. 'I advise you', the commissar of defence wrote, 'to put an end as soon as possible to your extremely literary abstractions and to direct all your knowledge and energy to practical work.'[60]

In Stalin's eyes, Tukhachevsky represented a constant reproach, a potential threat, a man who embodied many of the characteristics that Stalin could not abide in a subordinate. Son of a nobleman, a former officer in the tsarist army, a brilliant thinker in a field where Stalin had pretentions, a rival in the civil war, he was elegant, cultured, worldly, yet still a proletarian internationalist in his political views. He came as close as anyone in the ruling elite to being indispensable. But this was a status Stalin had reserved for himself.

By 1937 Tukhachevsky's most powerful patrons had been removed from the scene: Kirov had been assassinated; Ordzhonikidze had committed suicide; Kuibyshev's death was apparently normal, but suspicions linger about the real causes. All three reportedly had sought to restrain Stalin's excesses as early as 1933–34. With Stalin's approval, Voroshilov and Nikolai Ezhov, commissar of the NKVD, concocted a plot with the assistance of the Nazi security services which supplied fabricated documents implicating Tukhachevsky and his command group in a 'military-political conspiracy against the Soviet power encouraged and financed by the German fascists'. In a farcical examination and trial held in secret, three of the five marshals of the Soviet Union – Tukhachevsky, Iakir and Uborevich – were condemned along with a number of their closest aides and associates in June 1937 and shot. Stalin then called for the extirpation of 'enemies of the people' who were hiding in the army.[61] A veritable orgy of arrests and executions followed. The Soviet officer corps was decimated. All the corps commanders, almost all division and brigade commanders, about half the regimental commanders as well as most of the political commissars of corps, divisions and brigades, and about a third of the regimental commissars were arrested.[62]

The 'healthy elements' in the party perceived the damage the indiscriminate purges were causing in the armed forces. At the January 1939 plenum, the Central Committee condemned the mass exclusion of party members in general and in particular in the army. As a result the party commission of the Political Administration of the Red Army reversed decisions by the district party commissions to purge 63 per cent of communists in the Leningrad military district and 67 per cent in Belarus.[63] Despite these 'corrective measures', military commanders on the eve of the war complained of insufficient numbers of political officers, a situation recognized by Ivan Zaporozhets, who recommended measures to fill the more than 13,000 vacancies in the middle ranks of the Political Administration of the Red Army.[64] But it was not until the outbreak of the war that urgent measures were taken to reorganize and complete its staffing.[65]

Estimates vary on the number of officers and political personnel who were purged. Scholars without access to Soviet archives gave inflated numbers.[66] But even with access, specialists on the topic disagree. Roger R. Reese proposed a more modest figure of 34,301 expulsions from the army and air force for political reasons. But he pointed out that of this number 11,596 had been reinstated in rank before the outbreak of war.[67] Whatever the final numbers may turn out to be, if indeed they can ever be established, the effect on the morale of the army was incalculable. The military academies were devastated; hundreds of teachers and students were arrested and disappeared; retired officers did not escape the denunciations. Stalin did not even spare the dead. He ordered the names of many of the leading generals of the civil war extirpated from the historical records. As Roy Medvedev has pointed out, 'never did the officer staff of any army suffer such great losses in any war as the Soviet Army suffered in this time of peace'.[68] By the summer of 1938 even Voroshilov joined others in the Politburo in complaining that the repression had begun to undermine the economic and defence potential of the country.[69]

Even before the war broke out, Stalin considered himself something of an expert in military affairs. He read widely if unsystematically in translated French and German as well as Russian works. As Geoffrey Roberts has demonstrated, his wartime comments drew heavily on his interpretation of these works.[70] But he did not develop a military doctrine, to say nothing of operational concepts. In fact, Stalin reversed some of Tukhachevsky's reforms and tactical innovations. He misunderstood the lessons of the Spanish Civil War. He ordered independent tank formations to be broken up and redeployed as infantry support. The powerful Soviet long-range bomber formations developed by Iakov Alksnis and others were severely weakened by their purge and the arrest of the designer Andrei Tupolev, the brains behind the bomber designs. The Soviet Air Forces never fully recovered from these blows. Strategic bombing, which Tukhachevsky supported as an integral part of the strategy of 'deep penetration', did not play a major part in the Soviet military effort in the Second World War.

Yet even in the army, the purge of the battered officer corps was not without a paradoxical effect. It opened the way for upwardly mobile peasants who managed to obtain some military education or enter the army and work their way into positions of command. By the outbreak of war the overwhelming number of generals came from peasant stock.[71] They led the country to defeat the invaders.

Moreover, Stalin stopped short of embracing Voroshilov's outmoded ideas.[72] He was not blind to the lessons of the early Nazi campaigns in Poland and France. Once the battle for France had demonstrated beyond the shadow of a doubt the superiority of mass tank formations, the Red Army began quietly to reintroduce Tukhachevsky's doctrines, although too late to have a decisive effect on Soviet dispositions in 1941. The General Staff completed its work on creating a new mechanized army corps in early 1941. It proposed the formation of an additional twenty corps. But this would have entailed the production of 30,000 tanks, a long-term project that at existing production schedules would have required four to five years. Other changes involved a drastic reduction in men and horses at the divisional level in order to introduce greater mobility and firepower. But these innovations, like so many others, were still in the process of being introduced when the Germans struck. Many divisions were only at 60–85 per cent of their authorized strength in 1941. The superb artillery parks lacked mechanical traction. The new models of tanks and aircraft, more than a match for their German counterparts, were just coming off the assembly lines in the spring of 1941. They were too few and their crews too inexperienced in handling them to compete on equal terms with the battle-hardened panzer units and Luftwaffe.[73] The entire picture reveals an army in the midst of a fundamental transformation from order of battle to operational planning.

Between 1924, when the General Staff of the Red Army was created, and 1941, the planning of military operations in the Soviet Union underwent fifteen revisions.[74] The most complete and highly original plans for 'deep penetration' were worked out by Vladimir Triandafilov, the chief of the Operational Section of the General Staff, in the period 1926–29, when the chiefs of staff were Tukhachevsky and Egorov. Over the following years the plan underwent several fine-tunings. Following the Nazi-Soviet division of Eastern Europe into spheres of influence, the plan was again revised in June 1940 by General Aleksandr Vasilevsky and Marshal Shaposhnikov. Semeon Timoshenko, the commissar of defence, opposed Shaposhnikov's conclusion that the main theatre of operations would be the northwestern front (north of Warsaw and in East Prussia), which proved to be the correct forecast of the German invasion. Timoshenko and his subordinates in the commissariat and the General Staff, including Nikolai Vatutin and Georgy Zhukov, expected the main sphere of operations to be in the south. They may well have been influenced by the fact that they had all begun their service in the Kiev military district. Stalin supported this view, believing that Hitler could not fight a prolonged war without the grain and iron ore of Ukraine.[75]

Other strategic factors were also in play. Timoshenko's October 1940 draft for future military operations indicated that an offensive along the southern line would cut Germany off from the Balkans and deprive it of its important economic base (presumably Romanian oil) and influence the Balkan countries to come in on the Soviet side.[76] Moreover, it is important not to forget that Stalin's experience in the Soviet-Polish War had come on the southwestern front, which he believed at that time was more important politically than the advance on Warsaw.

The operational plan underwent two revisions in March and May 1941. The latter version included a proposal to forestall a German offensive by 'attacking the German army at that moment when it would be at the stage of deployment and would not yet have succeeded in organizing its battle front and the co-ordinated action of different branches of its forces'.[77] This had no practical result and was never approved by Stalin, although it has been interpreted to mean that a pre-emptive strike was being prepared.[78]

This misconception of Soviet intentions may have had its roots in the idea advanced by advocates within the party of the so-called 'red intervention' or doctrine of offensive war. The foremost champion of this view was Andrei Zhdanov, who gathered around him a group of like-minded civil and military officers of the Leningrad military district, including General (later Marshal) Kirill Meretskov, commander of the district, Lev Mekhlis, the chief of the Main Administration of Political Propaganda of the Red Army, and the political commissar of the first rank Ivan Zaporozhets, who were critical of the strategic thinking of the Red Army leadership. Despite the fact that Zhdanov had been pressing for a pre-emptive attack on Finland that led to the humiliating Winter War in 1939–40, he and Meretskov escaped censure by managing to place all the blame on the leadership of the Red Army. They convinced Stalin of the need to remove his old friend Voroshilov as commissar of defence. Zhdanov and his group, now including young Nikolai Voznesensky, the future economic planner, mounted a major political offensive to hasten preparations for war.[79]

In Zhdanov's view, the main enemy were the Anglo-French imperialists who had condemned the Winter War and given moral support to the Finns. He believed, like Stalin, that Germany would never fight a two-front war and that the Soviet Union had time (Meretskov believed at least another year) before Germany could reduce England and be ready to attack. In the wake of the Nazi invasion in 1941, Zhdanov's prestige plunged to new lows. As an advocate of close ties with Germany, the alliance with Britain further discredited him. Never appointed to the State Defence Committee (GOKO), he was assigned the dangerous task of defending Leningrad in the autumn of 1941. Determined to hold on to the city at all costs, he was belaboured by his chief rivals in the Politburo, Georgy Malenkov and Lavrenty Beria, who advocated that the city be abandoned to concentrate all forces for the defence of Moscow.[80]

In the face of conflicting advice on the eve of the German invasion, Stalin merely ordered additional reinforcements of the southwestern front. The whole series of revisions represented a variation of the operational plans of Tukhachevsky and Triandafilov, namely an active defence followed by counter-attacks. The main operational design remained constant throughout these adjustments. Some confusion has arisen because Stalin did not sign either the March or the May revisions. After the war, General Vasilevsky explained that the operational plan of 1940 remained in force with minor adjustments and was communicated on the eve of the war to all commanders and staffs of military districts.[81]

On the eve of the war Stalin began reluctantly to approve measures strengthening the frontier defences. In April and May 1941 the General Staff started to organize the mobilization of 800,000 reservists. In May additional divisions reinforced the western and southwestern borders. Orders were issued to speed up the construction of the frontier fortresses. Beginning on 12 June, Marshal Timoshenko and General Zhukov repeatedly urged Stalin to bring the Soviet forces up to full combat readiness. Stalin, fearing this would provoke the Germans, only agreed to issue the orders on the evening of the German attack.[82] But Timoshenko's independent initiative to mobilize the Kiev military district on the eve of the war was blocked by Beria, who denounced the move to Stalin as fraught with dangerous consequences for Soviet-German relations. Beria lost no chance to criticize the professional cadres and Stalin always lent a ready ear.[83]

The real problem was not the lack of a plan or even the damaging assumption that the main direction of the invasion would come in the southwest. Rather it was the unforeseen and unintentional breakdown of operational defence, the key element in all the strategic plans. And this reflects another paradoxical aspect of Stalin's preparations for war.

Operational defence depended upon the creation of a strong defence line facing the western frontiers. Beginning in 1923, fortified regions were constructed as the backbone of such a line with the aim of slowing down and canalizing enemy formations so that they could be destroyed by counter-attacking mechanized forces on their flanks. But this was a huge under-taking and construction was slow. In January 1939 several reports by the deputy commissar of the NKVD of the Ukrainian Republic, Bogdan Kobulov, sharply criticized the condition of the fortified regions in the southwest. This rapidly led to the creation of special departments of the NKVD which were given extraordinary powers, not only to investigate subversive activities in the Red Army and the navy, but also to report on the military and moral shortcomings of the armed forces at every level.[84]

Following the expansion of the Soviet Union from 1939 to 1940 in the Baltic states and eastern Poland, another massive undertaking was launched to move the fortifications westward into the newly acquired territories which were designed to serve as a military buffer zone. The construction work resumed at a high tempo, but the new fortifications were not provided with a sufficient number of large-calibre guns. Out of 2,500 pillboxes only 1,000 were armed with artillery. Consequently, the decision was taken in the spring of 1941 to shift the planning back to rely on the old fortified regions as the basis for operational defence. On the eve of the war, their restoration had not reached a level of combat preparedness:[85] the fortified regions were occupied by only 34 per cent of the required officers, 27.7 per cent of the non-commissioned officers and 47.2 per cent of enlisted men.[86] In addition, the operational rear also required reorganization in order to support the new lines of defence, but the underdeveloped transportation networks, especially roads, were inadequate to rapidly move fuel and food, not to speak of munitions, to the forward areas.[87] When the German attacks struck the forward positions and broke through, their momentum could not be contained by the underequipped and undermanned fortified regions; counter-attacks, frantically ordered by Stalin and the central command, could not be organized and the entire front collapsed in the summer of 1942.[88] Thus, the buffer zone of borderlands acquired by diplomacy turned out in military terms to be a trap.

Another paradoxical situation arose in the field of intelligence, where the very abundance and reliability of information helped to obscure rather than clarify Hitler's intentions. Despite the massive arrests and executions, Stalin continued to show a profound distrust of the information gathering by the professional military cadre right up to the outbreak of war. His suspicions contributed in no small way to the unpreparedness of the Red Army in June 1941 and the disastrous defeats of the summer. Stalin insisted that military intelligence be subordinated to the Commissariat of Defence rather than to the General Staff. Even then Marshal Timoshenko, the commissar of defence, complained that he was not informed about all intelligence-gathering operations. It was his deputy, Filipp Golikov, who headed the Main Intelligence Administration (GRU). He reported directly to Stalin and cultivated close ties to Beria, with whom he often presented joint reports. The General Staff had to be satisfied with bits and pieces of intelligence that Golikov deigned to scatter before them. Stalin's reaction to the massive inflow of intelligence reports on German intentions has given rise to a great deal of debate.

In the months before the invasion, the Soviet leadership was bombarded by intelligence reports from agents in Germany and Japan warning of an impending attack.[89] The information was collected and analyzed by several Soviet intelligence organizations. But there was no central clearing house or even a systematic exchange of information within the intelligence community. Stalin appears to have relied more on Beria, who was 'filtering out' material on the threatening situation on the Soviet frontiers, than on General Golikov.[90] Like most intelligence, the material that Stalin was reading contained raw information, some of it contradictory or mistaken in specifying the date of the attack. But there were other reasons why Stalin failed to credit the mass of accurate intelligence and was taken by surprise on 22 June 1941. David Holloway has identified three factors that lessened the value of Soviet intelligence. They were, first, suspicions about the reliability of certain well-placed agents, such as Richard Sorge in Tokyo; second, the lack of an agent at the centre of the Nazi decision-making elite; and third, the success of the German campaign of disinformation which had already worked so well in defaming Marshal Mikhail Tukhachevsky.[91]

These shortcomings of Soviet intelligence were magnified by Stalin's own erroneous assumptions about Hitler's strategic plans and intentions with respect to the Soviet Union. He believed that Hitler would not repeat the mistake of Imperial Germany in 1914 by fighting a two-front war, and that so long as Britain remained unconquered the Soviet Union had time to perfect its military preparations. He also suspected that Britain, desperate to draw the Soviet Union into the war, was feeding it false information on an

impending attack. He further assumed that Hitler would precede an attack
by issuing an ultimatum demanding more economic concessions. Finally,
he was led to believe that the German leadership was divided over the question of war with the Soviet Union and that it was imperative to avoid giving
a provocation which would tip the balance in favour of the more aggressive
military planners in Germany.[92] Whatever motivated Stalin, his greatest
mistake was to believe he had more time to prepare for the German attack.
What he appeared to have gained in diplomacy through the Nazi-Soviet
Pact and the advance of the Soviet frontiers, he forfeited because of this
miscalculation. That Stalin believed he still had time to prepare for the
German attack gains additional confirmation from his views on weapons
design and procurement.

DEFENCE INDUSTRIES

Beginning with the second five-year plan (1933–37), a clear shift in budgetary allocation toward defence priorities took place. Before that the Soviet
Union lacked an industrial base – including a modern metallurgical industry
– that was capable of supplying the needs of an army and air force that could
stand up to the military forces of Western Europe. The Sixteenth Congress
planned for 'forced development' of industries directly connected to the
defence establishment. Basic weapons production increased dramatically.
From 1930–31 to 1932–33, the average annual production of aircraft practically quadrupled and that of tanks and aircraft almost doubled.[93] After 1936,
however, the buildup of the defence industries was entangled in a complex
bureaucratic rivalry between the Kaganovich clan and the group of former
clients of Sergo Ordzhonikidze. In the five years preceding the war, Stalin
pursued a policy of decentralizing the administration of defence industries
with the result that the production of weapons was distributed among four
new commissariats. He also intervened personally in the aviation industry,
where he had long taken an active interest. He became incensed on receiving
information – which later proved false – that Germany was daily out-
producing the Soviet Union in military aircraft by a factor of three. He
ordered a crash programme which created eighty-six new factories. By the
spring of 1941 the Soviet aviation industry surpassed the German in its
productive capacity by one and half times.[94]

The purges struck the defence industries with the same indiscriminate effect as other branches of the economy. Heavy industry, upon which the production of weapons depended, was especially hard hit. In 1937–38, for example, the commissariats replaced more than 5,000 heads of enterprises, trusts and *glavki* (subordinate administrative units). Ordzhonikidze struggled in vain to protect his best subordinates, but ended up falling victim himself. The 1937 show trial of Georgy Piatakov, deputy commissar of heavy industry, as a member of the so-called 'Trotskyite Parallel Centre' was, as Jeremy Azrael has put it, 'in effect a trial of the entire Communist managerial elite'.[95] The chemical and transport chiefs went down with Piatakov.

Stalin exploited the natural rivalries between the professional specialists and the *praktiki* with devastating effects on the level of technical innovation and the introduction of new inventions.[96] Experienced replacements were impossible to find. About 20 per cent of the graduates of higher technical schools in the second half of 1938 were immediately placed in responsible leadership posts. Promotion from the factory floor to the front office became customary. The turnover rate was, consequently, extremely high. For example, 85 per cent of all *glavki*, the entire executive apparatus, was replaced. The absence of trained personnel drove up accident rates, demoralized the workforce and led to a decline in production and heavy imbalances in the production of key items. The constant shifts in personnel and the atmosphere of suspicion and fear had a pronounced effect upon heavy metallurgy with its complex technology and production process. Two examples will suffice. In the worst years of 1937–38 iron ore production declined by 64,000 and 1,185,000 tons in comparison to previous years. The figures for manganese ore were almost as bad: declines of 248,000 tons were registered in 1937, and 479,000 tons in 1938.[97]

High-technology defence industries were badly hit. The purges of specialists in radar design deprived the country of a vital anti-aircraft defence until units had to be imported from the USA and Great Britain at the end of 1941. Leading designers in the earliest Soviet rocket weapons, along with individual experts in tank and artillery production, many of whom had worked with Tukhachevsky, were eliminated. Railways suffered the loss of most of the trained executives in the central apparatus.[98]

High rates of turnover linked to accusations and denunciations gave rise to pathological traits in the bureaucracy. The tendency for each new chief of a department to ignore all the work of his predecessor – 'to rediscover America' – gained strength as the predecessors were identified as enemies of the people. Mediocre or incompetent officials sought to save their own skins by currying favour with Stalin and discrediting their colleagues. In a series of striking cases on the eve of the war, the innovative work of the Commissariat of Armaments was seriously disrupted. The chief of the Main Artillery Directorate, Grigory Kulik, a narrow-minded opportunist who had come to office in the dread year of 1937, insisted on substituting for the 76 mm gun a new unproven large-calibre cannon, mounted on the T-34 tank. Stalin supported him. The people's commissar of armaments, Boris Vannikov, objected strenuously. The 76 mm gun had undergone the most strenuous tests and was clearly superior to any German cannon mounted on a tank. On the eve of the war, it was just reaching its peak of production. Stalin arbitrarily appointed Zhdanov, who knew nothing about armaments, to chair a committee to resolve the question. Taking his cue from Stalin, Zhdanov accused Vannikov of sabotage; Vannikov shot back: 'you are allowing the disarmament of the army on the eve of a war.' Stalin overruled him.

In the early months of the war, the predictions of Vannikov proved correct, and it was necessary to order forced production of the 76 mm gun. But the conversion from the large-calibre model favoured by Kulik was time-consuming and costly, and the prewar production figures were reached only in 1942. Vannikov also attempted to protect his military engineers against baseless attacks, ultimately at the cost of his own career. He defended B.I. Shavyrin, the brilliant designer of the powerful Br-5 field mortar, against accusations of wrecking, preventing his arrest, only to be arrested himself the very month that the war broke out.[99]

Despite the carnage in the heavy industry cadres, the Eighteenth Party Congress in 1938 announced new priorities for defence in the third five-year plan, reflecting the deteriorating international situation after Hitler's annexation of Austria increased the possibilities of war. Four measures have been identified as characterizing the initiatives taken to strengthen the Soviet defence sector.[100] First, the size of the armed forces was slightly increased by the addition of NKVD units. Second, military establishments were subjected to firmer control, for example by enlarging and strengthening the frontier zones and eliminating the 'abnormal' number of Germans, Poles, Estonians and Latvians employed in defence industries; third, measures were taken 'to introduce modern technology into all sectors of the national economy and into all forms of national defence', particularly in the production of aircraft; and fourth, efforts were initiated to improve the performance and facilities for troops. Capital investment in the defence industry increased to a quarter of overall investment. According to one of the few sets of statistics comparing the defence outlays of 1940 and 1941, the allocations to the Commissariat of Defence and the Naval Commissariat increased from 56.8 billion to 83 billion rubles. This represented a greater annual increase than during any one of the subsequent war years.[101] Newly built factories and plants to manufacture non-military goods were designed for easy conversion to defence industries. All enterprises were obliged to work out mobilization plans. When war broke out in the West in September 1939, a partial mobilization of Soviet industry was carried out. In characteristic fashion Stalin demanded increased tempos above the levels set at the congress. He demanded increases in production of 17–18 per cent in 1941 alone before the war broke out. He exerted heavy pressure in the form of threats and coercion on both the industrial and party cadres to improve poor discipline and labour productivity.[102]

The new plan emphasized the industrial development of the east, partly for economic reasons but mainly to improve the country's strategic position and strengthen industrialization among the less developed economies of the national republics. The majority of the new metallurgical, energy and chemical industries were constructed east of Moscow, including some of the largest and most modern plants in the Soviet Union. On Voznesensky's recommendation, with Stalin's approval, investment in the defence industry east of the Volga rose to 12 per cent of the total.[103] The search for fresh sources of minerals and coal spurred co-operation with the scientific community that proved enormously fruitful in the war years. In the Karaganda region, the most technologically sophisticated coal industry in the country began operations on the eve of the war. A crash railway construction project, spearheaded by 18,000 Komsomol volunteers, laid down over 8,000 kilometres of track linking Karaganda with the expanded metallurgical combines of Magnitogorsk. A successful drive was launched to make the Soviet Union self-sufficient in aluminium production. Similar breakthroughs were reported in the production of tin and copper in the Urals. The oil fields at Emba, called 'the second Baku', rapidly expanded production in 1938 and 1939.[104]

The damage to the metallurgical industry caused by widespread arrests of industrial managers during the purges was largely repaired by 1940. The design and manufacture of new weapons occupied a major place in the third five-year plan, and the growth of major heavy industrial sectors facilitated mass production. Stalin took a close personal interest in weapons procurement and fancied himself a specialist. Modern weapons technology fascinated him, but his technical knowledge was often faulty. In the thirties he fostered the image of himself as a great patron of aviation. He pressed for advanced types of fighters and bombers, yet at the same time he ordered or permitted the arrest of leading aircraft designers like Tupolev. Moreover, Stalin's insidious insistence on increased tempos for production of planes, including prototypes, was responsible for a sudden surge in aviation accidents on the eve of the war. In the first quarter of 1939 alone, accidents claimed the lives of 141 airmen, with the loss of 138 machines. It became the subject of a special inquiry, but Stalin blamed the commanders and ordered heads to roll.[105]

Long before the conflict broke out, Stalin had predicted that the future war would be 'a war of motors'. But this was merely a hollow echo of Tukhachevsky. Like many of Stalin's banal maxims, it was broadcast as great wisdom. He was obsessed by advances in the explosive power of munitions, though his pronouncements on this as well as other technical matters often appear commonplace. 'Everything comes down to the destruction of the objective,' he stated, 'and that leaves it up to munitions. The explosive force of munitions defines the power of all types of armed forces including aviation and serves as the standard of the military and economic expedience of investing in one or another combat technique.'[106]

The first sign of urgency in weapons procurement came at a high-level conference in August 1938 on tank production. The participants included members of the Politburo, military leaders and weapons designers. The production of tanks was not concentrated in one commissariat until the very eve of the war, delaying the implementation of the planners. More than a year of discussion, debate and trial runs culminated in the decision to mass-produce two new types; the KV-1 heavy tank and the T-34 medium tank, both equipped with diesel engines. Production began belatedly in the spring of 1940, when the big plants at Stalingrad and Chelyabinsk began production, and over 1,800 were in service when the war broke out.

A whole set of technical improvements were introduced into small-arms production in the year preceding the war. New systems of artillery were developed, especially in heavy-calibre weapons and mortars. The first experiments with rocket field artillery proved successful, and the famous Katiusha went into mass production as the war began. There was a strong push to design new model aircraft, particularly fighters. The Central Aero Hydrodynamic Institute was reorganized just before the war. New bureaus for the design of military aircraft produced two excellent models, the MiG-3 and Il-2, but production only began in 1940 and small numbers were in service when the Germans invaded. Rewards were now showered on the remnants of the talented group of designers who had been recruited by Tukhachevsky.[107]

Thus on the eve of the war, in spite of the wasteful and wholly unnecessary disruption of defence industries by the purges, the Soviet Union had succeeded in erecting a modern metallurgical base and specialized factories for producing the most modern arms in large quantities. Soviet weapons designers and inventors, who had sustained heavy losses during the purges, continued to turn out new models of small arms, tanks, artillery and aircraft that proved under battle conditions to be equal and in some cases superior to the German matériel. Soviet weapons technology had, no doubt, benefited from contacts with German engineers in the twenties. But contacts had been broken off after 1933. The new Soviet weapons were not copies of foreign models, but the products of domestic inventiveness. And innovation in weapons technology did not stop with the outbreak of war.

Although Stalin killed off many of the innovative army and air force leaders and weapons designers, he ultimately appropriated most of their ideas. He was shrewd enough to understand their value and their power. There is a chilling parallel here to his relationship with the Left Opposition in the area of economic planning: initially he opposed rapid industrialization, but after he had liquidated its most ardent supporters, he cannibalized their ideas. The way in which he expropriated the major economic, technological and military ideas of his victims shows all the earmarks of a demonic intelligence. In Stalin's hands the subtle and complex proposals of the economic planners and military innovators became coarsened, unbalanced and distorted. He turned each of the major transformations of Soviet society, industrialization, collectivization and modernization of the army into so many costly victories that almost defeated the purpose for which the great sacrifices had been made. Nevertheless, by the eve of the war the Soviet Union had achieved the rank of a world military power comparable to Germany, out of all proportion to its level of general economic development.[108]

DIPLOMATIC SERVICE

In the world of Soviet diplomacy, the loss of personnel during the purges and the extent of disorganization were as great as in the army, but the recovery was even slower and the damage done to relations with the outside world was in many subtle ways more lasting. In the late thirties, Stalin's growing recourse to extralegal means was beginning to complicate and undermine the policy of collective security.[109] It is estimated that about two thirds of the top Soviet diplomats, including all heads of department and directors of services of the Commissariat of Foreign Affairs and a majority of *polpredy* (ambassadors) and commissars, were arrested and executed. The leadership of the Commissariat of Foreign Trade was also destroyed. The Litvinov cadres were decimated, and the foreign commissar himself lived in dread of arrest, a revolver tucked under his pillow at night. It was not simply a question of replacing seasoned diplomats with less experienced men, or of restoring shattered morale, as in the army. The entire ethos of the diplomatic service was profoundly altered, and a return to the spirit of the twenties only began to take place in the 1980s.

There were three waves of purges that decimated the diplomatic corps. The first came in 1930 among Soviet embassies and commercial missions in response to defections by Soviet diplomats prompted by the shock of collectivization. The second struck at the top ranks in 1937 and 1938. All Litvinov's deputy commissars were arrested – Lev Karakhan, Nikolai Krestinsky, Boris Stomoniakov, Khristian Rakovski and Gregor Sokolnikov – as well as a whole series of veteran Soviet representatives in embassies abroad. It was enough to have 'been in contact' with an enemy of the people at some time in one's career to guarantee repression. Several of the top figures – like Krestinsky, Rakovski, Sokolnikov, deputy commissar of foreign trade, and Arkady Rozengoltz, commissar of foreign trade – featured prominently at the show trials, where the chief prosecutor Andrei Vyshinsky accused them of spying and planning to dismember the USSR. Stomoniakov attributed his arrest to a 1907 meeting with Trotsky, who had visited him in Vienna on his way back from Bulgaria. Morale plummeted in the commissariat; denunciations, suspicion and fear virtually paralyzed diplomatic activity. Many embassies were reduced to a skeleton staff, deprived of all their responsible personnel. Consular services in Iran, China and Germany ceased to exist. There was no one left in embassies in Saudi Arabia and Greece. In January 1939 Litvinov complained to Stalin that eight Soviet embassies were without *polpredy*: Tokyo, Warsaw, Bucharest, Barcelona, Kaunas, Copenhagen, Budapest and Sofia, some of them for more than a year. The situation was worse among the support staff, which had been decimated. In the central offices of the commissariat, only one out of eight section chiefs was left. Courier service had been cut because twelve couriers had not received permission to travel abroad before a review of their personal files. Too many specialists had been recruited for secret work and not replaced. Litvinov saw no chance of replacing the staff abroad because of the long delays in verifying their credentials. Within the commissariat, fewer and fewer documents analyzing the international situation were being produced.[110]

Beginning with the first show trials in 1936, the process of isolating the foreign community from the population within the Soviet Union and the Soviet diplomatic personnel from the population of foreign countries accelerated. By 1937, 'an anti-foreign campaign of almost unparalleled intensity', according to the American diplomat George F. Kennan's Moscow dispatch, made no effort to distinguish between democratic peace-loving states and fascist aggressors. A wave of arrests and deportations of foreign nationals swept indiscriminately through the foreign community. Arbitrary arrests of Soviet citizens who worked for foreign missions further reduced contact. Protests from abroad over arrests of foreign as well as Soviet citizens working for embassies were ignored. Statements by leading Soviet officials in the press and radio warned the public that all foreigners were secret agents. Harassment of foreign diplomats turned their lives into a nightmare. When Litvinov returned from one of his trips abroad, Krestinsky informed him that Soviet diplomats were no longer accepting invitations to foreign embassies because 'they were afraid'. Litvinov admitted to the German ambassador that he lacked any means of restricting the internal authorities, that is the secret police, from arresting German citizens. Even the French ambassador, representing a country allied to the Soviet Union, was helpless to prevent the expulsion of French nationals.[111]

Litvinov's courageous attempts to defend his subordinates ran into a wall of hostility. In one case he demanded a personal meeting with Stalin. 'Comrade Stalin, I vouch for Stomoniakov. I have known him since the beginning of the century and together with him carried out the most difficult assignments from Lenin and the Central Committee. I vouch for Stomoniakov.' Stalin listened in silence, pacing the room. Then he fixed Litvinov with 'a cold piercing glance', and said, 'Comrade Litvinov, you can only vouch for yourself.'[112] A seasoned diplomat, Stomoniakov had played a major role in shaping Litvinov's policy of collective security in the Far East. By the autumn of 1937, however, the rising number of unexplained arrests in the Foreign Commissariat began to affect Litvinov's morale; the burden of work, which increased as his collaborators disappeared, not to be replaced, wore him down physically. He was not surprised when his deputy, Krestinsky, was arrested that Vladimir Potemkin was chosen as his successor. Potemkin was an experienced diplomat and he had no black marks on his record. He had not been an émigré in the West before the revolution, and after he joined the party he had no contacts with members of the 'opposition'. Meanwhile, feeling himself 'the last of the Mohicans', Stomoniakov attempted suicide. He was removed from office and after a few months arrested. He died in prison in July 1941.[113]

By contrast, the case of Boris Shtein, another veteran diplomat and associate of Litvinov, took a different turn, although again the reasons remain obscure. After a brief special assignment in Helsinki, he returned to Moscow to be informed in May 1939 by Vladimir Dekanozov, Beria's man in the Foreign Commissariat, that he had been dismissed from his duties as *polpred* in Italy, where he had served for four years. His party card was withdrawn. He confided to Litvinov that he was in limbo. After several unsuccessful attempts to recover his card, he volunteered to teach in the Higher Diplomatic School. The party bureau examining his request for restitution concluded that he had engaged in 'anti-Soviet activity in 1918'. It demanded an account of a journal he had edited at the time in Zaporozhe. Several special commissions met in 1940, broadening their investigation to cover 'errors' in his lectures at the Higher Diplomatic School, and accused him of weakening the activities of the trade union. Subject to continued harassment, nonetheless he was not arrested, continued to teach and died peacefully in 1961.[114]

By 1938 the Foreign Commissariat was also deprived of its unique source of information about the outside world. The purges had decimated its press department. Staffed by experienced specialists with excellent linguistic training, it had provided news and copy to government organs including *Izvestiia*. The purgers were beginning to close in on Litvinov himself. In 1939 Beria took charge of fabricating a case against Litvinov, attempting to extract denunciations from close associates like G.A. Gnedin, the former deputy commissar for the press. Within the year Litvinov was expelled from the Central Committee. But he did not go quietly. When verbally harassed by Molotov, he defended his policy of collective security towards Britain and France and predicted a German attack on the Soviet Union. Stalin rose to refute him. Litvinov demanded to know whether he was considered an enemy of the people. Stalin answered deliberately: 'We do not consider "Papasha" an enemy of the people but an honest revolutionary.' Stalin knew that Litvinov had never associated in any way with an opposition or factional group.

The third wave of purges followed Litvinov's replacement by Molotov. It virtually turned over the entire staff of the commissariat.[115] Molotov was extremely suspicious of Litvinov. He believed his predecessor was a 'decent diplomat, a good one', but ideologically unsound. 'In spirit', recalled Molotov, 'he took up a different position, rather opportunistic, [and] he sympathized a great deal with Trotsky, Zinoviev and Kamenev.'[116] This was patently absurd. But Molotov acted upon this assumption. By the outbreak of the war there were few survivors among the '*Litvinovtsy*' in the Foreign Commissariat. Many had been recalled or demoted in the period just before the war, including his closest associates: Iakov Surits in Paris, Boris Shtein in Rome and Oleg Troianovsky in Washington (although his ill health would probably have soon forced him to leave his post). Even Potemkin, who had moved up to deputy commissar following the second wave of purges, was obliged to retire. Among the last holdovers were Ivan Maisky in London and Aleksandra Kollontai in Sweden. But after the Nazi-Soviet Pact, Maisky was marginalized. He was subjected to a severe attack by the young, inexperienced party stalwart Fedor Gusev, who had been appointed head of the West European Department of the Commissariat. Gusev reprimanded him for his diplomatic work, ordering him to restrict his meetings with top-level officials and only transmit information from the press.[117] He was probably saved from being recalled by the Nazi attack on the Soviet Union and the prospects of an alliance with Britain. Litvinov himself was recalled to service after the outbreak of war to serve as ambassador in Washington. He and Maisky were recalled to Moscow in 1943 as a sign of Stalin's displeasure over the postponement of a second front.[118] But both men retained their rank in the Foreign Affairs Commissariat. Moreover, in another example of how Stalin could recognize the value of special skills, he appointed them to chair two committees planning for postwar Europe. Possibly, too, he was holding them in reserve for a restoration of closer ties with the West.[119] However, Litvinov nourished bitter feelings throughout the rest of his life.

Reminiscing about his dismissal, Litvinov subsequently claimed that the management of Soviet foreign policy had fallen into the hands of three men. 'None of them', Litvinov lamented, 'understands America or Britain.' Molotov, Stalin's longtime friend and supporter, had no diplomatic experience. He never even considered himself a diplomat, he admitted, because he had no command of a foreign language. But his qualifications were limited by more than his narrow definition of the profession. He also held the view that the struggle against the Trotskyites and the 'Rights' who were 'politically very literate people' qualified him to conduct foreign policy as though representatives of foreign powers were the equivalent of defeated party leaders. An early example of Molotov's contempt for Litvinov and diplomacy was his attempt in 1935 to go behind the foreign commissar's back in trying to work out a deal with the Americans over debt settlement. The second man, Andrei Vyshinsky, a lawyer by training, had a notorious reputation among the foreign community as the xenophobic prosecutor in the purge trials. Litvinov considered him a sheer opportunist with no fixed views on any question. Vladimir Dekanozov was a former police official who, together with Vyshinsky, was responsible for the purges in the Baltic states; later as ambassador to Nazi Germany he 'sat next to Ribbentrop for a year', in Litvinov's sarcastic evaluation, 'and that's all he knows about foreign countries.'[120]

Stalin had never displayed much interest in the operational aspects of foreign policy. Litvinov and his predecessor, Georgy Chicherin, had enjoyed a good deal of leeway in implementing the general lines of foreign policy, occasionally even taking surprising initiatives. This was also the case with the leadership of the Comintern. The evidence suggests that Stalin was sceptical about the twin policies of collective security and a popular front against fascism, but he allowed them to develop as their advantages became clearer to him. But after 1936, he appeared to retreat more and more into isolation. He created a sensation in the diplomatic corps, for example, when he surprised American ambassador Joseph E. Davies with a visit in Molotov's office.[121] Combined with his personal indifference, Stalin's repeated pronouncements on the renewed dangers of capitalist encirclement produced a gloomy reaction among Western – especially American – diplomats, who interpreted it as a prelude to the abandonment of the policy of collective security.[122]

Yet at the same time that Stalin was reducing his foreign contacts he gathered the threads of foreign policy more tightly into his own hands. Without experienced diplomats who understood foreign languages, the Soviet leadership, in the words of Molotov, feared 'being swindled'. In order to avoid costly errors, Soviet diplomacy in the thirties, forties and fifties was highly centralized. The *polpredy* were only executors of specific orders. Stalin decided everything and exhibited extreme caution as he groped his way through unknown territory. Even during the war he somehow found time to read most of the incoming dispatches.[123]

The effect of the purges and isolationist tendencies upon the Soviet diplomatic corps itself is more difficult to document than in the case of the army, because the revelations by Soviet diplomats in the 1960s were not as numerous or detailed as those of the generals, and rehabilitations were fewer and less significant. Gleaning from the memoirs of Alexander Barmine, Ivan Maisky, Nikolai Novikov, Valentin Berezhkov and Zinovy Sheinis, it is possible to sketch a picture of a service that became disoriented, demoralized and distrustful. As in the army, the elimination of knowledgeable veterans forced promotion of young or inexperienced individuals to high ranks for which they were not adequately prepared. Most of the new diplomats were drawn from the middle ranks of the bureaucracy and the professorate.

Andrei Gromyko, a professor of economics, had no idea why he was plucked out of the academic world in 1939 to head the USA department in the Commissariat of Foreign Affairs. Perhaps it was because he knew some English and his party credentials were impeccable.[124] When Andrei Vyshinsky was appointed first deputy commissar of foreign affairs in 1940, he had had no previous diplomatic experience. Semeon Tsarapkin entered the diplomatic service in 1937 and was still in his late thirties when he took over from Gromyko as head of the USA department of the Commissariat of Foreign Affairs. Gromyko at thirty-four and Fedor Gusev at thirty-eight became *polpredy* to the USA and Britain after only four and six years of service, respectively.[125] Nikolai Novikov, who had enjoyed a successful career in the metals industry, acquired only two years' service before he was appointed counsellor at the London embassy and ordered to accompany Maisky to all top-level meetings; Anthony Eden regarded him as 'a Kremlin watchdog'. He was probably an agent of the NKVD.[126] After two years in that post he took charge of the Second Section for European Affairs of the Foreign Commissariat at age thirty-eight. Aleksandr Bogomolov was already thirty-nine when he was assigned to the service and, after two years, became ambassador to the allied governments-in-exile in London. When the war broke out with Germany, the Foreign Commissariat was caught short-handed and scrambled to find former diplomats with some experience, on one occasion plucking the wounded E.D. Kiselev out of a hospital to become general-consul in New York.[127]

The autobiography of Nikolai Novikov gives a vivid idea of the new diplomats. He had only seven years' formal schooling before he joined the Red Army and then enrolled in a two-year adult education course before entering the Institute of Red Professors, not a higher school in those early years but a middle school. He was recruited out of his third year to serve in the Foreign Commissariat. His interview with Litvinov was a disaster. After reading him a lecture on the necessity of a political education, a solid cultural preparation and irreproachable literacy as prerequisites, Litvinov summarily dismissed him. But Malenkov picked him up and appointed him to the Political Section of the Far Eastern department, a position for which he had no training. He relied heavily on the guidance of his superior, M.S. Mitskevich, 'whose competence in foreign relations was also not high'. Mitskevich, in turn, was dependent on his deputy, A.F. Miller, a veteran of the Foreign Service, professor, linguist and author. But Miller was soon purged. Novikov then approached Boris Stomoniakov a few days before he too was purged. Promoted to replace Miller, Novikov became deputy of the Turkish section of the department. After Molotov took over the Commissariat, he was made head of the newly created Middle East section. In the absence of a trained Arabist, responsibility for preparing the survey of current events in Arab countries rested solely on Novikov, who at least knew some Turkish.[128] When Litvinov was recalled from Washington, Novikov became chargé under Gromyko and then succeeded him as ambassador, also serving as Gromyko's deputy on the Far Eastern Commission in 1946.

Bogomolov and Novikov were two of the harshest critics of British and American foreign policy during and immediately after the war. In the key position of ambassador to all the allied governments in exile in London, Bogomolov also felt free to comment on British and American influence on these governments. In his view the two Western powers sought to gain 'exclusive influence on the affairs of postwar Europe'. He advised a policy of reserve in dealing with de Gaulle; Sikorski was a 'puppet' in the hands of the more reactionary Poles; he dismissed plans of a Czech-Polish federation as contrary to the will of the people.[129] In October 1943 he wrote to Vyshinsky of 'things coming to a dénouement'. The British were planning to install in Europe their own governments-in-exile, dispatching the Free French to Algiers and Greek monarchists to Cairo, the key jump-off points for Europe. In Cairo, according to Bogomolov, the Anglo-Americans were gathering strength to descend on Central and Eastern Europe at the moment when the Germans withdrew to their frontiers as a result of the defeats inflicted on them by the Red Army. The American military government would create all kinds of puppet regimes, he predicted. He urged strong Soviet representation in Cairo to make contact with the Egyptians, Greeks and Yugoslavs.[130] He followed this up with an even stronger denunciation of Anglo-American policy as an attempt to prolong the war in order to weaken Germany and the Soviet Union, encouraging the most reactionary French circles in support of General Giraud against de Gaulle, siding with Mihailović in Yugoslavia and the 'pro-fascist' Polish government of Edward Raczyński, attempting to undermine the Soviet-Czech rapprochement, encouraging the Vatican in its anti-Soviet policy in Eastern Europe and in general directing most of their activities not towards defeating Germany but towards bolstering the counter-revolution.[131]

In his capacity as ambassador to Washington, Novikov was the author of the famous dispatch of 27 September 1946 on US foreign policy that has often been interpreted as the Soviet equivalent of Kennan's Long Telegram.[132] He was also one of the early Soviet critics of the Marshall Plan. On 9 June 1947 Novikov attacked it as 'sketching the clear contours of a Western bloc directed against us'; he repeated 'the accusation on 24 June.[133] Stalin had given instruction for Molotov and a large Soviet delegation to attend the preliminary discussions on a plan for economic reconstruction of Europe. But on 9 July he informed a Czech delegation to Moscow that 'on the basis of materials received from our diplomats we are convinced that behind the screen of financial aid to Europe something like a Western bloc is being organized against the Soviet Union'.[134] Although it is not possible on the basis of the available materials to determine the extent to which reporting by men like Bogomolov and Novikov influenced Stalin, there can be little doubt that the change in tone of dispatches by the Soviet diplomats since the time of Litvinov's tenure as foreign commissar weighed heavily in the calculations of the Soviet leader.

Another problem arising from the purges and the atmosphere they created was the decline in the quantity as well as the quality of the information received in Moscow. Beginning in the late thirties, the network of informal communications and trust among colleagues within the service was badly disrupted. A conspiracy of silence descended; the purges were simply not discussed. Aleksandra Kollontai, an Old Bolshevik, Soviet ambassador to Sweden and a great admirer of Litvinov, dared only to confide laconically to her diary in 1937: 'It is a difficult, anxious time . . . I do not remember such a tension-filled atmosphere.' Reports from the field that ran counter to accepted wisdom in Moscow were ignored. When Kollontai returned to Moscow in order to warn Molotov that a Soviet attack on Finland would turn all 'progressive Europe' against the USSR, he reacted with cold indifference and abruptly rebuffed her.[135] Formal instructions from the centre became terse and were often delayed for long periods because of the excessive centralization that replaced individual initiative. Ambassadors were no longer trusted with confidential information. The announcement of the Nazi-Soviet Pact struck them like a bolt from the blue.

Individuals were abruptly recalled and reassigned without warning or consultation. Outside of formal diplomatic receptions, social contact with foreigners was rare. These habits and procedures continued even after the wartime alliance was consolidated by the summit meetings at Tehran and Yalta. Western diplomats discovered that negotiating with the Russians was a baffling and frustrating task. The smallest changes in wording in original Soviet drafts had to be referred to Moscow. Sometimes embarrassed by lack of instructions and their own inability to respond, Soviet diplomats resorted to extraneous arguments, misleading comparisons and mendacious evasions; then, when instructions arrived, they were perfectly capable of blithely reversing themselves without batting an eye. Traditional diplomatic practices and procedures were ignored or poorly understood. Agreements by Soviet diplomats 'in principle' were rejected in practice; but when Allied diplomats agreed in principle for the purposes of discussion, Soviet diplomats including Stalin took this to mean acceptance in practice.[136] These Stalinist traits of negotiation became deeply ingrained in the Soviet diplomatic service. They were re-enforced by the onset of the Cold War and the anti-cosmopolitan campaign of the late 1940s, and only gradually began to change after Stalin's death, although strong traces of them remained characteristic of Soviet diplomacy into the 1980s.

Stalin's complete domination over foreign policy and the imposition of his mentality, backed by fears among his diplomats that the slightest error would be misconstrued as weakness or sabotage as exemplified in the purge trials, had the effect of re-enforcing rather than creating the anti-Soviet feelings that permeated the British and American foreign services. The American specialists on Russia were, by and large, well trained in the language and steeped in the culture, but they had little sympathy with the new Soviet regime. Whatever sympathy there might have been was quickly dissipated by Stalinism. Their experiences in the thirties added a stiff dose of personal frustration, humiliation and anger to their political and ideological predispositions. They sympathized with ambassador William Bullitt's disillusionment and scorned Joseph E. Davies for his naivety. They had little patience for Roosevelt's policy and, consequently, he sought to circumvent them. The president succeeded only partially; the Russian specialists exercised strong influence on all his ambassadors except Davies and, after he passed from the scene, their advice and counsel were eagerly sought by an administration that was drawing up the battle lines for the Cold War.[137]

The longer experience of the British Foreign Service was even more volatile, agitated by the anti-Russian sentiments that pre-dated the revolution and powerfully re-enforced by such incidents as the Zinoviev letter and the Arcos Raid in the twenties as well as the purges that came later.[138] Despite the heavy legacy of these traditions, the Stalinist style – from which, ironically, only Stalin himself was occasionally free – created unnecessary difficulties for

Soviet foreign policy, often projecting the image of the diplomat as a rude, uncompromising automaton and turning every negotiation into an ordeal of patience and a test of will.

With the withering of the Soviet diplomatic service, Stalin and Molotov took over the making of foreign policy. They worked well as a team. Stalin set down the broad lines and on occasion entered directly into negotiations at the highest level, where he proved to be a shrewd and skilful bargainer. He relied heavily, however, on Molotov to carry out his detailed instructions in dealing with foreign diplomats and occasionally with foreign leaders. Molotov acquired a reputation as a tough, often inflexible but effective negotiator, earning the sobriquet 'stone bottom'.[139] Their efforts to keep the Soviet Union out of a general war seemed crowned with success in 1939–40 with the signing of the Nazi-Soviet Pact and the Neutrality Pact with Japan. They had obtained, without a shot, substantial territories on their western border and settled the frontier disputes in the Far East. But their expectations of a breathing space for the Soviet Union to strengthen defensive preparations behind the newly acquired buffer zone were upset by two unanticipated events. First, the rapid defeat of France made possible massive concentration of Axis forces on the Soviet frontier. Second, Hitler launched his invasion before Stalin believed that he would. Fortunately, the Japanese remained quiescent, in part the result of Stalin's decision not to weaken the Far Eastern forces of the Red Army. Fortunately, too, the negotiations with Germany and Japan, which had alienated many in the Atlantic world and which could have led to complete isolation of the Soviet Union in the face of a possible two-front war, did not prevent Churchill and Roosevelt from signalling their unqualified support of the Soviet Union. Stalin and Molotov were then able at the diplomatic level to help forge the Grand Alliance that won the war.

*****

In preparing for war and simultaneously building socialism, Stalin embarked upon a course marked by paradox at every turn. As industry was nationalized and farms collectivized, the administrative tasks facing the party and the state agencies multiplied many times. Stalin's response was to launch a second round of expansion of the Soviet bureaucracy. It unfolded rapidly amid an enormous social transformation that was only in part designed and co-ordinated from above. In many situations, the changes were wholly improvised, despite the principle of planning that in theory was officially designated as the basis for building a new order. The amalgam of the planned and the improvised became a hallmark of the Stalinist system. Within the bureaucracy itself there were also conflicting tendencies. The rapidly rising number of officials in the party and state agencies took place under conditions that were hardly conducive to meeting the classic formulation of the Weberian model of the bureaucratic phenomenon. Instead of a gradual and orderly introduction of a rational order based on merit, the recruitment and in-house training of the new generation of Soviet bureaucrats proceeded in a cyclonic atmosphere. The proliferation of offices and officials to staff them was accompanied by a very high and rapid turnover in personnel marked by successive waves of purges beginning in 1929 and culminating in the Great Terror of 1936–38, diminishing at a slower rhythm but still taking a toll in 1939 down to the outbreak of war. Thus, the building of an orderly, centrally planned economy and a modern army was carried out by civil and military servants of the state living in a constant state of uncertainty, anxiety and fear.

A decade of experience acquired by a skilled corps of diplomats in building a security system was virtually wiped out. The result was a peculiarly lopsided system in which the rules, lines of command, procedures and functional distinctions were blurred and overlapping, further dislocated by intimidation, denunciations, arrests and violations of the fundamental legal norms.

The transformation of the educational system aimed at training a new generation of officials and workers was characterized by a similar paradox. Among industrial personnel the ranks of engineers and technicians expanded at a great rate and received proportionally higher material rewards than manual or white-collar workers. The new cadres, the so-called 'red directors' produced by the Soviet educational system, began to occupy key posts in the economy and government, replacing the so-called 'bourgeois specialists' left over from the old regime.

While the bias in favour of *praktiki* in educational and industrial policy had a negative effect on the quality of production, it contributed, paradoxically, to the formation of a new working class through upward mobility of the peasantry moving out of the farm to the factory and also providing the recruits for a new elite among the intelligentsia.[140] A similar process was taking place among the army officers. The foreign service was staffed by amateurs. Among the new men and women who had identified themselves with Stalin in his rise to power, very few had been members of the opposition. Yet, despite their proven loyalty, they too were not spared from the sweeping scythe of the purges that carried off some of the best of them. Their dedication to a rigorous scientific rationality, their independent thinking on industrial and strategic problems, as well as their keen awareness of the limits of the possible, appeared to place many of them at odds with Stalin's governing style. On the one hand there was his obsession with forced tempos of production and mobilization embodied in his slogan 'Bolsheviks can storm any heights'. On the other hand, there was his equally powerful obsession with uncovering internal enemies and threats to his own power. The exercise of his personal rule cut deeply into the ranks of the technical intelligentsia, the army leadership and ambassadorial ranks, and the gaps were filled by upwardly mobile and ambitious men and women who owed their advancement to Stalin's paradoxical policies of instability and renewal.

In the Bolshevik party, the ordeal by fire was if anything more harrowing. In the decade between 1928 and 1939 approximately 1.75 million members were removed from the party rolls. During the same period, the party increased its size from 1.25 million to 2.5 million, and jumped another 1.5 million in the two years just before the war. Given that there had been a four-year suspension of recruitment between 1933 and 1937, the flood of new recruits that inundated the party after 1937 could not be easily absorbed. The social composition of the new recruits reflected a departure from earlier practice. The old bias in favour of the working class lost much of its appeal, to be modified in favour of the intelligentsia and white-collar workers in the civil bureaucracy and peasants in top ranks in the officer corps.

As a governing body, the party had lost much ground to the police and economic bureaucracy. Its two main representative organs, the party congress and the central committee, met more irregularly and the congress was reduced to performing a ceremonial function. They played little role in the preparations for war. Although the party was the central governing body, its institutional relationship with the other state agencies, the army, economic bureaucracy and diplomatic corps was never firmly or clearly established. Stalin devoted his energies to building socialism and preparing for a war he believed was inevitable while weakening the forces most necessary to defend the country against a powerful antagonist.

CHAPTER 2

MOBILIZATION AND PURGES ON THE PERIPHERIES

In the decades leading up to the war, Stalin rallied his loyal supporters to follow a paradoxical policy aimed at consolidating Soviet power among the nationalities. On the one hand, he initiated intensive propaganda campaigns to mobilize the populations of the non-Russian republics by stressing unity and equality in building socialism, opening up opportunities for political advancement in the party and state bureaucracies, promoting local cultures and economic development. On the other hand, he conducted extensive purges of veteran party leaders among the nationalities, imposed restraints on perceived nationalist deviations and ordered selective deportations of nationalities on the frontiers of the country. The gradual shift that took place towards the more coercive aspects of his dual-nationality policy intensified as Stalin anticipated a coming war. Although foreign relations had played a role in motivating his actions on the periphery as in the centre, this factor assumed greater importance with the passing of every year. A reverse turn would only take place when the war actually broke out.

THE NATIONALITIES AND THE BORDERLANDS

In the early thirties, the policy of promoting non-Russian nationalities to administrative and party positions in their republics – *korenizatsiia* ('indigenization') – crumbled under a combination of internal and external pressures. Within the Soviet borderlands, peasant resistance to collectivization and the attempts of local party leaders to protect their regions from arbitrary and unreasonable quotas for the collection of grain were interpreted by the centre as proof that class enemies and the 'nationalist deviations' were joining forces. This had always been Stalin's greatest nightmare, which he had sought to dispel by promoting indigenization. At the same time, the Piedmont principle – a term used at the time to refer to the role of the Kingdom of Piedmont-Sardinia as the core of the movement for Italian unification – which had been intended to attract elements of the nationalities outside the Soviet borders, was being appropriated by Germany and Japan to exercise a centrifugal pull on the Soviet borderlands.[1]

In the national republics and autonomous republics of the USSR the decimation of party cadres was no greater than in the Russian Soviet Federated Socialist Republic (RSFSR) during the purges, yet there was one essential difference. Most of the victims in the non-Russian republics were condemned for nationalist deviation; none was so condemned in the Russian Republic. In the words of the Soviet historian Roy Medvedev, 'by destroying tens of thousands of good Communists among the minority nationalities, the charge of nationalism helped to revive many nationalistic moods and prejudices'.[2] These were, it should be added, never very far below the surface.

Along with the retreat from the high point of indigenization, Stalin launched a strong revival of Russian patriotism, beginning with the recasting of Russian history and spreading rapidly to other sectors of cultural and intellectual life. The purges were in one sense merely a continuation – albeit in radically intensified form – of the prolonged struggle between the Great Russian centre and the periphery over cultural issues. Statistics tell only part of the story, but even by themselves they are eloquent. In the 1920s there was a steady rise in the percentage of indigenous Communists in all the republics, except the Volga German Autonomous Soviet Socialist Republic (ASSR), but especially in Ukraine, Belarus and the Crimean Tatar ASSR. After the mid-1930s, when the purges cut deeply into their membership, the percentages declined in most of them. In the Central Asian republics, the drop was from 5 per cent in Kazakhstan to 15 per cent in the Kirghiz SSR. Only in Ukraine did no decline take place, although the pace of indigenization slowed and the earlier steady increase in numbers of Ukrainians in the Communist Party of Ukraine ceased altogether.[3]

At the end of 1934, the year of ominous signs for Stalin, the Politburo introduced a new regime for the western borderlands. Terry Martin has argued that this was the prelude to a shift in Soviet policy to large-scale ethnic cleansing. The new regulations created a 'forbidden border zone' of varying depth 'into which no one could enter without special NKVD permission'.[4] But even before this, the security organs detected a potentially dangerous link between the resistance to collectivization in Ukraine and Belarus and Polish intervention. As a precaution, in 1930 the Politburo ordered a vigorous campaign against deviations from the party line in the frontier districts of the two republics and a series of operations to strengthen border security. The arrest and deportation of kulak elements was to be carried out with great speed, but quietly (*bez shuma*), avoiding any indication of a mass deportation.[5] The campaign gradually gained momentum, but up until 1936 the security organs were still more involved with internal actions. By the end of 1936 approximately half the German and Polish inhabitants in the border districts had been deported throughout the Soviet Union. At the same time, similar policies were applied to the Finnish, Estonian and Latvian populations of the Leningrad border region.[6]

In the Inner Asian borderlands, the NKVD finally carried out the long-planned deportation of the Korean population inhabiting the frontier districts. In the process, however, they rounded up almost all the Koreans – at least 175,000 – in the Far Eastern region (*krai*) and packed them off to the Central Asian republics. About 8,000 Chinese were also snared by the NKVD nets. Especially hard hit were those associated with the army, secret police or defence industries.[7] Similar deportations were taking place almost simultaneously along the Caucasian and Trans-Caspian frontiers.

At Stalin's behest, beginning in January 1938 the secret police unleashed a new wave of mass repression against the so-called 'national contingents', targeting a hitherto unprecedented range of ethnic groups – Poles, Germans, Latvians, Estonians, Finns, Greeks, Romanians, Bulgarians, Macedonians, Iranians, Afghans and Chinese.[8] These were essentially the peoples of the borderlands.

The dual mania directed against foreign spies and domestic class enemies in the borderlands was not limited to the nationalities. In the early stages of the raids on the national contingents, Nikolai Ezhov, the commissar of internal affairs (NKVD), targeted hired workers and refugees from abroad who had entered the Soviet Union in recent years as 'defectors'. Following up his warnings to the party and military leaders in the first half of 1937, Stalin ordered Ezhov to arrest all Germans employed in defence industries and to deport numbers of them. The targets were originally German citizens but the campaign rapidly engulfed Soviet citizens of German nationality or those who had some contact with Germans or Germany. The Poles and those who were in any way linked to Poland were next, followed by numerous other nationalities.[9] Instructions to purge extended even to large numbers of 'Kharbintsy', the approximately 25,000 ethnic Russians who had been repatriated in 1935 following the sale of the Chinese Eastern Railway. They were suspected of harbouring anti-Soviet sentiments dating back to the civil war and of collaborating with the Japanese.[10]

It soon turned out that the deportations and purges in the western borderlands were insufficiently thorough. This at least was the message that the Politburo member Andrei Andreev relayed to Stalin in 1938, during his whirlwind tour of potential trouble spots throughout the Soviet Union. In the frontier districts of Belarus he uncovered weak party structures and subversive elements among the Poles and families of purge victims. He recommended that these elements be deported farther into the interior. Although the secretary of the Belarus Communist Party, Panteleimon Ponomarenko, received a passing grade, Andreev fingered Belarus's commissar of education as 'a traitor and probably a Polish spy', and its commissar of agriculture as a 'suspicious character'. He suggested the removal of many party secretaries in the frontier districts who were Poles or Latvians. He also pointed out weaknesses in the frontier defences and proposed a series of measures to prevent cross-border movement.[11]

Ukraine was particularly hard hit by the purges because of its large party organization, the number of prominent Ukrainians in the central apparatus and the vigorous cultural life within the republic. The nationalist character of the Ukrainian purge was etched clearly from the outset. During the 1920s the Ukrainians were second only to the Georgians in their criticism of centralization and Great Russian chauvinism. The strongest voices came from two of the many factions and tendencies that had gone on to make up the Communist Party of Ukraine during the early years of the revolution and civil war. There were, first of all, the Old Ukrainian Bolsheviks like Mykola Skrypnyk, a staunch defender of Ukrainian cultural autonomy and an outspoken critic of what he called the 'unified-indivisible change of land-mark striving of our Soviet apparatus'. Second, there were the former members of the Borotbist Party, a Ukrainian socialist revolutionary party that had co-operated with the Bolsheviks and then fused with them in 1920. These included Grigory Grinko, the commissar of education in the Ukraine, who also deplored the 'centralizing inertia' in the party that crippled the cultural-national work of the Ukraine. At the Twelfth Congress they and the Georgians provided the main backing for Rakovsky's proposed amend-ments that forced some minor concessions from Stalin on the draft of the Soviet constitution. An unexpected source of support for their position came from Bukharin, who emphasized the dangerous consequences of a dogmatic Great Russian chauvinist position. He warned that turning away from a policy of indigenization would only redound to the benefit of Mensheviks in Georgia, Petliurists in Ukraine and Basmachi in Central Asia; in other words, to the centrifugal forces that still threatened the integ-rity of the state.[12]

Ukrainian resistance to the centralists did not come to an end with the adoption of the new Soviet constitution. The leaders, joined now by Vlas Chubar, who had replaced Rakovsky as chairman of the people's commis-sars of the Ukraine in 1935 and was soon to become a candidate member of the Politburo, maintained a drumfire of criticism against administrative, budgetary and judicial procedures that deprived the republics of their rights; in several cases they gained their points.[13] A muted struggle continued over the question of bringing the Ukrainian republic's constitution in line with the Soviet constitution. It required five years of intermittent discussion before a revised Ukrainian constitution was approved. It retained the formula that the Ukraine had entered the USSR as an 'independent treaty state limited only in matters reserved to the USSR under its constitution'. As E.H. Carr has stated: 'This was a stronger affirmation of formal independ-ence and sovereignty than appeared in the constitution of any other Union republic.'[14] It also kept alive, if only feebly, the hoary question – dating back to the treaty of Pereiaslav in 1649 – of the precise constitutional relationship between Russia and the Ukraine.

While the Soviet leadership was firmly in the hands of centralists, Bukharin having abandoned his endorsement of republican rights, it perceived the need to strengthen the cultural identity of the nationalities under the

Bolshevik aegis as a method of neutralizing nationalist sentiments. In Stalin's view, the spread of Ukrainian cultural institutions was an important hedge against accusations of Great Russian chauvinism that could weaken the border regions and endanger the dictatorship of the proletariat. He admitted that the Ukraine was a test case for Soviet nationality policy that would have as great an effect on 'the peoples of the West as Turkestan has for the peoples of the East'.[15] But there were, inevitably, growing disagreements over the interpretation of the policy of 'Ukrainianization'. The existence of small, strongly pro-nationalist elements within the Ukrainian party and the outspoken statements of Ukrainian intellectuals were used by Stalin to compromise the more moderate elements represented by Chubar.

As tension mounted, the issue of cultural autonomy was swept up into the debate over industrialization, where the leaders of the Ukrainian party were in a weaker position to defend the interest of Ukraine against the imperative of an all-Union policy of central planning.[16] Resistance to collectivization in Ukraine further blurred the distinctions between cultural rights and political opposition. The first purges of Ukrainian intellectuals took place in 1930–31; a wholesale replacement of party cadres followed; in 1933 Skrypnyk, under relentless fire, took his own life. He had been accused of a raft of errors, including his support of the Piedmont principle which might lead, in the words of Pavel Postyshev, the newly appointed second secretary of the Ukrainian party, to 'the separation of Ukraine from the Soviet Union, [which] would be the beginning of the end of the entire Soviet Union, the beginning of the end of proletarian and peasant power'.[17] The Ukrainian Communist Party was thrown into confusion. Did this mean the demise of indigenization? Was this a shift in the official policy that had identified great power chauvinism as a greater danger than local nationalism to the internal stability of the country?

In a characteristic move, Stalin now assumed the position of absolute arbiter in defining the middle road. The 'man of the borderlands', speaking ex cathedra at the Seventeenth Party Congress in 1934, indicated that the questions had been badly posed. 'It would be stupid to endorse a formula that would be valid for all times. Such formulas do not exist. The greatest danger is that deviation against which one ceases to battle and which therefore grows into a danger to the state.'[18] He offered the cadres no clear guidance for the future. The implication was clear. They would have to fight it

out among themselves while he remained above the battle until it was necessary from his point of view to intervene.

The problem facing the local leaders in Ukraine and elsewhere at this
crucial moment was similar to that which historically had complicated relationships between the borderlands and the centre. No matter that they were
handpicked by Moscow (or Saint Petersburg); no matter that they may not
have shared ethnic identities with their subjects; no matter that they professed
their primary loyalty to the centre: they had to operate within a distinctive
cultural milieu shaped by historical memories. The tradition of wavering
loyalties went back to Count Kirill Razumovsky and Prince Ivan Mazepa in
the era of the tsars. A successful career in Ukraine demanded some accommodation with the local elements, and more often than not officials appointed
from outside the republic took on the coloration of their new environment.
The centre was bound to interpret any form of resistance to its commands as
tinged with nationalist sentiments; Peter the Great, Catherine the Great and
Nicholas I had reacted in similar ways. The difference with Stalin came from
the extent and violence of his reaction. While he maintained many of the
formal aspects of indigenization and some of its educational policies, he
unleashed a violent campaign against the local cadres. In the terrible year
1937 the Ukrainian apparatus was destroyed several times over. Almost all
the leading officials of the party and soviets of the republic were arrested, and
most of them were executed. Over 180,000 party members – representing 37
per cent of the total – were repressed.[19] Old opponents of Stalin like Grinko,
moderate defenders of Ukrainian rights like Chubar and even loyalists like
Postyshev who could not, however, conceal their distaste for Stalin's excessive demands for subordination, were swept away, as were their immediate
successors. A group around Grinko was accused at the trial of Rights and
Trotskyites of having organized a 'National Fascist Organization' that plotted
with foreign agents to detach Ukraine from the USSR. It was the only case
in which the Ukrainian leaders were publicly identified with nationalist
deviation, but it was enough to taint the entire Ukrainian party, which
had failed to discover and eradicate it. As if to confirm this identification
of political opposition and culture, the purges of the leadership were accompanied by a campaign to moderate 'Ukrainianization' and to inject a dose
of russo-centrism through the medium of language.[20] The combined assault
on the Ukrainian party apparatus and use of Ukrainian language were

the kind of mistakes in Soviet nationality policy that, as Bukharin had warned, played into the hands of the real nationalist enemies of the Soviet Union.

On the eve of the war, the purges of the Ukrainian communists could only have benefited the number of Ukrainian nationalist organizations outside the Soviet Union active in Ukrainian communities in the Western Ukraine, in the Carpatho-Ukraine under Czech sovereignty, in the Bukovina under Romanian control and scattered in smaller émigré colonies in Germany and France. Of these the most militant and best organized was the Organization of Ukrainian Nationalists (OUN) whose main strength was in the Western Ukraine. When Red Army forces occupied the area in 1939 as the Soviet share of the partition of Poland with Germany, Moscow discovered the supporters of the OUN bitterly divided and demoralized. The party confronted a strong network of underground opponents of Sovietization. After the German invasion in 1941, they became the core of an anti-Soviet resistance that fought a civil war within the larger war of the great powers over the fate of Ukraine.[21] In Belarus, the purges made an almost complete sweep of the party leadership; half of the membership lost their party cards. By 1937 there was no one left to work in the Central Committee in Minsk, and replacements were chewed up within a year of their arrival.

Moscow's reaction to the perceived threat of Ukrainian cultural autonomy had traditionally sparked a reaction on the Polish side of whatever territorial demarcation existed at the time. And vice versa; if Ukrainianization had its counterpart in Warsaw's 'Volhynia experiment' of extending cultural rights to Ukrainians in Poland, then the Soviet repression of nationalist deviation had its cross-border counterpart in the 'revindications of souls'. In December 1937 the Polish Defence Corps put into play its plans to encourage Ukrainians to convert from Orthodoxy to Roman Catholicism. The inspiration came from the military rather than the clergy. In the mix of incentives and coercion employed to restore 'their true nationality', there were no harsh measures of arrests and deportation comparable to those taking place across the border. But the aims were more radical. There were plans to Polonize the entire Ukrainian population of Volhynia by 1944.[22] The main beneficiaries of the attempts of both Moscow and Warsaw to impose their control over the fractious peoples of the Ukrainian borderlands were the extreme nationalists in the OUN and the deviant communists in the remnants of the Western Ukrainian party.

The North Caucasus, like the Ukraine, suffered enormously from collectivization; the purges inflicted greater suffering, disorganization and demoralization on the local cadres. In Ossetia almost the entire obkom (regional committee) bureau was arrested and a large part of the small intelligentsia wiped out. The Checheno-Ingush Autonomous Republic was decimated in two massive waves of arrests that may have amounted to 3 per cent of the population. In the Kabardino-Balkarian Autonomous Republic, the popular hero of the civil war and first secretary of the obkom, Betal Kalmykov, was arrested and executed. Because of the relatively small numbers of Old Bolsheviks and party intelligentsia in these less advanced regions, the losses were probably more damaging than in the Ukraine, where replacements could be found more easily. In any case, the purges severely weakened local resistance to the German invader during the Second World War, contributed to widespread disaffection and delayed the re-establishment of Soviet power in these areas after the liberation.[23] Recent evidence from the Soviet archives reveals that Beria assigned over 100,000 NKVD troops in the midst of the war to organize the deportation of 650,000 Chechen, Ingush, Kalmyk and Karachai people; they were packed into railway wagons and dispatched from their homeland to Central Asia under conditions of great hardship.[24]

In the South Caucasian borderlands Stalin took a personal interest and played a direct role in the destruction of the old cadres. Knowing Stalin and the region as he did, Beria presented Stalin with a picture that he was all too ready to accept of close links between internal subversion and the threat of external intervention assisted by old political enemies in the emigration. The potential existed for exploiting widespread disaffection with Moscow, and Stalin was never one to underestimate potential opposition, especially when he had been responsible for inciting it. Stalin's conflict with the Georgian Mensheviks before the revolution and during the civil war, together with his dispute with Lenin over the Georgian Communists in 1922, had provided him with many old scores to settle. He had appointed Beria as first secretary in 1931 to carry out a more or less continuous purge of the local cadres. During the Great Purge Trials, some of the survivors of these quarrels, like Budu Mdivani, an Old Bolshevik and member of the Caucasian Bureau from 1920–21, were implicated with the leading oppositionists, Trotsky, Zinoviev and Bukharin, as well as being denounced as British agents. Massive replacements for the top posts of the Georgian

Communist Party in 1937 suggest that virtually the entire leadership from the 1920s perished. But the executions were not limited to party members. Prominent writers, poets, dramatists and intellectuals also disappeared.[25]

During the period of the Nazi-Soviet Pact and tense relations with the Western powers, Beria reported on the creation in Istanbul of a branch of the Council of the Confederation of the Caucasus, an émigré organization formed in Paris in 1934, under the leadership of Noe Zhordaniia. Its members included Georgian Mensheviks, Muslim Musavatists and North Caucasus mountaineers. (One of the last group, Sultan-Girei Klych, collaborated with the Germans in an attempt to raise the Adyghe and other tribes in revolt against the Soviet power.) After the fall of France, the Paris group had scattered and together with remnants of the Prometheus group had found refuge in a number of European and Middle Eastern countries. These groups were allegedly connected to Trotskyite elements supported by the Turkish government.[26] Given the belief, widespread among the Soviet leadership, that Turkey, and possibly Iran, would join in an attack on the Soviet Union if German forces penetrated deeply enough into the North Caucasus, such reports could not but reinforce and intensify suspicions of nationalist deviations. To be sure, in 1942–43 the German army fell short of its objectives in the region. Moreover, although there were German-sponsored anti-Soviet movements among the mountaineers (see p. 222), the Germans bungled efforts to expand their contacts with Georgian émigrés which dated back to the Georgian independence movement they had supported at Brest-Litovsk. But this could not have been foreseen in 1939–41.

Armenia, like Ukraine, was particularly singled out for having harboured a 'Right-Trotskyite national centre'. In 1938, a see-saw struggle over the review of party documents had revealed the resistance of some local party leaders to wholesale repression. Then Nersik Stepanian, one of the Armenian party leaders, denounced Beria's book *The History of the Bolshevik Organization in the Transcaucasus* as a blatant falsification. Beria's published reply attacked the party leadership and demanded their physical elimination. This sealed their doom. Veteran Bolsheviks like S.N. Martikian, hero of the Baku Commune and president of the Sovnarkom in Armenia, and A. Khandzhian, the first secretary of the party, were executed; less than six months earlier, both had received the Order of Lenin. After ten months of massive repressions, Stalin sent a letter to the bureau of the Armenian Central Committee expressing dissatisfaction that the leadership was protecting enemies of the people; he declared that certain executions had been 'premature, with the aim of preventing the unmasking of the remaining enemies who remained at large'. A wave of arrests followed which destroyed most of the top leaders of the party, government, armed forces and cultural establishment in the republic. The purge reached down to the local level, where one third of the secretaries of primary organizations and of party organizers were eliminated. Even after 1938 the process continued.[27]

The Azerbaijan party organization suffered greater losses than any other republican organization except for Georgia. In Azerbaijan the role played by Beria in Georgia was filled by Mir Jafar Baghirov, a close associate of Stalin who had also entered the secret police during the civil war. Baghirov wiped out the entire leadership of the party, government, local military commanders and much of the older generation of the Azerbaijan intelligentsia. From 1937 to 1938 over 10,000 officials were removed and presumably shot. Baghirov also denounced as 'politically suspect' the entire émigré colony of Iranian Azerbaijan, which had fled to Soviet Azerbaijan after the collapse of the Gilan Republic in northwestern Iran. These purges had a pronounced effect on the Soviet position in northern Iran during and after the Second World War.[28] During the period of tension with France and Britain following the Nazi-Soviet Pact, Beria's reports emphasized the threat to the oil industry of Azerbaijan of émigré diversionists directed by the French and penetrating Soviet territory across the Turkish and Iranian frontiers. He urged a thorough purge of the personnel of the big industrial complex Azneft, especially the distilling plants, and the recruiting of additional agents to combat sabotage.[29]

In the five republics of Soviet Central Asia the purges had no direct effect on foreign policy except in so far as they played a role in the evolution of Soviet nationality policy during the war. The party organizations in Central Asia were small and the arrests so sharply reduced their numbers that in certain districts of Tajikistan, for example, only one out of four members were left alive. As was the case throughout the national republics, the top leadership of the party and soviets was destroyed; again the Old Bolsheviks – who were even rarer here than elsewhere – were among the first to go. For several months in the winter of 1937/38 the Central Committee of the

Turkmen party ceased to exist. Recruitment of new party members virtually came to a halt in this period. In Uzbekistan the first secretary, Akmal Ikramov, a Bolshevik since 1918 and member of the All-Union Central Executive Committee, perished with most of the Uzbek leaders of the party, soviet, Komsomol and main army units. Ikramov and his chief rival in the Uzbek organization, Faizulla Khodzaev, a Bolshevik since the revolution and chairman of the republic's Narkom, were implicated in the trial against Bukharin as the leaders of a nationalist plot to work for an independent local economy and ultimately secession of Uzbekistan under British protection.

Kazakhstan passed through the greatest ordeal. In the late thirties all members and candidates of the Central Committee Bureau were executed along with most of the Central Committee itself, almost all the secretaries of the gorkom and raikom organizations in addition to many rank-and-file communists. The Kazakh intelligentsia lost many of its leading figures. Rigid centralization was imposed in the administration and economic life of the republic. These measures retarded recovery from the terrible losses inflicted on agriculture, primarily the herds of livestock by collectivization.[30] The Tajik frontier was particularly vulnerable to penetration from Afghanistan, Iran and Turkey by kulaks and Basmachi, tribesmen raiding across the frontier. Stalin's trouble shooter, Andreev, recommended the transfer of Tajik army units to the European part of the Soviet Union to remove them from subversive influences.[31]

Stalin's purges of the nationalities, as with other targeted groups, spared individuals whose talents he recognized, valued and rewarded by promoting them to the heights of their professions. The army provided a few such outstanding examples. General Aleksei Antonov, born into a family of Volga Tatars, rose to become Army Chief of Staff and one of Stalin's top advisers on strategic planning, including the assault on Berlin. Ivan Bagramian, from a lowly Armenian family, was the only non-Slavic front commander. Displaying a ruthless attack mentality on the Baltic sector earned him Stalin's respect and won him marshal's baton after the war.[32]

Despite these paradoxical success stories, the picture was a grim one for the nationalities on the eve of the war. The fact that Russians in the state and party organizations were not spared, the removal of the national cadres who had been the founders of the local parties and ardent supporters of the Bolsheviks in the civil war, when their cause was not popular among many of the local populations, created widespread and deep bitterness in the republics which only surfaced after the denunciation of the Stalin cult. Stalin's indiscriminate assault on the national parties weakened Soviet influence in all the borderlands on the eve of a war that would test and strain the bonds of the 'great friendship'.

THE COMINTERN

The purge of the Comintern did not strike a healthy organism, but the treatment hastened its decline. Its history had been marked by intense factionalism, periodic purges, rapid volte-faces and, up to 1935, a general decline in membership. The Seventh Congress of 1935 bid fair to reverse the declining popularity of communist parties by demoting world revolution to a secondary concern and identifying the fortunes of the communist parties with a broad anti-fascist front. But the gains in membership and electoral successes in the few countries where they were still legal were offset by resentment among the professional cadres over the apparent indifference to revolutionary goals, and the ever-deepening sense of complete subordination to Soviet security interests.[33] Moreover, the leaders of the parties that were illegal in their own countries were obliged to shelter in Moscow where they were vulnerable to direct Stalinist pressure. In 1929 the patient took a turn for the worse. The removal of Bukharin as head of the Comintern changed the way in which decisions were reached. Stalin was determined to eliminate all traces of open disagreement and dissension. In a series of spiteful measures, he demonstrated that the Comintern would no longer play a prominent role in international politics. He placed the Comintern administration under his personal control and created a special section of his secretariat to bypass the established chain of command; no decisions could be taken without his sanction.[34] He turned the full force of his dark suspicions on the activities of the local parties. The old factional fights in the Comintern centred on real policy differences. Beginning in 1929, a new wave of repression began as a purge of the moderates or 'Rights', that is, Bukharin's supporters, but rapidly degenerated into an orgy of personal denunciations that crossed factional lines. For his own dark reasons, Stalin did not turn over the Comintern to the left doctrinaires. A number of prominent supporters of Bukharin, including a few – like the Swiss pastor and member of the Swiss Communist Party Jules-Frédéric Humbert-Droz – who did not openly recant, were not removed but merely transferred. The Stalinists came down hard on the German, Czech and Polish parties. The Italian and Bulgarian parties enjoyed relative immunity because the Italian leaders had chosen exile in France and the Bulgarian leader Georgi Dimitrov was able to protect some – if not all – of his countrymen. The ferocity of the purges can be explained in part by the factions and personal animosities inside the exiled parties.[35]

Stalin had drawn the clumsy distinction between the right as a tendency not yet well defined which should be exposed and chastised and the right as a group or faction which should be repressed by the same harsh measures that he had imposed on the Trotskyites. His agents in the Comintern defined 'the right' in the German Communist Party as a faction and demanded its destruction by 'organizational methods'. The hammer fell next on the leading rights in the Czech party.[36] The Polish party was the most deeply shaken, foreshadowing its complete destruction eight years later. It was accused of having worked for the Polish secret police by establishing links with the Western Ukrainian party in order to infiltrate the Ukrainian SSR. Mass arrests followed. The savagery of these purges in the years before the assassination of Sergei Kirov, which precipitated the Great Terror, may be in part attributed to Stalin's grave concerns over the loyalty of Ukrainian communists to the regime during the worst years of collectivization and the real fears that the Polish secret police would exploit discontent in the borderlands for their own aims. In fact, the wave of denunciations merely facilitated the Polish secret police infiltration of the Polish party; the provocateurs then helped destroy it by denouncing its leaders.[37] Increasingly feeble and dominated by sectarians, the Polish party showed little enthusiasm for embracing the popular front. Dimitrov prodded them to get rid of their image as 'Moscow's agent'. He urged them to build bridges to other parties and mass organizations and find an authoritative and self-confident leadership.[38] The Comintern Executive also encouraged them to address the question of an incomplete bourgeois democratic revolution in Poland and thus to abandon the policy that had brought the Stalinist minority to power. Yet at the same time it announced the need to undertake 'a surgical intervention' in order to remove from party leadership the Trotskyites and agents of the class enemy. The policy of class collaboration was undermined almost immediately by revival of the old methods. The rising drumbeat of accusations against the Polish communists resonated in the bitter struggle over the Ukrainian borderlands.

Several new factors in the mid-thirties changed the tone of Soviet-Polish relations and signalled a general shift in targeting enemies of the people. Ethnic considerations mixed with and then superseded class factors in selecting the victims. In 1934, shortly after the rise of Hitler to power, the Poles signed a non-aggression treaty with Germany. In the eyes of the Soviet leaders, Poland had suddenly become less of a potential ally against Nazi Germany and more of an opportunist, waiting for the best offer before moving to one side or the other. A year later, Marshal Józef Piłsudski, the strong man of the Polish government, died, and with him perished his policy of accommodation with the Ukrainian minority in the border province of Volhynia. A nationalist reaction set in, appealing more directly to Polish sentiments in Volhynia and beyond its frontiers to the east. During the same period, the Communist Party of Western Ukraine proclaimed its own insurrectionary line against the Volhynia experiment of the Polish government. Their action was taken independently of the Comintern and in defiance of the official policy of the popular front. These events coincided with Hitler's reoccupation of the Rhineland and the outbreak of the Spanish Civil War with the two fascist powers, Germany and Italy, supporting the Nationalist rebels. There could be little doubt in Stalin's mind that the threat of war had increased exponentially.[39]

Stalin's first response, in August 1936, was to orchestrate the trial of the 'Trotskyist-Zinovievite Centre' around the central theme of linkage between the accused and foreign intelligence agencies throughout the world, but mainly in Germany and Japan. The following year, at the trial of Karl Radek and Piatakov, members of the Left Opposition, Vyshinsky embroidered the idea of a conspiracy to weaken the Soviet state. He falsely accused them of promising territorial concessions in the western and eastern borderlands to Germany and Japan. He also stoked the fires of a campaign to liquidate the POUM (Partido Obrero de Unificación Marxista) in Spain, an anarcho-syndicalist group sympathetic to Trotsky.[40] In 1937, as the mass repression and decimation of the Comintern reached a climax, Stalin summed up his views on terror in private remarks to Dimitrov. He identified five historical turning points: 1905, 1917, Brest-Litovsk, civil war and collectivization. At each point, he explained, weak elements fell away from the party, especially during collectivization. They went underground and 'being powerless themselves, they linked up with our external enemies, promising the Germans Ukraine, the Poles Belarus, the Japanese our Far East'. Stalin hammered at this theme at the February and March 1937 plenum of the party, when he urged his colleagues to remain aware at all times that under conditions of capitalist encirclement the threat of spies and saboteurs was constant.[41] At a banquet following the 7 November celebrations in 1937, Stalin amplified his remarks by justifying the terror as the necessary means to preserve the Russian state, what he called the 'legacy of the tsars':

> We, the Bolsheviks, for the first time, united and strengthened this state, making it one and indivisible . . . We united the state in such a way that any part that might be torn away from the common socialist state, while a loss in itself, could not exist independently and would inevitably fall under foreign domination. Anyone, therefore, who attempts to destroy this united socialist state, who strives to separate it from its single parts and nationalities, is an enemy, a sworn enemy of the state and of the peoples of the USSR.[42]

Against this background, the focus of the terror on linking internal and external enemies stands out in stark outline.

Beginning already in 1936, the NKVD launched a campaign to uncover agent provocateurs within the Communist Party of Poland and to root out members of the alleged Polish Military Organization in the USSR, which by this time no longer existed except as a convenient fiction in the fertile imagination of the NKVD. Stalin had long harboured suspicions of the Polish Communist Party, perhaps dating as far back as its formation when it combined three distinct elements of the pre-revolutionary left in Poland, and re-enforced by his experiences in the Soviet-Polish War of 1920. Ominously, from his point of view, the Polish party was the largest communist party in Eastern Europe and its members occupied important posts in the Comintern. By 1936 the Comintern Executive responded to mounting pressure to exert greater vigilance by notifying Ezhov that the Polish Communist Party was 'the major supplier of spy and provocateur elements to the USSR'.[43] Simultaneously, on orders from Moscow, the Ukrainian Communist Party organized the deportation of over 8,000 families, more than a third of them Polish, from the frontier with Poland. This action was followed up in early 1936 with the even larger deportation of 15,000 Polish and German families to Kazakhstan and a final 'cleansing' of the frontier districts later that year. As many as 60,000 Poles were deported.[44]

In 1937, when the mass purge reached its climax, Ezhov organized with the approval of the Politburo the 'Polish Operation'.[45] This unleashed the most devastating attack on a single national group within the Soviet Union and the destruction of the Polish Communist Party. Approximately two thirds of the more than 600,000 Poles living in the USSR were residents of Ukraine, among them unrecorded numbers of refugees from Poland. Beginning its campaign against 'Polish spies', the NKVD spread its net of arrests to sweep up all Poles who had 'links with abroad. The alleged crimes of those living in the frontier areas ranged from sabotage and wrecking to planning uprisings in time of war'. Although exact figures remain elusive due to the irregular process of recording, it has been estimated that 143,000 Poles were convicted of crimes, of whom 111,000 were shot; the rest were sent to camps in the two years from 1937 to 1938.[46]

At the same time, the NKVD was carrying out arrests of members of both the Polish Communist Party and the Comintern apparatus. Within Poland, the purge wiped out the remnants of the old majority, which had been sympathetic to Bukharin, and then crushed the minority. Members of the Politburo in exile in Paris were recalled to Moscow and arrested. Other Stalinist loyalists considered it their duty to return from Prague, Spain and Warsaw to defend themselves. They too perished. The entire leadership was engulfed in the cataclysm including the last member of the Polish Politburo, who had endorsed the arrests of all his colleagues. Yet the operations were carried out in secrecy so that neither the Comintern executive nor the rank and file of the Polish party knew about them.[47] Nevertheless, in November 1937 the Comintern Executive ordered the dissolution of the Polish Communist Party. Reorganization was out of the question because 'the central party organs were in the hands of spies and provocateurs'. Stalin approved but noted that 'the dissolution is about two years late'. The Comintern urged the re-creation of the party by Polish members of the International Brigades fighting in Spain.[48] Comintern agents fanned out over Europe with orders to persuade the remnants of the party to accept and endorse the decision. Discipline prevailed but doubts remained. Elements of the *aktiv* remained sceptical; there had been no factual evidence to prove the accusations of treason.

The communist parties of Western Belarus and Western Ukraine had been weakened by fierce attacks in the early 1930s when the top leaders were denounced as agents of Ukrainian nationalist organizations, recalled to Moscow and executed. In 1938 the parties, decimated by further denunciations and arrests, were dissolved and officially ceased to exist. The communists in Western Ukraine, always mavericks, continued their active operations against the Polish state. They even went so far as to form a working alliance with the Ukrainian nationalists of the OUN. The two groups intermingled in typical borderlands fashion and mutually endorsed a policy of social and national revolution.[49] Was it here that the seeds were sown of a separate path to Polish socialism?

In 1937 the Polish and Hungarian sections of the Comintern were reduced to one man each. The two parties were so badly mauled that they virtually ceased to exist. The Chinese and Bulgarian sections of the Comintern also lost almost all their personnel to the 'conveyor', a euphemism for the process of secret killings. The German Section was reduced by 70 per cent. Of the Yugoslav party cadres in the Soviet Union, numbering about 900, at least 800 were arrested and only forty of them survived the camps. The party was virtually decapitated, leaving Tito unchallenged at the top. The leaders of the Romanian party in Moscow were almost all shot, including Marcel Pauker (whose wife Ana survived, adopted Soviet citizenship and emerged after the war as a leader of the Romanian party). The Iranian communists who had fled to Moscow following the collapse of the Gilan Republic in 1921 were already under suspicion as nationalists in 1932, and little was heard of them after that date. Their most prominent leader, Avetis Sultan-Zade, who had crossed swords with Bukharin at the Sixth Comintern Congress, was secretly executed in 1938 along with almost all the Iranian exiles in the Soviet Union.[50]

The Latvian party, many of whose members had played a key role in the Bolshevik taking of power in Petrograd in 1917, was treated with particular brutality. Driven underground by the government in 1934, its Central Committee was abolished by the Comintern and replaced by a provisional secretariat which was then also liquidated. Pēteris Stučka, who had been head of the short-lived Latvian Soviet government of 1919 and its representative to the Comintern, was posthumously denounced. In 1936 the Foreign Bureau of the Central Committee in the Comintern was wiped out, including Lenin's former colleague, the Old Bolshevik Jānis Lencmanis (Lentsman), who had occupied positions in the Soviet government as well. A massive purge of party members followed, reducing the Riga party organization to 150 people. A brief period of renewal followed the decisions of the Seventh Comintern Congress to rebuild the organization with workers, but the purging continued; all the Latvian cultural organizations in Moscow were also abolished and their members killed. In 1940 there were only 1,000 members of the party left in Moscow. They were completely cut off from the Comintern and unprepared to assist in taking power, which was mainly the work of the Red Army, Soviet police and party elements.[51]

The Estonian Communist Party was also crushed by the purges of 1937–38. A large number of Estonian communists lived in the Soviet Union in the 1930s, including many of the Old Bolshevik leaders of the revolution in Estonia and veterans of the civil war and many communists from the ranks of ordinary workers. In a rising tide of suspicion, large numbers of them were accused of maintaining links with the 'bourgeois police of Estonia', and executed. Among the most prominent of these were Jaan Anvelt, a Bolshevik since 1907, one of the founders of the first Estonian Bolshevik newspaper and in 1917 a leader of the Estonian soviet, and a veteran of the civil war. He survived four years of illegal work in the underground, led the rising of 1924 and finally emigrated to the Soviet Union where he served as a commissar in the Zhukovsky Military Academy and as a high official in the fleet and the Comintern. His close colleague, Hans Pöögelmann (Pogelman), another journalist and party veteran since 1905, had suffered arrest and exile before 1917 when he returned and plunged into revolutionary work, leaving Estonia after the civil war to become prominent in the Comintern Executive. With them perished the rest of the Estonian leadership. Along with the other Baltic parties, the Estonian party was so badly crippled by the shootings that the Central Committee simply ceased to operate after early 1938; the Estonian party's links with the Comintern were severed. Scarcely a year later, when the Nazi-Soviet Pact placed Estonia in the Soviet sphere of influence, the absence of experienced local party members was keenly felt. Zhdanov, who was sent in to consolidate Soviet power, had to rely on numerous Russian cadres who backed up the low-level and politically ineffective surviving Estonians.[52]

The Lithuanian Communist Party, numbering no more than 2,000, lost its entire leadership in the purges and was a negligible factor in the Soviet incorporation of Lithuania into the USSR in 1940. More seriously, as was the case in Estonia, the absence of any reliable communist cadres required the use of Russians including army officers to command the Lithuanian units incorporated into the Red Army. At the same time the Soviet authorities carried out an extensive policy of mass deportation of those suspected of being anti-Soviet elements, which numbered, according to some Western sources, approximately 35,000 people. According to subsequent Soviet admissions, these measures were 'insufficiently prepared and organized' so that 'dangerous opponents' were left at large and many innocent people were swept up in the nets. Acting as foreign invaders without any significant local support, the Soviet Union attempted to compensate for its 'errors' by nationalizing industry and redistributing land to over 200,000 poor and landless peasants.[53] It was a fruitless operation. The combination of Soviet blunders, the absence of reliable local cadres and the widespread hostility caused by the occupation and loss of independence destroyed any Soviet hopes of transforming the Baltic states into a defensive glacis.

The purges struck hard at the elite Comintern training schools in the Soviet Union. The Communist University for the National Minorities of the West was dissolved; it had enrolled about 600 students from the western nationalities of the USSR in the period 1933–36. Most of the students were sent to Spain, except for the Volga German contingent, who were arrested. A handful of the German graduates survived, however, and occupied important posts in the German Democratic Republic after the war. The Communist University of the Toilers of the East suffered fewer losses but the Chinese students appeared to have been singled out. The staff of the Lenin School training the upper ranks of the Comintern was decimated. The German-language newspaper published by the Comintern was purged, leaving only one person in charge by the end. When the paper was finally suspended most of its readership had also joined the staff in the camps. The most fortunate communists were those who had been imprisoned in their own countries, especially in Hungary, Romania and Poland, beyond the reach of the NKVD.[54]

The devastating effects of the Comintern purges on the national parties emerge most clearly from the complaints of a few communist leaders that important organizational work was being sacrificed and cadres demoralized. The eminent economist Eugen Varga wrote a personal letter to Stalin courageously arguing that the purges were leading to the demoralization of communist cadres in fascist countries 'who would have a prominent role to play in the forthcoming war!'[55] Dimitrov also tried to protect some of his colleagues in the Comintern but willingly sacrificed others in what amounted to triage.[56] Perhaps his most important rescue operation was Tito. No one was more keenly aware of the devastating effect of the purges on the organization. But he was unwilling to confront Stalin. The best he felt he could do was to point out that, following the arrests of the former leaders of the parties in Lithuania, Latvia and Estonia as well as Poland, 'sincere communists in those countries have been left disoriented and with no connection to the Comintern'. He requested assistance from the Central Committee in selecting a few comrades from the All-Union Communist Party (b) who spoke the native language to be used in reconstructing the shattered parties.[57]

Stalin had designed the purge of the nationalities and the Comintern as a radical means to eliminate potential sources of opposition at home linked to the growing threat of war on the part of an aggressive Nazi Germany and militarist Japan. These actions were not incompatible with a policy of collective security abroad. Paradoxically, they fit the propaganda of the popular front by exposing the threats posed by the aggressive policies of Germany and Japan, who sought by subversive means to undermine the loyalty of the most vulnerable international defenders of the Soviet Union. To be sure, the Western powers did not see it that way. As a theme of mobilizing the Soviet population to work harder and be more vigilant, the purges began to lose their appeal as the international situation began to change by the spring and summer of 1938. The Western powers were hesitant to support the embattled Spanish Republic and only the Soviet Union and Mexico sent substantial aid. The popular front government in France lost its majority, and French leaders showed signs of weakness in defending its closest ally, Czechoslovakia, in the face of Hitler's threats. In China once again, the Soviet Union was the only major power to send military aid to the Nationalists in their war to resist the Japanese invasion. Litvinov's voice rang hollow in the halls of the League of Nations. Sensitive to shifting winds from abroad, Stalin and his associates, especially Zhdanov and Molotov, grew uneasy and then alarmed at the prospect that the Soviet Union was becoming isolated in the first line of trenches against fascism.[58]

On 8 August 1938 two apparently unrelated events signalled to those with sensitive political antennae that Stalin was shifting his priorities in his preparations for war. The first was the appointment of Lavrenty Beria as deputy head of the NKVD; the second was the publication of the long-awaited *Short Course of the All-Union Communist Party (b)*. Within a few months Beria had replaced Ezhov as head of the NKVD – Ezhov was then arrested and shot. The purges did not come to a sudden stop, but gradually diminished over the next few months, never completely disappearing as an instrument of Stalin's rule.

In the months before the publication of the *Short Course*, Stalin had systematically gone through the first draft prepared by his subordinates to remove many of the references to the previously prominent international themes of mobilization, including the conspiracies and the role of the Comintern.[59] The impact of these two events on changes in domestic policy should not obscure their implications for the conduct of foreign policy. What is important for the main thesis of this chapter is that Stalin's radical editing included a revision in his theory of the threat of war. Reverting to his earlier concept, he again envisaged that a war among the imperialist powers – France, Britain and Germany – would be more likely than one directed against the Soviet Union.[60]

The purge of Comintern personnel in the borderlands annexed by the Soviet Union in 1939–40 also appears at first glance to have been highly dysfunctional. As Dimitrov had foreseen, the Baltic republics of Estonia, Latvia and Lithuania represented a special case. The destruction of the three small communist parties of the Baltic states hampered efforts to Sovietize these countries in the brief hiatus between their occupation by the Red Army in the summer of 1940 and the German invasion a year later. It is quite possible that one of the reasons that Stalin hesitated for over a year after having established protectorates over the Baltic states in 1939 following the Nazi-Soviet Pact was his inability to find suitable replacements for the 'bourgeois' officials and army officers of the independent governments. Instead, fellow-travelling intellectuals were chosen, like the writer Justas Paleckis (Poletskice) in Lithuania, the microbiologist Augusts Kirhenšteins (Kirchenstein) in Latvia and the poet and physician Dr Johannes Vares in Estonia. Vares was not even a member of the Communist Party until he became prime minister and then president of Estonia in the summer of 1940.[61]

When the deterioration of relations with Germany impelled him to occupy the Baltic states in 1940, Stalin had little choice but to leave most of the middle-level civil servants and army officers in place, obliging them only to take the oath of loyalty to Soviet power. This was a sharp reversal of his policies in the borderlands during the Russian Civil War; but in 1940 his military power was much greater, and was not – for the moment – challenged directly from abroad. He would face a similar situation in much of Eastern Europe in 1944–45 and would respond pragmatically in the same way.

In the long run, the implications of the Comintern purge for Soviet foreign policy proved profound. The killings in Moscow severely weakened the ability of the left to resist Hitler in Eastern Europe from 1938 to 1941. Their weakness persisted throughout the war. The leadership losses affected most of the East European parties like those of Poland, Hungary, Romania and Bulgaria, and complicated the tasks of liberation and reconstruction. The Yugoslav party was exceptional due to the ability of Tito to build up a powerful personal following among younger Yugoslav communists, and then to organize and lead a strong partisan movement. The victims among foreign – as among Soviet – communists cannot be categorized by ideological tendency; 'rights' and 'lefts' alike perished, and representatives of all factional tendencies also survived in the same parties. The wonder was that the international cadres were not utterly demoralized, that they did not simply crumble and disappear. But many in Eastern Europe and the Soviet Union quite literally had nowhere else to go; to attempt to escape from prison or evade arrest and flee would probably have meant falling into the hands of the Gestapo. In Spain and Western Europe, a subtler power held them in place. They were unable to conceive of a political existence outside the party which defined their entire worldview. Those celebrated intellectuals who denounced 'the God that failed' were exceptional both in the ability to rationalize their actions and to reconstruct their worldview on a different basis.[62] Yet even more astonishing than the behaviour of the rank and file was the attitude of the Soviet leaders towards the condemned. During and even after the Second World War, some survivors of the purges in the camps were permitted to return to their homelands and even to occupy positions of real responsibility in the new regimes. Of course, there were pressing practical reasons for this unofficial 'amnesty'. There simply were not enough trained communists to administer the liberated borderlands. Still, one has to admit that it is a curious employment of men and women who had been denounced as spies and saboteurs.

Focusing on Stalin's preparations for war reveals the paradoxical nature of his approach to questions of power. His policies may be summed up as a radical transformation of a backward agrarian society, deeply scarred and divided by revolution and civil war, into an industrialized society with a modern army. At the same time he embarked on an equally radical policy of neutralizing every real, potential and imagined opposition to his policies in the army, diplomatic corps, technical intelligentsia, nationalities and international communist movement, whose expertise and experience appeared to be vital – indeed indispensable – to the achieving of his aims. He attempted to resolve the contradiction between creative and destructive policies by employing mass mobilization techniques aimed at creating new and testing old loyalties through propaganda and centralized administrative measures on an unprecedented scale. His initiatives were often arbitrary, badly co-ordinated and wasteful of lives and resources. The design for a new society, however flawed, was beginning to emerge on the eve of the war. Yet more time was required to consolidate the gains and to settle down a population convulsed by violence imposed from above. The coming of war, so often invoked, had to be delayed. The deal with Hitler in 1939 was shockingly opportunistic to true believers in the moral superiority of the communist mission, but it made sense just so long as Stalin believed he had bought time, had acquired a defensive glacis and continued to have access to high technology through trade with Germany. He miscalculated the timing of Hitler's aggressive intentions, and almost lost everything as a result. The deal was made not because he trusted Hitler, but rather because he calculated that Hitler would not make the same mistake as Napoleon in 1812 or Germany in 1914 of fighting on two fronts. As long as Britain could hold out, Stalin thought the chances of a German attack were slight. And for Britain to survive, it needed the Russians to come in, which was one good reason to avoid doing so. Soviet intelligence was good, but not well co-ordinated; the 'noise' was distracting. Stalin had taken too much into his own hands.

Like his paradoxical policies in the central institutions of the Soviet Union, so too his preparations for war in the borderlands and the international communist movement undermined the basis of resistance to a foreign enemy. Initially an advocate of building a new loyalty among the nationalities who formed the outer perimeter of defence, he reversed course when it appeared to him that a growth of autonomy even in the cultural sphere would weaken his authority and expose the territories to penetration by trans-border, hostile foreign elements.

Although he had never put much stock in the international communist movement to serve as a forward, screening force in the defence of the Soviet Union, nevertheless, his deep suspicion of their reliability and unity drove him to decimate their ranks, thereby reducing their potential contribution to subverting the war effort of his potential attackers; exceptions like the Yugoslav and Greek communists were largely due to survivors and local conditions. To be sure, his actions made the local parties even more dependent in the postwar period on his authority and the liberating forces of the Red Army to pursue their bid for power.

PART II

FIGHTING THE WAR

CHAPTER 3

FORGING THE SINEWS OF WAR

Operation Barbarossa, the code name for the German invasion of 1941, came very close initially to destroying the Soviet system and breaking up the great multi-national state that the Russians had built up and ruled over for three centuries. The initial German attack, launched along three broad fronts, smashed through the Soviet frontier defences. In a series of sweeping encirclements, the Wehrmacht took more than 3 million prisoners, of whom over 2 million had died in captivity by February 1942.[1] The front-line air force was virtually destroyed with a loss of over 5,000 planes, many having been caught on the ground. The great tank force that rivalled the Germans in numbers was badly mauled; 10,000 tanks were destroyed in three weeks. Soviet artillery and gun crews sustained equally heavy losses. Most of the ammunition dumps crowded into the frontier areas were overrun or blown up. For a brief period, there was a shortage of ammunition that chillingly recalled the dark days of 1914–15. The railway network was heavily damaged, especially in the period October–November 1941, when twenty-five lines were bombed simultaneously, creating a crisis of supply.[2] The army suffered enormously from the disorganization of the rear.[3]

Stalin's initial reaction to the German invasion was hesitant and disbelieving. He questioned the first reports in the early morning of 22 June; wasn't it a provocation? However, discussions of his subsequent behaviour have become as controversial as the debates over the 'preventative war' thesis. The much-cited version of his shock and virtual nervous breakdown relies on dubious sources, most prominently Khrushchev's self-serving memoirs. When the war broke out, why didn't Stalin immediately deliver an appeal to the Soviet people instead of leaving the task to Molotov and delaying his own radio broadcast for twelve days? According to Khrushchev, 'He was totally paralyzed and could not collect his thoughts . . . he was in a state of shock.' But Khrushchev was not in Moscow at the time and had to rely on the second-hand testimony of Beria and Malenkov.[4] Moreover, Khrushchev himself was not immune to panic and shock in the initial days of the war. On 9 July, while serving as the political commissar for the south-western front, he issued orders to carry out a scorched-earth programme including the destruction of all machinery in factories and reserves of grain and other goods that could not be evacuated by the Red Army in a zone 100–150 kilometres from the front. The following day, Stalin counter-manded this order, asserting that it failed to account for the situation at the front and 'threatens to demoralize the rear and create in the army and population a mood of retreat rather than a decision to repulse the enemy'. Stalin's instructions were to evacuate agricultural machinery, cattle and grain; to destroy the rest except for fowl, small animals and other products necessary to sustain the population. He further ordered that factories and electrical stations were not to be blown up, but to have their key functioning parts removed. All of this in a zone 70 kilometres from the front.[5]

In a film for television made in 1992, General D.A. Volkogonov, who had access to the Presidential Archive for his post-Soviet study of Stalin, presented a different version. He insisted that Stalin did not collapse in the early days of the German invasion but only a week later on 28 June, after he received news of the fall of Minsk. Then he retired to his dacha and cut himself off from everyone. He only recovered when members of the Politburo visited him and insisted he take command. Volkogonov too appears to have relied on an unnamed member of the Politburo for his interpretation. Who was this source?[6] Certainly not Molotov, who remembered these days differently, insisting that Stalin was biding his time, waiting for the situation to clarify so that his public response would be the appropriate one. 'It is not possible to describe him as distraught [rasterialsia], upset, yes but he didn't show it.'[7] Nor was it Kaganovich, who was even more forceful. 'They say he received nobody. Lies! He received us . . . [he] gave assignments to each of us.'[8] To be sure, Molotov and Kaganovich were two of the most loyal Stalinists. But there is additional evidence to suggest that their versions may be closer to the truth.

In 1990 researchers uncovered an appointments book maintained by the duty secretaries of visitors to Stalin's office in the Kremlin. For 22 June, the day of the German attacks, he met twenty-nine times with members of the Politburo and Central Committee and military commanders, from 5:45 in the morning to 4:45 in the afternoon. The following day he met with them thirteen times, from 3:20 to 6:25 in the morning, and again from 6:45 in the afternoon to 1:25 in the morning. A similar pattern shows up for 24 June until 28 June.[9] He found time to issue twenty different decrees and orders. He created several emergency organs including the General Headquarters of the Supreme Command (Stavka) and the Soviet Information Bureau (see below, pp. 113–14 and p. 168).[10] Nor did he neglect to keep in touch with key figures at the front. A few hours after the Nazi attack, Stalin called Ponomarenko, the secretary of the Belarusian party, and gave him instructions on the need to act 'boldly, decisively, taking the initiative without waiting for orders to come from above.'[11] Called to the Kremlin at 7:00 a.m. on 22 June, Georgi Dimitrov found Stalin with a group of associates: 'Striking calmness, resoluteness, confidence of Stalin and all the others.' The decision was made to have Molotov broadcast over the radio and his speech was being edited. Stalin gave orders to evacuate all diplomatic representatives. The Comintern was 'not to take any overt action . . . the issue of socialist revolution is not to be raised. The Sov[iet] people are waging a patriotic war against fascism.'[12] If all these key decisions were made as Dimitrov described them, then what is left of the story of Stalin's collapse?

The most probable source for Volkogonov's version was the longtime Politburo member Anastas Mikoian, who later wrote that when Stalin was informed of the invasion he simply did not know what to say to the people: 'Let Molotov speak', he declared.[13] In a more spectacular revelation, Mikoian declared in his memoirs that when Stalin faltered after the fall of Minsk the initiative passed briefly to a small number of his lieutenants. The situation was rapidly deteriorating, especially on the Belarusian front where communications with the centre had been cut. Stalin flew into a rage, rebuking Zhukov, who was reduced to tears. A few days later, Mikoian's account continues, an informal meeting of Politburo members called by Molotov debated the need to create a supreme organ – the State Defence Committee

(GOKO) – to concentrate all the powers of the state. They agreed that only Stalin had the prestige to head it, but Molotov worried about Stalin's depressed state. The young economist Nikolai Voznesensky made the startling proposal that if Stalin continued to hesitate then Molotov should take over; 'we will follow you', he said. The rest disregarded him. When they confronted Stalin in his dacha he appeared to be taken aback; Mikoian was convinced he was afraid they had come to arrest him. Stalin seemed surprised they offered him the leadership.[14] Beria insisted that five men be appointed to the GOKO, Stalin as head, along with Molotov, Voroshilov, Malenkov and himself. Stalin suggested adding Mikoian and Voznesensky, but Beria argued that they were needed in the commissariats and Gosplan. Voznesensky and Beria then got into a heated discussion. It turned out that Beria and the others had already agreed on the membership among themselves. Mikoian intervened: let the five be members of the GOKO. He would do what he did best by assuming authority over supplying the front with food, fuel and clothing as a plenipotentiary of the GOKO. Voznesensky proposed taking responsibility for the production of weapons and military equipment. Tank production was assigned to Molotov and aircraft to Malenkov. Characteristically, Beria was to take charge of maintaining domestic order and combating desertion, which it must be presumed was already perceived as potentially a major problem.[15] As described by Mikoian, the bizarre bargaining had no precedent. In the view of the memoirist, the re-affirmation of Stalin's leadership appeared to have fully restored his spirits. Three days later he broadcast his famous appeal to the Soviet population.

In the meantime, there had been no general call to arms except for Molotov's radio broadcast of 22 June. The purported resolutions of the Central Committee and Sovnarkom on 23 June mentioned in early Soviet historical accounts of the period have turned out to be inventions. The directive of 29 June from the same organs, which was compared to the public appeal of Lenin's government in February 1918 to defend the revolution against the Whites in the civil war, was in fact a secret document which applied only to the front-line units.[16] As a result, there were delays in transmitting orders, a serious lack of detailed information from the fronts and disarray among the leaders that cost the army and civilian population terrible losses in the first two weeks.

Few measures can better convey the sense of desperation than the release of 600,000 people from the labour camps, of whom 174,000 were immediately inducted into the army.[17] Among them were tens of thousands of Polish citizens who had been deported as prisoners of war in 1939 to widely scattered camps in inhospitable climes. They were released under the terms of the Sikorski–Maisky agreement of July 1941 by which the Polish government in exile was recognized by Moscow. Over the next few months, Polish delegates, also released from captivity, scoured the country for survivors who would serve as the core of a Polish army under General Władysław Anders, which was allowed to leave the Soviet Union through Iran and later to join the British forces fighting in Italy. But Poles who had lived in those parts of Western Belarus and Western Ukraine that had been incorporated into the Soviet Union as a result of the Nazi-Soviet Pact of 1939 were not allowed to join, but had to serve as labourers in war work.[18] In Nazi-occupied Poland (the General Government), a Polish underground army was also forming, but it had no relations with Soviet forces until the tragic days of 1944.

In the early days of the war, Stalin turned with fury against the Volga German population. He had received unreliable reports from the Southern Front Command of sniping at retreating Red Army units. He ordered Beria to 'boot them out' of their autonomous republic. Within two months, from 438,000 to 446,000 Volga Germans had been piled into railway wagons and sent to Siberia. Meanwhile, 8,000 Soviet Germans had flocked to the militia and fought in the legendary defence of the Brest Fortress.[19] The Volga Germans had been living in Russia since the time of Catherine the Great and had never shown any signs of disloyalty. Their villages were among the most prosperous and productive in the country. Over the next few months, Soviet citizens of German nationality were rounded up throughout the country. In September Beria reported that his agents had arrested 141,249 anti-Soviet and doubtful Germans living in the Krasnodar and Ordzhonikidze *krai*, the Tula oblast, and the Kabardino-Balkarian and North Ossetian autonomous republics. More arrests and deportations took place in the Azerbaijan and Georgian republics. Several thousand were picked up in Moscow and Leningrad as well.[20] The sweeps had taken on a racial character similar to the deportation of Germans and Jews near the front undertaken by the tsarist government in 1914. Meanwhile, elsewhere in the western borderlands, real resistance to the Soviet occupation broke out immediately.

SHOCK, PANIC AND DEMORALIZATION

Despite the purges in the Baltic republics directed by the Soviet government in 1940–41 against the leadership of right-wing nationalist parties, large numbers of the rank and file survived in the underground. In June 1941 they emerged to attack the retreating Red Army, launch pogroms against the Jewish population, and attempt to establish or re-establish national independence. In Estonia the NKVD reported the activities of 60,000 members of the semi-military organization Kaitseliit, formed originally in 1918, and now armed with 40,000 Japanese rifles and twenty-two batteries of artillery.[21] The Soviet command of the northwestern front reported two days after the German attack that 'diversionary groups' led by 'bourgeois nationalists' in the Baltic republics were 'rupturing lines of communication' and 'sowing panic among the local population'. In Lithuania, a major anti-communist revolt broke out. Lasting eight days and involving from 100,000 to 125,000 men, including at least half of the Lithuanian army units incorporated into the Red Army, the rebellion took over the capital of Kaunas before the German arrival and set up a provisional government.[22] The revolt touched off smaller and less well-organized insurrections in Latvia, leading to a premature seizure of Riga before the Germans arrived. In Estonia, the first secretary of the party, Karl Säre, defected to the Germans and betrayed the whereabouts of several partisan units. Meanwhile, the Germans, having brushed aside the provisional government of Lithuania and other independent groups in Estonia and Latvia, established direct military rule with the assistance of a small number of fascists and attempted to create 'self-defence' detachments, especially in Lithuania, to fight the Soviet partisans.

Counter-measures proved feeble and quickly petered out. Over the signatures of the central committees of the three Baltic republics an appeal was issued in June for volunteers for regular additional army units. Presumably the order and the organizational work were directed by GOKO and the Defence Commissariat. In any case, two Estonian, one Latvian and one Lithuanian rifle division were formed in Soviet territory and sent into combat. The NKVD, with some assistance from the much-weakened party cadres and Komsomol, attempted to organize resistance against the 'diversionists' and German forces, but these efforts proved much less successful. Scattered, poorly armed, ignored, and occasionally betrayed by the local population, they suffered heavy losses. Most were destroyed within six months.[23] By the end of 1943, there were only about 1,800 Soviet partisans in the region, scattered in seventy-four small groups.[24]

In Belarus, there was evidence of the same pattern of hasty, panic-stricken retreats and the breakdown of local authority. A week after the German invasion, the party organization in the Gomel region notified Stalin of the demoralized behaviour of the army command; the departure of commanders from the front with the excuse of supervising the evacuation of families; mass desertion from units spreading panic among the population in the rear areas; the arrest and disarming by punishment battalions of 200 men who fled the airfield without having seen the enemy; and the lack of critical information by the command on the number and armament of units that had disintegrated, sowing confusion in the organization of defence and threatening a collapse in the Gomel region and endangering the flank of the Kiev front. A district secretary of Pinsk province recorded an equally desperate situation: individual units fighting without any co-ordination, unlike an organized army; the whereabouts of the commander of the Fourth Army unknown; key points on the railway lines not protected; individual units, lacking commanders, not knowing what to do and piling into their vehicles and retreating to the east; individual aircraft sent off without a destination and being called back. In Pinsk the panic affected the operation of local arms and supply depots, leaving many of the mobilized without arms; everywhere there were demands for immediate and co-ordinated action.[25] Confused and contradictory reports streamed in on the reaction of the local population.[26]

The Belarus anti-communist emigration provided leadership for the civil administration of the population and helped to recruit local police battalions (*Schutzmannschaften*) of 20,000 men, which later became the nucleus for the Belarusian Home Guard (*Heimwehr*). There is abundant evidence that the local population participated in denunciation of the Jews and offered no objection to their expropriation and humiliation. The collaboration of the Belarusian auxiliary police and local administration facilitated the escalation of the murderous policies of the German occupation authorities. Without their assistance, for example, it would not have been possible to organize so swiftly the ghettoization of the Jewish population of Belarus. As the evidence of mass killings became known, however, there was a growing sense of revulsion among the local population.[27]

In Ukraine, several nationalist groups rode in the baggage trains of the Wehrmacht. The Ukrainian Central Committee was the most consistently collaborationist. Formed in the former Polish districts of western Galicia under German occupation, it promoted cultural activities to break the monopoly of Polish culture while quietly laying the political groundwork for a future Ukrainian state. After June 1941 the Germans allowed it to spread its activities into occupied eastern Galicia. The metropolitan of the Ukrainian Greek Catholic Church, Andrei Sheptyts'kyi, preached an anti-communist line that appealed to disaffected elements in the rural popula-tion.[28] His letters both to Hitler and the Vatican expressed his fervent support for the German army. In his letter of 23 September 1941, congratu-lating Hitler on the taking of Kiev, he wrote: 'The business of liquidating and extirpating Bolshevism, which you as the Führer of the great German Reich have taken upon yourself as the goal in this campaign, has earned your Excellency the gratitude of the entire Christian world.' Similar sentiments were repeated on 14 January 1942.[29]

Panic spread rapidly into the interior provinces, most seriously of all in Moscow in October 1941, when Politburo member Aleksandr Shcherbakov admitted that the party agitators were preoccupied with evac-uation work and had failed to counter the rumours of the leadership deserting: 'in several cases there was disorganization, the cadres of organ-izers lost their heads'.[30]

In Ukraine, the party secretary Nikita Khrushchev reported to Stalin that the local party and soviet organizations located in the front-line areas had reacted passively to the German attack, independent of the military command. In the face of the advancing enemy, they had abandoned their duties and evacuated prematurely, leading to demoralization of the rear at critical moments. To bring the situation under control, he proposed a series of measures which would subordinate the party and soviet organization within a zone up to 300 kilometres behind the front to the Military Council of the Southwestern Command of the Red Army for specialized duties relating to the conduct of the war.[31] In Odessa oblast, the panic-stricken party leadership ordered a mass evacuation, leaving thousands of acres of grain fields unharvested despite the fact that the front was hundreds of kilo-metres away. Some party leaders were accused of seizing kolkhoz and sovkhoz funds and fleeing on trucks into the interior. Those workers in trade and banking enterprises who did not get passes to leave their posts plundered offices and stores and fled to Mariupol.[32]

The psychological impact of the Stalinist policies and propaganda in the immediate prewar period had a devastating effect on the officer corps and rank and file of the soldiers, contributing to the mass surrenders and widespread panic among the civilian population.[33] The emphasis in propaganda on the high level of military preparedness and the impressive figures on investment in military hardware and the formation of the largest army in Europe gave the impression of invincibility, reinforced by the belief, mainly cherished by the youth, that Stalin had eliminated all the internal enemies of the regime and was master of the international situation. Although the pact with Germany was not popular, it led to an expansion of the frontier zone and seemed to presage a breathing space. The purge of the army command had removed a significant proportion of the senior officer corps, but it had also deeply affected the morale of the survivors. Marshal Zhukov later reminisced on the decline in discipline, and rising numbers of absence without leave up to the point of desertions.[34] The fear of taking the initiative without orders from the centre was proven to be widespread following the initial German attack. The emphasis on the military doctrine emphasizing offensive operations that had been strongly promoted did not prepare the army for the shock of the Nazi blitzkrieg. Propaganda had worked too well in drawing a picture of success; in fact it was a recipe for disaster.

The magnitude of the Soviet recovery from these dark days to victory may best be illustrated by a comparison with the experience of Stalin's wartime allies who had also suffered initial defeats. The Americans were driven out of the Central Pacific by the Japanese and the British forced off the continent by the Germans. But neither had been invaded. Britain had suffered heavily from aerial bombing, but except for a few weeks in 1940 had not faced the imminent prospect of losing the war. The USA and Britain were able to maintain high levels of defense spending without impoverishing their populations. Rationing was introduced in both, but there was no hunger in the countryside. All this contrasted sharply from the Soviet experience. The Soviet Union also bore the brunt of the fighting on land for three years, not only against Germany but also against armies of Hitler's European allies like Finland, Hungary, Slovakia, Romania and units from France and Spain which did not engage either the USA or Britain.[35] After the defensive victory at Stalingrad, the Red Army seized the initiative at Kursk, the largest tank battle in history. The great Soviet offensive from June to August 1944, code named Bagration, was timed as Stalin promised to correspond to the Allied cross-channel invasion. This operation inflicted a mortal wound on the Wehrmacht, destroying Army Group Centre. The Soviet campaign against Japan in Manchuria may well have contributed as much to ending the war in Asia as the two atomic bombs, by destroying the million-man Kwantung Army, although this view has not been adequately explored. Only Nationalist China suffered as great a loss of territory and population and industrial potential as the Soviet Union. For the first four years of the Sino-Japanese War, Stalin had supplied the Nationalist government with arms and pilots, ending the arrangement only on 22 June 1941, when he mobilized the entire resources of the country for the defense against Barbarossa.[36] Nationalist China never recovered from the conflict and sunk into civil war. The recovery of the Red Army was all the more startling because it was unexpected, not only by the Germans but also by many military experts in the West who predicted an early Soviet collapse. The war had also shifted the image of the Soviet Union throughout the world. Soviet propaganda had much less to do with the transformation than the fighting spirit of the Red Army and the human drama of the Russian people, as they were invariably called in the West. In Britain the Ministry of Information took an active part in promoting Anglo-Russian friendship. In the USA the Russian War Relief was the largest of its kind. *Time* magazine selected Stalin as 'Man of the Year' in 1942. Frank Capra's award-winning documentary *Battle for Russia*, which rationalized the Russian defeats in 1941 and 1942 as strategic withdrawals, was endorsed by Generals George Marshall and Douglas MacArthur. Stalin approved and ordered the printing and distribution of 100,000 copies. American ambassador to Moscow from 1936 to 1938, Joseph P. Davies wrote a largely uncritical appreciation of the Stalinist regime, which was made into a film in 1943. Pipe-smoking 'Uncle Joe' became an almost genial figure as portrayed by the cartoonists in the USA. At liberation the majority of the French ranked the Soviet Union as deserving the most credit for the victory over Nazi Germany. In 1944, the Soviet Union re-entered the world community of nations as one of the founding members of the United Nations Organization. That the Soviet Union would emerge from the war as the world's second greatest military power and the rival of the USA in exercising political influence throughout the globe could hardly be imagined in June 1941.

Once Stalin's emotional appeal to the country for help had been broadcast on 5 July 1941, he resorted to the methods that had served him best in the internal struggles for power. In the first few months of the war, when whole armies were chewed up while their commanders looked on helplessly, Stalin imposed draconian measures to punish those who failed 'to stand and die'. A month into the fighting, he ordered the arrest, trial and execution of the commander of the western front, General Dmitry Pavlov, his chief of staff, Vladimir Klimovsky, the chief of communications of the western front, A.T. Grigorev, and the commander of the Fourth Army, A.A. Korobkov, one of the best of the younger generals who had survived the purges. Pavlov and his subordinates were rehabilitated after Stalin's death, and exonerated of any irresponsible or treasonable activities. In fact, Pavlov had warned Stalin of the impending attack. On the eve of the war, he telephoned Stalin requesting – in vain – permission to place his troops on a wartime footing. But Stalin was not about to take the blame for the disasters which followed.

As catastrophe enveloped the Red Army, Stalin dictated a series of punitive measures to stem the rout. Retreat without per mission or surrender even after encirclement was defined as defeatism, panic-mongering and treasonable, and was punishable by death and confiscation of all property. In the heat of battle, with hastily organized defence lines disintegrating in the face of panzer attacks, it was impossible to verify denunciations coming from the police organs. By the end of 1941 fourteen generals and numerous other high-ranking officers had been arrested. The records are not clear as to their fate.[37]

From the outbreak of war, the NKVD swung into action. The security organs issued a flood of orders to carry out operations against parachutists, diversionists, spies, deserters and bandits and instructions to secure important installations.[38] No doubt the reports on the mixed reception of citizens in the Moscow region to Stalin's speech encouraged the police organs to redouble their efforts.[39] Beria instructed the Moscow city and district units of the Frontier Forces to 'uncover the counter-revolutionary underground'.[40] The police organs carried out a draconic policy of arrests that included the families of traitors even if they were ignorant of the involvement of their kin in what was subsequently denounced as a brutal violation of legality.[41] It would appear there was no breakdown in their communication network. In the first year of the war, the Frontier Forces operating in the rear swept up 700,000 suspects. From the third day of the war, they mounted guard in the rear of the Red Army, arresting deserters, clearing the roads of refugees and assisting in the evacuation. At the same time, Beria sought to broaden the scope of their activities. In the first few months of the war, the political organs of the Frontier Forces were mobilized to conduct propaganda in the national republics of the South Caucasus. The Central Committee of the party responded to requests to increase the firepower of the Frontier Forces by supplying them with tanks, artillery and automatic weapons. Their value was further recognized by orders increasing their numbers by 22,000 men.[42] In Ukraine NKVD units and Frontier Forces played a key role in repressing the nationalist bands after territory had been liberated by the advancing Red Army. In 1943 the chief of the Political Administration of the Frontier Forces ordered the district commanders to strengthen the offensive against 'ideological diversionists'. These forces took over all propaganda and agitation in the newly liberated territories. The army officers were considered too inexperienced to do the job correctly; 'the needs of defending the frontiers involved complicated political tasks'.[43] They were the most active Soviet protagonists in what had become a veritable civil war.[44]

The fear and awe inspired by Stalin (and the police) runs like a thread through the memoirs of those who came into his presence during the war. But there was a limit to the effectiveness of coercion in mobilizing the energies of the population. Stalin faced two apparently contradictory tasks: first to impose from above a strict, even ruthless, mobilization of the population; and second to stimulate from below a genuine emotional response to accept the sacrifices needed to win the war.

One of the earliest measures to mobilize the population in a literal sense was to organize a massive evacuation from the urban centres in the zones of military action. The apparent aim was to deprive the enemy of a labour force and to preserve the cadres of skilled workers and the creative and scientific intelligentsia necessary to fight a long war. The first railway convoys left Riga, Tallinn, Minsk and Kiev at the end of August. By February 1942 10.4 million people had been evacuated to the rear by rail and another 2 million by water transport. During the 'wild flight' of the army in the summer of 1942, 8 million more were evacuated. The problems of housing, providing medical assistance and feeding this dislocated mass of people had no precedent in world history. The burden fell on the local population of the unoccupied territory.[45]

More structural changes were introduced in order to mobilize a population that was already psychologically and physically drained by the ordeals of collectivization, forced industrialization and massive repression. A drastic change was required to transform the prewar mentality of the leading social strata and to reorder the administrative structure of the country. The crucial task which overshadowed and subsumed all the rest was to revive the shattered alliance between the party and groups within the intelligentsia. In the 1930s, Stalin and his closest associates had turned against both the civilian and military specialists who had laid the foundations for the modern industrial power of the Soviet Union. Stalin's natural inclination to over-centralize and bureaucratize political and economic life, married to his morbid suspicions and lust for personal power, had seriously undermined the vital balance in the ruling elite between the ideological-organizational elements in the party and the creative and innovative elements in the technical and literary intelligentsia. During the war, he was able to repair enough of the damage that he himself had imposed on that relationship while at the same time retaining his real monopoly of power in order to ride out the crisis.

In the course of the 'great recovery', a super-centralized government reorganized, with the powerful assistance of the intelligentsia, the centres of industrial production, re-equipped the Red Army and air force, revitalized and broadened a moribund ideology and inspired a revival of the international communist movement. Yet stunning as the recovery was in comparison with the dark days of 1941, it did not resolve the fundamental paradox of power that lay at the heart of the Stalinist system.

THE COMMAND ECONOMY

There were three keys to the economic recovery of the Soviet command economy after the invasion. The first was the super-centralization of the war effort in the hands of a few leaders; the second was the revival of an alliance with the scientific and technical intelligentsia; the third was a series of improvisations, which were in certain sectors – like agriculture – a relaxation of the centralized state controls of the prewar period. The efforts of the streamlined central organs were concentrated on solving critical problems that had fatally undermined the tsarist monarchy in its greatest test during the First World War, namely: breakdown in transportation; shortage of arms and munitions; and inadequate supplies of food, fuel and raw materials. Their effectiveness can only be fully appreciated by recalling two salient characteristics of the Stalinist system as they evolved in the thirties. The first was the long lead of the Soviet Union over the other belligerents in preparing for modern war. The second was the shallow roots of state institutions and the absence of factions – though not of personal rivalries – within the party. The exact timing of the German invasion might have taken Stalin by surprise, but the inevitability of war had long been recognized as a fact of life in the Soviet Union. Ever since the second five-year plan, the country had been engaged in creating a powerful military infrastructure in the armed forces and the defence industries. This survived the purges of individuals, massive and costly as these were with respect to the qualitative performance of the army and defence industry on the eve of the conflict. The factories, research institutes, level of tactical training and above all cadres of skilled workers, however, had escaped unscathed.

The second feature, Stalin's personal dictatorship, had eliminated not only all forms of political opposition, but had also destroyed the basis for any potential resistance to his reordering of the state system. There were few if any bureaucratic traditions, customs or entrenched ways of thinking in a world of institutional constraints left to delay or block his radical changes and super-centralization. Stalin did not have to deal with powerful party satraps or institutional survivals of the old regime, as did Hitler. Nor did he have to bargain and compromise like Churchill and Roosevelt. The Soviet political order had such a short history and had been rendered so malleable in his hands that he could literally reshape it to meet the urgent needs of the moment. That was not true of any other modern society in the mid-twentieth century.[46]

The top leaders of the wartime institutions outside the army rarely met as a body. Stalin reserved for himself all the major decisions in the economic as in the military and diplomatic sphere. As his deputy, Molotov remained his faithful instrument in shaping foreign policy. Voroshilov, who had forfeited any 'operational' confidence, was kept close, presumably for moral support.

Malenkov and Beria were only candidate members of the Politburo, but had proven their mettle in the purges and would not shrink from the most extreme measures. Malenkov carried out Stalin's orders in the apparatus; he had absolutely no competence in military matters, as shown by his ineffective appearances on the Stalingrad front. Beria increased his authority, moving from 'cleansing' the rear areas of diversionists and organizing the deportation of unreliable elements among the nationalities, to operating the forced-labour camps and running the camps for German and later Soviet POWs – the latter those who had been caught in German encirclements and had fought their way out, only to be arrested as traitors. His authority in the defence sector was also increased when Stalin put him in charge of developing an atomic bomb. Mikoian and Kaganovich, added subsequently, were wholly involved in transportation and production problems. Other members of the Politburo were assigned to specialized tasks outside the centre. Zhdanov and Khrushchev as members of the Military Council shouldered responsibilities for liaison with the army on the northwestern and southwestern fronts. Andreev was occupied with supplying the front with food. All of them reported personally to Stalin and took no major initiatives without his explicit orders.[47]

Of all the top wartime leaders, only Voznesensky had formal economic training and extensive experience at the levels of planning and operational aspects of the economy.[48] A member of the younger generation of Soviet leaders, he owed his meteoric rise to his skill in interpreting and refining the broad lines of Stalin's views on Marxist economics and industrial development. A protégé of Andrei Zhdanov, who appointed him in 1935 to take charge of the Leningrad Economic Planning Commission, he had already made his mark as an analyst of the Soviet economic system in party journals. He adhered closely to Stalin's views against Bukharin and further demonstrated his loyalty by reversing his own view to follow Stalin's sudden shift on the role of money and trade at fixed prices in a socialist economy. As an economic planner in Leningrad he set an example for his staff of direct involvement in the practical applications of the plan. His success in adjusting planning targets to changing conditions and unforeseen problems brought him to the attention of Stalin at a critical moment in 1937. The economy was undergoing a slow-down; the growing complexities and purges of the economic apparatus and multiplication of administrative subsections threatened the stability of the system. Voznesensky's appointment as deputy and then full director of Gosplan was part of Stalin's decision to recruit a new generation of leaders including Aleksei Kosygin, Dmitry Ustinov, Mikhail Suslov and Dmitry Shepilov, who were to distinguish themselves during the war and go on to dominate Soviet politics for forty years. In implementing the general goals set forth in a new Gosplan statute issued shortly after his appointment, Voznesensky introduced the same measures that had gained him respect in Leningrad. In order to ensure the smooth operation of the plan, he instituted frequent checks, oversight and information flows including a network of Gosplan agents bypassing other local institutions to report directly to the centre. The aim as always with Voznesensky was to achieve a 'balance of the national economy' within the law-governed structure of the plan. Voznesensky had been elected to the Central Committee in 1939 and delivered the main economic report to the Eighteenth Party Congress, when he was also made a candidate member of the Politburo. Temporarily relieved of his responsibilities as chairman of Gosplan, he remained a central figure in wartime economic planning.

A recently published collection of documents gives a clearer picture of Stalin's governing style as he exercised his enormous power through a revised organizational structure and decision-making process. The creation of the State Defence Committee (GOKO), while proposed by members of his inner circle, fitted perfectly his style of governing in a crisis situation. Initially made up of Stalin, Molotov, Voroshilov, Malenkov and Beria, its composition would change over time.[49] GOKO was modelled in certain respects on the Council of Workers' and Peasants' Defence created during the civil war. It was an ad hoc organization with no fixed rules superimposed on the rest of the Soviet system. There was no special administrative machinery to implement its decisions. Instead, Stalin resorted to the use of plenipotentiaries – much in the style of Peter the Great – as a way of exercising direct control and cutting through cumbersome bureaucratic procedures.[50] The method enabled him to focus great power on a particular situation while keeping responsibility fixed on specific individuals. GOKO became part of a three-cornered system together with the Politburo and the newly formed Commission of the Bureau of the Council of People's Commissars (Sovnarkom) on Current Affairs, also changing their personnel during the war. There was no clear set of rules governing their interaction or the specific duties of the political leaders, which frequently overlapped. The need for quick decisions meant that decrees were often terse rather than being burdened with excessive detail.[51]

The loose administrative arrangements and personal, interventionist style of Stalin were well suited to deal with the series of crises that threatened to overwhelm the system. The breakdown in normal lines of command and information, the terrible losses of equipment and production capacity demanded emergency measures. Governing had become the equivalent of fighting fires. GOKO moved from one emergency to another, pouring resources first into weapons production then into transport.

The enormous centralization of power in Stalin's hands meant a further atrophying of the party organs.[52] The Central Committee ceased to function. Most of its members were scattered far and wide, some at the front, others in the partisan movement. Even those who remained in the centre were preoccupied with tasks that gave them no time to spare. Nor did Stalin care to consult such a large collective body. Two plenums were supposed to meet in 1941. But the October meeting was postponed and the committee was never summoned again.[53] Even the Politburo no longer gathered as a group, except insofar as five of its fourteen members were associated with the GOKO. The Orgburo (Organizational Bureau of the Central Committee) met a similar fate. It lost most of its functions to the secretariat, which reached out into every nook and cranny of the bureaucracy. Most of the decrees bore its imprint and its members occupied key posts in the ad hoc agencies. Although the Central Committee as a collective body withered away, its staff grew rapidly in size and strength. The Administration of Cadres proliferated into forty sections with responsibility for placing people at all ranks in every branch of the national economy, health, education, science and the press. At its head was Malenkov, who also served as a secretary of the Central Committee and member of GOKO, thus gathering enormous administrative authority into his hands.[54] His political alliance with Beria created a concentration of power second only to Stalin. But Stalin checked the police penetration of the top military command. Even after the conclusion of hostilities, when Beria concocted a dossier accusing Zhukov of plotting against Stalin during the war, the ageing leader rebuked him: 'No, I will not give you Zhukov to arrest. I do not believe in all that. I know him well. I knew him for four years of war better than myself.'[55] Beria was more successful in undermining Voznesensky, as shall be seen below (p. 257).

The unwieldy Sovnarkom apparatus suffered an eclipse, but its bureau spawned numerous commissions, meeting frequently and issuing a stream of orders mainly concerning economic problems. Voznesensky and Molotov shared the duty of presiding officer.[56] Individual commissariats gained enormous power. The decree of 1 July 1941, 'On Broadening the Rights of People's Commissars in Wartime Conditions', allowed individual commissariats to reallocate resources assigned to approved projects and reorganize their finances to facilitate investment in new crash projects. At the same time a decree on economic mobilization ordered the regrouping of the workforce around clusters of projects in the Volga, Ural and Western Siberia regions and suspended all long-term projects that were not directly connected with the war effort. Capital construction was reduced by 300 per cent; the number of projects included in the third five-year plan was radically cut from 5,700 to 614.[57]

Gosplan was reorganized in order to streamline its functions, shorten the chain of command, increase controls over orders and expand the mobilization of resources. Reflecting reverses in the field, new plans in the third and fourth quarters of 1941 drastically reordered priorities. Special emphasis was placed on energy resources, especially the opening of new mines to replace the loss of over half the coal production of the country to the enemy. But the reign of emergency measures could no longer continue without leading to breakdowns in the basic industries. If nothing else, it was necessary to co-ordinate and regulate the mass of orders coming from on high. The changes that were introduced over the first year and a half were, in a sense, an intensification of peacetime methods. Over the previous twenty years, right up to the outbreak of the war, radical changes continued to be introduced in the productive process, repeatedly creating imbalances that always had to be corrected; there were certain fortresses even Bolsheviks could not storm. Stalin and his associates had to turn once again to the specialists, in this case the professional economists and planners, who alone could reintroduce some kind of rough economic equilibrium.[58]

The key figure in the re-emergence of the planners was Voznesensky. Gosplan chief for three years before the war, he was reappointed in 1942 to that post, where he served until 1949. Appointed to GOKO he sought to introduce a greater degree of rationalization in the war effort. The first sign of his new influence was the creation of the Operations Bureau of GOKO at the end of 1942. The role of Gosplan in basic industries such as steel, energy and transport was crucial to the recovery of productive levels. It drew up reconstruction plans for the restoration of recaptured areas in January 1943, beginning with the Donbas and besieged Leningrad. Gosplan steadily expanded its control over the allocation of resources. Voznesensky rapidly acquired an authoritative position in economic decisions second only to Stalin.[59]

However, Voznesensky's youth, his sudden rise to prominence and his access to Stalin aroused jealousy among the small band of Stalin's intimates. Beria, the master weaver of conspiracies, uncovered Voznesensky's weakness, his predilection for schematic planning. As production levels fell in the early months of the war, Voznesensky's frequent redrafts of monthly and quarterly plans projected increases. When Beria brought the discrepancies to Stalin's attention, the general secretary was outraged. Although Voznesensky was not replaced, he lost some of his influence and control over several branches of industry which Beria and others distributed among themselves.[60]

In the construction industry, the key figure was Semeon Ginzburg, who had been placed in charge of a new Commissariat of Construction in 1939. All major construction projects were concentrated under his authority, and each trust and enterprise was headed by an experienced specialist. He developed what he called a wholly new type of organization within the commissariat, the Construction Assembly Section, self-contained and highly mobile units that could be thrown into one major project after another to bring them to rapid completion. About 100 of these innovative organizations were fielded with over 400,000 construction specialists and workers. Other innovations in organization of design and drafting shops and bringing the research institutes into direct and close relations with the production units significantly speeded up the process of moving from research to development.[61]

The mass production of weapons and introduction of advanced models was made possible in part by the administrative centralization and specialization of weapons procurement that was already well under way before the outbreak of war. The Commissariat of Armaments and Military Supplies had been split off from the Commissariat of Heavy Industry. Changes in the organization of Soviet defence industry and training of specialists were aimed at raising the quality of production. On the eve of the war, Stalin, after some hesitation, came down on the side of the new commissariat against the protests of the Commissariat of Foreign Trade in allocating 200 million gold rubles for the purchase of special lathes and other equipment from abroad for the production of artillery barrels. It took several years in some cases to prepare the orders; much of the equipment only arrived as part of Lend-Lease in 1944, but in time to make a significant contribution to wartime production. For example, all artillery and machine-gun factories were placed in special categories of enterprises and granted extensive privileges that attracted the best workers and technicians and sharply reduced labour turnover. Stalin held conferences with the directors and party chiefs of defence plants to improve efficiency. Various specialized instructional techniques and courses were devised to improve skills. The reorganization of the state labour reserve provided more flexibility in pulling talent into defence industries. A special effort was undertaken to recruit women for high-quality precision work. Specialists who had been arrested before the war were plucked out of the camps and restored to leading administrative positions. One case was Vannikov. Beria succeeded in persuading Stalin to release his former classmate and friend, who been arrested by Ezhov, and to appoint him commissar of munitions. Thanks to the general improvement in the quality of defence workers, the conversion, evacuation and reconstruction of key factories proceeded much more smoothly than might otherwise have been the case.[62]

The shift of economic resources into the defence industry on the eve of the war facilitated the tremendous production increases in the plants beyond the reach of the enemy in the early months of the fighting. In the last three years of the third five-year plan, defence production rose 39 per cent, as compared to a general rise of only 13 per cent for all industry. During the war, the expansion of arms production by the Commissariat of Armaments to full capacity was virtually completed by the end of 1942, demonstrating how extensive the prewar planning had been. A new commissariat, created solely for the production of mortars and mines, carried out the conversion to defence of textile and other factories with the same production profile.[63] The role of Lend-Lease in Soviet wartime planning and production was critical in certain areas. In the early bargaining over deliveries Mikoian set priorities in light of special needs for raw materials and communication equipment as well as massive numbers of trucks and jeeps. These items helped to free the Soviet planners to concentrate on arms production.[64]

Super centralization that combined both emergency measures and elements of planning managed to check the disastrous slide of the Soviet wartime economy. Within six months it had begun to carry out the evacuation, conversion and new construction that enabled the country to increase substantially the production of all types of weapons during the period of defeat and retreat. Stalin personally directed the evacuation of industry from Leningrad, giving specific details on the relocation of factories producing tanks.[65] The evacuation of existing industrial plants to the east saved from 1,200 to 1,700 enterprises. This heroic improvisation has acquired legendary proportions, although its real economic significance has been questioned. Organized by the Evacuation Council headed first briefly by Kaganovich and then by Nikolai Shvernik, its achievements were accompanied by appalling losses and confusion. The most successful operations were carried out by Aleksei Kosygin in Leningrad. Left behind in the occupied areas were almost 32,000 other enterprises, representing almost 80 per cent of the region's industrial production. But in military terms, the contribution of the evacuated plants was vital. They constituted the bulk of the defence industries; the tank and aircraft plants were especially significant.[66] Tanks produced by reassembled plants from Leningrad and Kharkov were already rolling into combat by the time the crucial battle for Moscow reached its critical phase in December 1941.

Conversion and the construction of new plants were relatively simpler matters. The prewar contingency plans were rapidly put into effect. Giant tractor factories of the second five-year plan like that at Chelyabinsk that had been designed with conversion to tank production in mind made the changeover smoothly. Typewriter factories shifted to the production of automatic rifles and ammunition, bicycle factories made flamethrowers, and various die-stamping plants converted to manufacturing parts for grenades. There were undeniably delays and unexpected problems here too. The construction of new plants was not anticipated, but within less than a year over 850 new enterprises – including many for basic industries like mines, blast furnaces and electric stations – were completed. By the autumn of 1942, Soviet factories were producing, in comparison with the prewar period, four times the number of rifles, six times the number of artillery pieces, eight times the number of tanks and ten times the number of mortars. This accelerating tempo continued relentlessly to the beginning of 1945. By the end of the war the Soviet Union had far out-produced Germany and Great Britain in tanks, aircraft and self-propelled guns.[67]

This achievement resulted from a conscious policy of concentrating on a reduced repertoire of standardized weapons. In contrast to Nazi Germany, Soviet arms production avoided expensive and risky experiments with new technologies, forgoing the production of such items as heavy bombers and complex naval vessels. For example, the Red Army already possessed at the beginning of the war the T-34 tank, which was superior to the German panzers. Its production continued unchanged and in large numbers. Meanwhile, in 1943 and 1944 the Germans introduced superior models in the Panther and Tiger but they could not produce them in adequate numbers or quickly enough to overcome the massive quantitative edge of Soviet tanks.[68]

In other sectors of the economic infrastructure, the heroes were army officers and nameless technical personnel on whom the burden of improvisation fell. Nowhere was this more vividly demonstrated than in the field of communications, particularly the railway network. Recognizing that transportation was 'the twin brother of the army', in Voroshilov's phrase, the leadership had thoroughly modernized and reorganized the railway system in the 1930s. But the purges had seriously disrupted the administration, and there remained strategic gaps in the western network. Reflecting the strategic plans to give primacy to offensive operations, too little attention had been given to constructing lateral north–south lines in the central provinces and too great a percentage of strategic lines remained concentrated in the exposed western provinces. The rapidity of the German advance deprived the defenders of lines carrying 40 per cent of the prewar traffic.[69] The losses in locomotives and rolling stock were staggering and could not quickly be replaced, since most of the factories producing them also fell into enemy hands.

By February 1942 the situation on the railway was so critical that Stalin decided to militarize the entire transportation system. He appointed General Aleksandr Khrulev as commissar of transportation, who brought in his own team of officers. They converted the railway network to exclusively military needs and integrated it into the rest of the transportation system. When Khrulev took over, the northern railway from Moscow to Arkhangel'sk was virtually paralyzed. Almost 3,000 railway wagons stood idle, deprived of locomotives.[70] Having reintroduced by herculean efforts some semblance of order in the rear areas, the new chiefs were overwhelmed once again by the German summer offensive which broke all communications between the centre and the oil of the Caucasus. An entirely new supply route across the Caspian Sea, to a major distribution point at Orenburg, and then throughout Central Asia had to be improvised. In order to construct spur lines to facilitate the transport of oil drums it was necessary to tear up a little-used existing line between Kokand and Namangan in order to lay down track between Krasnovodsk and Iletsk. Faced by a shortage of merchant ships on the Caspian, the teams of specialists from the commissariat experimented with floating drums towed by barges. The smaller Caspian ports were hastily enlarged to handle the new freight. But the long-range problems needed time to resolve.

In the first year and a half of war, only eight locomotives were built to replace the 3,900 that had been destroyed. In the early stages of the fighting, over 150,000 freight wagons had been destroyed and yet not a single replacement was produced in 1942. The GOKO ordered the creation of new factories but their construction required several years. In the meantime, improvisation was the order of the day. Railway men experimented with varieties of fuels that helped avert a fuel crisis in the early years of war. Machinists organized their own flying columns of repair teams equipped with their own locomotives, like the famous Chelyabinsk Depot Group. Dispatchers played a key role in developing ingenious new ways of regulating traffic; Soviet personnel showed themselves to be superior to the Germans in overcoming problems caused by bottlenecks, shortages and destruction of equipment. To replace the 100,000 railway workers drafted into the armed forces new cadres were rapidly trained. Women plugged most of the gaps among the unskilled. In certain areas like electro-mechanics, they soon constituted a majority of the workers.[71] A crash programme of construction balanced the loss of the main north–south trunk lines. The Kazan–Stalingrad line was completed just in time to play a crucial role in supplying Soviet forces on the Middle Volga in the winter of 1942–43. Overall, approximately 9,000 kilometres of new rails were laid down in the USSR during the war. The figure includes many short strategic spurs, but also a number of important trunk lines, particularly in the Urals, Western Siberia and Central Asia. The average annual tempo of construction during the war exceeded that of any of the prewar five-year plans. It was no wonder that despite the greater

Table 1. Commodity Output in Key Industries in the USSR, 1941–45+ (in billions of rubles)[73]

	1941a	1941b	1942a	1942b	1943a	1943b	1944	1945+
Electricity	27.4	19.3	14.1	15.0	29.1	32.3	39.2	43.3
Coal	91.9	59.5	35.7	39.8	75.5	93.1	121.5	149.0
Oil	17.3	15.7	11.7	10.3	22.2	18.0	18.3	19.4
Iron	9.0	4.8	2.3	2.5	4.8	5.6	7.3	8.8
Steel	11.4	6.5	4.0	4.1	8.1	8.5	10.9	12.3
Rolled ferrous metal	8.2	4.4	2.6	2.8	5.4	5.7	7.3	8.5
Iron ore	16.6	8.1	4.6	5.1	9.7	23.3		

(a and b refer to first and second half of the year)

destruction of railway in the Second World War, the period of postwar recovery was much shorter than after the First World War.[72]

Despite the achievements of central planning, improvisation and heroic sacrifices, the Soviet economy recovered only in a relative way. Production was adequate to supply the armed forces with their needs, but in most sectors prewar levels were not reached until the war was over. The low point came in the first half of 1942, when it also appeared as though the military front would crack. After the *annus terribilis*, a slow recovery began to take hold.

AN ECONOMY OF SCARCITY: FOOD

The impact of the war on the agricultural sector was disastrous and left permanent scars on the countryside. Hunger and starvation were the lot of millions of Soviet citizens. When the army and war industries took 6 million men from the collective farms, not enough women and children and older people could be found to fill the gap. The tremendous decline in mechanical work, draught animals and human labour caused a precipitous fall in the amount of cultivated land and the gross value of the harvest which was, at the end of the war, less than half the 1940 figure – yet that was an improvement over 1943.

It was something of a miracle that the Soviet Union was able to feed its army and civilian population in the face of frightful losses in livestock, a severe drop in productivity and a massive decline in mechanical and human labour on the collective farms. Two of the most striking figures are the decline in grain production from 95.5 million tons in 1940 to 29.7 and 29.4 million tons in 1942 and 1943 respectively, with a partial recovery to 49.1 and 47.2 million in 1944 and 1945 respectively; and the decline in meat production from 7.5 million tons in 1940 to 3.4 million tons in 1942.[74] Sugar beet cultivation dropped from over 1.1 million hectares in 1940 to 266,000 in 1943.[75]

The rapidity of the German advance forced the evacuation not only of industry but also of the great livestock herds of the western provinces. With no preparation, tens of thousands of cattle, goats, horses and pigs were driven east, often strafed by enemy planes. It was the most poignant and unsung heroic exploit of the war. In the first phase only 13 per cent of the herds in the occupied areas were brought out safely. Government requisitions and sale to the army further depleted their numbers, so that by 1942 only 3 per cent of the original herds survived in the non-occupied areas. During the second phase the terrible evacuation in the southern Ukraine at the height of the summer of 1942 subjected the herds of these areas to great losses from heat, thirst and heavy slaughtering. Only about 30 per cent of the horned cattle and horses, and practically no pigs at all, made it to winter quarters.[76] The following year a massive re-evacuation of replenished herds into the liberated areas was better planned, with veterinary assistance provided along well-supplied tracts. One cattle drive of 120,000 had covered 350 kilometres between West Kazakhstan and Stalingrad. Losses were comparatively small.

By mid-1942, 40 per cent of the tractors in the country had been lost. Agricultural equipment proved more difficult to evacuate than the herds. Almost all tractor plants were converted to producing tanks and the production of tractors was only started up again in 1943. Production was up to 7,700 by 1945, though this was less than a third of the planned target.

The concentration on the production of weapons and military hardware could not have been achieved without a drastic shift in resource allocation away from the production and distribution of food. To be sure, the armed forces could not be deprived of the calorific intake necessary to produce the high levels of energy required in combat. This did not mean that all the troops were supplied with an adequate diet all the time. Still, the front-line troops took first priority, then the rear echelons. The civilian population was placed under great pressure to provide food for the army. They were left largely to fend for themselves.

The introduction of rationing had the psychological effect of equalizing the burdens of war. But it discriminated among different types of work that contributed to the war effort, and rations were used as rewards.[77] The main sources of food supply for the civilian population were a variety of private food markets. Excluded from rationing, deprived of the most productive age groups of the male labour force, lacking replacements for worn-out equipment, and faced with increasing obligatory deliveries to the state, the collective farms were forced to fall back on their own resources. The government permitted a rapid expansion of the private plots on both kolkhozes and sovkhozes in order to avoid large-scale hunger in the countryside. The peasants fed themselves from these plots and supplied substantial food to the urban population. Even under highly disadvantageous conditions, the free market provided 40 per cent of the butter and potatoes, a third of the meat and a quarter of the milk and vegetables for the urban population. The party vigorously encouraged private gardening in and around cities. In 1942 almost a third of city dwellers had their own garden or participated in a collective garden. The war also gave an impetus to the expansion of subsidiary farms attached to industrial enterprises as an important source of food for the urban population.[78] All of these improvisations demonstrated that the government was incapable of fighting the war and feeding its own population.[79]

The kolkhoz system never recovered from the wartime damage. The prewar process of narrowing the gulf between the workers and peasants slowed down. The size of the private plots was sharply cut back; the improvised market mechanisms were closed down. Despite the government's massive increase in investment in the agricultural sector in the postwar five-year plans, the kolkhoz population never returned to its prewar levels. Only some of the demobilized soldiers and evacuees came back to the villages. The decline was greatest in the territories occupied by the enemy. The losses were greatest among kolkhoz directors.[80]

MILITARY RECOVERY

The recovery of the Red Army from its initial disastrous defeats in 1941 and again in 1942 depended not only on a steady supply of weapons and munitions but also upon a radical reorganization of the command structure. The key to success here, as elsewhere in the war effort, was Stalin's readiness to re-establish the supremacy of the professional specialists over the *praktiki*. At the top of the command hierarchy he acted swiftly to form a centralized military counterpart of GOKO. A newly created organ under the title General Headquarters of the Supreme Command (Stavka) became the strategic planning and operational centre for the duration of the war. Yet the functional distinction between GOKO and the Stavka was often blurred. According to Zhukov, who became a member of both, they had overlapping jurisdiction and personnel. Stalin's style was to consult individuals and small groups, not institutions, and it was difficult to tell which hat the generals were wearing when he consulted them. In any case Stalin would not permit any protocol to be kept. All the documentation of the Stavka activities has to be drawn from memoirs.[81]

The name and form of the Stavka was borrowed from the pre-revolutionary army and symbolized to many the restoration of the army to a position of equality with the party and police in the institutional structure of the Soviet system. The Stavka drew its technical support from the General Staff, 'the brains of the army' in Marshal Shaposhnikov's ringing phrase. The Staff provided information, organized the supply and movement of troops, and kept in close touch with the fronts in order to intervene at a moment's notice in the development of operations.[82]

Stalin's relationships with the Stavka and General Staff evolved throughout the war as he came to rely on the advice of the professional soldiers. Up to September 1942, Stalin placed too little reliance on the work of the General Staff, which cost the army dearly. But even after that he never surrendered his arbitrary power to the demands of routine. Instead, he fashioned the military bureaucracy to fit his style of governing. Shortly after the outbreak of the war, he assumed the title of supreme commander. He made certain that no major decision was taken without his approval and that he was kept fully informed at all times of the situation at the front.

Stalin experimented with the structure and function of the Stavka in order to strike the right balance between military efficiency and his personal control. Initially, the Stavka was composed of a dozen or so senior commanders. But this arrangement soon proved to be unwieldy. The numbers were pared down. The Stavka did not function as a permanently sitting board. Members had their own assignments and responsibilities. They were often on the move, mainly to the fronts. Even after the military situation stabilized, Stalin did not like his deputy supreme commanders, Zhukov and Vasilevsky, 'sitting too long' in Moscow. In the thirty months that Vasilevsky was a member of Stavka he could not recall a single occasion when the body met as whole. Thus it could not act as a group; Stalin as the supreme commander was the hub that held its individual members together. Stalin never was a slave to fixed rules. The ad hoc selection of advisers from a small, specialized pool of talent enabled him to observe, test and ultimately come to trust his immediate circle of subordinates (insofar as he ever trusted any group of men). Stalin never took a major decision without an elaborate series of consultations beginning with members of Stavka. He called them together in small groups, sometimes only by twos or threes. Then he would widen the circle of consultation, taking the preliminary decisions to the GOKO or the Politburo for further discussion. There was real give and take at all levels, and not everyone agreed with Stalin's proposals. In GOKO, for example, Voznesensky and Stalin had sharp exchanges over the ability of the defence industries to meet the ever-growing needs of the front.[83]

The rapid advance of the Nazi forces in the early days of the war threatened to plunge into chaos the entire strategic rear of the Red Army. In the thirties, the General Staff was responsible for general supervision of stockpiling and supplying the combat fronts. But the shock of war overwhelmed the Staff. Zhukov had to admit at the beginning of July that he himself no longer knew what the needs of the troops were. Relying on the experience of the First World War and the civil war, General Khrulev of the Staff took the initiative of proposing a plan for organizing the supply of the army. On Zhukov's strong recommendation, Stalin approved the decree of 1 August 1941 that created the Main Administration of the Rear of the Red Army, which brought under centralized authority a number of agencies including the Quartermaster Corps, the Administration of Military Communications, the Highway Administration, and the Military-Medical and Veterinarian administrations. Khrulev, the deputy commissar of defence, was named the chief of the rear areas of the Red Army. Under his command the new agency established strict controls over the supply of virtually all necessities for the army: military equipment, food, transport, fuel, medical supplies and hospitals. Close working relations were established with the commissariats. Mikoian personally selected and dispatched teams of specialists from various branches of the central economic apparatus. At the beginning, emergency measures and improvisation carried the day. The chief of the rear areas sent his own plenipotentiaries to uncork bottlenecks; in the absence of supply roads, horse-drawn vehicles and even camels and reindeer were pressed into service in the north and in Central Asia. Gradually, a more systematic hierarchical organization replaced the plenipotentiaries and expansion of the railways took up much of the burden of transportation. In addition to his other duties, Khrulev also became commissar of transportation.

One of the chief concerns of the new agency was to supply the troops with decent hot food. Often improvisation again played an unexpected role. On the Volkhov front, encircled Russian troops were supplied with air drops of *pelmeni* (dumplings) on the initiative of a battalion cook whose recommendation reached Mikoian. But the centre had, as usual, to intervene on a large scale in critical moments. In 1943 a breakdown in the supply of food on the Kalinin front prompted the GOKO and the Commissariat of Defence to issue a stern warning against commanders who skimped on food in order to increase shipments of shells, promising stern punishments for those who failed to provide adequate rations for troops.[84] Once again super-centralization, combined with a greater freedom to improvise and experiment at the local level, worked effectively to solve most of the problems and stabilize the rear areas within a year after the initial attack. Whenever a military or civilian specialist showed extraordinary talents Stalin rewarded him by piling more responsibility on his shoulders. Only the strongest were able to bear the strain.

Stalin kept his generals in line by a combination of intimidation, fear and charm; he also won their respect by his phenomenal memory, grasp of details and iron will. Stalin was far more brutal than Hitler in punishing commanders for defeats in the field. The disgrace of Marshal Grigory Kulik was only the most notorious case. Following the loss of much of the Crimea along with the town of Kerch in early 1942, Beria cooked up one of his conspiracies and denounced Kulik for defeatism. Kulik attempted to defend himself, but was brought to trial and forced to confess to having acted contrary to orders. He was stripped of his medals and his marshal's baton, excluded from the Central Committee, removed as deputy commissar of defence and demoted to major-general. The rest of his life was an ordeal. Demoted again at the end of the war, excluded from the party and arrested in 1947 for anti-Soviet activities, he was finally shot in 1950.[85] His example hung like a sword of Damocles over the field commanders. Stalin was a stickler for formal reports from Stavka members sent on missions to the front. Woe to the man whose report was tardy or slipshod. He would find himself mercilessly reproached by Stalin, even threatened with dismissal. Even Zhukov, Vasilevsky and Nikolai Vatutin, Stalin's favourites, felt the sting of his rage.

Gradually, however, Stalin's trust in the Soviet generals increased, as Oleg Khlevniuk has demonstrated, a tribute to the enormously expanding role of the army fighting the war. The 'memory of repression' that lingered from the prewar purges gave way to greater stability in the officer corps, milder penalties for mistakes and setbacks, and greater rewards for achievements in the field. As a result, the top command gained greater confidence in their actions and proposals for change in the military culture. The abolition of political commissars was a visible sign of the growing trust, although surveillance by the secret police continued. This did not mean that Stalin relaxed his hold over strategic decision-making or his concern about the postwar role of the army.[86]

Stalin pushed his generals to the very limit of their endurance and sometimes beyond, insisting on greater speed, more audacity, sparing no one, working eighteen hours a day. As a military thinker, he was as in all things a bundle of contradictions. Zhukov, in the most recent revision of his memoirs, asserted that Stalin was at home in strategic questions from the beginning of the war; in operational matters it took him longer to master the fundamentals. At the beginning of the war, he displayed a frank ignorance of the most elementary operational problems such as the two-pronged attack. He felt comfortable with such matters only after the battle of Kursk in mid-1943. Throughout the war, he briefed himself with the help of junior officers of the General Staff, calling them in one after another, so that he was normally well prepared when he met with the commanders of the fronts. Occasionally he would, like Hitler, memorize a situational problem in great detail in order to catch out the professional soldiers, but his knowledge was more systematic than that of the Führer.[87] His chief commanders were impressed by his analytical keenness during meetings of the Stavka, GOKO or Politburo, his unhurried manner, attentiveness, rapid response to questions, and ability to summarize a discussion and arrive at a concise and penetrating conclusion. He personally knew all 100 front commanders and the leading figures in the Commissariat of Defence. Early in the war, he began to show himself to be well informed on the general situation on all fronts, the disposition of forces and reserves available. Khrushchev's accusation at the Twentieth Party Congress that Stalin often planned operations on a globe has been completely refuted by the testimony of those like Vasilevsky and Sergei Shtemenko who worked with him every day. Quite to the contrary, the General Staff in its daily briefing of Stalin made use of extremely detailed maps of 1:200,000 scale, and had to be prepared for the supreme commander's pointed questioning and demand for the most precise information. In the early months of defeat and retreat, Stalin was often explosive and inconsistent. As the war progressed, he became calmer and more restrained, less certain of his absolute correctness, more willing to tolerate dissent on military matters.[88] Yet his military knowledge even at the end of the war was insufficient, according to Zhukov, and did not reach the level of a professional military man. Moreover, he became increasingly jealous, feeling that the great victories should be associated with his name.[89]

Stalin's skills as a military administrator also improved under the pressure of war. As in operational fields Stalin profited from his mistakes while Hitler compounded his. When the war broke out, Stalin divided the front into three commands under his old cronies, Budenny, Voroshilov and Timoshenko. Only Timoshenko displayed any effectiveness as a commander by holding up the German attack for three crucial weeks.[90] Stalin gradually removed all of them from positions of command. He relied more and more on Shaposhnikov, then Zhukov and later Vasilevsky as his closest advisers. Shaposhnikov was the only senior officer of the Imperial Russian Army who survived in Stalin's entourage. Stalin held him in high esteem and treated him with a mixture of politeness and deference that was unique. Shaposhnikov was undeniably a talented military thinker, but he probably owed his survival and Stalin's trust to the fact that he had come down on Stalin's side in the debate over the responsibility for the defeat of Poland in 1920. In any case, it was probably Shaposhnikov more than anyone else who was able with his combination of tact, erudition and quiet persistence to begin to teach Stalin the art of modern warfare.[91]

Zhukov too was politically reliable, having served under Budenny's and Stalin's command in the First Cavalry Army during the civil war and Polish campaign. But he was also an admirer of Tukhachevsky and Uborevich, the fallen marshals, the former 'for his erudition and profound analytical mind', the latter for his operational and tactical skill.[92] Zhukov learned from both. He was a man of enormous military ability and had already displayed his mastery of modern armoured warfare in his stunning victory over the Japanese Kwantung Army at Khalkin Gol. Vasilevsky had also been trained in the tsarist army tradition and served as a junior officer in the First World War. In the twenties, he had studied at the feet of Shaposhnikov and became his favourite student. It took time for their influence to have the desired effect. In the meantime, Stalin staggered from error to error. The mass surrenders of troops who had been encircled in the first battles and the ineffectiveness of his top commanders aroused all Stalin's morbidly suspicious instincts. He reached out for political solutions. In July 1941 he reintroduced the dual-command structure. Side by side with the professional military men, the party appointed a political commissar who assumed full and equal responsibility for the unit's conduct in battle. The commissar was authorized to denounce commanders who were 'unworthy of their rank' and to 'wage a relentless struggle against cowards, panic-mongers and deserters'. This was, as John Erickson suggests, 'the language of the civil war'.[93] Stalin never entirely freed himself from this mentality that viewed those who surrendered or fell under German control as internal enemies of the state. By October 1942, the political commissars lost most of their independent position and were subordinated to the military commander.

Stalin learned after the terrible defeats in the summer and autumn of 1941 not to commit his reserves piecemeal. During the defence of Moscow, he doled out his reserves like a miser. Zhukov, writing at the height of the anti-Stalin campaign in the sixties, admitted that 'Stalin was in Moscow organizing men and material for the destruction of the enemy. He must be given his due . . . he performed an enormous task in organizing the strategic reserves and the material and technical means for the armed struggle. By means of his harsh exactitude he continued to achieve, one can say, the well nigh impossible.'[94] But the military defence of Moscow and the counterblow that forced the Germans back for the first time in the Second World War was the product of professional staff work. Stalin gave Zhukov and the General Staff broader latitude in planning the operation than probably at any other time in the war.[95]

But Stalin had not yet learned all his lessons. He still displayed a lack of realism, bouts of frenzied impatience, impetuousness and a disregard for professional advice that recalled his irrational decisions during forced collectivization and the drive for excessive production norms in the first five-year plan. After the successful defence of Moscow his overweening self-confidence led him to order a general offensive along the entire front, despite opposition from Zhukov, Shaposhnikov and Vasilevsky. When the offensives quickly petered out, he disregarded the repeated warnings of his top commanders that his refusal to order a retirement behind the Dnieper would lead to a disaster at Kiev. The huge encirclement cost the Red Army 300,000 men. Zhukov resigned as chief of staff in disgust.[96] Stalin was also a bad forecaster of German intentions. He expected the main blow in 1941 to fall on the southern front, but it came in the centre. He reversed his prediction in 1942, but Hitler changed his strategic objectives. The main attack came in the south while Stalin was waiting for a renewed assault on Moscow.

The creation of Stavka and the appointment of professional officers were not enough to save the Red Army and the country from defeat. It was necessary to create a viable command structure. The most serious consequences of the purges emerged with blinding clarity. It was not simply the liquidation of well-trained officers knowledgeable in modern armoured warfare that contributed to the debacle of 1941 and the errors of 1942; it was the absence of a command group that shared a history of working together, freely exchanging ideas, refining their strategic thinking, planning for contingencies. This was normally the product of years; in 1942 it had to be created in months. Yet it was the very kind of group that in the thirties Stalin had come to fear as the embryo of conspiracy. He was not about to change his thinking during the war, even though defeat was staring him in the face.

Stalin settled on a compromise between his obsessive suspicion of self-contained, specialized working groups entrenched in the power structure and the strategic requirements of modern warfare. But he reached it only after the German offensive in 1942 brought the country once more to the brink of collapse. Stalin's attempts to conduct a general offensive after his forces had won some local victories in the winter of 1941–42 led to the series of defeats in the south that resembled at times 'a wild flight' to the Volga. Stalin was forced to dismiss his personal favourites. Budenny was eased out of the Stavka. Voroshilov, stumbling from one blunder to another, was removed from active operations and provided with work in the rear areas.[97] A beneficiary of Stalin's personal favour, he was among the fortunate. Others who had committed lesser errors were summarily shot. Timoshenko also faded from the scene. The dual command was abolished, and the political commissars were restricted to an advisory role. In August 1942, Stalin appointed Zhukov deputy supreme commander. After Shaposhnikov retired for genuine reasons of ill health, he was succeeded by his pupil Vasilevsky. Stalin gave the two generals plenipotentiary powers and subsequently appointed them first and second deputy commanders.

A professional chain of command was taking shape. In planning the Stalingrad counter-offensive, Stalin placed the generals of the air force and chiefs of artillery and armour under the command of Zhukov and Vasilevsky. Previously, their role had been largely administrative within the Commissariat of Defence. With these appointments military professionals were installed in all points of the chain of command above the operational level. There was to be no more ad hoc consultation on Stalin's part, first with one and then with another of the members of Stavka. Stalin still set the rules and defined the relationships between himself and his deputies. This was hardly a routinized military bureaucracy. But a regular, hierarchical order came into being in the High Command. Later, Vasilevsky's first deputy, the erudite, self-effacing and brilliant workhorse General Alexei Antonov succeeded as chief of staff and became Stalin's invaluable aide. By the end of 1943, the majority of directives issuing from Stavka bore the signatures of Stalin and Antonov, or else Antonov signing for Stalin.[98]

There was a striking contrast between the responses of Stalin and Hitler to the problem of managing the relationship between political power and the armed forces. As Earl F. Ziemke succinctly puts it, 'Stalin's response was rational and self-serving; Hitler's only self-serving.'[99] Like the Stavka the creation of GOKO fused into one structure elements of Stalin's personal despotic rule and a bureaucratic order. The arrangement survived as long as he thought it necessary. He kept it in place until the end of the war, then dismantled both GOKO and the Supreme Command, replacing them with another system.

The internal organization of the armed forces did not remain static during the war. It changed in response to the demands of modern warfare and the shock of the initial defeats. Caught in the middle of structural changes initiated in 1939, the military leadership found it necessary at first to improvise, at times in desperation. In the first few months, the front-line units of the Red Army disintegrated. One hundred and twenty-four divisions were so badly chewed up that they had to be abolished as operational forces. There were not enough officers with adequate training to staff corps headquarters. All rifle and tank corps had to be temporarily disbanded; inexperienced divisional commanders were overwhelmed with problems in attempting to manoeuvre their units in the highly fluid situation of hasty retreat.

There had been no plans for a strategic withdrawal. Little co-ordination existed above the divisional level. The army commands were obliged to redeploy with smaller tactical units and to supply these with new equipment as it began to arrive. Hastily assembled reserves could not be organized into divisions for lack of officers and communications equipment. They had to be committed often piecemeal as brigades. The People's Home Guard, little more than an untrained militia at first, often led by zealous but untrained Communist Party volunteers, was also thrown into battle in an effort to gain time.[100] Its losses were appalling. But the picture was not uniformly grim. Units fought their way out of encirclements; the skeletal structure of command did not collapse; most of the troops did not surrender until their position was hopeless. More systematic reorganization slowly took hold.

Nevertheless, there was one more military crisis to face in the summer of 1942, when the German army launched a major offensive in Ukraine. The Red Army was driven back to the Volga and a German spearhead reached the Caucasus mountains. Stalin reacted by issuing order no. 227, famous for its hortatory phrase 'Not one step backwards. Stand or Die'. It is seldom noted that this demand was followed by an order, emulating the example of the German Army, to create blocking or barricade battalions in the rear of the front lines to prevent unauthorized withdrawals. According to Stalin these innovations by the German High Command had a salutary effect in stiffening discipline in the ranks of the Wehrmacht after its failure to take Moscow in December 1941. Stalin's order also authorized the creation of penal battalions on each front, composed of commanders and commissars who had been found guilty of cowardly or confused actions and assigning them to the most dangerous sectors of the front lines. Finally, he ordered the creation of defensive squads within divisions that displayed signs of wavering.[101] The order was never printed but read aloud to all fighting units. Its effect has been variously interpreted and often exaggerated in attributing subsequent victories to fear. Certainly, this was not the case at Stalingrad.

Meanwhile, in 1942, the flow of new weapons from defence plants and fresh reserves made possible the formation of larger and better-equipped units. The reorganized rifle divisions, the tank and motorized corps and finally the tank armies constituted a powerful field force that had the potential, for the first time since the outbreak of war, to penetrate the enemy's defences and conduct offensive operations on a large scale. The Red Army learned through bitter experience the lessons that the Tukhachevsky command group had preached in the thirties: the necessity of providing a great variety of support and special units including engineer brigades, vastly increased numbers of signal units, ski troops and battalions of road maintenance and railway troops. The functional specialization reflected the increased influence of the professional soldiers. The air force was almost totally reorganized into air armies in order to overcome the weaknesses of a divided command.[102]

At the level of military operations, a similar process of learning from experience and adjusting to changing circumstances produced a Soviet-style offensive. The strategic ideas of Tukhachevsky were quietly restored, with suitable modifications, to a place of honour. But this took time. The Moscow counter-offensive of December 1941, though largely successful, consisted of improvised attacks by separate units rather than a well-co-ordinated action. The same shortcoming showed up during the winter offensives all along the line. The army command had little or no experience in conducting operations on such a large scale. They lacked the necessary skill, firepower and force levels to mass powerful concentrations at the points of breakthrough. They gradually learned, too, the art of directing offensive operations on several fronts (rather than just one, for which prewar planning had prepared them). They increased the strategic depth of their defences as fresh forces became available to them. But the lessons were costly. And Stalin did not hesitate to rebuke the military leaders publicly and repeatedly for having failed to learn the techniques of modern warfare.[103]

He, of course, took no responsibility for having eliminated those who had. The commanders had finally learned to lead, he declared on the twenty-fifth anniversary of the Red Army on 23 February 1942, 'having discarded the foolish and harmful linear tactics and having finally adopted the tactics of manoeuvring'. But he was still urging in November 1943 that 'all Red Army men must perfect their combat skills . . . commanders must acquire mastery in the conduct of battles'. He urged greater obedience, organization and order.[104]

By mid-1943 the Soviet command began to match its limited operational skill with its growing superiority of mass. It combined the 'salient thrust' or 'cleaving blow' with the modified encirclement. Following Tukhachevsky's views incorporated in the 1936 field regulations, it involved a series of deep penetrations along parallel lines that forced the enemy back along a broad front. Its application turned out to be a less sophisticated and more ponderous manoeuvre than the German blitzkrieg in the early months of the war. Only in unusual circumstances could these repeated frontal assaults by an overwhelming mass of infantry and armour be converted into a double envelopment or encirclement, a difficult tactical operation that required speed, precision and considerable experience in manoeuvring. The Stalingrad encirclement was exceptional because of Hitler's refusal to allow the withdrawal of the German Sixth Army. Later, even when the Soviet superiority reached four, five, or even six to one, mass encirclements were rare.[105] Stalin appeared to harbour some deep-seated bias against the manoeuvre, telling Zhukov on one occasion that it was 'not your business to encircle German forces on our territory'. He insisted that they should simply be driven off Soviet territory so that the spring grain could be planted; it would be possible then to encircle them on their own territory.[106]

The number and quality of military manpower steadily increased throughout the year. In the first year of the war, the armed forces grew from just under 3 million to 5.5 million. By the end of the war, the figure had doubled again. A more serious problem was training officers to replace the heavy losses from the purges and the first six months of the fighting which reduced officer cadres to 34 per cent of authorized strength. In the first year the need was so great that officer training courses had to be streamlined in order to permit accelerated graduation. In 1942 half a million officers were trained under the new programme. By 1943 the emergency had lifted and the course of studies in all ground forces was lengthened from twelve months to two years.[107] But the inadequate prewar training of officers for command positions, the rapid expansion of the army and the wartime losses, more than the prewar purges, created a situation in which ill-prepared replacements were often rushed into combat, quickly sustaining further losses in what Roger R. Reese has called 'a vicious circle' that delayed mastery of the art of war.[108]

By the summer of 1943, the Red Army underwent another major reorganization accompanied by a massive re-equipment. In the words of John Erickson, the 'Soviet infantryman had become a walking arsenal, equipped as no other for anti-tank fighting'. By this time too Stalin was finally persuaded by the tank men to create the tank armies that had been the dream of Tukhachevsky. Artillery was also reorganized into a separate corps; this reform represented a breakthrough in military organization that recognized the importance of its firepower. There was still the shortage of jeeps and trucks that had hampered every offensive operation, but Lend-Lease was beginning to supply these in large quantities: 183,000 by mid-1943 and 430,000 by 1944.[109]

The great battle at Kursk in the summer of 1943 was the first real test for the new Red Army that had gradually emerged from the deep shadows of the purges and early defeats. By this time the army had been largely re-equipped and re-staffed; the Stavka and the General Staff had given Stalin ample proof of their professional competence. The Kursk operation was the first example of collective planning, taking into account a discussion of strategic alternatives, a systematic evaluation of intelligence and a complex combination of premeditated defence in depth with a co-ordinated counter-offensive. The professionals in Stavka, the General Staff and the front commanders had to overcome Stalin's reservations about the ability of the army to sustain the shock of mass tank attacks by the German forces. They repeatedly reassured him that the experience and skills had been acquired to avoid a repetition of 1941 or 1942. Unprecedented in size and scope, the operation provided for a multi-level defence zone of 250–300 kilometres, and the largest concentration of troops and matériel in the war.[110]

In planning the operation, Stalin entrusted Mikoian as early as March with the organization of the Reserve Front (later called the Steppe Front), a new special operation reserve in the Frunze tradition to back up the planned counter-offensive three months later. Mikoian summoned a team of civilian and military specialists from all branches of supply, ordnance and transport, as well as commanders of units withdrawn from the front for replacements and re-equipment. As planned, the Soviet defence in depth checked the German attacks and launched their powerful counterstroke with devastating results. Numbering about 1.25 million men, supported by 20,000–24,000 artillery pieces, 2,700–3,400 tanks and 3,000–5,000 aircraft and half a million men from the Reserve Front, the Soviet offensive shattered the vaunted German Army Group Centre. German losses were catastrophic.[111] The strategic initiative had passed to the Red Army. It never relinquished it. For the Germans it was a greater defeat than Stalingrad.

From Kursk to the end of the war, a rough balance was struck between Stalin and his generals over the conduct of the war. Strategic and operational planning on all levels settled down into a fairly predictable pattern. But Stalin reserved and exercised the right to intervene at any point in order to assert his personal prerogatives as supreme commander. At times he opposed his top-level advisers without making clear why.[112] For example, in July 1944 he insisted that the Soviet forces take Lvov (L'viv) before reaching the Vistula, while Zhukov and Konev wanted to reverse the priorities.[113] Was Stalin thinking back to that fateful moment in the civil war when the First Cavalry Army under Budenny and his command had pressed their attack on Lvov while Tukhachevsky's offensive on Warsaw failed at the gates of the city? Or was it merely a political move to strengthen the Soviet claim on Lvov as early as possible? The supreme commander did not share his deepest motivations with his generals.

The last two great strategic operations of the war – the Belarus breakthrough and the final assault on Berlin – were masterpieces of planning and execution on a colossal scale. According to Zhukov, the Belarus operation demonstrated the ability of the Soviet commanders to execute the most difficult of all tactical manoeuvres, the encirclement and destruction of large enemy formations. The commanders had gradually weaned Stalin from his attachment to frontal blows. The battle for Berlin gave further proof of the kind of working relationship that had developed between Stalin and the professionals. Stalin was determined to allow Zhukov's First Belarus Front to reap the glory of taking the Nazi capital. But the General Staff agreed with Marshal Konev that his First Ukrainian Front should participate in the assault from the south in order to guarantee the most rapid and decisive results. Only Stalin could decide. Hearing out his advisers, Stalin silently crossed out the section of the demarcation line between the two fronts that cut off the First Ukrainian from Berlin. 'Let the one who is first to break in take Berlin', he said.[114]

Stalin's recognition of the professional soldier took on an elaborate symbolic form during the war. He restored the lustre of an army tarnished by the purges and introduced a series of rituals and rewards to mark acts of individual and collective heroism. The officer corps, as the repository of military tradition, was the main beneficiary. The reforms of 1942 not only abolished dual command, which had offended the pride of the officers, but also restored epaulets and gold braid, creating a 'cult of the uniform'. New decorations were created for officers only. Even more startling was the restitution of the etiquette of the tsarist army in forms of address and behaviour. The following year a series of new military academies – named the Suvorov Schools after the great eighteenth-century commander – was opened. Their curriculum, discipline and general atmosphere were, according to the military newspaper *Krasnaia zvezda*, modelled 'after the manner of the old cadet schools'.[115]

Following the battle of Kursk, Stalin proposed an elaborate ritual to celebrate every victory. He recalled that in Muscovite Russia victories were marked by the ringing of bells. He suggested that artillery salvos and some kind of illumination should serve the same purpose. The General Staff worked out three categories of salutes to match the significance of each victory: twenty-four salvos by 324 guns, twenty salvos by 224 guns and twelve salvos by 124 guns. The salutes were carried on national radio broadcasts and accompanied by congratulatory orders giving the names of commanders and units. The solemn communiqués listed the liberated cities, adding their pre-revolutionary names where appropriate, honoured the leading commanders and ended with the same refrain: 'Eternal glory to the heroes who fell in the struggle for the freedom of our country. Death to the German invaders!' As Moscow reverberated to the thunder of the volleys, cascades of fireworks illuminated the sky above. Stalin was consulted on every one of these, and on occasion even edited the text of the broadcasts. He did not easily forgive mistakes. When the consecrated formula was altered Stalin flew into a rage, as in the case of Marshal Konev's name inadvertently having been omitted in the victory broadcast.[116]

The awarding of medals, decorations and titles to individuals and units went far beyond pre-revolutionary custom. The number and variety probably exceeded those of any other army in the Second World War. By 1942 the process of making awards had to be speeded up in order to meet the demand by extending the right to commanders of units down to the regimental level. In addition to the older decorations, Hero of the Soviet Union and the Order of the Fatherland War 1st and 2nd Class appeared for both officers and men. For officers only the Order of Alexander Nevsky and three classes of the orders of Suvorov and Kutuzov were introduced. This was followed by the creation of the Order of Bogdan Khmelnitsky for operations in the Ukraine, separate decorations for naval and air force personnel and finally the new Order of Glory and Order of Victory. There were also special medals for the defence of the great cities, and for partisans. Altogether more than 35 million decorations were awarded to men and women in the fighting services. In 1943 collective awards were introduced. Almost 11,000 individual units and formations received one or more of these. The creation of Guards Divisions for units which distinguished themselves in special ways first made their appearance during the defence of Moscow. The designation carried special rewards and privileges for officers and men. Stalin attached great importance to these forms of incentives and rewards. On occasion he would reduce the level of a decoration to one of the General Staff or front commanders in order to demonstrate his reservations or annoyance over an error or an infraction of rules.[117] In all of this there was something highly stylized, ritualistic and hierarchical. The formal portraits of the marshals and senior officers bedecked with medals and decorations formed a new pantheon of secular saints to take the place of the old iconostasis. One could judge by the frequency and class of awards the correct place in the general hierarchy. Stalin finally placed himself at the apex of the pyramid by adopting the title of generalissimo. He appeared in a resplendent uniform covered with gold braid and decorations. Yet he wore it only once. It was as though he had made his point to the professionals. He decided to adopt instead the rank of marshal. It was enough to demonstrate that he was still supreme while at the same time equating his military skills with those of the top commanders in the Red Army.

In forging an alliance with the professional soldier, Stalin invented a new, Soviet military tradition. The Red Army of Peasants and Workers of the 1920s with its egalitarian command structure, its international outlook and its civil war traditions gave way to a hierarchical and nationalistic Soviet army whose history began on 22 June 1941. In all other European armies, an essential element in the spirit of the army was regimental loyalty, developed over a long period and extending in many cases back into the eighteenth century. In Russia, these traditions had been destroyed during the revolution and civil war. The famous units and exploits of the civil war were short-lived because Stalin killed off most of its heroes who survived into the late thirties. What he had to do during the Second World War was to create a whole new set of traditions as he went along. The creation of decorations, the designations of guards divisions, the recognition of 'hero cities' and the elaborate celebration of victories in the communiqués, all of these had a profound effect on the officer corps and the rank and file, both drawn from the 'toiling masses'. The upper levels of the officer corps were recruited almost exclusively from families of peasants (Zhukov, Vasilevsky, Vatutin and Shtemenko) or workers (Rodion Rokossovsky and Ivan Bagramian). Trained in pre-revolutionary officers' schools and Soviet academies, they nevertheless owed Stalin their promotion to the command ranks and they remained loyal to him even in their memoirs. The glorification of the common soldier in Soviet propaganda and through the reward system was a vital if ultimately immeasurable force in binding the villages and factories to the fighting front. Stalin's political skill in building the new army out of the wreckage of the old for which he too was responsible is one of the strangest paradoxes of his rule. But it was not the only one that surfaced in the process of a military recovery.

The partisan movement represented a large potential for carrying out political as well as military tasks, by maintaining a Soviet presence in the territories under German occupation as well as disrupting German communications and gathering intelligence. It had started up spontaneously among soldiers cut off from their shattered or encircled units, Communist Party and Komsomol members overtaken by the rapid German advance and civilians antagonized by German brutalities, whose numbers increased when the tide of war began to turn; these included a substantial number of Jews. The problem for Stalin was how to control the activities of bodies of armed men and women outside the reach of the Soviet system, living and fighting in a liminal state, which paradoxically appeared to many partisans as personally liberating. Stalin's appeal in June 1941 for a mass uprising against the enemy was not followed up in practice. According to the most recent and comprehensive study of the movement: 'actual Soviet policy discounted and even discouraged popular initiative and participation'.[118] Moreover, the strategic planning for an eventual war, from Tukhachevsky and Egorov down to the much disputed draft of May 1941, anticipated frontier battles which would then be carried over into an offensive on the enemy's territory. No provision was made for a fighting retreat with provisions for the operation of partisan units behind the advancing enemy to disrupt communications and carry out diversionist attacks.[119]

As soon as information about the troops caught behind the front lines reached the regional and central leadership of the party, a sub rosa competition arose over the control of what was to become known as the partisan movement. In a letter to Stalin from a party member attached to a signal company on the northwestern front in August 1941, the situation behind the line of the German advance was vividly described. The writer's unit lost a third of its complement and was surrounded. Based on five days' experience behind the front lines, he concluded that there were abundant opportunities to organize partisan units to disrupt the extended German lines of communication and attack small units. But he observed that in the areas they traversed there was no trace of partisan activity. In the forest and swamps, scattered groups were seeking to break out of encirclement and avoid contact with even the smallest enemy units. But 'they were not psychologically prepared to conduct military operations behind the lines'.[120]

The first to recognize the potential for organizing resistance behind the lines was Ponomarenko, the secretary of the Belarus Communist Party. In letters and telegrams to Stalin in 1941 and 1942, he praised the resistance of the collective farmers in his region and proposed the creation of a separate administrative organ of the partisan struggle, offering to take command of it. Following up Stalin's instructions to take the initiative, he urged his party officials to remain behind the lines, there to organize and lead partisan units.[121] Not far behind him, Beria portrayed the situation differently in the early months of the war. He exaggerated the role of NKVD units in conducting partisan and diversionary groups behind the German lines on the northwestern front. Clearly he aimed at persuading Stalin to give him authority to take charge in organizing the partisan movement. In this he was successful.[122]

Ponomarenko's idea of a special organ to conduct partisan activities encountered resistance from the Main Political Administration of the Red Army, especially its head Lev Mekhlis, who promoted their own plans. Stalin's decision to reconcile the competitors by appointing Ponomarenko to head a Central Partisan Staff in Moscow with deputies from the organs of the secret police did not end the bureaucratic in-fighting or allay the suspicions of the army and police over the trustworthiness of armed forces outside their immediate control.[123]

By August 1942 the situation in the western borderlands seemed critical. Ponomarenko reported that the Germans were making every effort to recruit elements of the Soviet population 'in order to draw the partisans into battle not with the Germans but with the formations of the local population, and to withdraw their own units from battles with the partisans to send to the front'. These formations, of which he listed ten, were bombarded with propaganda displaying slogans like 'For an Independent Ukraine', 'Free Belarus from forced russification', 'Independent Latvia', 'Crimea for the Tatars'; in the case of the Crimean Tatars, inter-ethnic rivalries were stirred over access to arms and supplies. Ponomarenko urged efforts to counter these groups through propaganda and specially trained personnel.[124] On the second anniversary of the war, Ponomarenko could proudly report to Stalin that there were 10,000 partisans in the forests around Bryansk, although there were still problems of command and organization. The number grew rapidly, reaching a total of about 100,000 by the end of the year, but only 60 per cent were armed.[125] As the Wehrmacht retreated under the hammer blows of the Red Army, a flood of fence-sitters joined the partisan ranks, bringing their number in Belarus up to 374,000 by the time the region was liberated.[126]

From the outset, the central authorities had wrestled with the dilemma of how to tame the spontaneous spirit and direct the local activities of the partisans while increasing their efforts to recruit new members and extol the achievements of individual heroes and heroines.[127] The great danger, for the central leadership, was that the men and women who had elected their own leaders, decided on their own personnel and set their own missions might not easily be reintegrated into Soviet society as it had existed in the prewar period. Like the members of the intelligentsia whose initiatives had played a crucial role in the economic recovery, many partisans regarded the war as a time of personal freedom and tended to identity the movement as their primary reference group. They were shortly to be disabused of these ideas, though a residual pride in being a partisan lived on in their collective memories.

By authorizing the recruitment of women for combat roles, Stalin tapped into a large reservoir of support for the war effort. But he took the decision only after the disasters of the first year of war meant that many men desperately needed to be replaced. The measure was not carried out without resentment and even resistance on the part of male soldiers, and disappointment and even disillusionment on the part of the women themselves. Prewar Soviet propaganda and education had stressed the special role of strong women in every aspect of society, and had made paramilitary training available for women as well as men, mainly through the Komsomol organizations.[128] A few female warriors from the past were widely celebrated. As soon as the war broke out, many young women, especially in the universities, rushed to the recruiting stations. They were assigned mainly to auxiliary roles as nurses and medical assistants, although an undetermined number was accepted into the militias that were hastily formed, thrown into combat without proper training and chewed up in the early weeks of the fighting. There were exceptions. From Stalin's first authorization of a women's air regiment to the introduction of women into anti-aircraft units, the orders were issued in secret, presumably to avoid the impression among the Germans that the Soviet armed forces were suffering unsustainable losses.[129] There were also contradictions in the policy of mobilizing women. The sniper movement, for example, was launched early, and was highly touted abroad. The training of women snipers was quickly organized on a professional basis. Paradoxically, these skilled killers were lauded as model fighters at the very time when the regime was re-affirming the primary role of women as guardians of the family.[130] Women were also celebrated as active participants in the partisan movement, although here too there were serious problems of sexual discrimination and harassment, causing bitter disappointments. On the eve of Stalingrad, Stalin issued a secret order that the partisan movement must be an 'all-people's movement'. The partisans drew in increasingly large numbers of women, although they still formed a small minority by the end of the war.[131]

Ponomarenko again took the lead in advocating women's active role in the partisan movement. He evoked the patriotic upsurge in the war of 1812 and sanctified the names of martyred heroines like Zoia, executed by the Germans, and others. 'Without the massive involvement of women in the partisan detachments,' he wrote, 'it is impossible to radically expand the movement and make it a genuine all-people's movement.' He insisted women could be trained in every combat specialization and declared that these measures be re-enforced by the strictest disciplinary measures against 'dissolute behaviour' and 'incorrect attitudes' toward women.[132] In the postwar years, however, women warriors 'virtually disappeared from view'.[133] As was the case with other groups in the Soviet population who responded to the call to fulfil their patriotic duty even in the face of great sacrifices, women veterans of the war found themselves blocked from expanding their wartime gains as Stalin re-imposed social controls that harked back to the prewar era.

*****

It would be wrong to attribute the paradoxical character of Stalin's policies solely to his leadership. His personal rule was, to be sure, a decisive element in shaping the responses of the party and state to underlying structural problems. These persistent factors that confronted Russian policy-makers since Peter the Great were deeply rooted in the country's geography, economy and society.[134] As the state expanded it never reached a natural frontier and by the early eighteenth century its frontiers, the longest in the world, were porous, open to penetration, difficult to defend. Expansion brought large numbers of different ethnic groups into borderlands, without succeeding in integrating them into a Russian identity. As a result, the multi-cultural society with clusters of well-defined cultural differences on the periphery presented an additional problem for the defence of the country.

Finally, the absence of access to the open sea and the overwhelming agrarian character of the population under climatic conditions that kept the peasantry living at subsistence levels periodically threatened by regional famine conditions, along with transportation problems stemming from large distances and severe weather conditions, created a situation of relative economic backwardness in comparison with Western and Central European societies. Overcoming these problems in preparing the country for war led Stalin to take decisions often based on impulse rather than socialist planning, irrational in their hasty application and costly in human and material terms. As a result, his building of a socialist economy and a modern army, integrating the nationalities and conducting a foreign policy aimed at distancing external enemies from the vulnerable borderlands, was deeply flawed. In order to eke out a victory under these conditions, he was driven to undertake a mobilization of unprecedented scope and to gain through compromise the support of the social elements crucial to success that he had subjected to an equally unprecedented series of controls and punishments in the years leading up to the German invasion.

CHAPTER 4

THE SCIENTIFIC AND TECHNICAL INTELLIGENTSIA

Stalin's relations with the scientific and technical intelligentsia during the Second World War throw into bold relief several major features of his style of governing as warlord.[1] His policy may be defined along four main lines: first, intensifying their mobilization, employing a mixture of both blunt instruments and rational selectivity; second, an increase in the level of centralization of power together with a devolution of authority along functional lines; third, a re-affirmation of the primacy of collective action and practical tasks alongside a recognition of the value of innovation and scientific theory; fourth, application of severe repressive measures – with notable exceptions – and an increase in incentives. This chapter seeks, first, to illustrate the interplay of these paradoxical and even contradictory elements as a contribution to addressing the larger question of how the Soviet Union managed to survive crushing initial defeats and massive losses of resources and population, and to achieve a significant victory on the battlefield. Second, it offers some conclusions on the evolving relationship created by wartime conditions between Stalin and the scientific and technical intelligentsia.

Lenin had early recognized the signal importance of science and technology in defending advancing revolutionary ideals. He was drawing on three traditions: the nature of Marxism as a scientific method of analysis of social and economic relations; the pre-revolutionary professional intelligentsia including scientists and engineers committed to the transformative power of scientific discoveries and practical inventions; and finally, the enthronement of 'technique' in imperial Russia, inherited from Peter the Great as an instrument of bolstering autocratic power at home and abroad, and sustained by his successors erratically and less energetically developed over the long term in state-supported institutions from the Academy of Sciences to special institutes and lastly the universities.

THE TECHNICIANS

Stalin's views on the scientific and technical intelligentsia were both more complicated and more primitive than Lenin's. Over the course of the twenties and thirties, two ideologies associated with representatives of this community fell under his suspicion. He dismissed those who advocated pure theory as distinct from practice; they could not contribute to solving the basic tasks of building socialism. At the same time, he rejected the ideas of the technocrats as constituting a dangerous opposition to the supremacy of the party embodied in his personal rule. In the debate over the guidelines for secondary education he sided with Kaganovich who endorsed practical over theoretical training and work (*praktiki*) against A.V. Lunacharsky, the first commissar of education, who defended a broader approach which recognized the importance of theoretical courses and who, like Lenin, warned against political intrusion in the scientific disciplines.[2] A leading spokesman and main victim of the technocratic approach was the mining engineer Petr Palchinsky, who had been trained in pre-revolutionary Russia and served in the provisional government as president of the Special Council on Defence. An active member of the Russian Technological Society, he had become increasingly critical of Russian capitalists and embraced the Soviet regime along with other members of the society's left-leaning Electrical Section. In the 1920s he promulgated his ideas of the technocrat-engineer as an economic and industrial planner, actively engaged in the direction and form of the country's development. For this heresy he was shot in 1929, having been accused of being a leader of the so-called Industrial Party, and of planning to overthrow the state.[3] Faced by the exigencies of war, Stalin was obliged to reconsider his disdain for theoretical science and his opposition to anything that smacked of technocracy in the scientific and technological intelligentsia by giving way, however grudgingly, to accepting the importance of theoretical work, especially in physics, and endorsing more willingly a directing role for the Academy of Sciences in solving problems related to defence.

Reaching beyond the commissariats, Stalin repaired the frayed ties between the government and the scientific and technical intelligentsia by granting its members a larger role than ever before in economic development, permitting them a degree of autonomy which, though not extensive by Western standards, was greater than any they had enjoyed since the twenties, as well as according them a distinguished place in his pantheon of war heroes.

Early in the conflict, Stalin – and, following his lead, the propaganda apparatus – celebrated the role of the scientific and technical intelligentsia in the war effort, lifting its prestige, which had suffered so grievously from the prewar purges, to new levels. In his annual reviews of the wartime state of the Union, Stalin accorded a more prominent and honoured place to the intelligentsia with the passage of every year.[4] Towards the end of the war he ranked the importance of its members' contribution to the war effort in third place behind the army and working class: 'Our intelligentsia was able to take the road to innovation in the areas of technology and culture, successfully developing contemporary science, creatively applying it to the achievements in arms production for the Red Army. The Soviet intelligentsia by its creative labour made an inestimable contribution to the task of crushing the enemy.'[5] During the conflict, *Pravda* published a long series of articles dealing with the contributions to the war effort of the intelligentsia in general and the scientific and technical cadres in particular.[6]

THE SCIENTISTS

Despite Stalin's suspicions of the potential for opposition among the scientific and technical intelligentsia, he had allowed the Academy of Sciences to expand its membership and institutional structure in the prewar decades. As a result, it had already evolved into a powerful organizational base for deploying the intellectual resources of the country in support of the war effort. Woven into a network of institutions were the forty institutes and seventy-six independent laboratories, councils and other scientific establishments.[7] Within their walls worked 123 academicians, 182 corresponding members and 4,700 scientific and technological assistants. In the prewar years many of its members were engaged in work of a military nature. Their co-operation with the Commissariat of War and the Naval Commissariat extended to about 200 projects.[8] What was remarkable – indeed extraordinary – about the role of the academy in contributing to the defence sector was its emergence during the war as a semi-autonomous force in Soviet society. By taking the initiative in setting up and expanding new forms of organization, the academy virtually replaced the party in the direction of several sectors of the economy. To be sure, this was done with Stalin's approval, but it was nonetheless an even more extreme case than that of the military revival in Stalin's policy of derogation of decision-making within an overall concentration of his power and authority.

The day after the German attack, an unscheduled meeting of the Presidium of the Academy of Sciences met, presumably on the initiative of its leadership. More than sixty scientists and scholars took part. Among them were Petr Kapitsa, the Old Bolshevik Gleb Krzhizhanovsky, the head of the academy's Institute of Energetics Ivan Bardin, one of the first engineers ever elected to the academy and an advocate of the close relationship between theory and practice, Vladimir Komarov and Otto Shmidt. In an eloquent statement to the people, party and government they pledged to commit all their efforts, energy and knowledge to winning the war. In early July 1941, GOKO appointed Sergei Kaftanov to head the Committee for Higher Education and to serve as its liaison with the scientific community. He appointed a special Scientific-Technical Council composed of the eminent scientists Petr Kapitsa, Abram Ioffe, Nikolai Bruevich, Nikolai Semenov and Sergei Vavilov. It was subdivided into sections on chemistry, physics, geology and biology. The council identified three main directions for its activities: direct involvement in meeting the needs of the military; assistance to industry and solving problems of production; and mobilizing the country's natural resources and finding domestic substitutes for material shortages. Embodying the vaunted ideal of Soviet science, the council took responsibility for organizing scientific research and addressing practical problems.

The council created a number of specialized committees headed by leading scientists in almost all commissariats and government agencies including Gosplan. Scientists were appointed to high government posts as commissars and deputy commissars of war-related branches of industry. The armed forces created their own scientific commissions and appointed scientists to high military rank.[9] The proliferation of activist as well as consultative bodies and the network of contacts woven by the scientific community greatly enhanced their authority and their ability to intervene in promoting the war effort as they saw fit.

The evacuation of the academy from its main centres in Moscow and Leningrad in 1941 was carried out in stages, under extremely difficult transport conditions, often under aerial bombardment. The dispersal of the institutes and staffs concentrated them in three centres. The largest centre in Kazan brought together the physical, chemical and technical institutes. In the Urals the mining, metallurgical and geological-geographical establishments were located near the major sources of raw materials for the defence industries. The biological units, located in Central Asia, addressed questions of cultivation and improvement of strains of plants and livestock and increase of agricultural production. The humanities institutes were also moved to Central Asia. The need to co-ordinate the activities of research groups dispersed in forty-five separate locations spurred the leadership to undertake a massive reorganization and rationalization of the academy's work along five innovative lines.[10]

First, the general assembly of the academy, meeting in May 1942 at Sverdlovsk, elected six vice-presidents to manage the activities of the three regional centres. Second, to head the institutions of the academy in the Kirghiz, Kazakh and Uzbek republics, it appointed a number of fully empowered delegates. It was their responsibility to establish links with the local party and state organs to decide organizational questions connected with the expansion of the work of the academy. Third, a series of commissions were set up that cut across the traditional lines of the research institutes by recruiting personnel from different branches of the academy. A special commission was created in beleaguered Leningrad which continued to operate throughout the siege. A series of defence commissions forged links with military organizations to meet the needs of the army. A Special Commission for Scientific and Technical Questions relating to the Fleet was initiated and headed by the distinguished academician Ioffe with the young Ivan Kurchatov – who later became one of the fathers of the atomic bomb – as his deputy.

As early as July 1941 a special commission of the Geological-Geographical Section of the academy went to work on military questions in the full range 'from geology to technology concerned with the implementation of ideas from the factory and the front and finally participating in the direct application of the proposals', in the words of the president of the section, the academician Aleksandr Fersman.[11] Geography was a much neglected discipline in the Soviet Union before the war. Military geography in particular suffered from its low status. The military academies devoted little attention to the subject, including the making and interpretation of maps in the western borderlands, a consequence of the prevailing doctrine that the next war would be fought on the territory of the enemy. Geographers were preoccupied with the economic aspects rather than topographical descriptions. It was only after the central leadership began to explore the possibilities of evacuating vital industries to the east that Soviet geographers began to assume an important role in military-related operations.

A major part of the Institute of Geography of the academy was evacuated to Alma-Ata in Kazakhstan by the late autumn of 1941 and attached to the Kazakh branch of the Academy of Sciences. The handful of scientists who remained in Moscow following the evacuation worked in close co-operation with the Soviet military through the medium of the newly formed Commission for Geological-Geographical Services to the Red Army, under Fersman's leadership. It co-ordinated their activities with the Commission on Aerial Photography and Engineering Geology. Together they responded to orders from a range of military departments to produce hundreds of maps. The major part of the geographers in the academy in Kazakhstan integrated their work with the institutes of soil and botany and also forged links with local academics.[12] They played a major role in the Commission for the Mobilization of the Resources of the Urals which stands out as the most ambitious and active of the special commissions sponsored by the academy during the war.

The Commission for the Mobilization of the Resources of the Urals was initiated and organized by the president of the academy, Komarov.[13] Taking an unprecedented set of initiatives, the commission analyzed the condition of the most important branches of the regional economy and drafted a plan for mobilizing human and material resources to meet the country's defence needs and compensate for the huge losses in the productive capacity of the occupied territories in the western provinces. Within a few months, it became clear to the leadership of the academy that the connections between the Urals and Western Siberia required an expansion of the commission, which was achieved in April 1942 with the creation of the Commission for the Mobilization of the Resources of the Urals, Western Siberia and Kazakhstan. The party and government once again officially acknowledged and welcomed the initiative. Specialists in the commission excelled in locating new sources of strategic raw materials. Not limited to opening new mines, but also to improving extractive techniques, and removing transport bottlenecks, their proposals were accepted by the respective commissariats and substantially increased production of coal, bauxite, wolfram, copper and oil in the Urals and Western Siberia.[14] Many of their proposals went far beyond the normal recommendations of research scientists. They were making economic policy.[15]

Special expeditions were particularly important in discovering resources for the development of a whole new industrial base in Kazakhstan. The commission's exemplary success sparked a new initiative in June 1942 with the creation of the Commission for the Mobilization of the Resources of the Middle Volga and Kama Regions. Its eight sections were all headed by an academician. Still a third major commission was responsible for the discovery of a vast new source of oil in the so-called 'New Baku' in the Middle Volga region, winning the appreciation of the Presidium of the Supreme Soviet of the Tatar Republic for the future development of the region. A Commission for the Expansion of Food Supplies contributed to the more efficient exploitation of the ample but under-exploited plant and animal resources of the Kazan region. And in early 1942 the academy introduced another innovation by dispatching flying squads of scientists and technicians to industrial flash points. Their function was to 'fight fires' by solving in record time problems which surfaced in the relocation of industry and its efficient functioning. In sum, throughout the east, commissions of the academy virtually usurped the normal functions of the party and the economics commissariats in developing natural resources and solving major industrial problems. Thanks largely to the efforts of the academy the share of war industry in the eastern regions climbed from 18.5 per cent in June 1941 to 76 per cent in June 1942.[16] In the long run, the war forced a trend – already modestly under way – of greater economic integration of the regions, and substantially reduced the great disparities in the rate of industrialization between the Slavic centre and the Muslim republics on the periphery.

During the war, the academy accelerated its efforts to establish permanent institutional centres outside the European parts of the country. On the eve of the conflict, important steps had already been taken to strengthen and encourage the scientific community in the non-Slavic republics of the borderlands. Branches of the Academy of Sciences were opened in Uzbekistan in 1939 and in Turkmenistan in 1940, although the scientists in the latter republic accompanied their petition with a memo of self-criticism focusing on the gap between science and the practical needs of socialist construction. In January 1941 a Georgian Academy of Sciences was established, the first of the full-fledged republican academies, and then in 1943 an Armenian academy.[17] The president, Komarov, used the opening of a branch of the academy in the Kirghiz Republic in 1943 as an opportunity to refute Nazi propaganda on the discord among nationalities of the USSR. Branches in the Central Asian republics benefited from the evacuation of scientists from Moscow and Leningrad who helped to organize research and local war production.[18]

In the sphere of weapons technology, the Academy of Sciences demonstrated that its guiding principle of combining theory and practice yielded important results. Most of its contributions came in response to direct requests from the military organizations. In 1942 alone the Commissariat of Defence sought assistance in solving problems in 175 subjects, of which only twenty-two could not be addressed. Throughout the war, commissariats assigned theoretical problems ranging from ballistics and optics to aerodynamics to the academy, where teams of researchers attacked them. For instance, the academy team on aerodynamics was able to devise solutions to overcoming wind resistance that aircraft designers could then apply to increase speeds of Soviet fighter aircraft by 100 kilometres an hour. A group headed by Mstislav Keldysh, who later became an academician and the president of the Academy of Sciences, applied mathematical formulae to solve the problem of extreme vibration at high speeds. Their contributions were critical in designing the new models of Soviet aircraft, especially the Ilyushin Il-2 ground-attack aircraft (best known in the West as the Stormovik). The geographers and astronomers prepared precise operational maps and meteorological charts for assistance in air defence, greatly appreciated by the Soviet Air Forces. The compilation of a 'Large Astronomical Calendar' for 1943, 1944 and 1945, reportedly superior to the English equivalent in scope and precision, was carried out at great sacrifice by the Astronomical Institute in Leningrad. Their work was immensely important in planning the defence of Moscow in 1941 and offensive operations in 1943 and thereafter was given full recognition by military authorities. Their work was also praised

by the naval commands. Employing sophisticated mechanical and mathematical models, other groups perfected the rocket artillery, improved
armour-piercing shells, hardened artillery barrels and perfected the heavy
machine gun.

The workers of the academy were deeply engaged in the defence of
Leningrad. They helped develop techniques for dealing with the effects of
incendiary bombs and the construction of reinforced concrete defensive
structures. The Optical Institute under the academician Sergei Vavilov
designed superior models of range-finder, stereoscopic telescopes and a
whole variety of optical instruments for military purposes. The Physical-
Chemical Institute developed an effective early warning system in defence
against aerial attack. It invented anti-icing devices that helped keep open the
ice road to the besieged city over frozen Lake Ladoga. The Military-Sanitary
Institute had close ties with special units of the army and the Fleet
Commissariat of Health. Half the work of the commission in the areas of
surgery, epidemiology, hygiene and aviation medicine was carried out by
members of the academy. The commission introduced new techniques for
improving sanitary conditions in the hospitals, where its work was largely
responsible for reducing deaths; an estimated 70 per cent of patients were
restored to service, as compared to 40–50 per cent in the First World War.[19]
The academician Nikolai Burdenko, the chief physician of the Red Army
and a veteran of two previous wars, was an innovator in neurosurgery and
the use of drugs in treating the wounded. Fearless, he carried out thousands
of the most difficult operations at the front. As the result of his method of
employing a sulphamide preparation, battlefield deaths from wounds were
reduced from 65 to 25 per cent.[20] Severely wounded, Burdenko nevertheless
designed plans for the USSR Academy of Medical Science and became its
president shortly before his death. But Burdenko like all scientists was
obliged to submit to Stalin's political agenda. As the head of the official
commission to investigate the Katyn massacre of 22,000 Polish officers, he
turned in a report that falsely accused the Nazis of the crime, which in fact
had been carried out by the NKVD.[21]

In industry, academicians perfected a whole range of technological
improvements in steel production, fractionating of oil to obtain toluene for
TNT and other processes. These included the invention by two academicians of the defectoscope, which detected flaws in artillery shells, saving

time and increasing levels of production. The academician Nikolai Gudtsov's contribution to the improvement of the operation of motorized vehicles, especially tanks, earned him the Order of Lenin and the Red Star.[22]

Recording the achievements of the academy is not to ignore serious shortcomings in planning that continued to arise, such as the technical imbalances that led to a 'contradiction between operational concepts and equipment on the one hand and command and control practices and facilities on the other hand'. But these problems were caused by decisions of the political leadership, Stalin first and foremost, which created what Jacques Sapir has called a specific 'technological culture'.[23]

The Academy of Sciences responded to the new opportunities with loyalty, dedication and enthusiasm.[24] But it also made claims for the unique place of science in Soviet society. The two most cherished aims of the academy were to preserve its international ties and its internal autonomy. In responding to Stalin's praise, the academy took pains to point out that world science was a 'single, indivisible whole'. Its wartime conferences celebrated Newton and Copernicus as well as Timiriazev.[25] The academy took great pride in its unique privilege of electing its members after a thorough investigation of credentials and achievements. Komarov, the president of the academy, declared in 1943 after the election of thirty-six new academicians and fifty-eight corresponding members that 'It is difficult to exaggerate the significance of the fact that at a time of war, the Academy of Sciences of the USSR was afforded the opportunity to organize these elections and in this way substantially increase its membership'.[26] However, the academy remained cautious in selecting candidates for membership.

One glaring example of its self-policing was the case of Lev Landau. One of the truly great theoretical physicists of the twentieth century, Landau had been arrested in 1938 for publishing a leaflet comparing Hitler and Stalin. He spent several months in prison where, allegedly, he continued to work out in his head the main ideas for his world-renowned ten-volume *Course in Theoretical Physics*, which would appear in the 1950s. After he was released in April 1939 thanks to the intervention of Kapitsa, he returned to head the Theoretical Section of the Institute for Physical Problems, where he continued to produce original work in solid-state physics. Just days before the German invasion he submitted a paper on liquid helium that won him the Nobel Prize in 1962. But the shadow of his arrest hung over him. In

1943 when the institute proposed him for membership in the academy, the academic secretary, Bruevich, wrote to the head of the Science Section, referring to Landau as 'capable' but 'undesirable as a candidate for political considerations.'[27] His election was delayed until 1946. Although he was reluctant to work on the atomic bomb project, he made substantial contributions to its fruition and to thermonuclear dynamics, a paradox, too, explained by those who knew him as being due to his inability to do shoddy work. Despite the suspicions of the NKVD, he was awarded Stalin Prizes in 1949 and 1953 and the title Hero of Socialist Labour in 1954.[28]

Among the older generation of scientists there were a few who were convinced that the best guarantee for the autonomy of science would be their freely given dedication to the needs of the state. The strongest voices in favour of universal values issued from Vladimir Vernadsky and Kapitsa. Like many scientists who had made their reputation before the revolution, Vernadsky elected to remain in the Soviet Union, although he was suspicious of the early Bolshevik commitment to promoting science.[29] In an essay written in 1942 but not published until thirty years later, Vernadsky envisioned a postwar utopian world in which scientific free thought would flourish. He advocated closer co-operation with the United States to create a world community of scientists.[30] No one, meanwhile, was more bold and daring than Kapitsa, who called into question the entire organization of research and development in Soviet science. Undoubtedly, his views were strongly influenced by his anglophile inclinations. He had emigrated to England and spent ten years (1924–34) as an associate of the distinguished British scientist Ernest Rutherford at his laboratory in Cambridge. On a visit to the Soviet Union in 1934, Kapitsa had been prevented from returning to Britain at the express order of Stalin. But the decision was also taken to offer Kapitsa extraordinary professional and personal privileges, including the creation of his own Institute for Physical Problems in the academy, the purchase of his entire laboratory at Cambridge, and living quarters that were lavish by Soviet standards.[31]

Although Kapitsa's prewar work was primarily in the field of theoretical physics, he applied himself to solving one of the most difficult productive problems facing the country's industrial development during the war. The rapid expansion of the metallurgical and chemical plants and the manufacture of tanks and other military supplies vastly increased the demand for liquid oxygen. Kapitsa organized the most powerful turbine installation in the world, which produced 2,000 kilograms of liquid oxygen in one hour, increasing more than six times the previous level in a considerably smaller space.[32] In 1943 Kapitsa was awarded the Order of Lenin and twenty of his associates in the institute were decorated with lesser awards for their work in inventing an inexpensive method of producing liquid oxygen and the production of acetic acid. Unstated in the award were his numerous other inventions in weapons technology and several medical techniques.

Kapitsa used his privileged position and favour with Stalin to raise questions about other issues which appeared to challenge conventional practices and hierarchical rules. Even before the war, he ventured into dangerous waters by undertaking the defence of scientists like the arrested Landau. In a letter to Beria on the eve of the war, he requested that Landau be released from prison under his 'personal guarantee', assuring the dreaded head of the NKVD of his readiness to guarantee that Landau would not undertake any counter-revolutionary activity inside or outside Kapitsa's institute. A few months later he wrote to Stalin expressing regrets that a young scientist in his institute Arkady Migdal had been denied a Stalin 'Studentship' (fellowship) after having won a place in an open competitive examination. The excuse of the committee was that Migdal had once been arrested by mistake in the mid-thirties but had not informed it at the time of his application. Kapitsa found this unfair and requested Stalin's intervention. A week later the committee received an 'appropriate instruction', in the words of Stalin's secretary, and Migdal's fellowship was restored.[33]

Kapitsa also attempted, with the approval of the Soviet leadership, to recruit Western scientists to follow his example and emigrate to the Soviet Union. But both Niels Bohr, who had fled the Nazis to Sweden, and Jules Langevin, who had escaped imprisonment in Paris for Switzerland, politely declined.[34] Kapitsa also reflected on the possibility of bringing the brilliant Hungarian scientist Leó Szilárd – also in exile, first in Great Britain and later at Los Alamos in the USA – to the Soviet Union. But he complained to Malenkov that 'it would be difficult to imagine a worse system of encouraging inventiveness than we have in the Soviet Union'.[35]

Kapitsa also defended the dignity of scientists when confronted by bureaucratic interference with their work, even by the highest officials. He reproached Malenkov for the lack of respect with which officials in his department treated him. 'It seems to me,' he concluded, 'that officials of the Central Committee should treat scientists with respect, i.e. *sincerely* and not condescendingly and patronizingly as they usually do. Such treatment makes my gorge rise.'[36]

Kapitsa wrote several highly critical letters to Stalin during the war. He deplored the fact that 'although we have built a great deal and mastered many techniques in the 27 years since the Revolution, how little of major significance of our own have we introduced into technology! Personally I can think of only one major achievement – synthetic rubber'. This was in contrast to the achievement of capitalist countries, where twenty fundamental new developments in technology were recorded in the same period. Kapitsa complained to Stalin that the implementation of his innovative methods for producing liquid and gaseous oxygen on a large scale in order to speed up the treatment of metals and chemical products had been delayed by bureaucratic inertia. New forms of industrial organization were required, he argued.[37]

Kapitsa took advantage of his privileged position and the restored prestige of the scientific technological community to reopen the perennial debate over theory versus practice that had run like a thread through the long history of the academy, but which had disappeared into the thicker warp and woof of Stalinism in the thirties when the *praktiki* appeared to have emerged victorious over the professional specialists and theorists. The debate had implications for all fields of Soviet culture and intellectual life. It was ultimately a political question involving the extent to which the party could claim and exercise control over other autonomous realms of thought. Kapitsa may be said to represent the theory side, though he was not rigid about the distinction. In defending the autonomy and internationalization of science, science 'as one indivisible whole', Kapitsa was critical of what he called the 'vulgarization' of the debate over the relationship between science and technology. He argued that it was incorrect to assume that every scientific problem ought to have an immediate practical application. The superiority of Soviet military equipment over the enemy, which Stalin himself acknowledged, was due in Kapitsa's view to the superiority of Soviet science. In almost every area of weapons technology the key breakthroughs had been made by scientists, not engineers. Kapitsa did not deny the value of scientists acquiring certain engineering skills (such as his own) in order to work out the practical applications of their discoveries. War naturally accelerated this process. But war was a special condition and could not serve as a model for scientists.[38]

At the other end of the spectrum of debate, Trofim Lysenko, an anti-Darwinist agronomist and biologist who embraced Lamarck's view on inherited characteristics, asserted that the only criterion for judging the value of science was practical results. Lysenko was still far from achieving the unassailable position he secured for himself after the war. But even some of his fiercest critics admitted that during the war he made an important contribution to averting widespread famine. He promoted with great energy the traditional peasant practice of increasing the yield of potatoes by cutting off the productive sprout (eye) of the tuber, preserving it throughout the winter and spring, while using the rest as food, and planting it with results that gained him great popularity among the public. He also travelled extensively in Siberia during the unusually cold autumn of 1941 broadcasting the idea that immature wheat could survive under snow and be harvested in the spring as if it had matured successfully. To be sure, he used his success to denigrate theory and extol practical methods which had long been observed by the pre-revolutionary peasantry.[39] On the defensive in scientific circles in response to attacks on his theoretical weakness, he did not confront Kapitsa directly. It was clear that his main backing came from party circles, but the support was not unequivocal.[40] Most of the remaining participants in the debate shied away from identifying with either extreme, distancing themselves from Kapitsa's dangerously sharp distinction between science and technology. Instead, they defended the value of theoretical research.

Kaftanov, the president of the Committee for Higher Education, took up this theme in celebrating the award of 250 Stalin Prizes to engineers. He acknowledged their contribution to the design of new weaponry but stressed the importance of the 'creative work of Soviet scientists who had enriched by virtue of their new achievements the treasury of world science'. He returned to this theme two years later when he wrote: 'Side by side with the practical questions of the day on the agenda of the institutes of higher learning . . . work of large scientific theoretical significance should be pursued, and scientific technical problems should be worked out for the future development of the national economy.' He went on to criticize the commissariats for insufficient financing of scientific research in the higher schools.[41] Even more powerful voices were raised against the vulgar practices of Lysenko. On the initiative of Voznesensky, soon to become a member of the Politburo, an article appeared in the American journal *Science* in 1945 by the well-known Soviet geneticist Anton Zhebrak, which openly criticized Lysenko. Voznesensky and others recognized the damage inflicted by Lysenko on both Soviet agriculture and the international reputation of Soviet science.[42] These voices were muted, fell silent or were silenced in the postwar atmosphere of ideological conformity.

Most Soviet scientists preferred to justify their work by stressing the vital role that they were playing in the war effort; they attributed that success to the unique organization of Soviet science. Baptizing the conflict 'a war of physics', the academician Ioffe had praise for the formation of the Scientific-Technical Committee in the USA but maintained that Soviet science, with its four specialized institutes of physics under the unifying administrative umbrella of the academy, was the model for mobilizing resources.[43] At least as far as this debate was concerned, the scientific intelligentsia expressed a broadly based consensus over the desirability of a new relationship between itself and the government. It accepted implicitly the centralization of political power and the administrative centralization of science under the control of scientists. Although members of the scientific-technical community voluntarily accepted the social command, they reserved the right to debate and define the limits of its obligation. They made no claims for absolute independence; even Kapitsa accepted the need of a social conscience. The young Andrei Sakharov, later a famous dissident, shared these views, accepting the idea that the best way to guarantee peace and stability in the postwar world was for scientists to help assure the security of the state and, at the same time, to carry on practising 'superb physics'.[44] Beyond this, the scientific community sought an active role in drafting the social contract that bound them to the Bolshevik party and Soviet state. Stalin did not challenge this view during the war; nor did he endorse it. The assumption among scientists appeared to be widespread that what was not forbidden was acceptable. It proved to be a faulty assumption.

Although repressive measures sharply declined during the war, a number of members of the academy as well as lesser lights in the scientific community were accused of espionage because of their German names or else their pre-revolutionary associations. The distinguished geneticist Nikolai Vavilov, who had been arrested in 1940, remained in prison despite the fact that his brother, Sergei, was a member of the prestigious Scientific Council. As an opponent of Lysenko, now at the height of his power, he died behind bars in 1943 and was not rehabilitated until after Stalin's death. Others who had been in prison were only allowed to pursue research related to defence in closed institutes run by the NKVD (sharashkas), as made famous by Aleksandr Solzhenitsyn in his novel *The First Circle*.[45] Among them were two figures who were associated with the spectacular postwar achievements in rocketry, Sergei Korolev and Valentin Glushko.[46] The end of the war did not signal the end to Stalin's repressive measures against leading figures in the defence industries. The most glaring example was the replacement and arrest of Aleksei Shakhurin, the people's commissar of aviation, after Stalin had rejected his proposal to put the German Messerschmitt Me 262 jet fighter into production in favour of a Russian design.[47] The extent of Beria's role in these and other arrests is not always clear.[48] On occasion Stalin reined in Beria, but his motives were often obscure. Shortly after the war, Beria attempted to undermine Kapitsa's position in the institute, and asked for permission to arrest him. Stalin replied: 'I will remove him for you, but don't you touch him.'[49]

Shortly after Beria had been appointed commissar of internal affairs in 1938, he proposed the creation of several specialized technical bureaus, which were reorganized and renamed the Fourth Special Department of the NKVD at the outbreak of war. As part of his internal empire-building, Beria had grasped the significance of using camp inmates with scientific or technical training in order to help strengthen the defence industries, especially in the construction of aircraft, aircraft engines, naval vessels, the production of artillery and artillery shells, and the use of and defence against chemical warfare. From 1939 to 1944, the Fourth Special Department compiled an impressive record of achievements in all these sectors. Major innovations in the design of dive bombers, fighters and the first Soviet jet engine were credited to imprisoned engineers. Out of the Gulag came improvements in the design of tank turrets, gun mountings on railway wagons and artillery systems, the latter contributing to the defence of Leningrad in 1941. A new model of anti-tank gun from the same source was widely employed on all fronts in 1942, and in the following two years larger-calibre tank cannon were successively introduced. A new design for submarines was being tested in 1944. A better gas mask provided with a new type of absorbent entered the manufacturing phase during the war. Experiments with new types of radio communication were in the early stage of development, while night fighters were equipped with better instruments.[50]

Prisoners under the direction of the Fourth Special Department made important contributions to the operations of factories engaged in war work. Once again, the hand of Beria can be seen clearly in the construction and equipping of a dozen major plants nominally attached to the Commissariat of Defence. The Fourth Special Department took pride in the record of its specialist prisoners in introducing higher norms in the production of steel, coal and other vital products. Beria took special credit for organizing the resources of the Fourth Department in supplying radio communications for NKVD troops defending mountain passes in the Caucasus. For outstanding services, the commissariat recommended the release with full restoration of rights of 156 incarcerated specialists, twenty-three of whom received medals. Three men received Stalin Prizes for their work on special projects; six others were similarly decorated for their individual contributions.[51] Others were not so fortunate. But no one, to be sure, took note of the supreme irony of decorating men accused of sabotage and wrecking for having contributed within a few years to the design and manufacture of precision weapons and equipment that helped win the war.

The mobilization of prisoners in the Gulag for war production involved hundreds of thousands of workers in all branches of the defence industry. It is difficult to determine how many of these were technical intelligentsia, but certain official figures are suggestive. According to the famous report of Viktor Nasedkin, the chief of the Gulag Administration, to Beria in August 1944, 40,000 specialists and qualified workers from the camps, including 'engineers, technical specialists, metalworkers, railway workers and miners', were identified and assigned to factories under the administration of the NKVD. In order to train additional qualified personnel, the camp administration organized a large-scale programme of technical training which in three years turned out 300,000 qualified workers.[52] However, evidence from dozens of memoirs gives the impression of an enormous waste of talent due to the arbitrary and cruel camp practices directed against prisoners with high levels of technical and scientific education and training.

Stalin's paradoxical view of the scientific and technical intelligentsia was nowhere more evident than in his attitude toward the relation between theory and practice with respect to the development of new kinds of weapons, from the laboratory to the drawing board and on to the finished product. His approach to the construction of the atomic bomb and the development of missiles illustrates the point. In the field of theoretical physics, Soviet scientists were pioneers in investigating the problem of nuclear fission. But their research was largely ignored until Stalin learned from Truman at Potsdam that the Americans had perfected a new and devastating weapon which could revolutionize warfare. The Soviet leader immediately instructed Beria to launch a priority programme to develop an atomic bomb.

The groundwork had been laid much earlier.[53] The significance of uranium as a potential source of great energy if harnessed was first pointed out in Russia before the revolution by the multi-talented Vladimir Vernadsky. With the help of two future academicians who played an important part in the Second World War, Vitaly Khlopin and Fersman, he was instrumental in establishing the Radium Institute in Petrograd in 1922. Inspired by important discoveries in the West on the release of energy by splitting the atomic nucleus, Soviet scientists embarked on a number of projects to develop the field of nuclear physics. The academician Ioffe led the Leningrad Physicotechnical Institute, a nursery of future leaders in theoretical work and practical applications including the development of an atomic bomb. Among them the physicist Kurchatov stood out. Put in charge of the nuclear project in 1943, he became the leading figure in the postwar development of the atomic and nuclear bombs. Others included Gregory Flerov, the co-discoverer of nuclear fission, Iakov Frenkel', Iuli Khariton – who had also studied at Cambridge on Kapitsa's recommendation and who together with Iakov Zeldovich carried out important work on fission chain reactions – and many others. Although they sought to justify their work in terms of practical outcomes, according to David Holloway their main interest in the 1930s was in 'doing interesting physics' and being part of a worldwide scientific community. Most of them were sceptical about 'the possibility of utilizing atomic energy'.[54] As the result of an unlikely and accidental incident of cultural exchange, the situation changed dramatically. Vernadsky was apprised of the real possibility of exploiting atomic energy for military purposes by a report of an American journalist sent to him by his son

George, a historian at Yale. In characteristic energetic fashion, Vernadsky rallied his old collaborators Khlopin and Fersman to help him draft memoranda to the Soviet government to establish the research facility which became the Uranium Commission in 1940. It was staffed by a stellar group of scientists including Khlopin (chair), Vernadsky, Ioffe, Fersman, Kurchatov, Khariton and Kapitsa, bringing together representatives of industry and geology as well as physicists. Their plans still did not include any reference to an atomic bomb. The wheels ground slowly. Vernadsky complained of the 'routine and ignorance of Soviet bureaucrats'. The group lobbied hard to reverse the government's suspension of exploring uranium deposits in Central Asia.[55]

With the outbreak of war, scientists dispersed, meeting immediate defence needs. The Uranium Commission closed down. In the early years, Stalin made inquiries about the possibility of building a bomb as information began to trickle in from his agents in Britain that research on the topic was being strongly pushed. When Kurchatov was appointed head of the small nuclear project in 1943, he was still not certain that a bomb could be constructed, until Molotov supplied him with the intelligence material from Britain. The memoranda Kurchatov then drafted persuaded GOKO (which meant Stalin) to issue a secret instruction authorizing him to set up a research laboratory (code-named No. 2). Kurchatov was frustrated by the slow progress and hampered by an inadequate supply of uranium and lack of active support from Molotov, so he turned to Beria for assistance. Ironically, Beria did not believe the intelligence reports gathered by his own agents on the progress of the Manhattan Project at Los Alamos. Stalin returned from Potsdam determined to compete with the Americans by developing a Soviet atom bomb. In the presence of Marshal Zhukov, he remarked to Molotov: 'We'll have to talk to Kurchatov about speeding up our work.'[56] Preoccupied with implementing the Soviet entrance into the war with Japan, Stalin still delayed taking decisive action until after Hiroshima and Nagasaki had made it irrefutably clear that the Americans had succeeded in changing the balance of forces in the world. It was now necessary to restore it.

After Stalin held conversations with Kurchatov and Vannikov, the people's commissar of munitions, GOKO issued an order to set up a special committee under Beria to pursue an atomic bomb project. The postwar development of atomic and nuclear weapons in the Soviet Union lies outside the limits of this study. However, the main features of its history retained all the elements of the paradox of power that characterized Stalin's wartime policies. On the one hand, he placed no limit on the human and material resources necessary to achieve the desired end. On the other hand, he continued to express suspicions about the loyalties of the experts responsible for carrying out his orders.[57] In the postwar atmosphere of repression, the attack on 'cosmopolitanism' and the rise of Lysenko put at risk many of the leading physicists with Jewish names or foreign contacts.[58] The main textbooks of theoretical physics, including the famous ten-volume work by Landau, came under severe criticism for kowtowing to the West. Only by the slightest of margins did nuclear physics as a discipline survive the attacks on ideological grounds that devastated biology and genetics. Sheltered in the atomic bomb project under Beria's protection, the scientists worked in secret, to be fully recognized and lavishly rewarded shortly after Stalin's death.

Rocket science in the Soviet Union during the war, like atomic physics, was entangled in the fraught relationship between theoretical and practical lines of development with links to pre-revolutionary traditions. The interest in developing missiles stemmed from the pioneering theorist of space travel, Konstantin Tsiolkovsky. An autodidact, he investigated the major problems of constructing missiles, including the relationship between mass and velocity, although his work was not recognized until late in his life. Tukhachevsky was one of the few in the top echelons of the Red Army who recognized the potential use of rockets in delivering explosive projectiles at great distances. As we have seen above, the work of the Reactive Research Institute created under his supervision was responsible for the invention of rocket artillery. Tsiolkovsky also inspired two men who would be responsible for major advances in Soviet rocket and missile development in the postwar years. Sergei Korolev and Valentin Glushko had been two promising researchers at the institute until 1938, when they were caught in a large-scale purge that wiped out the leadership. (The head of the institute was shot, together with his deputy.) Their major contributions came only after they had endured arrest and long terms of imprisonment.

Stalin suspended his prejudice against theoretical work when he recognized the close connection of theory to the development of rockets as well as the atomic bomb. As would be the case with nuclear fission so with rock-etry: Stalin belatedly woke up to the close connection between theoretical work and weapons development, but only after foreign countries provided compelling examples. Within two months of the first launching by the Germans of the V-1 and V-2 rockets on London, Stalin ordered Soviet design bureaus to begin work on long-range missiles. Beria recommended to Stalin the release of thirty-five specialists from detention to staff a special Construction Bureau of the NKVD. Among them were Korolev and Glushko, both of whom had been sentenced to eight years' imprisonment. Initially, Korolev was on the list sanctioned by Stalin to be shot. After his arrest, Glushko was beaten and tortured before being sent to an aircraft factory outside Moscow to work on improved designs for heavy weapons. Transferred from time to time, he ended up at a sharashka in Kazan with Korolev and other former colleagues who had been arrested. Under the supervision of the NKVD, he continued to work on propellants for rockets, which he perfected after the war. He was released after serving most of his term. Like Glushko, Korolev pursued his research in a sharashka, where he was appointed to head a group on rocket design. Working under conditions of hardship, he drafted and submitted a plan for organizing work on long-range missiles. While Stalin agreed to free him, he withheld the right to rehabilitation, still suspicious or reluctant to admit a mistake. Korolev was then appointed one of the first instructors on rocket engines at the Kazan Institute of Aviation Design, at the time unique among all Soviet institutes of higher education in teaching rocket design.

In April 1945 both Glushko and Korolev were included in a commission to collect information in Germany on the research and development of the German rocket programme. After the war, their careers soared. In September 1945 half a dozen of the former prisoners were awarded medals for their work in the Construction Bureau. After Stalin's death, Glushko developed large liquid-propellant rocket engines. Korolev, meanwhile, became the central figure in the dramatic postwar development of Soviet rockets and satellites. He was responsible for designing Sputnik and has been credited for the world's first intercontinental missile. Both men were repeatedly decorated, but Korolev's name was not made public until his death in 1966.[59]

The wartime experience led to a new relationship between Stalin, the political elite in the party and state apparatus, and the scientific-technical intelligentsia. A military-industrial complex had come into existence during the thirties; the war added a third dimension, creating a military-industrial-scientific complex – not unlike that which emerged in the United States and Great Britain. The contribution of the nuclear physicists in the postwar period is well known and amply documented. But this development merely reinforced a process – a developmental spurt – launched during the war. Stalin recognized the value of the scientific and technical intelligentsia by granting them a degree of autonomy, only partially cut back after the war, co-opting them into areas of economic planning, vastly expanding their research and training facilities, and heaping rewards on outstanding achievements that rivalled those given to his marshals. But they had to accept the terms offered to them, whatever their private reservations about the party's ideological pretentions and administrative restraints; Kapitsa and later Sakharov were exceptional in their outspoken criticisms. And the risks were great. Kapitsa earned the dangerous hostility of Beria.

But there were others with distinguished war records, even in biology, who helped to weaken Lysenko's position after the war. Their defence of 'pure' science helped to expose the charlatanry of Lysenko, who rejected Darwinian theories of evolution, and his counterparts in physics, who rejected Einsteinian theories of relativity. But it took years to discredit his ideas.[60] The achievements of the war years were not entirely extinguished by Stalin. After his death the natural scientists of the wartime generation recovered their voices, speaking out, as Loren Graham has stated, 'on topics outside their own special realms, a clear indication of their growing influence and ambitions.'[61] The All-Union Congress of Scientific-Technical Societies, established in 1933, was finally able to convene its first congress in 1959. Attempts to establish the validity of specialized professional roles were increasingly articulated by individual scientists and technicians.[62] The academy won its fight to concentrate on pure research, as Kapitsa had advocated. Eventually, the technical institutes were removed from the academy in 1961 and 1963. Administrative reorganizations supplemented by an expansion of research and development helped improve links between industrial organizations. In 1965 Kapitsa, the Cassandra of Soviet science, warned that 'the gulf in science between our country and the USA has not only stopped declining but has increased.'[63] The new system had serious flaws inherited from Stalinist times. It continued to suffer from what Moshe Lewin has called *mekhanizm tormozheniia*.[64] In the absence of Kapitsa's 'new forms of industrial development', long delays between research and development sharply reduced the impact of innovative ideas. The combination of these internal structural faults and the reaction of the party to external challenges to the Soviet model of socialism from Hungary, Czechoslovakia and Poland had a crippling effect on the ability of the scientists to transform Soviet society in the utopian spirit which continued to inspire so many of them.

THE ECONOMISTS

During the war, a group of economists concentrated in the Institute of World Economics and World Politics directed by Eugen Varga proposed an alternative explanation of the postwar development of capitalism to the Cold War model that Stalin embraced in 1948. It was paradoxical that Stalin had previously expressed great respect for Varga and had appointed him to his secretariat only to allow his enemies to criticize him, and then to abolish his institute, yet to retain his services as an economist specializing in the economies of capitalist countries. In 1927 Varga was appointed director of the newly created institute, where he remained in charge for the next twenty years. He had been a member of the short-lived communist government under Béla Kun in Hungary in 1919. Forced to flee the White counter-coup, he emigrated to the Soviet Union. There he became the chief economist in the Comintern, and supported Stalin in his conflicts with Trotsky and Bukharin. Varga shared with Rosa Luxemburg the concept of the chronic problem of markets and predicted a major crisis in capitalism. Bukharin at the Seventh Comintern Congress in 1928 endorsed the idea that the strong role of the state would contribute to the stabilization of capitalism. This meant that the Soviet Union could continue to pursue the New Economic Policy. The depression the following year cut the ground from under Bukharin's views and justified Stalin's claim that 'rotten stabilization' would lead to renewal of imperialist wars. Stalin was able then to rationalize collectivization as the basis for industrialization.[65] Ironically, Varga would return to Bukharin's ideas during the Second World War.

Under Varga's leadership, members of the institute produced a stream of monographs on the history of crises in the capitalist world, among them Varga's own contribution, *Novye iavleniia v mirovom ekonomicheskom krizise* ('New Phenomena in the World Economic Crisis'), which came out in 1934. With colleagues he then began work on a projected six-volume institute publication which was two-thirds complete by the beginning of the war. The object was not simply to analyze but also to offer prognoses. The strong emphasis on the sharp contradictions among capitalist countries, inevitably leading to a clash with fascism and another imperialist war, seemed to be borne out by events in 1939. Another set of studies pursued the technological and economic advances of capitalism, a favourite topic of the disgraced Bukharin. Others 'uncovered laws of capitalist development' relating to the decline in the number of employed workers and also of highly qualified workers under the pressure of rationalization. The narrowing down of the labour aristocracy and the increase in low-paid workers had political implications which were not fully drawn at the time. Beginning in 1942, a team of institute economists was employed in preparing a series of works on capitalism during the Second World War.[66]

As a member of Stalin's private secretariat, Varga survived the purges that carried off Kun and his closest associates.[67] Dimitrov, who had worked with Varga in the Comintern, considered him a man 'of proven worth'. As late as 1943, Stalin praised Varga's report at the Academy of Sciences. According to Dimitrov, he found it 'good, Marxist'. Dimitrov concluded: 'Any criticisms of that report in the Central Committee secretariat are no longer valid.'[68] During the war, Varga developed his main theory of postwar capitalism. In an article published in the institute journal he argued that one of the most important results of the war was the fact that in bourgeois countries the state acquired a decisive role in the military economy and that this 'profoundly changed the very nature of the economy'. The totalizing character of the war, in his view, had forced the state to take full control of those sectors of the economy necessary for military production. Its intervention varied but everywhere led to a contradiction in social relations; the greater the state control and the role of bureaucracy, the less active and autonomous the workers' movement and the more the workers were removed from productive labour.[69]

Varga then presented an expanded view in a report that was the subject of a debate. He indicated that the main problem for the United States after the war would be an excessive productive capacity and a struggle with unemployment. He predicted that delayed demand would be rapidly met; inflation would be temporary. In Europe, however, wartime damage would create a crisis of under-production and real inflation. Britain would occupy an intermediate position, experiencing greater demand than in the USA but with more productive capacity to meet it than in Europe. The outcome would depend on the willingness of the USA and to a lesser extent Britain to export capital for the purposes of reconstruction and to plan for the establishment of an international financial organization to serve these ends. Would the USA then accept the importation of European finished goods? Or would a cycle of over-production by the restored markets repeat some of the features of the prewar period? In the discussion, there was general agreement on the cyclical nature of capitalism, but also an optimistic view on state intervention to stabilize the currency, export capital and stimulate the international exchange of goods.[70]

Throughout 1945 the economists embellished Varga's thesis. They generally provided an optimistic view that the greater stabilization of international capitalism, though not free from crisis, created new possibilities for the international order. In a burst of optimism, the economist I.M. Lemin proclaimed that the defeat of Nazi Germany had been the work of a coalition, with the Soviet Union taking the brunt of the conflict in achieving a 'moral-political victory'; the term became a leitmotif for the group. He attributed the Soviet victory to its economic organization, technological-economic independence and unity of the people, with the Bolshevik party bringing up the rear on his list, and no mention of Stalin made at all. He also paid homage to the diplomatic preparation for the coalition, going back to the diplomacy of the period from 1933 to 1939 and its stand against the anti-national policy of isolationism, a transparent homage to the diplomats associated with Litvinov. He reiterated Stalin's view on the longevity of the coalition. The 'powerful moral authority' of the Soviet Union facilitated the economic transformation of Eastern Europe through agrarian reform, a new politics and a resolution of the national question. He boldly asserted that the Soviet postwar aims were a 'democratic order based on the peaceful coexistence of people and the organization of an effective international system of security'.[71] It was an extraordinary statement, going beyond the cautious implications of the Varga thesis. But caution did not spare Varga from some rough handling, even though he too, like his friends Litvinov and Kapitsa, survived. Other economists in the institute tended to follow Varga's lead of cautious optimism, being careful to hedge their prognoses.[72]

Economists made explicit the connection between economic development and the political reconstruction of Europe. Again, the emphasis was
on the importance of co-operation, exemplified, for instance by an analysis
of the Yalta Conference. The mistakes of the First World War had been
avoided; the principle of collective responsibility had been established
among the Big Three for maintaining the peace and resolving every political
problem arising from the transition from war to peace. A decisive blow had
been struck against isolationism and the tendency to create spheres of influence. The Declaration on Liberated Territories would serve as the basis for
the democratic reconstruction of the liberated countries. The efforts of the
reactionary émigré governments-in-exile to split the Big Three were refuted
at the Crimean Conference; unity had prevailed, the analysis concluded.[73]
This was surely one of the most optimistic prognoses of the path not taken,
an alternative to the Cold War. The economists celebrated plans for agrarian
reform in Romania and Italy already drafted before the end of the war as one
of the major indicators that this transition was taking place, although they
acknowledged the resistance of reactionary forces.[74]

******

Coming from plebeian origins and a modest education, but nourishing
aspirations as an original interpreter of Marxist theory following in the foot-
steps of Lenin, Stalin viewed himself as a worker-intelligent. Yet he under-
regarded the genuine intelligentsia, especially those with a 'bourgeois' class
background. He tended to dismiss their claims for independent thinking
based on specialized knowledge, whether in strategic thinking, economic
planning or diplomacy. In general, he preferred to surround himself with
subordinates similar in background to his own: men with a practical rather
than a theoretical education and approach to solving problems, favouring a
Kirov over a Bukharin in the party; a Zhukov over a Tukhachevsky in the
army; a Molotov over a Litvinov in the foreign service; a Lysenko over a
Vavilov in biology. There were exceptions, but even then, as with the physicists, he appointed his own men like Beria to monitor their activities. Or else
he tolerated an economist like Varga, whose views he perceived as similar to
his own, or Kapitsa, whose contribution to winning the war had immediate
practical results. With the coming of the war, he exhibited an even greater
degree of flexibility in judging the value of men who may not have met his

own rigorous standards of trust and reliability so long as they were whole-heartedly committed to the war effort. As the next chapter will show this was also true of his treatment of the cultural intelligentsia. As a result, the paradoxical character of his rule diminished and an illusion of greater unity of purpose took hold. But the paradox would surface again after victory, when many who had served most loyally during the war were dismissed, demoted or purged, jeopardizing the winning of the peace.

CHAPTER 5

ON THE CULTURAL FRONT

Under the pressure of a war for survival, Stalin realigned the cultural front. Paradoxically, the greater the centralization and restrictions he imposed on the cultural front, the less effective the results he sought; the greater the autonomy he extended to the practitioners of cultural production, the greater success in mobilizing the population for the war effort. As a typically Bolshevik military metaphor, the cultural front had taken on a meaning in the early years of Soviet power of a struggle between the party, aiming for control over the institutions and expression of cultural values, and various groups of the pre-revolutionary intelligentsia ranging from proponents of a radically new proletarian culture to defenders of the old values of autonomy and freedom for creative individuals.[1] There was no clear-cut outcome, either in the early years or later down to the end of the Soviet regime. The struggle extended along a broad spectrum. On occasion, it took the form of a general offensive, other times, it cut back to local actions as in a real war. This was an ongoing campaign with retreats in some sectors and advances in others. But the firing rarely ceased altogether. To extend the metaphor, the intensity of the fighting depended to a large measure on the combatants involved and the degree to which they were unified in their own ranks as well as the changing conditions in the outer world. From time to time there was a relative pause, when the action subsided to a state of what Sheila Fitzpatrick has labelled 'cultural orthodoxies'.[2] But these pauses were temporary, generated by the imperatives of domestic and foreign policy as perceived by Stalin.

The prewar attempts to impose control on the activities and thoughts of the creative intelligentsia by centrally organizing them into unions and imposing on them a unified aesthetic was part of Stalin's practice of mobilization. According to one account, Stalin first defined the term 'socialist realism' in 1932 during preparations for the first congress of Soviet writers. He rejected the use of the term 'proletarian' to define the creative method, proposing instead a term which would express the continuity in the development of literature of critical realism of the nineteenth century changing over into a method (*partiinost'*) that would define the position of the party on questions of literature and the arts.[3] The first congress of the Union of Soviet Writers took place two years later. Although Gorky and Bukharin both spoke, Zhdanov's keynote address became the classic formulation of the doctrine. The principal components of his definition were *partiinost'*, *ideinost'* (Bolshevik ideology), *tipichnost'* (typicality) and *narodnost'* (national character). These were interpreted as a commitment to the depiction of reality in its revolutionary development by emphasizing the positive values of socialist society, expressed in clear, uncomplicated and inspirational prose. These elements were subsequently applied, with appropriate emendations, to musical composition, painting and architecture as unions for these professions were formed over the following years.

From the outset, however, both the organization of unions and the practical application of the doctrine ran into problems. First of all, a number of leading writers were extremely unhappy with the decisions of the congress.[4] Second, the unions proved difficult to manage. They were designed like other institutions of Soviet life to combine democracy, that is elections by their constituents, with the concentration of real power in the hands of a few.[5] Third, Socialist realism had proven to be an elusive doctrine, difficult to interpret and apply to works of art.[6]

The nature of the war created a whole new situation between the party and the cultural groups. The threat of an external enemy, so frequently invoked in Soviet propaganda, had become terrifyingly real. The enemy defined it as a 'war of annihilation'. The top officials in the German political, military and economic hierarchy envisaged this as a different kind of war involving mass slaughter of prisoners and civilians, followed by mass starvation and deportation to the east to reduce further the population. These sentiments were shared, as events soon confirmed, by the German troops, who conceived of the civilian population as barbaric or inhuman, justifying terrible brutalities and atrocities.[7] This kind of war required new weapons from the Soviet cultural armoury to mobilize the entire population in defending the country.

It would be a mistake, however, to assume that the organizations of the cultural front were merely waiting for instructions or inspiration from above. Even before the party and the government issued orders and appeals, the Union of Soviet Writers, the Union of Soviet Composers, the Academy of Sciences and the Orthodox Church all spontaneously and immediately volunteered their talents and issued calls to rally the people. These were just the institutional reactions. Scattered evidence drawn from memoirs and literary accounts attributed the spontaneous upsurge of patriotic feeling to a paradox in the prewar popular mood cultivated by the state. The building of a society on the basis of strict discipline, strong hierarchy and subordination to command had been diluted by a spirit of romantic idealism, especially among the youth. The Soviet historian Mikhail Gefter characterized it as a 'strong blend of plenary power and accountability [which] conferred a kind of shock-brigade mentality.'[8] Other, more sceptical commentators rejected the idea of an immediate coming together of the people as a myth of unity.[9] The two positions were not necessarily contradictory. Rather they illustrate the difficulty of characterizing the psychological state of 100 million people in the face of a massive attack from abroad.

Directives from above were not long in coming. Two days after the German invasion, a directive of the Sovnarkom and Central Committee of the Communist Party established the Soviet Information Bureau to centralize the wartime propaganda within the country and abroad. It faced two major problems. The first was the shortage of paper. The second was self-imposed. The increasingly obsessive involvement in detail by Stalin and his subordinates contributed to the stifling of initiative. The attempt to impose rigid censorship and restrictions on distribution imposed by shortages in transportation and communication facilities meant that the goal of achieving complete control over the flow of information was paradoxically undercut by the means devoted to achieving it. The number of publications at the centre was cut in half, only eighteen out of thirty-nine newspapers survived; a similar winnowing out took place in the provinces. Even *Pravda* was reduced from six to four pages. However, the shrinkage of the press also reduced the percentage of non-Russian newspapers to a level hovering from slightly less than a quarter to a third of prewar levels.[10] In the first few years, up to Stalingrad, under the pressure of censorship the main organs of the media, press, radio and documentary film displayed a reluctance to describe the full scale of the military disasters. It was important then to find other means to bolster public morale. Radio was particularly effective in developing new approaches to programming. Two daily series, 'Letters from the Front' and 'Letters from the Rear', read out by leading actors and actresses, reached the homes of millions. Classical culture, not socialist realism, dominated the airways with readings from Leo Tolstoy, and symphonic performances including the works of the great German composers were among the most popular broadcasts.[11] An extensive campaign to encourage letter writing between Uzbek villagers and front-line soldiers was vigorously promoted in order to enhance the patriotic image of the war of peoples.[12]

The Sovinformburo (the leading Soviet news and propaganda agency) supervised a number of subsidiary groups including the All-Slav Committee, the Anti-Fascist Committee of Soviet Scientists and the Jewish Anti-Fascist Committee. In the press, the most active and influential group of journalists was recruited from the leading lights in the Union of Soviet Writers, many of whom became war correspondents. Aleksei Tolstoy, Ilia Ehrenburg, Mikhail Sholokhov, Konstantin Simonov, Leonid Leonov, Marietta Shaginian and Evgeny Surkov were the most familiar names in a long roster. Their writings were disseminated by radio to foreign audiences as well.[13]

It was these groups who were largely responsible for introducing a new, eloquent and militant spirit into what had become before the war a dull and sterile field of propaganda. To be sure, Stalin was still the last court of judgement, but much initiative had passed to organized groups and informal associations of individuals outside the party and commissariats. A new cultural orthodoxy was emerging in which Marxism-Leninism was muted though never absent, always standing in the shadows.

In addition to permitting a greater range of expression, Stalin's main contribution to strengthening the cultural front was to broaden the range of mobilization themes, thereby further stimulating the new relationships between ruling institutions and ideology on the one hand, and diverse cultural groups and the mass of the population on the other. He had already employed three of these before the war: *partiinost'*, russo-centrism and

Soviet patriotism.[14] During the war he added the theme of Slavic solidarity. He spread the deadly strain of 'demonology', which had already infected his mental outlook in the purges, to infect the external enemy – the fascists. But as a counterpoint, he allowed a minor, humanitarian theme to characterize Soviet civilization as distinct from the inhumanity of fascism. He reconfigured the role of religion in general, and the Orthodox Church in particular, into a moral force in the service of the state. Finally, he introduced changes in the ideology and structure of international communism by abolishing the Comintern and reviving the prewar theme of different roads to socialism. A leitmotif in all of them evoked distant echoes from different periods of imperial Russian history, suitably revised to fit new circumstances.

Soviet propaganda had begun the process of making the war 'the great event' of the Soviet experience. The Bolshevik revolution, despite having been enshrined in official propaganda, was ill suited for the purpose of a founding myth. It had been the achievement of a minority of the population, leading to civil war. The defeats of the Whites and interventionists did not reconcile or eliminate the disaffected elements within the country or dispel the hostility of the capitalist world outside. Within two decades, most of its prominent leaders except for Lenin had been tarred by Stalin with the brush of treason. By 1938 large numbers of the rank-and-file Old Bolsheviks had also been condemned. The revolution was lavishly celebrated on 7 November, and Lenin's mausoleum and the burial niches in the Kremlin Wall were venerated; the red star was prominently displayed. But there were very few other rituals and visible symbols of the revolution.

In this scenario, Stalin played the dominant role of leader (*vozhd*), matching Lenin's achievement. He did not seek so much to replace the myth of revolution as to overshadow its significance.[15] The war, with all its terrible immediacy, provided him with a unifying context, in which he could anchor the society; for all its paradoxical character Stalin's war offered the country an eerie spiritual stability.[16]

PARTIINOST'

The public place of Marxist-Leninist theory and the role of the Communist Party as the hegemonic cultural as well as political force in the country were already in a state of crisis before the war broke out. Despite Stalin's savage and contemptuous treatment of the party in the prewar years, it remained the most reliable and compelling instrument of his power for reconciling the contradictions that sprang up when Stalin allowed or emphasized different themes in his efforts to mobilize the population. While the country could be governed during the emergency by an ad hoc committee run by a dozen powerful men under Stalin's command, the hard local organizational work demanded the revitalization of the party. No other state organ could be entrusted with running the daily life of the country; certainly not the police, not even the soviets, which lacked experience, *esprit de corps* and discipline. Restoring the old enthusiasm and initiative of the party members was no easy task in the wake of the purges. Where the provincial party organizations remained intact under strong leaders, like Ponomarenko in Belarus, the ideological work went smoothly. After the initial panic, at critical moments like the siege of Leningrad and the battle of Stalingrad, party morale held firm under the most extreme pressure. But there was always the danger that moving too far ahead on one or another sector of the cultural front would undermine the pre-eminence and coherence of the party's organizational and ideological work. For example, the traditional relationship between party and army was in danger of being reversed.

In 1941, the government had, in a moment of panic, re-established the dual command in the army by the appointment of political commissars. Once the Red Army commanders had proven their reliability, the system was changed back to the principle of a unified single military leadership with a deputy political officer. Just as important was the relaxation of party membership requirements for Red Army men, especially those in combat. As a result, a flood of raw peasant recruits entered the ranks of the party. In 1941, the military accounted for 20 per cent of party effectives; by 1943, they numbered 50 per cent, and by the end of the war slightly more than that. Another problem arose as the party lost many of its seasoned activists in the initial fighting when they were hastily thrown into combat; overall, the party lost 3 million members during the war. There was no time for the more than 3.5 million new recruits to study the Marxist-Leninist classics, and the party leadership complained of their appalling ignorance.[17] The main organ of the party to guide ideological work, *Propagandist*, interrupted publication briefly in March 1942 in order to revise and revitalize its message in light of the new challenge.[18]

An equal cause for concern was the erosion of the party's authority in the autonomous republics. In the peripheral republics under German occupation, the drop in party membership caused by battle losses, Nazi executions and flight was often catastrophic. By the end of the war, despite wartime recruitment, the Ukrainian party had lost 43 per cent of its prewar member-ship and the Belarus party 34 per cent. In both parties, the substantial majority was composed of young communists, inexperienced and untested. Overall, very few of the nationalities in the USSR had more Communist Party members than they did on the eve of the war – only the Mari, Buriat Mongols, Estonians and Iakut, all numbering below 10,000 members. The party organizations of the territories annexed by the Soviet Union on the eve of the war were so weak and small that the party took the extraordinary measure in the autumn of 1944 of creating a party bureau for the Moldavian, Estonian, Latvian and Lithuanian Soviet republics. For a historical prece-dent, it was necessary to go back to the dark days of the civil war when similar bureaus had been set up for Central Asia and the Caucasus.[19]

To meet the challenge, the party leadership overhauled the entire propa-ganda structure of the army. It shook up the stodgy Main Administration of Political Propaganda, replacing Lev Mekhlis with the vigorous Aleksandr Shcherbakov, a member of the Politiburo, and creating a high-powered advisory Council of Military-Political Propaganda. An 'Institute of Agitators' was created to raise the level of political workers in the armed forces and the number of agitators throughout the country was increased by two to three times.[20]

While the inner circle around Stalin maintained their firm adherence to his version of Marxism-Leninism, there were signs that not all the party organs were toeing the same line, although overt deviation was, of course, not possible. As the implication of the Stalingrad victory became clearer, the party organs re-affirmed the legacy of Leninist theory on the nature of war. They followed the familiar reinterpretation of Clausewitz by Lenin and Stalin, stressing the need to go beyond the simplistic reaction of 'the enemy is invading my country' to find out 'where war comes from, from which classes, [and] owing to which political goals'.[21] In the wake of the Yalta agree-ments, the implications for Soviet foreign policy were being driven home. In a clear foreshadowing of Stalin's well-known election speech of February 1946 on the inevitability of war, the party's leading theoretical organ declared that 'War arises from the phenomenon of antagonistic class contradictions: wars have accompanied the entire history of class struggle. The possibility of war will exist as long as the antagonistic contradictions exist.'[22] The full implications of the return to the theme of class struggle and the party revival did not emerge clearly until after the war.

RUSSO-CENTRISM

In Soviet wartime propaganda, russo-centrism and Soviet patriotism were closely linked, but subtle differences distinguished one from the other. Stalin played on both themes, alternating from one to the other, in mobilizing support for the war effort. But a latent tension remained between them. In his first public address to the Soviet people after the German invasion he employed a very specific term to define the war as a '*Velikaia Otechestvennaia voina*'. This is conventionally translated as the 'Great Patriotic War', but this misses the symbolic meaning of the word; 'Great Fatherland War' better captures the historical reference of the term. The war of 1812 against the aggressor from the West, Napoleon, had a long and honoured pedigree as an *Otechestvennaia voina*.[23] Stalin first employed the term '*Otechestvennaia voina*' in February 1918, when the Austro-German forces threatened to occupy Ukraine. He was indicating that it would be a defensive, territorial war as opposed to an international revolutionary war at a time when the term 'patriotic' (*patrioticheskaia*) was still associated with the old regime and the provisional government.

Stalin never used the term *Velikaia Patrioticheskaia voina*, which has a foreign ring. Its use in Soviet propaganda for foreign consumption in its anglicized form might have been a conscious choice to resonate in the ears of foreign allies. Another indigenous alternative used by Stalin was captured in the cry '*Za Rodinu!*', which could only be translated 'For the Motherland!', evoking another highly emotive gendered term.[24] The employment of such phrases as 'brotherhood of peoples', 'Fatherland War' and 'defence of the motherland' could hardly be accidental. The implication was clear: the Soviet people were a great family of nations.

In seeking new ways to redefine the national purpose, Stalin wove together Russian, multi-national and international themes. For many years afterwards Russians who heard his radio broadcast remembered his startling salutation: 'Comrades, citizens, brothers and sisters . . .'[25] The man who had subjected his people to a succession of social traumas – collectivization, industrialization, the terror – all in the name of building socialism and glorifying himself in the process as the peerless leader, was now humbling himself, asking for their help to defend the motherland by employing the vernacular of the Russian peasantry: 'brothers and sisters'. It was with that broadcast that Stalin began the long and painful process of mobilizing the population, legitimating the war and justifying the terrible human losses in the battle for survival. He began with the only means at his disposal in those grim June days: an exhortation, but cast in a new spirit and foreshadowing the emergence of a new ideological synthesis.

Before Stalin's June 1941 speech, his revival of russo-centrism was well under way.[26] It was part of his domestication of Marxism-Leninism that had commenced with his doctrine of 'socialism in one country'. He was already moving away from the high point of his 'affirmative action' policy. His attention had been drawn to signs that this was exacerbating ethnic tensions rather than resolving them. He moderated the Soviet nationality policy by introducing the idea of the 'friendship of peoples', guided by Russia as the first among equals.[27] From 1936 to the outbreak of war the russo-centric theme shifted in emphasis from proletarian internationalism to national Bolshevism as the leading, if not exclusive, theme in party propaganda.[28]

In his first wartime speech, Stalin took the additional bold step of combining universal with national themes in defining the war. In his new formulation, he appealed not only to 'brothers and sisters' but to all 'freedom-loving peoples'. The war was no longer for him an imperialist war between competing forms of capitalism, but 'a war of national liberation' with international implications. As in the war against Napoleon, the aim of continuing the fight into 1813 was, in his words, 'not only to repel the threat to Russia but also to help free all European people struggling under the yoke of the tyrant'. Even his rhetoric echoed the proclamation of Tsar Alexander I, with 'fascism' replacing Bonaparte's imperialism as the enemy.[29]

The propaganda campaign followed and embellished his lead.[30] The Soviet historian Evgeny Tarle struggled to find the right combination of patriotic elements in his 1938 book, *Napoleon's Invasion of Russia, 1812*, which was praised and then attacked after the Second World War. Sergei Prokofiev grasped the symbolic significance of the parallel with 1812. He had already embarked on an ambitious plan to write an opera on the theme of Leo Tolstoy's great epic of the Napoleonic invasion, *War and Peace*. Backed by the Committee on Arts Affairs, he worked with renewed energy.

Evacuated first to the Caucasus and then to Western Siberia, he struggled to find the right balance in his music between the heroic and comedic elements. After completing parts of the piano score, he responded to criticism by shifting to the more heroic element, building up the character of General Kutuzov. In the seventh scene he employed a folk song, 'The Expulsion of Napoleon from Moscow', from a well-known Russian collection. But the enormity of the undertaking and the difficulty of reconciling the ideological with the musical defeated him.[31]

As Stalin began his rhetorical appeal in 1941, so he ended it in 1945 with an even more flamboyant flourish. When he raised his glass in a victory toast, he singled out 'the Russian people because it is the most outstanding of the nations that reside in the Soviet Union ... the leading force in the Soviet Union ... because it has a clear mind, firm character and endurance'.[32] In between the two incantations Stalin multiplied his symbolic gestures of russo-centrism and offered up to the Russian people a series of concrete concessions. On the first wartime anniversary of the October Revolution, of all days, Stalin unveiled his cult of heroes. These were six pre-revolutionary military leaders, all Russians, who had defended the homeland against foreign invaders. 'Let the images of our great ancestors,' he said, 'Alexander Nevsky, Dmitry Donskoi, Minin and Pozharsky, Suvorov and Kutuzov, inspire us in this war.' It made no difference that Nevsky and Donskoi were canonized saints of the Orthodox Church or that Suvorov had repressed the Poles in their struggle to save their national homeland. Right on cue the Propaganda and Agitation Department of the party turned out a million copies of popularly written pamphlets on each one of these heroes. A stream of novels and plays drew upon traditional accounts of their exploits in order to extract moral principles and guides to right action. Three new military orders bearing the names of Nevsky, Suvorov and Kutuzov were introduced with great fanfare to reward emulation of their achievements: the Order of Suvorov, for example, to commemorate the 'battle of annihilation'. Nine newly established military academies were named after Suvorov, 'the great captain'. The glorification of lesser military leaders like Admiral Pavel Nakhimov and Prince Petr Bagration followed later, but Stalin's six maintained their special distinction.[33]

Behind the scenes Stalin encouraged an even more startling rehabilitation of the two tsars with whom he felt a close affinity, Ivan the Terrible and Peter the Great.[34] The film producer Sergei Eisenstein had already created

Alexander Nevsky as an early warning to the Germans before the war. Now he undertook to direct part one of *Ivan the Terrible* expressly on Stalin's orders: 'The main idea of the film is the might of Russia and the great struggle which took place in order to consolidate this might', wrote Eisenstein. During the war four major historical novels, several of them trilogies, appeared on Ivan. Aleksei Tolstoy's two plays about Ivan set the tone, portraying him as a defender of national unity against both internal enemies, the boyars, and in the Livonian War against external attack. Tolstoy's earlier plays on Ivan enjoyed a revival. Pavel Sokolov-Skalia contributed several historical paintings on Ivan. The more serious but highly flattering historical work on Ivan by Robert Vipper was republished in two separate editions with several quotations from Stalin embellishing the text.[35] Formerly, Stalin was eager to appear as the heir to Lenin's mantle, but now he extended his lineage by 400 years and tapped into a familiar historical tradition.[36]

Yet even here there was an inconsistency rising to the level of a paradox in Stalin's manipulation of history. In August 1941, Vipper had written an essay entitled 'The Historical Roots of German Fascism', which he began by declaring that 'the war was not a struggle with the German people, but with German fascism'. Drawing on his expertise as a medievalist, he sought the reasons why a people 'who had given so much to universal culture had fallen back into a state of barbarism'. His answer was to trace the roots of fascism in Germany to the feudal-militarist traditions in the German states dating back to the tenth century. The essay was not published until 1997. The reasons may be surmised from his response to his critics written in 1942 as an addendum to the essay. By implication, Vipper had challenged the party line on the origins of fascism as an outgrowth of Lenin's stage of imperialism. Yet in the addendum, when Vipper applied his long-term historical analysis to the Russian state from Ivan the Terrible to Stalin, his views were not only accepted but widely praised.[37]

The creation of a Soviet Russian pantheon of heroes was a culmination of the process of reintroducing the individual in history that had been under way in school textbooks and popular literature since the mid-thirties.[38] Running parallel to this trend was the construction of the cult of Stalin which peaked just before the war. It was briefly suspended and then revived when the tide of battle shifted to the Soviet side.[39] To be sure, Stalin, the Georgian, did not fit in any real way the image of a Russian *bogatyr*, or frontier knight. But then again, Hitler was hardly a specimen of the Nordic superman. As in every aspect of the revival of ideology cum propaganda, it is difficult to arrive at any scholarly consensus on the role of the cult in shaping the moods and attitudes of the population towards the *vozhd*.[40]

The words 'Russia' and 'Russian' were given more and more prominence in official propaganda. A new national anthem was unveiled on 1 January 1944, replacing 'The International', which was relegated to the position of party hymn.[41] The new anthem contained a verse that was offensive to many Old Bolsheviks and representatives of the nationalities: 'Great Russia (*Velikaia Rus'*) had built an eternal and indestructible Union of Free Republics.' Those who could remember Lenin's extreme distaste for the reactionary term *Velikaia Rus'* with its chauvinistic and anti-Semitic overtones could only shake their heads in wonder. The British correspondent Alexander Werth declared that a 'virtual orgy of nationalism' flared with renewed vigour after the great victory of Kursk. But as the verse of the new anthem announced, the Soviet theme was not ignored but rather subordinated to the russo-centric theme. In the same way, the famous poem by Aleksei Surkov placed the dynamic Russian people at the head of their passive brethren: 'Avenging Russia is advancing / Ukraine and Belarus, wait and hope.'[42]

Stalin completed the process, already under way in the thirties, of expanding the timescale of the brief Soviet tradition. He moved back the 'great time', in Mircea Eliade's sense of the word, from 1917 to the sixteenth century. But he broke the timeline, consciously or not, in the early nineteenth century, thus leaving a gap of 100 years from 1812 to 1917. What he had created then was a mythic past linked by six 'great ancestors' and separated by a century without heroes, a century of decline, until the real events of the revolution.[43] From his point of view novelists and playwrights were better suited than historians to portray the mythic past and infuse it with lessons – national and patriotic – for the present. The writers of fiction carried the main burden of firmly anchoring the Soviet experience, which lacked any event of truly national significance that transcended proletarian revolution, with the long and glorious episodes of unity against the external enemy.

Under Stalin's tutelage, another rich current in the Russian national tradition, folklore, was diverted into the mainstream of wartime propaganda. Beginning with Gorky's speeches at the first congress of the Union of Soviet Composers, folklore was rehabilitated as an 'oral poetic expression of the folk masses' after a decade of having been dismissed by left-wing critics who derided it as a feudal survival. On the eve of the war, Russian folklorists had enjoyed a renaissance. Efforts were made to revive the tradition of the village tale-tellers. Their performances of *byliny* (traditional epic poems) were recorded, taught in schools and broadcast on the radio. The theme of repelling the foreign invaders was embellished with epic tales of the frontier knights (*bogatyry*) like Ilia Muromets, Aleksei Popovich and Dobrynia. An anthology of folk songs composed by Red Army soldiers in the 1920s was published in 1938.[44]

The popularity of folk tales reached a climax during the war with the famous recitals by Marfa Kriukova, who had mastered the technique of transposing the language and imagery of the *byliny* into contemporary life. She had a repertoire of about two hundred such poems, three quarters of which were original and the rest her own compositions. During the war, she gave 13,000 performances to Red Army units. Shortly after the war ended, a two-volume collection of her tales, *About Heroes Past and Present*, was published, in which traditional heroes appeared to help fight the Germans.[45] The tradition of the lamentation (*plach*) was also revived in the villages of the north on the occasion of a soldier's departure for the front or death in battle.[46] It was only a matter of time before a flood of pseudo-folk tales about Soviet leaders, with Stalin in first place followed by Voroshilov, began to appear.[47]

Drawing on a related genre, musicians responded by composing thousands of war songs, another powerful vehicle for transmitting patriotic emotions.[48] The term 'war song' covered a wide range of genres, evoking emotions from the lyrical to the militant. Like the folk tales, the simplicity of the music and verbal structures made them easily accessible even to the illiterate. Their origins were firmly rooted in pre-revolutionary military traditions, when every battalion in the imperial Russian army had its group of 'soldier-singers'. During the war, the propaganda apparatus lost control of the genre and many of the songs continued to enjoy popular acclaim, and do so to this day.[49] Among the most notable composers writing war songs, Prokofiev immediately responded to the appeal by the leadership of the Union of Soviet Composers to 'mobilize all composers for the creation of anti-fascist songs'. He refocused his activities to compose 'The Song of the Brave' on a text by the poet Aleksei Surkov and another to a text by Vladimir Mayakovsky, one of Stalin's favourite poets. The exaltation of national and patriotic themes in wartime songs and literature, particularly in poetry and short stories, invoked the plain folk as heroes and heroines. Perhaps the most famous war poem was 'Vasily Terkin' by Aleksandr Tvardovsky, which celebrated the courage and optimism of the simple soldier. Awarded a Stalin Prize, it was published chapter by chapter in newspapers sent to the front and read over Radio Moscow.[50] Other poems celebrated the exploits of the working class, the partisans, and the sacrifices of old people in the villages, all embodying the unity of the whole country.[51]

SOVIET PATRIOTISM

The distinction between nationalism and patriotism has been widely recognized in the scholarly literature.[52] It is critical in analyzing Soviet wartime propaganda. Russo-centrism was an ethnic principle based on a strong sense of belonging to a Russian nation and the role of the Russian people as the leading element in the multi-national Soviet Union. The words 'Russian nationalism' were never used by Stalin or the party to define the basis for sovereign rule or to justify the right to self-determination or separatism. For many years, Stalin opposed the creation of a Communist Party of the Russian Republic. Soviet patriotism was a political not an ethnic principle. It defined loyalty to a homeland composed of a union of national republics of which the Russian was only one, albeit the pre-eminent one. Both principles served as a rallying cry for mass mobilization in a multicultural state where one nationality, the Russians, occupied a special role, having built the state into a great power under the tsars and constituting the leading element in rebuilding the state into a socialist great power. The term 'national Bolshevism' sought to incorporate the two principles, as did the concept of the friendship of peoples and russo-centrism on different occasions. Soviet patriotism, as it evolved in the twenties, particularly after the official acceptance of Stalin's 'socialism in one country', aimed at overcoming the persistent and disturbing absence in the state's previous history of a justification – morally superior to brute force or historical accident – for assembling under one authority the many people who constituted the old tsarist empire and the USSR. Its guiding idea was a fusion of class and ethno-linguistic identities in a new form of citizenship.[53] Its institutional bulwarks were the parties of the federal republics and the All-Union Communist Party, which had – significantly – changed its name to the Communist Party of the Soviet Union.

In the first year of the war, when the fronts in the Baltic, Belarusian and Ukrainian republics collapsed, the leadership sponsored meetings of representatives of the union republics and appealed to their patriotism.[54] In a seldom recognized effort to include the nationalities in the cultural front, the music of the nationalities was promoted by the Union of Soviet Composers. Created in 1938–39, the union took as its motif the co-ordination, production and interpretation of new music; a sub-theme was to unleash the creative potential of the whole Soviet population. Toward this end, it set up chapters in the Central Asian republics. Soon after the outbreak of hostilities, most of the Soviet composers were evacuated to Sverdlovsk and Central Asia.[55]

Just before the war, Prokofiev had composed a panegyric to Stalin on the occasion of his sixtieth birthday, the *Zdravitsa* cantata, which consisted of seven folk poems from Russian, Ukrainian, Belarusian, Mari, Mordvinian and Komi sources in hopes of repairing the damage to his reputation as a loyal Soviet citizen.[56] When he was evacuated in the autumn of 1941 to the Kabardino-Balkarian Autonomous Republic in the Caucasus, he became interested in the 'oriental' style of Tatar music. While working on *War and Peace*, he also composed his Second String Quartet on Kabardino-Balkarian themes drawn from dances and songs of the region in a transcription made by the nineteenth-century Russian composer Sergei Taneev. It was these combinations and their lyrical quality that Prokofiev invoked when attacked after the war for formalism.[57]

At the height of the war, with victory in sight, Stalin gave the idea of the multi-national state its fullest expression in a speech to the Moscow Soviet and party organizations: 'The strength of Soviet patriotism consists in that its base does not rest on racial or nationalistic prejudices but on the profound devotion and faith of the people in their Soviet motherland [*rodina*] and the fraternal friendship of the toilers of all nations of our country ... Soviet patriotism does not divide but on the contrary unites all nations and nationalities of our country into a unified fraternal family.'[58]

Soviet patriotism served Stalin as an instrument for stiffening the resolve of the nationalities, especially those exposed to the pressures and temptations of living outside Soviet power under German occupation. In order to reconcile national and multi-national loyalties, the leadership appealed to 'the unbreakable friendship of peoples', with the Russians occupying the position of the first among equals.[59] It was not difficult for propagandists to embellish this theme with examples from the Soviet period. But the party pressed for glorifications of the military tradition among the non-Russian nationalities and these, for the most part, could only be found in the history of their resistance to Russian conquest. In order to resolve the embarrassing paradox, the historians tasked with this glorification had recourse to the 'lesser evil' formula. They explained that the nationalities fared better under the Russians than they would have under the alternative rule of the Turks, or the Chinese, or the Poles, and that, ultimately, they benefited from the greatest bounty of all – participation in the Bolshevik revolution.[60] There were other problems in interpreting Stalin's dual formula of russo-centrism and Soviet patriotism. In attempting to bridge the gap, propagandists in the Political Administration of the Red Army strained to distinguish between love of the Russian people and the Russian land from national chauvinism. While acknowledging the equality of nationalities, the emotional ties that held the USSR together were linked to the same love for the Russian people expressed in the work of non-Russian national poets.[61]

Not surprisingly, Andrei Vyshinsky emerged as the foremost propagator of Soviet patriotism as the foundation for a state of the new type. An ex-Menshevik, he had been Stalin's blunt instrument in humiliating and liquidating the Old Bolshevik leaders in the purge trials (see above, p. 67). Repeating his denunciations of them, particularly Bukharin, he gave pride of place to the state as the 'decisive factor' in building socialism, relegating the party to a subsidiary role. His exaltation of the state, particularly its federal character as 'a voluntary and equal union of peoples', did not fit easily into a picture dominated by russo-centrism nor does it jibe with the theme of *partiinost'*.[62] No one chose to take notice of the contradiction.

One of the most popular propagandists for Soviet patriotism was the president of the USSR, Mikhail Kalinin, a deft touch considering that he was, to many, the embodiment of the 'pure Russian peasant type' among the governing elite. In his frequent appearances before Komsomol leaders and front-line agitators, he insisted that the Soviet Union was 'a single harmonious family of nations, forging a unity such as the world has never seen'.[63] Kalinin boasted that the state was not afraid, as the tsarist monarchy had been, of recruiting from all the national groups. .

The State Defence Committee decided to give more visible and dramatic expression to the vitality of the Stalinist nationality policy. Stalin had already recognized in 1937 the need to introduce obligatory Russian into the teaching curricula of the schools in the union republics. He pointed out that in recruiting for the army in Uzbekistan, Kazakhstan, Armenia, Georgia and Azerbaijan the lack of knowledge of Russian was a severe handicap. 'With such a situation, one is forced to leave them in their local regions and then our divisions and brigades are transformed into territorial ones. This is not an army'.[64] In November 1941, the Red Army recreated the national units that had been abolished in 1937. The task was placed in the hands of republic and oblast party commissions which, it was specified, had to contain at least a minimal representation of the local nationality. Russians were permitted to join the units only if the necessary technical personnel were lacking. Units of divisional strength were formed in the Central Asian, Transcaucasian and North Caucasian nationality areas.[65]

But the Commissariat of Defence quickly realized that the '"non-Russians" in the ranks of the Red Army [had] poorly mastered or entirely [did] not know the Russian language', with devastating effects on their fighting capabilities. As a result, Shcherbakov, the vigorous head of the Political Administration of the Red Army, called for an intensification of a propaganda campaign to better integrate the non-Russian soldiers into an understanding of the nature of the war. By recognizing the specific cultural needs and celebrating the exploits of heroes of the non-Russian fighting men, the programme was also designed to overcome the prejudice directed against the non-Russians and to instil in them a sense of pride. As if to balance the equation, the teaching of Russian was to be vigorously promoted. These moves resembled a restoration of the indigenization policy of the early Soviet years, embodied in Stalin's formula of 'national in form and socialist in content'.[66]

When the Nazi advance broke through to the Caucasus, the Soviet press sought to repair the damage done by the purges in the region on the eve of the war. In the effort to mobilize support among the indigenous people, the theme of defending their national traditions under Russian leadership was given prominence. Once again Ehrenburg led the charge. But *Pravda* also went all out in celebrating the heroic warrior tradition of the mountaineers without, to be sure, mentioning that these had been developed in the wars against the Russians of the nineteenth century. The propaganda agencies also publicized the awarding of medals of patriotism to non-Russian nationalities in the region, including 313 Heroes of the Soviet Union during the battles for the Caucasus alone. Almost 13,000 Dagestanis were awarded state decorations for heroic labour in the rear areas.[67] Occasionally, there was a pathetic and cruel irony – not to say paradox – in all this. At the very time that the Chechen and Ingush people were being deported, the press noted that 36 awards of Hero of the Soviet Union had gone to young Chechen and Ingush soldiers.[68] In fact, the restoration of the warrior tradition of the mountaineers was only partial and temporary.

At the tenth session of the Supreme Soviet in February 1944, Molotov was still complaining that only 'partial induction' into the Red Army had been carried out in recent years in those regions of the Soviet Union 'where in the old days military inductions did not occur' (presumably meaning Central Asia). The Central Committee then drafted a law for the creation of military formations in the union republics and for the reorganization of the People's Commissariat of Defence from the All-Union to the Union-Republic Commissariat of Defence. The law also granted each union republic plenipotentiary rights to maintain diplomatic relations with foreign powers and changed the name of the All-Union Commissariat for Foreign Affairs to the Union-Republic Commissariat for Foreign Affairs.[69] The establishment of republic academies of sciences outside the Slavic republics was a more substantive effort to strengthen the loyalties of the non-Russian nationalities and exploit the intellectual resources of the entire country. The first step had been taken on the eve of the war with the creation of the Georgian Academy of Sciences. The relocation of scientists from the western war zones was instrumental in the organization of Uzbek, Armenian, Azerbaijani and Kazakh academies from 1943 to 1945. Shortly after the war, republic academies were founded in the reincorporated Latvian and Estonian republics.[70] The Central Asian academies also provided a haven for scientists evacuated from Russia and the western republics, thus bolstering the notion of unity in diversity. By building the institutional infrastructure of a multicultural society, the state gave credence to the Soviet ideal and rebuffed the Nazi racist myth of the inferiority of the Slavic peoples.

By 1944, however, contradictions began to show up between aspects of russo-centrism (emphasizing the supremacy of the Russian language and the Russian historical experience) and Soviet patriotism (extolling the supranational character of the struggle). Russo-centrism exhibited its negative

1. Anticipating Stalin as Warlord: propaganda poster by Arkady Arkady, 1939.

2. The great strategist Marshal Mikhail Tukhachevsky on the eve of his arrest in 1937.

3. Struggling on the ice road across the frozen Lake Ladoga to feed the people of Leningrad during the siege of the beleaguered city, winter 1941–42.

4. The deportation of Volga Germans, who were forced to
leave their ancestral homes for exile in Siberia, 1941.

5. The renowned Soviet journalist Vasily Grossman
reporting from the ruins of Germany, 1945.

6. 'Kill Him!' Kukryniksy's portrayal of the Nazi beast, with excerpt from a poem by Konstantin Simonov, 1942. The climactic line of the poem is, 'No one will kill him, if you do not!'

7. '1812–1943', propaganda poster by Kukryniksy. Echoing Stalin's invocation of history, the poster reduces Hitler to a puny figure who will share the defeat of Napoleon.

8. Pilots of the all-female 'Taman' aviation regiment. Known to the Germans as 'Witches of the Night', they were the only female combat flyers in any belligerent country of the Second World War.

9. A staged photograph illustrating typical Soviet partisans active in the forests of Belarus in November 1943.

10. The Soviet economic planner Nikolai Voznesensky before his arrest in 1948.

11. Lev Landau and Petr Kapitsa at Nikolina Gora. The two Nobel Prize winners relax at the well-known resort northwest of Moscow.

12. Stalin and Churchill reviewing Stalin's favourite regiment in 1944. Molotov is at Stalin's left and Vyshinsky at his right behind Churchill.

13. Marshal Zhukov leading the victory parade, May 1945. 'The man on the white horse' held clear implications for Stalin as he watched from the platform of the Lenin mausoleum.

14. Vyacheslav Molotov talks to Stalin while watching a Physical Culture Day parade at the Moscow Dynamo Stadium in 1943. Molotov seems deferential, as always, while Stalin appears to be looking into the future.

15. Homage to Stalin on the 66th anniversary of his death, Red Square, Moscow, 2019. An official celebration that inspired spontaneous reactions: note the woman crossing herself.

side when it was employed to denounce aspects of local nationalism as excessive. Front-line newspapers in national languages were reproached for not giving sufficient credit to the Russian contribution to the war. The campaign to create a pantheon of epic Tatar heroes ran up against the nature of their exploits in resisting imperial Russian expansion and occupation. Among other faults, the Tatar ASSR party organization was rebuked for 'serious mistakes in evaluation, the military-political and international position of our country, denigrating the role of the Red Army in the destruction of the German-Fascist predators and bowing before the military power, technical achievements and culture of the bourgeois', as well as 'serious shortcomings and errors of a nationalist character in illuminating the history of Tataria [glorifying the Golden Horde and popularizing the khanate-feudal epic of Idegei]'. The party organization of the Western Ukraine was taken to task for a series of nationalist errors including the failure to combat the 'Ukrainian-German nationalists' and overcoming the attitudes of the older generation of intelligentsia, 'who were educated in German, Austro-Hungarian, Polish and Romanian schools in the spirit of bourgeois ideology'. A similar decree of the Central Committee criticized the Bashkir ASSR for failing to distinguish between the Bashkir national liberation movement and bandit raids, and for having 'distorted the history of the participation of the Bashkirs in the Patriotic War of 1812, setting against one another the Russians and the Bashkirs'.[71]

Even historians whose party credentials seemed irreproachable could find their work sidetracked if it did not conform to the image of Russia as the progressive force in creating a multi-national state. Perhaps the most egregious example was the fate of *The History of the Kazakh People*, written in 1943 by a collective headed by the highly regarded historian Anna Pankratova. Nominated for a Stalin Prize, it was attacked by other professional historians for its negative portrayal of tsarist colonialism. This led to a fierce exchange, a virtual stand-off between Pankratova and her critics, and an uncharacteristic unwillingness of the party leadership to resolve the debate.[72] The latent conflict between Ukrainian and Russian national mythologies had already broken to the surface in 1943 and 1944. Stalin had contributed to the confusion over the historic relationship between the two Slavic peoples. He had approved Nikita Khrushchev's proposal to create the military Order of Bogdan Khmelnitsky (the medal bore his name in

Ukrainian) and appeared to encourage the mounting nationalist excitement of the Ukrainian Communist Party as the Red Army liberated one city after another. As party secretary, Khrushchev attempted to square the circle of permitting two nationalisms to claim equal status. Then Stalin came down hard on the novel and film script *Ukraine in Flames* by Oleksandr Dovzhenko, accusing the film producer of 'revising Leninism' by emphasizing national pride over the class struggle. The rehabilitation of classic Russian historians of the nineteenth century ran counter to the rehabilitation of Ukrainian historians writing on the incorporation of Ukraine into the Russian Empire.[73] But the campaign to denounce Ukrainian nationalist excesses had to wait until the war was over and the rift in the 'great friendship' could not be exploited by the nationalist opposition to re-Sovietization of Ukraine. Finally, even artists were condemned for slighting the creative role of the Russian literary classics. Meanwhile, the slogan of the 'great friendship of peoples' continued to be invoked.[74]

A major effort was made to mobilize the Jewish population under the banner of the 'friendship of peoples'. The loyalty of the Jews during the war was unquestionable. During the war, no Jews collaborated with the enemy, the only nationality (including the Russians) of whom that can be said. To be sure, they had little choice given the Nazi aim of exterminating them. But many Jews had benefited greatly under the Soviet regime in ways that were unthinkable in tsarist Russia. They had risen to occupy positions of influence in the sciences, arts, diplomatic corps and police.

In the prewar decades, many Jews had taken the earliest opportunity to gain from the social mobility facilitated by the spread of literacy and education. By 1926, 70 per cent of the Jews in Ukraine and Belarus were literate; in Moscow this figure reached 85 per cent. This enabled them during the first two five-year plans to escape from the shtetls by joining the industrial labour force as skilled workers and then moving up the ladder as they acquired experience. In 1930 they were the largest group, except for the Russians, in the *technikums* of the Higher Soviet of the National Economy of the Russian Republic, the faculties preparing engineers and a number of postgraduate candidates in the sciences. On the eve of the war, Jewish men held the directorships of the six major military academies. They were particularly prominent in the management of industrial enterprises, and the design and improvement of aircraft, artillery and tanks. More than fifty Jews in various branches of industry and scientific organizations achieved the rank of general. During the war years they constituted 22 per cent of the directors of scientific institutes of the Academy of Sciences, 23.5 per cent of directors of the machine construction enterprises and 14 per cent of directors of metallurgical enterprises. During the same period, they won 21 per cent of the Stalin Prizes. This in a period during which they constituted just over 2 per cent of the population.[75]

To be sure, prominent Jewish party stalwarts like Trotsky, Zinoviev, Lev Kamenev and Genrikh Iagoda had been expelled, arrested and often shot. Writers like Isaac Babel and Osip Mandelstam had perished in the camps. But these were individual cases; there had not been a systematic anti-Semitic campaign. The purges fell indiscriminately on all the nationalities. This is not to suggest that anti-Semitism did not exist among Soviet civil and military officials. A case in point was the treatment of Polish Jews in the formation of the so-called Anders Army, composed of Polish prisoners of war and deportees sent to remote camps after the Soviet occupation of Belarus and Western Ukraine in 1939. The Jews suffered discrimination at the hands of the representatives of both the Soviet and Polish officers and officials involved in organizing the recruitment and dispatch of the troops under General Anders, himself a notorious anti-Semite, to Iran and on to the western fronts.[76]

The formation of the Jewish Anti-Fascist Committee (JAFC) appeared to promise more salutary results on the cultural front. But its fate revealed another dimension of the paradoxical face of Soviet patriotism. The idea for forming an Anti-Fascist Committee had a bizarre origin with tragic overtones. Jews constituted about a third of the population of the territories annexed from Poland in 1939. Many were deported to remote camps and a number were arrested, included two leading members of the Jewish Bund, Henryk Ehrlich and Wiktor Alter. Two years later, in September 1941, they were released from prison and approached by an officer of the NKVD who advised them to forget the past and contribute to the common struggle against the Nazis.[77] He suggested creating a worldwide organization called the Jewish Anti-Fascist Committee and requested a plan for the organization. Their draft proposed activities in three areas, Poland, the Soviet Union and the West, to disseminate information and raise material support for the Jews in the Soviet Union. They even suggested the creation of a Jewish

Legion composed of volunteers from the US and Great Britain to fight side by side with the Red Army. It was clear from their draft that they envisaged that the leadership of the committee would include a number of socialists who like themselves had been members of the Second International with previous ties to the Bund. Within two months, however, both men were arrested again; Ehrlich committed suicide in prison and Alter was shot in 1942. Meanwhile, Shcherbakov, the head of the Moscow party committee and member of the Central Committee, and Solomon Lozovsky, the deputy foreign minister and head of Sovinformburo, were developing plans for what became the Jewish Anti-Fascist Committee, following a mass rally of Jews in Moscow supporting the war effort. Stalin's decision to proceed with the creation of the Jewish Anti-Fascist Committee illustrates once again his determination to employ every means of mobilizing the population, to the point of extending an unprecedented degree of autonomy to a group which in a different form had aroused his opposition in the past. Stalin had vigorously supported Lenin's sharp criticism of the Jewish Bund before the revolution on the grounds that its claim to be the sole representative of the Jewish workers placed national identity over proletarian internationalism.

After a brief period of silence, in April 1942, the formation of the JAFC was announced with the renowned actor Solomon Mikhoels, people's artist of the USSR, as chairman; Alter and Ehrlich had envisaged him as vice-chairman of their organization. Mikhoels had been evacuated to Tashkent where he served as the director of the Moscow Yiddish Art Theatre and became one of the most active and internationally connected advocates of Soviet Jewish interests. In 1946 he was awarded a Stalin Prize.

Lozovsky took the JAFC under his wing and helped to promote its activities at home and abroad. In 1943 it was considered safe enough to send Mikhoels and the poet Itsik Fefer, the Yiddish poet with ties to the police, on an official mission to the United States (where Mikhoels met Albert Einstein), Canada, Mexico and Great Britain to raise funds and promote the Soviet war effort. Yet the pair were forbidden to accept an invitation by the Yishuv to visit Palestine. The official journal of the JAFC, *Eynigkayt*, published in Yiddish, carried news on unofficial contacts with Jews abroad and the heroic exploits of Jewish soldiers. Large numbers of books in Yiddish were published in the Soviet Union. Mikhoels became a kind of universal adviser to Soviet Jews from all walks of life.[78] Among all the officially designated nationalities, the Jews had risen to a position of prominence that exposed them to the suspicion that they sought, with Western support, to occupy a position in Soviet society that placed them side by side with the Russians. This soon proved to be a dangerous location.

THE CULT OF HATRED

Measured by its sheer visceral impact, a cult of hatred, with its folkloristic images of the 'fascist beast', was designed to arouse the most powerful emotional response to the German attack on the Soviet Union. Stalin had already tested what Moshe Lewin calls a 'demonological theory of history' in his internal war against the opposition.[79] In orchestrating the purge trials, his instructions inspired Andrei Vyshinsky's vicious denunciations of the opposition. Vyshinsky turned himself into an inquisitor whose mission it was to destroy every vestige of genuine political motivation or even of human behaviour in the actions of the accused. The opposition, he raged, was 'not a political party', but 'a gang of criminals'. They were hardly if at all to be distinguished from highwaymen who waylaid unsuspecting travellers. They wove their conspiracies like invisible demons. 'The roots of this group', Vyshinsky went on in a passage remarkable for its popular imagery, 'are not in the masses of people of this country, whom this gang fears, from which it runs away like the devil from holy water. This gang hides its face from the mass of the people: it conceals its brutal claws and ferocious fangs. The roots of this gang must be sought in the secret recesses of the foreign espionage services'. The oppositionists were often accused of resorting to poison, the symbol of witchcraft, as a favourite method of wrecking and subversion; the most vivid image of their victims was the mutilated child.[80] Their conduct was inhuman, bestial. Yet once the war broke out nothing more was heard of internal enemies. But a similar rhetoric and imagery, intensified many times over, was turned with full force against the Nazi invader. In this case, unlike the purge trials, the crimes fit the accusations. But Soviet wartime propaganda was more successful than any other in transforming the terrible facts of Nazi atrocities into a systematic campaign of hating the enemy.

The Agitation and Propaganda (Agitprop) Department of the Central Committee threw all its weight behind the campaign to hate the enemy, but the real power came from the writers and artists who converted the dross of slogans into familiar visual devices drawn from popular traditions and early Bolshevik poster art.[81] The most powerful visual images emerged from the pens of the three most talented and popular satirist-cartoonists in the Soviet Union, Mikhail Kypriianov, Porfiry Krylov and Nikolai Sokolov, whose collaborative work, perhaps unique to the genre, appeared under the collective pseudonym 'Kukryniksy'. Their drawings were carried by *Pravda* and *Krasnaia zvezda*, but they also produced dozens of posters that were reproduced by the tens of thousands and pasted on the walls of Soviet cities. They designed special cartoons printed in German for massive distribution by air drops over enemy lines. Their work for Soviet audiences was particularly graphic in portraying the Nazi leaders and their fascist 'lackeys' in other Axis countries as animals with long fangs and claws dripping with blood. There were Nazi hyenas, wolves and monkeys (this role was reserved for Goebbels), snakes and spiders. Occasionally, these savage images would even be directed against German soldiers and their families at home. The trio of artists, like writers and Agitprop men, would pore over the captured diaries and letters of enemy troops seeking the appalling detail that would illustrate the bestial character of their conduct. This detail would become the focal point of the cartoon or story. Here too the folkloristic image burned most deeply, as in the case of the episode of the child's clothes: a German soldier sent home a Russian child's clothes (presumably stripped from her dead body), and apologized to his wife for the bloodstains. But she replied there was no need to worry, they washed out easily. From this exchange Kukryniksy drew a powerful cartoon portraying the well-dressed German *Bürgerin* as a witch-like creature scrawling her bloody reply while a ghostly image of her husband stripping the child hovers above her head.[82]

The three artists recruited the famous children's poet Samuil Marshak to write brief pungent verses to accompany their work. They insisted on brevity to enhance the impact: a few stanzas, but a single quatrain was best. The result was a twentieth-century wartime version of the Russian fabulist Ivan Krylov, who did some of his best work during the Patriotic War of 1812. Like Krylov, too, Kukryniksy's verses and drawings were imbued with a grim humour. Whenever Stalin used a folk image in his speeches, he could be certain that it would be picked up by them and embellished in different forms. For example, in his speech of 6 November 1944, he cited a proverb:

'We shoot the wolf not because he is grey but because he eats sheep.' Shortly thereafter Kukryniksy transformed it into a two-panel cartoon: in the first the Nazi sheep in wolf's clothing – a Wehrmacht uniform – impales a baby on his bayonet; in the second, the Nazi sheep, disguise abandoned, flees the bayonet of a Red Army man.[83]

Some of the most talented pens in the literary world refined the cult of hatred; Mikhail Sholokhov, Ilia Ehrenburg and Konstantin Simonov were the foremost among them. On the second anniversary of the war, Sholokhov's famous short story 'The Science of Hatred' appeared in *Pravda*.[84] It was immediately reprinted in the army newspaper, *Krasnaia zvezda*. The Agitprop Department snapped it up and churned out a million copies in pamphlet form. Soon after Sholokhov met Stalin, who told him that his story was as timely and necessary for 'the current phase' of the war as Gorky's *Mother* had been for the revolutionary movement. He urged Sholokhov to write a novel on 'the holy national war of liberation'.[85] Sholokhov found it difficult to write the short vivid pieces demanded of a war correspondent. Ehrenburg and Simonov took up the theme and developed it brilliantly in their feature articles for *Krasnaia zvezda*. Ehrenburg rapidly became the most popular and widely read of the war correspondents.[86] 'The Science of Hatred' shows why this was so. A powerfully evocative piece, it nevertheless made distinctions between the hatred of fascism and respect for the civilized values of old German culture. He and Simonov were masters at juxtaposing the brutality of German troops with the self-sacrifice of Red Army men. Few could equal them at giving the lie to Nazi propaganda about the Aryan myth. Their message was a simple one: the Nazis were inferior, not because of race, but because they were inhuman.[87] Aleksei Surkov turned out so many poems on the theme that they were compiled into a book on hatred.[88]

What endowed wartime films with a doubly powerful theme in the message of hating the enemy was the treatment of women as both the victims and avengers of Nazi brutality. Two films illustrate the extremes of violence inflicted on women and carried out by them. The first was Fridrikh Ermler's *She Defends the Motherland*, first screened in 1943. It portrayed a woman whose conversion to a murderous axe-wielding partisan is incited by the slaughter of her baby, shown on the screen, and by her rape, which is not. Another was Lev Arnshtam's *Zoia*, a film fable based on the arrest and execution of the famous teenaged partisan, Zoia Kosmodemianskaia.

Shostakovich wrote the music; much of the story was taken from a Stalin Prize-winning poem in 1942 by the young, soon to be famous, Margarita Aliger. Exhibited for only a month in 1944, it signalled both the culmination and the end of the cult of hatred, in the film and in general.[89] Few films were more effective in capturing the themes of hatred of the enemy and Soviet patriotism in its Ukrainian avatar than Oleksandr Dovzhenko's fiercely anti-German *The Battle for Our Soviet Ukraine* which, came out in 1943. Dovzhenko had produced several celebrated films in the 1930s on industrialization and collectivization in Ukraine. But like other creative artists who sought to show how these generally positive transformations of life also produced negative effects, he fell out of favour and his wartime masterpiece was attributed to his wife.[90]

In the battleground of emotions, the cult of hatred, designed to demonize the enemy, was counterbalanced by a celebration of basic humanitarian values as a fundamental characteristic of the Soviet people. The image of Mother Russia, carrying with it the sanctification of home and family, emerges from letters sent by soldiers to *Komsomolskaia Pravda*, selected and published by the editors. Developed further by official propaganda the theme acquired growing momentum after Stalingrad.[91] In wartime, creative artists also invoked the themes of humanism and lyricism. The inspiration for these themes was more complex, reflecting both the nature of their work and their patriotic feelings. In literature, the themes had appeared already in the first years of the fighting.[92] But they had their origins in prewar debates over the nature of socialist realism in literature and music.[93] By the thirties a shift was taking place in the direction of socialist realism in literature towards admitting the emotional responses of the individual as a legitimate component of a work of art linked to the intimate and lyrical elements. One of the most eloquent statements of this point of view was expressed by Konstantin Simonov in his essay 'Notes on Poetry: on the Rights of the Lyrical', published in *Literaturnaia Gazeta* at the very end of 1939. It was not surprising, then, that during the war he could evoke all the sentimental tenderness of a Red Army man writing to his wife that most famous of war poems, 'Wait for Me', and then spew out his fury in the story 'Kill Him!'

Some years earlier, Dmitry Shostakovich had already taken up the lyrical theme during the 'Discussion about Symphonies' of February 1935, when he spoke of symphonies as 'works of a lyrical character'. In his view, however, the First Quartet best expressed the inner life and intimate emotions of the composer. He sought to refute criticism that his work was 'formalist', meaning modern or too difficult for the average listener, by writing such works as the famous Seventh Symphony. The propaganda apparatus seized upon the work, which they dubbed the 'Leningrad Symphony', as a proudly patriotic expression of the heroic defence of the city, although Shostakovich had begun to compose it before the war broke out. The process of composition, however, continued during the war when Shostakovich remained in Leningrad for part of the siege and even served as a volunteer fireman before being evacuated to Kuibyshev. Once he had completed the symphony there, the party organized a performance in Leningrad which they recorded and broadcast over loudspeakers toward the German lines, as if to demonstrate that the city was the centre of a great culture holding out against the barbarian hordes: lyricism enrolled as the counterpoint of hating the enemy. Shostakovich continued, however, to write quartets, his second in 1944, with his third coming out a year after the war ended. The party exploited, praised and criticized him in the early postwar years. He defended himself by accepting the need for patriotic involvement – he actually called for 'ideological correctness' in music – while at the same time insisting that priority must be given to the musical values (echoing Kapitsa's views on physics) over any verbal or textual interpretation. His only concession on that score was to refer to his quartets as conveying sensations of spring-like moods and childhood, pointedly avoiding the use of the word lyrical.[94]

The cult of hatred, like some rare chemical element, possessed a short life. It had been launched by Stalin after a brief period when he vainly hoped for a strong anti-fascist movement to emerge in Germany after the outbreak of war. He encouraged individual artists and writers to pursue the theme; it then took on a life of its own in the hands of artists and writers.[95] By the end of the war, the cult of hatred became a political liability and Ehrenburg was singled out as the scapegoat. In April 1945 an article in *Pravda* by the rising star of the Agitprop Department, Georgy Aleksandrov, 'Comrade Ehrenburg Oversimplifies', signalled the end to the campaign. In the closing days of the war, it was important for Stalin to avoid driving a defeated Germany into the hands of Russia's Western allies. After an orgy of violence, inspired by revenge, the Red Army was issued instructions to maintain strict discipline in its relations with the German civilian population.[96]

What Stalin, in praising Sholokhov's 'The Science of Hatred', had called 'the current phase' of the war was over. It was characteristic of Stalin's political manipulation to make a scapegoat out of the most successful interpreter of his own ideas. Ehrenburg had become a symbol of the cult of hatred. Goebbels had singled him out in counter-propaganda as the embodiment of the Communist-Jewish conspiracy to exterminate all Germans. Stalin responded when it became politically expedient by disavowing him.[97] Others took the hint without having to be warned. The cartoons of Kukryniksy continued to portray Hitler and his entourage as shabby, pathetic and evil men, but the animal imagery faded away. At the Nuremberg Trials the trio of cartoonists sketched the accused as degenerates, but the fangs, the claws and the blood were gone. Across the Atlantic other demons were gathering.

THE PATRIARCHAL ORTHODOX CHURCH

Stalin's decision to add the Patriarchal Orthodox Church to his armoury of cultural weapons against the fascists strikes one even at this distance as extraordinary. The officially atheistic regime had subjected church and clergy to three waves of anti-religious campaigns from the moment of its inception. In addition to persecution, Stalin had welcomed and encouraged the split in the historical Patriarchal Church after the revolution, when a group of churchmen formed the Renovationist Church. They rejected Patriarch Tikhon's decree anathematizing the regime and accepted the secular authority of the state and its socio-economic policies. In 1927 a group of schismatics calling themselves the Josephite Church left the Patriarchal Church after Sergius (born Stragorodsky), the Moscow and Kolomensky district metropolitan acting as patriarch *locum tenens*, recognized the regime but not its policies.[98] The differences among them did not spare them from persecution. Two years later the Law on Religious Associations set strict conditions on the right to worship for all believers.[99] Much worse was to come.

Caught up in what became known as the Great Terror, between 1936 and 1938, the third and most extensive wave of church closings probably reflected the suppressed results of the 1937 census, which revealed that 56 per cent of the population identified themselves as believers. At the same time, about 150,000 clerical and lay officials of all the Christian faiths were arrested, half of them confined to the Gulag. The rest died or were executed, including most of the higher ranks of the clergy. Party and police officials co-ordinated their attacks right up to the outbreak of war, closing about 8,000 Orthodox places of worship and confiscating their properties. On the eve of the war, there were only 6,376 clergy in the Patriarchal Church and only four men in the hierarchy.[100] Stalin stopped short of implementing repressive policies in the western borderlands acquired under the terms of the Nazi-Soviet Pact, presumably to avoid encouraging support for German propaganda.

Under these dire conditions, Metropolitan Sergius took the bold step only twelve hours after the German invasion of calling upon the faithful to rally around the motherland. Like the head of the Academy of Sciences, he timed his appeal in advance of any public statement by a member of the ruling party or government; in his case, to be sure, he blended together nationalist and religious themes with implications for the celebration of russo-centrism. The same day, the Metropolitan of Leningrad issued a similar appeal, followed by the head of the Renovationist Church. Letters came into the Soviet authorities requesting information on the status of the church, the implication being that willingness to serve depended on an acceptable answer. Over the centuries at times of crisis – and particularly in wartime – the church had always assumed a prominent role in rallying support for government, a fact that Stalin, an old seminarian, knew only too well. Whatever the motives of the churchmen may have been, their reaction to the German invasion probably saved the Patriarchal Orthodox Church from extinction as an institution in Russian life.[101]

Later, in an epistle to the faithful in the occupied territories, Metropolitan Sergius instructed them to do nothing that would directly or indirectly give comfort to the enemy. However, the contribution of the church to the war effort went far beyond exhortations of spiritual support. It was active in raising funds to help meet a number of needs – military, charitable and medical – all connected to the war effort. The metropolitan organized collections for the Defence Fund and subscribed to the war loans. Church funds were donated to the army to purchase forty tanks to form the Dmitry Donskoi tank battalion and to the air force to finance the creation of the Alexander Nevsky squadron. Monasteries opened their doors to provide shelter and infirmaries for the wounded. The church raised funds for a variety of medical and charitable activities, ranging from providing food to assisting the families of soldiers. The total contribution in money and kind donated by the Patriarchal Orthodox Church to the war effort is estimated at 300 million rubles.[102]

Stalin responded by calling off the anti-religious campaign. After some hesitation he arranged an informal concordat with the church which led to the permanent re-establishment of the patriarchate in September 1943. Stalin appointed an NKVD general, Georgy Karpov, to head a Council on the Affairs of the Russian Orthodox Church, reporting directly to Molotov.[103] The installation of Sergius as patriarch in Moscow was a modest affair but the election of his successor, Aleksei, was attended by over 200 ecclesiastical dignitaries including the patriarchs of Antioch and Alexandria, the archbishop of Canterbury and metropolitan of North America. In his recommendations for the approval of Stalin and Molotov, Karpov included a mass of detail for the gathering of the church conference (*sobor*), ranging from the protocol at the airport to precious objects taken from museums as gifts to the patriarchs and the performers and programme of a music recital.[104]

In mapping his course for regulating church affairs, Stalin relied heavily on the advice and oversight of the NKVD. As early as 1942, Beria had suggested to Stalin that Metropolitan Sergius write a book, *The Truth about Religion in Russia*, to refute the Nazis' claim that they were liberating Christians from Bolshevik atheism. Under the scrutiny of the council, churches which had opened illegally were recognized and petitions for new churches were received. But the council, backed up by Molotov, was chary in its responses, allowing approval of only 6 per cent of the petitions. On the other hand, Stalin, characteristically, was not always willing to let the NKVD have its way. For reasons that are not clear, Stalin allowed the Renovationist Church to wither away, rather than following Karpov's advice to abolish it outright and incorporate its clergy into the Patriarchal Orthodox Church.[105]

In negotiations with Metropolitan Sergius, Stalin also departed from the views of his advisers by offering to open seminaries which would enable the church to train priests for future generations. In another unexpected concession, he gave permission for priests inducted into the army to return to their parishes.[106] From Stalin's perspective, however, the greatest service of the church was as an ally in the struggle over the loyalty of parishioners in the occupied territories of the western borderlands. The government relied primarily on the partisans and party organizers to maintain a Soviet presence in the occupied territories, but the church was useful in combating the defection of the clergy, especially in the Ukraine, and in resisting the proliferation of schismatics who opposed both the Nazis and the communists.[107] In the struggle for influence over the population of the western borderlands the church faced a new and challenging dilemma.

In 1940 after the incorporation of Lithuania, Latvia and Estonia as national republics into the USSR, Bishop Sergius (born Voskresensky) had been appointed metropolitan of Lithuania and exarch of Latvia and Estonia to heal the schism in the church. Their annexation increased dramatically the number of churches in the USSR to 3,021, of which about 3,000 were located in the newly acquired territories. Before 1940 there were no monasteries in the Soviet Union; the annexations brought in sixty-four.[108] Thus, when the Germans swept through the Baltic republics, Western Belarus, Western Ukraine and Bessarabia, they took possession of the overwhelming majority of the existing Russian Orthodox churches. The metropolitan remained in Riga, presumably with the sanction of Metropolitan Sergius of Moscow. He obtained permission from the German authorities to organize the administration of the church in the territories of the Russian Republic occupied by Army Group Centre. His official mission was to restore the Patriarchal Orthodox Church to its previous position, bringing the faith to a generation raised under the atheistic propaganda of the Soviet state. He sent out the first group of Riga 'missionaries' in August 1941; over the next three years, they succeeded in increasing the number of churches in the occupied territories tenfold, serviced by 175 priests. Their guiding idea of restricting their activities solely to religious life was, to be sure, compromised by the pressure of the Nazi officials to give religious propaganda an anti-Bolshevik direction and to recruit individuals for labour service in Germany or as members of the Russian Liberation Army composed of Red Army POWs organized and led by General Andrei Vlasov, a hero of the defence of Moscow who had gone over to the Germans. The extent to which the church resisted is a matter of some dispute.[109]

In the liberated territories of Ukraine, Stalin was personally involved in recruiting the church as part of the campaign to restore Soviet authority. Following the Yalta agreements which recognized the incorporation of Western Ukraine into the Ukrainian SSR, the oblast Agitprop Committee in newly occupied Galicia issued a 'short thesis'. In comparing the historical significance of the Patriarchal Orthodox Church and the Ukrainian Greek Catholic Church, it praised the progressive role of the Orthodox Church in unifying the eastern Slavs and, in the Second World War, of preserving Ukraine from Polonization and Romanization. It condemned the Ukrainian Greek Catholic Church for striving to separate Ukraine from the Orthodox East and the Soviet Union which 'would have meant handing it over to the capitalist West'.[110] In April, Stalin informed Khrushchev of the need to mobilize the Patriarchal Orthodox Church in the struggle against the Roman Catholic and Uniate churches, which had gained ground under the German occupation.[111] In a major step towards fulfilling these orders, an Orthodox eparchy divided into four parishes was re-established in Lvov (L'viv). A bishop was to be appointed from among Ukrainians and to be given the right to organize missionary activities. An initiative group in the Uniate Church was to announce a break with the Vatican. The Polish Autocephalous Church was to be disbanded and united with the Moscow Patriarch. The Mukhachevo Eparchy in the Zakarpatsky region, Mukhachersko-Pushevskoi (Zakarpatsky), was to be placed under Moscow's jurisdiction with the approval of the Serbian Church, which previously had jurisdiction over it.[112]

The implementation of these instructions was accompanied by extensive repression. A massive propaganda attack aimed to portray the metropolitan of the Ukrainian Greek Catholic Church, Andrei Sheptyts'kyi, as an ally of fascism and an instrument of Anglo-Saxon imperialism. Arrests of Metropolitan Yosef Slipyy and other leaders of the Ukrainian Greek Catholic hierarchy were carried out as the Initiative Group joined the campaign of the NKVD to bring pressure on its clergy to convert. By October 1945, 800 priests had joined the Initiative Group. Winning over the laity was complicated by the nationalist underground resistance and the massive Soviet counter-insurgency. From 1944 to 1951, the number of Ukrainians who were deported as the result of co-operating with the anti-Soviet resistance ranges from a Soviet account of 203,662 to an émigré estimate of about 500,000.[113] In any case, the Ukrainian Greek Catholic Church was broken at the end.

Stalin also recognized the value of playing the religious card in foreign policy. With his blessing, a delegation of the Orthodox Church visited Bulgaria. Karpov duly reported the favourable results to Stalin in great detail. The military and civil authorities of the newly established government coalition of parties, the Fatherland Front, expressed their gratitude to the Russian people for their liberation from the Turks in 1878 and the fascists in 1944. Some sceptical local priests were reassured by the April proclamation of the Sobor in Moscow. The re-establishment of ecclesiastical relations between the two countries was described as giving the lie to the provocative distortions of the position of the church in the Soviet Union. Karpov indicated that the delegation benefited from the great authority of the head of the delegation, Metropolitan Stefan of Pskov, who during the visit advanced the idea of *slavianstvo*, the unification of the Slavic peoples under the patronage of Russia. The remark was significant, Karpov noted, because the archbishop had been known earlier as an anglophile. On the basis of information received by the delegation, the head of the council recommended a secret subsidy be advanced to the patriarch of Constantinople, who was in financial straits. This would 'forestall a step by England which once it learned of the Patriarch's need would exploit the opportunity to strengthen its position'.[114] With Stalin's approval, the patriarch restored old ties to the Anglican Church. In another response to the patriarch's request, Stalin approved his proposal to send a delegation led by him to Palestine, Egypt, Syria and Lebanon as a prelude to organizing an international church conference in Moscow of all Christian faiths except the Roman Catholics. But Stalin made it an 'absolute condition' that the delegation be accompanied by 'a personal guard in civilian dress'.[115]

In Stalin's most ambitious attempt to employ the church as an instrument of Soviet foreign policy, he endorsed Karpov's plan in co-operation with Patriarch Aleksei to summon an Eighth Ecumenical Council of all Orthodox churches and to make the Moscow patriarch the equivalent of the Roman pontiff. But canonical problems raised by the Patriarch of Constantinople doomed the project. The fall-back position was to summon a pan-Orthodox conference in Moscow in June 1948. By accepting the dictates of conference, the Orthodox churches of the 'people's democracies' became subordinate to the patriarch in Moscow.[116] The Patriarchal Orthodox Church reaped no rewards. Stalin kept a strict control on the church's activities, wielding the instruments of surveillance to patrol the limits of church autonomy, similar to those he employed in dealing with the other cultural groups that had supported him in the war.[117]

SLAVIC SOLIDARITY

The idea of Slavic solidarity began to surface in party ideology just before the outbreak of the Great Fatherland War. It was part of a shift in Soviet ideology on two levels; first, toward reviving the historic and ethnic links among the three Slavic nations of the Soviet Union; and second, toward accommodating national differences within the international communist movement. In appealing to Slavic solidarity within the Soviet Union, Stalin was once again reaching back into Russian history for a long-standing if ambivalent idea and then reinterpreting it for his own purposes. In responding to Hitler's offer to divide Poland in the negotiations leading to the Nazi-Soviet Pact in 1939, Stalin grasped the idea that Soviet intervention could be justified and legitimized by the claim that it was necessary in order to protect the Belarusian and Ukrainian populations oppressed under Polish rule and exposed in the war with Germany.[118] Initially, his idea was to organize elections of deputies representing the Polish, Belarusian and Ukrainian populations to assemblies which would petition for the creation of a Polish Soviet Socialist Republic and incorporation into the Soviet Belarusian and Ukrainian republics.[119] He quickly reversed himself, redrawing the lines of partition between German-occupied Poland and the Soviet territories so that only the Belarusian and Ukrainian populations would be incorporated into the Soviet Union. There would not be a Polish Soviet Republic.[120] This meant, in effect, accepting the Curzon Line proposed in 1919 by the British foreign minister and subsequently restated by Stalin at Yalta to justify the postwar boundaries of Poland. In the negotiations that followed, the two powers arranged for an exchange of populations that would cement the ethnic boundaries of the Soviet Union and bury the Piedmont principle (see above, p. 60) represented by a Western Ukraine under Polish control.[121]

The first step to link Slavic solidarity to the Comintern was taken in February 1941, when members of the Central Committee secretariat, including Zhdanov, Andreev, Malenkov and Dimitrov, agreed that the principal aim of the newly organized Comintern schools should be 'to train for the most part cadres from the Slavic countries (Bulgaria, Yugoslavia, Poland and Czechoslovakia). In the curriculum: the emphasis is to be on the study of one's own country, one's own party, their problems, how to fight the enemy on one's home territory.' Zhdanov acknowledged that 'We got off the track on the national question. [We] failed to pay sufficient attention to national aspects.' In sum: 'our "internationalists" have to be trained.'[122]

Once the war broke out, Stalin adopted the pose of a champion of the Slavs.[123] By publicly invoking Slavic solidarity against the Germans, Stalin simply added another emotional dimension to his eclectic wartime propaganda. The premise of Slavic solidarity ran directly counter to notions of both international proletarian unity and Soviet patriotism. But even the Comintern organs came out rather shamelessly in favour of a special racial affinity of the Slavs against German expansionism, 'one of the most constant phenomena in the history of Europe'.[124] In appealing to the shared cultural values of Slavic people against the Germans, Stalin sought to avoid the obvious danger of reviving Pan-Slavism in its pre-revolutionary imperialist form. His recourse to Slavic solidarity as a theme in Soviet wartime ideology had two aims. It was, first of all, a counterfoil to Nazi racist propaganda which identified the Slavic peoples as second only to the Jews as the race enemies of the Aryan type, and promised their destruction. Second, it was a political weapon in combating 1,000 years of German expansion and cultural influences in Eastern Europe, and reversing it in favour of a Slavic advance to the west and – more importantly – Russian-Soviet cultural hegemony.

To propagate the idea of Slavic solidarity, the Soviet government sponsored the formation of an All-Slav Committee in September 1941. It supervised national radio broadcasts, held two congresses in Moscow during the war and a third in Belgrade in 1946. At the second congress in April 1942, the monthly periodical *Slaviane* was founded with a programme to rally all the Slavic people against fascism and recall the historic struggle against German imperialism.[125] The leadership of the congress was mediocre and the organization lacked any political muscle, as the Yugoslav communist, Milovan Djilas, was quick to notice. But there was a scattering of luminous intellectuals in its executive, including, among the Russians, Dmitry Shostakovich, Aleksandr Fadeev and Aleksei Tolstoy; among the Poles, Wanda Wasilewska, who later became a key figure in the restoration of the Polish Communist Party; and several Czech scholars.[126] In its many activities the committee emphasized Slavic humanism as contrasted with the predatory and militaristic character of its enemies both Eastern and Western. In his opening address, Aleksei Tolstoy 'rejected the old ideology of Pan-Slavism' as reactionary and contrary to the spirit of equality among the Slavic nations.

The passionate appeal for Slavic solidarity stressed the need to avoid crossing over to racism in reverse. This point was driven home by Aleksandrov in his remarks to the first congress of the Academy of Sciences held during the war. He too rejected Pan-Slavism but stressed the need to unmask the German aggression of the nineteenth as well as the twentieth centuries and to illuminate the struggles of the Ukrainian, Belarusian and Great Russian peoples against the efforts of Germany to destroy the Slavic peoples and establish German hegemony in Slavic lands.[127] It was important to mobilize the historians in particular. From the rostrum of the academy, Evgeny Tarle set the tone by reviewing and denouncing the distortions by Nazi historians of Germany's expansion in Eastern Europe from the Middle Ages to the present.[128] That these sentiments expressed Stalin's own views on the need for a Russian-Polish alliance emerged clearly from the record of his extraordinary two-hour conversation with the Polish-American Catholic priest Father Stanislaus Orlemanski in late April 1944.[129] In lecturing Orlemanski, Stalin appealed to the lessons of history, as he frequently did. He stressed the need for Slavic – in this case Russian-Polish – solidarity against a revival of German power in the future. This led him to argue for a reconstruction of the Polish government, one friendly to the Soviet Union. He concluded that the Polish people would surely not wish to welcome back those who had led them to disaster in 1939.

In practical terms, Stalin sought to use Slavic solidarity both in order to bolster political relations with the borderlands that had been for so long the contested zone between the Russians and the Germans and to weaken the influence of alternative sources of cultural dependency, in particular the French. The first step in this campaign was to encourage the leaders of Slavic states to expel the Germans bodily from Eastern Europe and to advance the Slavic frontiers and the movement of populations from east to west. In his dealings with the Poles over the postwar frontiers, Stalin revived the idea, first advanced by the Russians during the Seven Years' War and restated by the tsarist government in 1915, of expelling the Germans from East Prussia and annexing all or part of the province. As compensation, the Poles would be moved to the west. Stalin spoke of restoring the old Polish lands up to the Oder, thus reconstructing Poland as it had existed under the medieval Piast kings; this, in his mind, would be an anti-German Poland to replace the multi-national Poland of the Jagiellonian dynasty built by incorporating the Belarusians and

Ukrainians and repeatedly aspiring to a Dnieper frontier at the expense of the Russians.[130]

In an unusually frank and emotional speech in December 1943, honouring the Czech statesman Edvard Beneš, Stalin toasted the 'neo-Slavs', referring to the pre-revolutionary intellectuals who had favoured the complete independence of small Slavic countries, unlike the Pan-Slavs. He then turned his wrath on the Germans. 'I hate Germans,' he declared. 'Slavs footed the bill for the First World War and also the Second World War is being solved at their expense . . . But this time we will break the Germans so that never again will their attacks against the Slavs be repeated. We are attempting to make them harmless.'[131]

Early in the war, Stalin even toyed with the idea of a series of Slavic federations in Eastern Europe, one including the Czechs and Poles and the other the South Slavs. When the Poles resisted Stalin's offers to reconstruct their country, he torpedoed the west Slavic federation. During the war he expressed to the Yugoslavs his approval of their plans to create a federation with Bulgaria, but urged them to proceed slowly and, incredibly, to adopt the Austro-Hungarian model of a dualist state! He showed an interest in closer relations between the Yugoslavs and Albanians, making the extraordinary claim that 'the Albanians were also Slavs in origin'.[132] Stalin also pursued the expulsion of the Germans from the south Slavic states, particularly from Yugoslavia, and he sustained his interest in a south Slavic federation until after the war, when Tito's independent attitude led him to turn against that as well. These several abortive attempts to construct transnational Slavic associations in Eastern Europe suggest that Stalin sought to tap the genuine emotional force of fraternal relations among Slavic countries in order to raise a bulwark against a German revival and forge a powerful bond between these nations and the Soviet Union. Stalin was successful in exploiting feelings of Slavic solidarity in the peace negotiations after the war against the Germans, Hungarians, Italians and Greeks.[133]

Although the break with Tito doomed the All-Slav Committee, the Soviet policy of promoting Russian language and culture and the historic ties among Slavs persisted. Its legacy was mixed, because a certain result of the Russian cultural penetration of Eastern Europe was the sharp decline and almost complete disappearance of the strong prewar German orientation among the intelligentsia and the commercial-professional elements in the area. This cultural roll-back had nothing to do with Marxism-Leninism – quite the contrary in fact. But it did have a great deal to do with the consolidation of Soviet power in the western borderlands against the threat of a German political revival.

INTERNATIONAL COMMUNISM

The great traumas of the thirties had left the original Bolshevik ideology in tatters. Stalin's crude dialectics of intensifying state power and class struggle as the prelude to their disappearance made a mockery of Leninism. His assault on the Old Bolshevik leadership as spies and saboteurs shattered the myth of 1917. His sudden turnabout to embrace Nazi Germany as an ally disillusioned thousands of foreign communists. The German invasion was for Stalin an ideological windfall. Here was a cause around which he could construct a revised belief system.

The announcement of the Nazi-Soviet Pact passed like a tremor through the body of the international communist movement. Tactical flexibility was one thing, but to many communists a deal with Hitler was a betrayal. There had been almost no political preparation and only the most astute and cynical could have detected the faint signals in Soviet diplomacy that Stalin was ready to strike a bargain with the Nazis. Trotsky and his supporters had a field day at Stalin's expense. Trotsky's analysis did not, however, deny Stalin the right to make deals in the name of expediency. What he objected to was Stalin's proclaiming ideological solidarity with fascism. Moreover, he exposed the paradoxical character of Stalin's counter-revolutionary policy at home and his progressive policy in partitioned Poland, where he pushed the expropriation of the landlords and the nationalization of industry.[134] Widespread resignations in the local parties poured in, including of many prominent intellectuals. The revival of a flagging international communist movement after the German invasion was preceded by two years of uncertainty and confusion after the signing of the Nazi-Soviet Pact.

The communist parties of Europe were thrown off balance by the sudden reversal of Soviet policy toward Nazi Germany. They had not been forewarned, to say nothing of being consulted. Without clear-cut instructions defining a new line, they groped their way toward solutions reflecting local conditions. Their reactions took one of two basic directions, a trend that continued to develop sub rosa during the war and broke out into the open in the postwar years. The French and Italian parties, personified by Maurice Thorez and Palmiro Togliatti, re-affirmed the anti-fascist line in their own countries while at the same time supporting the pact as a political necessity for the Soviet Union. Initially, the French communists greeted the pact as a giant step toward peace which enhanced rather than excluded an Anglo-French-Soviet pact. They urged the British and French military delegations, which had been negotiating in Moscow with their Soviet counterparts, to reach an immediate agreement. They were uncompromising in their denunciation of fascism in general and Nazism in particular. This did not sit well with Moscow. On 1 September the Comintern Executive took the French and Thorez personally to task for having recommended incorrectly an unqualified support for the government of Édouard Daladier and Georges Bonnet.[135] Taking a more radical position articulated by Tito, the Yugoslav communists equally condemned both the fascists and democratic countries for unleashing a new imperialist war. They foresaw the outcome as a replay of the First World War and eagerly prepared for a revolutionary transformation of Yugoslav society.

The Comintern Executive was baffled by the '*exceptional difficulty*' of adopting the right tactical position and appealed for Stalin's '*immediate assistance*' (italics in the original). Stalin obliged: the new line stated unequivocally that 'the present war was an imperialist and unjust war in which the bourgeois of all the belligerent countries were equally guilty . . . the division of the capitalist countries into fascist and democratic has now lost its previous meaning'. The directive of the Comintern Executive singled out the parties of France, England, the USA and Belgium as those needing to correct their political line. Many of the other local parties, including those of Scandinavia and Canada, were also slow by Comintern standards in falling into line: the Comintern was still complaining in late October about their tardiness or reluctance to accept the new conditions.[136]

The Comintern instructions to the communist parties in Europe were to avoid engaging in either resistance to or open collaboration with the Nazi occupation forces. They could not be allowed to enter the fight against Stalin's ally, Hitler. That would, after all, risk antagonizing the Nazis at a time when Stalin was counting on their endorsement of his expansion in Eastern Europe. But neither could the local communist parties be encouraged to form any kind of political alliance with an ideological enemy that was bent on destroying their influence in Europe. In this short period of the pact, the delicate balancing act was difficult to maintain; the dangers were most striking in the case of Yugoslavia. Dimitrov urged Tito to be cautious in his revolutionary ambitions, a refrain he was destined to repeat many times over the following few years. Yet at the same time, the Comintern also gave clear signals that the Yugoslav party was in high favour due to the success of its clandestine organization in surviving the initial shock of the Nazi occupation. The contradictions continued to exist until the German invasion of the Soviet Union and were then replaced by another set.[137]

The condemnation of both sides in the imperialist war was an uncertain guide to action in the extremely dangerous circumstances created by the Nazi invasion and occupation policies. Among the communists, there were individual acts of resistance to the Germans. For example, in 1939, Władysław Gomułka and a few comrades escaped from a Polish prison and remained in the underground. In France Auguste Lecœur helped lead a strike in the spring of 1941 against the German occupation forces. But these were isolated incidents that only assumed importance in postwar polemics when both men, accused of national deviation, defended themselves as communist-patriots.[138] More serious was the plight of communist parties in small neutral nations. In Comintern and party literature, there were vague discussions about the rights of small nations to defend themselves against imperialist aggression. But, as we have seen, this form of resistance was really designed to justify the territorial expansion of the Soviet Union along its vulnerable western frontiers. The model was the Baltic states (see above, p. 38). It had nothing to do with mobilizing mass action and still less with revolution. The Comintern's anti-nationalist line, which was not even redeemed in the eyes of many communist militants by an active defeatism as the prelude to a revolutionary upsurge like that in Russia in 1917, had no appeal outside the ranks of hardcore Stalinists.

When it appeared that communist defeatism was contributing to the rapid victory of the Wehrmacht, especially in France, Stalin began to reconsider the usefulness of maintaining a homogenous international line reflecting 'the *parochial* interests' of the Comintern. In conversations with Thorez and Togliatti, Dimitrov raised the question of discontinuing the activities of the Comintern Executive 'as a *leadership body* for Com[munist] parties for the immediate future, granting *full independence* to the individual parties of Communists in their respective countries, guided by a communist programme but resolving their own concrete problems in their own manner, in accordance with the conditions in their countries and themselves bearing responsibility for the decisions and actions'. He even foreshadowed the creation of a Cominform by proposing 'an organ of *informational and ideological and political assistance for communist parties*'.[139] The whole idea of encouraging national communism was not only bold, but, as postwar developments would show, dangerous as well.

The shock of the German invasion, coming at a low point in the morale and organizational work of the Comintern, had an electrifying effect on the communist parties. Stalin's appeal for international help was not issued in the name of proletarian solidarity but of 'all freedom-loving people against fascism'. With those words he appeared to eliminate any and all barriers to co-operation among anti-fascists, whatever their class loyalty or party affiliations. For a year after the invasion, the Comintern Executive was still fumbling in search of a more precise formula to instruct the local parties; the Soviet leadership gave no clear doctrinal guidance. The local parties, in a repetition of events leading up to the popular front in 1934, began to take their own initiatives. Not surprisingly, the old tendencies re-emerged in accentuated form. What emerged from Stalin's general pronouncements was a new policy, the national or united front that proved more innovative in its open-ended appeal and organizational flexibility than the popular front. Its components were: first, partisan warfare in occupied Europe to pin down the enemy's armed forces; second, the broadest possible mobilization of society in support of the armed resistance and diversionary actions in the enemy's rear; third, the organization of all anti-fascist forces into a patriotic movement having auxiliary units for intellectuals, youth and women with the active participation and if possible direct guidance by Communist Party members; and fourth, the maintenance of the separate clandestine organization of the party. Almost all traces of the rhetoric of class struggle and social revolution disappeared from the communists' public discourse. The existence of the tightly knit clandestine party organization did not prevent all class co-operation on an unprecedented scale. The Comintern Executive hesitated to spell out all the political implications of the new strategy. But following the rapid German advance in the summer of 1942, Stalin's appeal for a second front and Churchill's first trip to Moscow, the contours of the

Grand Alliance became clearer. The Comintern publicized the long-term implications of the wartime alliance for the emergence of a new international system to guarantee the peace in the postwar world.[140]

The immediate goal was to weaken the Nazi war effort, to relieve pressure on the eastern front and to prevent the population from sinking into apathy or collaborating with the enemy. The Soviet leaders and the Comintern discouraged planning for the long term as a distraction from the overriding tasks of military victory. But they could not stop local communists from thinking about it. In fact, by extolling national resistance both in the Soviet Union and throughout the rest of Europe, the Soviet leadership encouraged local parties to fashion a programme best suited to local circumstances. The Soviet Union itself took steps to further the process of individualizing or domesticating the local parties in symbol if not yet in fact. It created special military units of volunteers from East European countries that were named after national heroes who had ironically won their glory in fighting the Russians. The example was taken up by the Communists throughout Europe. In France, the partisan units were called Francs-Tireurs et Partisans Français, echoing the name of guerrilla forces in the Franco-Prussian War. In Greece, they were called Andartes, in Italy the Garibaldi Brigades. It was a far cry from the International Brigades in Spain, who were named after communist heroes. Although the separate identity and discipline of the party was presumably adequate to protect against the infection of nationalism, emotional identification with the nation as a whole and the glories of its history proved stronger in many cases than the party leadership anticipated.

The policy of the national front opened the way for the growth of mass communist parties in Europe. In size and political activities, they surpassed the achievements of the popular front. To meet their equal, it was necessary to go back to the era of the splits in the old social democratic parties of Europe after the Russian Revolution and the end of the First World War. The most spectacular gains were registered in France, Italy, Yugoslavia, Greece and Czechoslovakia; in the Far East the Chinese communists had been practising a form of national front since 1937, and their numbers too had expanded greatly. But the success of the new tactics could not obscure another set of contradictions that they inspired, no less profound than that of the period of the pact. To put it bluntly, the idea of all-out resistance of an insurrectionary type was incompatible in most countries with the idea of a broad-based political alliance with elements of the peasantry and bour-geoisie that feared the destructive impact of insurrection on life and prop-erty. Where insurrection was muted, for one reason or another, as in France and Czechoslovakia, political co-operation along a very broad spectrum was generally successful. Where insurrection was the watchword, as in Greece and Yugoslavia, it was not.

The French and Yugoslav parties represented the opposite ends of the spectrum of variations within the national front. The French communists recognized the authority of the government-in-exile led by General Charles de Gaulle, a nationalist, and accepted two minor posts in his cabinet. By sharing ministerial responsibility, they traded freedom of action for political respectability. This did not prevent them from supporting active resistance movements. They helped found and sought to control the administration organ of the internal resistance, the Conseil National de la Résistance (CNR). But power-sharing meant that they had opted for what might be called the Spanish or parliamentary path to a new form of social republic, or, as it was to be called, a popular democracy.[141] This approach resurrected an idea first articulated by Stalin during the Spanish Civil War.

The Yugoslav interpretation of the national front was by contrast insur-rectionist. The Yugoslav communists refused to accept the authority of the royal government in exile. They went so far as to form their own de facto provisional government at Jajce in 1942. The communist-dominated National Liberation Committee in Yugoslavia included a number of prominent non-communists, but unlike the French CNR it recruited them as individuals and not as representatives of other resistance organizations. In contrast to a united resistance in France, there was civil war between the leading resist-ance movements in Yugoslavia. Almost from the very outset of the fighting in Yugoslavia, Tito and his associates committed themselves to a revolu-tionary course. That is, the national partisan war against the Germans and Italians was at the same time a social struggle aimed at taking power at the liberation. Given the peculiar historical circumstances in Yugoslavia, it was difficult to separate the two. This was not the case in France. Stalin may have reproached Tito and the Yugoslav communists for their overly zealous ideo-logical pronouncements and political assertiveness. Yet, at the same time, he strongly encouraged partisan war à outrance. In Yugoslavia this position was paradoxical and Stalin was never able to resolve the contradiction.[142]

Within the Comintern, both the French and Yugoslav models had their advocates. But the Yugoslav partisans were, throughout 1942 and 1943 up to the dissolution of the Comintern, the darlings of the international communist movement. In the absence of a second front, their style of guerrilla warfare offered the only hope of drawing off German divisions from the eastern front. During the spring and summer of 1942, the Soviet position was desperate. The Red Army was in headlong retreat that only ended at the Volga. Soviet diplomats urged the governments-in-exile to follow the Yugoslav example and unleash a general European insurrection that would force the Western allies to land on the continent.[143] The Yugoslavs were the only active guerrilla movement with any potential for large-scale operations, and the Soviet and Comintern press held them up as an example for all other European resistance movements. At times the Comintern placed them almost on a par with the Red Army. Their achievements were exaggerated, giving the impression that it was only a matter of emulating the will power exercised by the Yugoslav communists to mobilize the masses in their own countries and rise up against the occupiers. Even geography was unimportant. The Yugoslavs had demonstrated that partisan warfare 'was entirely possible and had a chance for success'. Success presumably meant the expulsion of the occupation forces, a dangerous fantasy which Stalin would later regret having encouraged.[144]

As part of its insurrectionist strategy, the Soviet government was determined to destroy illusions of stability within occupied Europe. It put heavy pressure on the Czech government-in-exile to demonstrate its worth as an ally through a blood sacrifice that would galvanize the passive Czech population into armed resistance. In May 1942, President Edvard Beneš responded reluctantly by ordering a specially trained team from London to carry out the assassination of Reinhard Heydrich, head of the Gestapo and the protector of Bohemia and Moravia. The killing touched off massive German reprisals, as Beneš had feared. The Comintern was exultant that the easy-going life in Prague had ended. The Germans felt themselves to be in an armed camp, while the Czech nation was united as never before. The world finally knew of the 'touching self-sacrifice hidden in the Czech people'. The Comintern interpreted the flight of many young Czechs from Prague as a move to join the resistance: 'One form of resistance leads to another.' Everywhere in Europe, passivity was the enemy.[145]

After the victory at Stalingrad and the dissolution of the Comintern, two events that may be more closely connected than we suspect, the insurrectionary theme faded from the communist press. But it continued to burn white hot in Yugoslavia and flared up from time to time elsewhere – as in Slovakia in 1944 – to embarrass the Soviet Union. It was one thing to launch an insurrection in order to relieve the pressure on a retreating Red Army. It was another thing to launch it as the Red Army was advancing in order to claim a share in the liberation. But having once let the genie of insurrection out of the bottle, it was difficult for Stalin to recapture it.

Although the insurrectionary spirit got dampened down, the long-range political aims of the resistance remained constant in Moscow's eyes. The Comintern pressed hard to prevent the consolidation of a mass base for fascism in the occupied countries. The smallest sign of resistance was given prominence, even magnified, in order to demonstrate that the 'new order' of Hitler lacked any social foundations. At all costs, it was necessary for the Soviet Union to dispel the illusion so sedulously cultivated by Goebbels that this was a war of civilized Europe against Bolshevism. In the early years of the war, the Comintern and Soviet press made a special effort to discredit Vidkun Quisling's puppet regime in Norway. It had no military or strategic significance for the Soviet Union. But 'Quisling' had become synonymous with a collaborator. The Norwegian Church's opposition to him was a valued proof that 'civilization' was not on the side of the Nazis.[146]

The size of the partisan movements outside the Soviet Union remains a subject of dispute. Estimates of the active participants in the fighting vary greatly. It was difficult to arrive at a generally accepted definition of a partisan. Was he or she an armed fighter involved full time in combat against the occupier? What about the auxiliary services that were called upon only occasionally, such as medical, communications, intelligence? In most areas, the number of partisans in the field at any one time fluctuated over time and in reaction to policies of the occupation forces. There was a dramatic jump in the number of those living *en clandestinité* – which is still different from being a partisan – after the introduction of the Nazi labour drafts in 1942. In order to escape forced service in German factories, tens of thousands of European youths went into hiding. Some joined the partisans. While the Soviet Union pressed vigorously for an expansion of partisan warfare, the Western powers were sceptical of the military effectiveness of large, badly

armed bands of irregulars. They much preferred the work of trained intelligence operators, clandestine radio contacts, networks for retrieving
downed airmen. But as liberation approached there was a rush to join the
partisans as the fence-sitters jumped to the winning side. These last-minute
resisters ran many fewer risks after the opening of a second front and the
approach of the Red Army to the 1939 borders of the Soviet Union.

The military contribution of the partisans is a controversial issue, but
their political significance was undeniable. In Eastern Europe partisan
warfare was the principal means of conducting the struggle for control of
the postwar governments. The communist parties were particularly well
suited to expand their size and influence under wartime conditions. By
virtue of their tightly knit, semi-clandestine organization and their militant
spirit nourished by strikes and demonstrations, the communists readily
adopted an underground resistance mentality and engaged in diversionist
activities. These qualities appealed in particular to youths who were driven
into the resistance by the Nazi labour drafts and the reprisals inflicted on
the civilian population by the occupation forces in response to partisan
attacks and individual acts of terrorism.

The strategy of the national front gave the communists enormous tactical
flexibility and enabled them to break out of the isolation imposed by the Nazi-
Soviet Pact. They succeeded in bringing together under their direct or indirect control substantial elements of the military and civil resistance in
Yugoslavia, Greece, Slovakia, northern Italy, France, Belgium, Albania,
northern China and Korea. Although they failed in Poland it was not for lack
of effort. Tens of thousands of non-communists served under their command
in these countries. This is not to deny the existence of large nationalist resistance movements in these countries, particularly in Poland, Yugoslavia, Greece
and China. But the communists were able to build a reputation – based in part
on real achievement and in part on myth – that they were the first and best
resisters. This gave them an enormous psychological advantage at liberation.

In addition to the parliamentary and insurrectionist tendencies, there was
a third variation of the national front that the Comintern sketched out during
the early years of the war. This applied to the fascist dictatorships themselves,
to Germany and Italy and their satellites, especially Hungary and Romania
where in the early years of the war there were no resistance movements. The
object here was to overthrow the leadership by a combination of forces

involving the masses but also including elements of the ruling circles, especially within the army. In the case of Germany, this approach elicited virtually no response at all from within the country. In his early wartime speeches, Stalin had sought to distinguish the German people from the regime and the Comintern picked up this theme. But hopes that the small remnants of the German Communist Party could re-establish some contacts with the working class and conduct acts of sabotage and diversion that might swell into an anti-war movement were never fulfilled. And the Comintern tacitly admitted it.[147] The prospect was only slightly more promising in the Soviet Union where small parties of communists and exiles made contact with German officers and soldiers in the POW camps. The process of organizing a national front in exile was painfully slow and its history belongs more properly in an analysis of Stalin's planning for postwar Germany.

In Italy and Hungary, the Comintern appealed to traditional elements in the ruling classes to abandon the fascist leadership and break with Nazi Germany as the only way to preserve national independence against German imperialism. The object was to encourage a separate peace that would break up the Axis front. In Italy the Comintern took heart from the news that there were three groups of opposition to Mussolini within his own camp: the monarchists, the Catholic conservatives and even 'part of the fascist party'. There was evidence that representatives of 'the fascist opposition' had met clandestinely in Milan with representatives of the liberals, Catholic republicans, socialists and communists. They had hammered out a programme to pull Italy out of the war, break with Germany, restore constitutional guarantees, establish civil liberties, revoke racist legislation and purge the fascists. Broadcasting from Radio Moscow, Togliatti called for overthrowing the fascists to save Italy from the catastrophe that was sure to come with Hitler's defeat. At the same time, he admitted that the partisan movement, largely confined to Venezia Giulia where it could co-operate with the Yugoslavs, 'still bears [in 1943] a sporadic and insufficiently broad character'.[148] The implication of Togliatti's message was that while the Italian Communists were doing their best to organize a mass movement against fascism they would accept a palace coup backed by the army and popular support in order to take Italy out of the war.

The Hungarian communists pinned their hopes on the army and the more traditional anti-German elements in the aristocracy who favoured a more independent Hungarian foreign policy. They too detected signs of a growing discontent among the liberals, the small peasants and the Christian and social democratic parties who resisted anti-Semitic legislation. In urging a separate peace, the communists appealed to the national pride of Hungary and its thousand-year history of struggles for independence. But their hopes that Hungary would become the first government to break with the Axis faded rapidly. They were forced to admit in 1943 that even 'in the working class the tendency to passivity and *attentisme* still prevails'.[149]

As spokeswoman for the Romanian communists, Ana Pauker found nothing to celebrate in the domestic politics of her country. This was ironic because within eighteen months, in August 1944, Romania would actually follow the third variation sketched by the Comintern for destroying a fascist regime: a palace coup with the support of all the major non-fascist parties, including the communists. But Pauker was a dyed-in-the-wool sectarian for whom this solution had no appeal up to that point in the summer of 1944.[150]

War had dramatically increased the range of political action available to the communists. But paradoxically, the variety of possible courses of action condemned the Comintern to irrelevance. By early 1943, its existence as an organizing centre appeared increasingly problematic. In May Molotov, Dimitrov and Dmitry Manuilsky discussed the future of the organization. Presumably, the initiative on taking such a major decision as its dissolution came from Stalin. Once Dimitrov and Manuilsky had prepared a draft resolution to that effect, Stalin explained the rationale. In two sentences, he dismissed the international ethos of decades and the authority of Marx and Lenin: 'Experience has shown that one cannot have [an international] centre for all countries. This became evident in Marx's lifetime, in Lenin's and today.'[151] He proposed instead wide consultation with European and Asian leaders like Mao in China. He carefully monitored the editing process. At a meeting of the Politburo, he expanded his earlier statement, adding that different national parties had different tasks: the German and Italian to overthrow their governments, the Soviet, American and British (*sic*) to support their governments. He admitted to an error in thinking that Moscow had the resources to direct the movement in all countries. Dimitrov noted that another reason for dissolution not mentioned in the resolution was to deprive the enemy of the 'false accusation' that the Comintern was the agent of a foreign state.[152] For Stalin the emerging 'pluralism' must have appeared as one more reason to confirm his long-standing doubts about the usefulness of the organization as a co-ordinating body.

On 23 May 1943, Moscow announced the dissolution of the Comintern. Stalin explained that this would demolish the lies of Goebbels's propaganda about communist subversion and facilitate the co-operation of all antifascist forces. No doubt the move was calculated in part to reassure the Western allies. In fact, the news was received with relief among some circles in Britain and the USA, though many remained sceptical that anything had really changed. In fact, the move enabled Stalin to score a propaganda victory while ridding himself of an organization that had caused him little but trouble. He had already transferred many of its functions to the Foreign Department of the Central Committee, the so-called 'ghost Comintern'. Henceforth, his relations with the communist parties were placed on a bilateral basis. This gave him greater flexibility and, he must have expected, greater control over them.[153] In this latter expectation he was to be sorely disappointed.

The Comintern organ, playing to a different audience, emphasized the 'demands of greater flexibility and self-sufficiency of its sections in the matter of deciding the problems facing them'. The workers' movement could take its cues from the peculiarities of each country. And those peculiarities were already quite evident. As might have been expected, the various parties greeted the announcement differently. It took several months for the Comintern Executive to round up a sample of opinions, and then it was only a sample.[154] Unanimity there may have been in principle, *mais c'est le tone qui fait la musique.* The Yugoslavs embraced the dissolution defiantly: 'Under the banner of Marxism-Leninism, the party will as in the past continue to fulfil its duty toward the people . . . [and] remain true to the principles of internationalism.' These sentiments were echoed by the Belgian, Spanish and Bulgarian parties. But the Italians, who were drawing ever closer to the French model, made no mention of Marxism-Leninism or internationalism.[155]

Despite Stalin's efforts first to eliminate factionalism and then to terrorize the various communist parties into subservience, there always remained stubborn pockets of resistance to complete homogenization. Under wartime conditions, these pockets grew in size and resilience. The international communist movement, like other instruments of Soviet foreign policy (the army, defence industry and diplomatic corps), was spared the ravages of purges on the prewar scale. Most important of all, Stalin had allowed the idea of a new form of transition from a bourgeois democratic to a socialist revolution in order to accommodate the changed international environment and the socio-economic peculiarities of the East European societies. 'Popular democracy' or 'democracy of a new type' not only represented a deviation from the Soviet experience by denying the necessity of a dictatorship of the proletariat, but also implied a variety of historical experiences leading to the establishment of a socialist state.[156]

The communist parties worldwide responded differently all along the spectrum from the parliamentary to the insurrectionary way, both cultivated by Stalin. Towards the end of the war, Stalin gave explicit instructions to the leaders of the French and Italian communist parties, Thorez and Togliatti, to cultivate allies among the republican and democratic parties, enter coalition governments without conditions and not to insist on preserving the irregular armed forces of the resistance period.[157] It was not until the formation of the Cominform in 1947 that Stalin made a concerted effort to impose conformity on all the European parties. Even then, the fierce criticism of the French and Italian party leadership was not accompanied by purges. Only after the show trials of 'national communists' in 1949 was the old prewar pattern of control re-imposed. By that time the tender shoots of national deviation had struck root and could not be easily extirpated.

By the end of the war, the activism and patriotism of the communist parties, combined with the prestige of the victorious Red Army, lifted their popular appeal to new heights in Europe, the Middle East and East Asia. The growth of party membership was one strong indicator of the 'great recovery'. Another was participation in postwar governments. In Asia, the Chinese party underwent the most spectacular increase in members, from 40,000 in 1937 to 1.2 million in 1945, and then doubling again during the first years of the civil war to 2.7 million in 1947. In Europe, the Italian party jumped from 5,000 in 1943 to 2 million in 1946. Yet these two parties stood at polar opposites in their interpretation of the national front. The Chinese were insurrectionists, and the Italians were well on their way down the parliamentary path that would lead to Eurocommunism. In France, the increase was more modest, from 300,000 on the eve of the war, a figure that was severely eroded during the Nazi-Soviet Pact, to approximately 1 million in 1946. The Yugoslav communists also made dramatic gains, going from an illegal underground sect to a mass party. Contrasting the two extremes of the parliamentary and the insurrectionist tendencies demonstrates the advantages of the pluralist outlook that settled over the international movement.

Other parties in Eastern Europe made large gains mainly after the liberation and under Red Army occupation. But the Greek party grew from 17,500 to 72,500, and the Finnish party from a minuscule 1,200 in 1944 to 150,000 in 1946, without the benefit of direct Soviet intervention.[158] In the early postwar elections, which were genuinely free, the communists won 20–25 per cent of the vote in Belgium, the Netherlands, France and Italy. Even in Finland, which had just fought two wars against the Soviet Union and lost important territories, over 23 per cent voted communist, while in Czechoslovakia, the communist share of the vote topped 38 per cent. In Yugoslavia there was no election, but the communists had proven their widespread support by winning their civil war unaided by outside forces. In Greece, the communist-dominated resistance controlled about two thirds of the country at the liberation and, judging by the first postwar plebiscite on the king, they could muster at least a quarter to a third of the electorate. In Iran, the newly created pro-Soviet Tudeh Party won only six per cent of the vote in the first really free election in the country held in 1944. Yet, within three years it had become the only mass party in Iran. In northern and eastern China, the communists commanded the overwhelming allegiance of the population. In Korea, by all accounts, the communists and their allies would have won a national election if it had been held in the second half of 1945. These achievements represented another 'great recovery' from the confusion and embarrassment of the Nazi-Soviet Pact.

As a result of the national front policies and the elections, the communists entered most of the governments of Europe during or immediately after liberation, accepting portfolios in France, Italy, Austria, Finland, Belgium, Denmark and Norway as well as all the governments of Eastern Europe liberated by the Red Army. In 1946 Tudeh members entered the Iranian government. A coalition government in China never materialized for internal political reasons, though it was accepted in principle by both the communists and the Kuomintang. The North Korean government was dominated by the communists from the moment of liberation. All these achievements reflected a greater degree of ideological openness, flexibility and pluralism within the international movement as well as a strong if often unfocused desire of the mass of the population in war-torn areas to bring about some kind of radical socio-economic change. But there was no longer an effective central representative organ that could determine a general line. Polycentrism was born of war.

From the outset, Stalin called it the Great Fatherland War rather than the Second World War. The implication was clear. The Soviet Union was fighting a different war than all the other belligerents. He also called it a 'war of all freedom-loving peoples against fascism'. But none of his allies adopted that definition either. Its dual meaning derived from Russian history and Marxist theory, not easy to synthesize, but Stalin was the master at combining them. He was determined that the war would be fought by means of mobilizing the population and its resources by methods that had been tried and tested in the prewar building of socialism, but with a difference. Because the enemy was external rather than internal, it required a more flexible employment of means to build the broadest base of support among the groups that held the keys to survival and then victory. Coercion remained; so too did hortatory propaganda. But they were supplemented by concessions of greater autonomy to the army command, the technical, scientific and cultural intelligentsia, the nationalities, the foreign communist parties and even to the Patriarchal Orthodox Church, extending beyond the last constraints of ideology. The General Staff was given greater freedom of operational planning, especially after Stalingrad, though always under Stalin's watchful gaze. Arrested officers, like Rokossovsky and Kirill Meretskov, were released and put in command of armies. Promotions, medals and commendations were showered on the new cadre of commanders, Stalin permitting their achievements to attain a public celebration close to his own. The intelligentsia responded to the outbreak of war with spontaneous declarations of loyalty and self-mobilizing activities. The technical and scientific cadres developed new weapons, explored and exploited material resources, and invented new chemical, biological and medical techniques for a variety of uses in warfare. The creative intelligentsia – writers, artists, musicians – introduced new themes with a powerful emotional impact to inspire the population to believe their cause was right. Except for the recently annexed western borderlands, the nationalities rallied behind the regime. There were far more Ukrainians who fought in the Red Army than in the OUN. There were no defections among the national units of the Central

Asian republics. Even among those nationalities that suffered deportation in the latter stages of the war, there were numerous loyal, decorated soldiers. The Jewish Anti-Fascist Committee spread pro-Soviet propaganda and raised funds abroad. The church raised funds for the welfare of soldiers' families and military hardware and assisted in the re-Sovietization of Ukraine. The foreign communist parties in occupied Europe threw themselves into the resistance, early on in Yugoslavia, Albania and Greece, and less actively in France. When allied armies drew closer, they took up arms in Slovakia, northern Italy and southern France. With the decline and then abolition of the Comintern, the local parties adopted more nationalist slogans.

While Stalin grasped the value of these initiatives, many coming from individuals and groups who had suffered from his attacks before the war, he did not diminish the role of the security services, but instead even expanded its range of activities. Beria exploited his unique sources obtained through surveillance and informants to furnish Stalin with information that he knew the *vozhd* would value. At the same time, he was building his own empire based on infiltration of state and party agencies. He secured authority to organize and deploy blocking units behind the regular Red Army units on the front line to prevent flight or desertion. He persuaded Stalin to grant military titles to all personnel under his authority in order to equalize their prestige with the military officers. His repressive operations led to the dismissal, disgrace or executions of hundreds of military officers, including Zhukov. As the following section will demonstrate, he intervened increasingly on the cultural front, denouncing those who were outside his control and promoting his own minions. On another level the Sovinform Bureau attempted to direct and control the lines of propaganda, and party stalwarts like Zhdanov and Malenkov already busied themselves denouncing writers and musicians who strayed too far over the fuzzy frontiers of Socialist Realism. Under the pressure of total war, the paradox of Stalin's rule took on a new dimension. The heavy reliance on coercion in preparing for war yielded to a greater reliance on compliance and a greater degree of latitude in what was permitted. But the agencies of repression also increased their authority. At the end of the war, the stage was already set for the pendulum to swing back in the direction of coercion as Stalin's preferred style of governing. But though many of the wartime gains of more autonomy in the society were wiped out, there were survivors among the wreckage, whose fate is not easy to explain.

PART III

WINNING THE PEACE

CHAPTER 6

A PYRRHIC VICTORY?

The paradoxical character of Stalin's policies during the war stems from the nature of the abrupt shifts that they represented. All the major belligerents in the conflict were obliged in one way or another to adjust the themes of their prewar public pronouncements and modify their political tactics in rallying their people. But in Stalin's case the shifts amounted to a rehabilitation of individuals and restoration of traditions, belief systems and institutions that had been rejected or denounced as inimical to the building of socialism. To be sure, the reversals were selective. For all the mass of documentation compiled by the ubiquitous security services, and the flood of memoirs and personal testimonies of citizens and émigrés, the question remains how successful this seismic shift was in mobilizing the mass of the population. Opinions differ.[1] One conclusion seems inescapable. The invasion and occupation, accompanied by extreme brutality, brought together in a common cause for the first time in the Soviet era the mass of the population and the party leadership personified by Stalin. He and his associates were able to channel the spontaneous upsurge of patriotism, resorting less than before the war to coercive means of mobilizing the population without ever giving them up. But it was enough to arouse great expectations for the postwar era, in terms of greater freedom of expression, relaxation of punitive measures to force obedience in the factory and the farm and continuation of tolerance for the Patriarchal Orthodox Church. Among foreign communists, the abolition of the Comintern, alliance with progressive forces in capitalist countries and fewer directives from the Moscow centre fostered the illusion that the Soviet model, so alien to the societies of Europe, would not be imposed upon them even when they took power. All these effects made it more difficult, paradoxically, for Stalin to reassert his control at home and within the international communist movement in order to renew the march to socialism in one country.

COUNTING THE LOSSES

The Soviet Union emerged as one of the principal victors from the ordeal of the Second World War, but the human and material costs inflicted by the enemy, and self-inflicted as a result of Stalin's leadership, may well have proved irreparable. No other state in modern history has survived the enormous losses in men, military equipment and productive capacity inflicted upon the Soviet Union during the first two years of the war, which were followed by a painful recovery sufficient only to defeat the enemy. In the first few months of wartime, the gross value of production fell by more than half, from 12 to 5.6 billion rubles. The Germans overran enterprises producing 71 per cent of Soviet pig iron and 60 per cent of steel, not to speak for the moment of agricultural losses in livestock and equipment. The figures continued to mount throughout the war at a terrifying rate. The most complete set of measurements now available has been calculated and summarized by Mark Harrison and G.V. Kirilenko. They do not differ substantially.[2] The losses of military equipment and weaponry were staggering. Of the 131,700 tanks from the prewar stocks, wartime production and Lend-Lease, over 73 per cent were destroyed, as well as 65 per cent of military aircraft and almost half the artillery. The size of the Soviet army at the end of the war was deceptive; its weaponry and equipment were obsolete compared to the Western armies, including the Wehrmacht, but the Germans had banked too heavily on technological innovations which could not be produced in sufficient quantity or with adequate lead time for testing under battlefield conditions.[3]

The estimated total of material losses of the war can be broken down into several categories, the critical one being direct losses of physical assets on occupied territory. The Soviet figures total 679 billion rubles, or about 30 per cent of national wealth. Destruction engulfed the homes of 25 million people, ruined 1,710 towns and cities, almost 32,000 industrial establishments and over 65,000 kilometres of railway lines. Harrison suggests that some of these figures may have been inflated in order to influence Western policy on reparations and credits for reconstruction. But his estimate of 25 per cent of the losses of prewar fixed assets is still devastating.

Demographic losses are even more controversial. Estimates have steadily increased from Stalin's low figure of 7 million to Gorbachev's over 25 million premature deaths. Because of the problem of whether to count emigration in the total, as well as the difficulties of measurement, Harrison arrives at an estimate of population losses of between 26.6 and 29.3 million, of which 7.8 were military.[4] Major problems in arriving at an accurate figure for military deaths remain insoluble. According to an order of the Commissariat of Defence in 1940, documents personally identifying soldiers and non-commissioned officers were abolished. Stalin admitted this was an error and ordered them restored. But technical problems relating to photographing millions of soldiers delayed the process. Beyond this, the rapid withdrawals and encirclements made it impossible to collect and identify the dead. Mass burials became the norm, often mixing German and Soviet dead. Similar problems occurred in counting deaths from wounds. Records for over 32 million soldiers treated in hospitals did not give information on the outcome of their stay. Many of the records were destroyed in the course of the fighting.[5] Consequently, estimates of the war dead fluctuate greatly. One Soviet scholar came up with the figure of 8.5 million killed in action and 2.5 million dead from wounds.[6] The burden on the state budget of support of veterans and their dependents cost the state an estimated 2 billion rubles as late as 1963, which represented about 12 per cent of the defence budget.[7]

The long-term demographic disaster can best be measured by declining fertility rates. The overall loss of 35 million people to war-related deaths, emigration and birth deficit 'was either not made up or continued to increase indefinitely throughout the postwar period'.[8] The disproportionate losses of men and women further impaired a postwar recovery. The imbalance was particularly striking in the countryside. In 1940 the proportion of women to men was 1.1:1; in 1945 it was 2.7:1. Over the next five years the number of children born out of wedlock ranged from 752,000 to 944,000. A large percentage of adolescents who had been employed in industry as the adult male population was drained for the front suffered from debilitating diseases.[9] The combination of wartime losses and the famine created long-term health problems and helps to explain the decline in life expectancy observed as late as the Brezhnev period.[10]

Whatever the exact figures, which will probably never be known, Harrison and Kirilenko reach the sobering conclusion that the wartime losses of population and fixed assets were permanent. Although the prewar levels of GNP and population were restored, 'the Soviet Union never returned to its prewar economic trajectory'.

The war had a devastating effect on the agricultural population. The collective farms suffered from a massive labour shortage due to conscription into the army and the Nazi policy in the occupied territories of deporting *Ostarbeiter* for forced labour in German factories. Demobilization did not bring large numbers of former peasants back to the land, even though there was large-scale unemployment in the cities after the war.[11] Almost 65 per cent of the demobilized veterans who had manned the machine-tractor stations did not return to their jobs. Agricultural equipment wore out without being repaired or replaced by new machinery as factories were devoting their production to armaments. The number of motor vehicles on the collective farms declined from 107,000 before the war to 5,000 in 1945. All major sources of food, from grain to sugar beet, suffered a massive decline.[12] There were insufficient food stocks in the state warehouses, and increases in the number of people on rationing drove up the price of food until Stalin was persuaded to reduce grain procurements and cut the number of people with ration coupons.[13] These measures were inadequate to cope with the natural disaster brought on by drought and bad weather, creating famine conditions in 1946 and 1947.

It is much more difficult to arrive at any general conclusions about the psychological impact of the war on the domestic population, on the individual men and women who fought, suffered or sought to opt out of the conflict in hope of surviving a cataclysm in which they perceived no preferable outcome.[14] Scholars have examined different social groups as they emerged from the wartime experiences: the front-line fighters, the youth too young to fight, women, nationalities, those living under occupation, others who endured deportation. The picture is one of deep psychological disorientation and disillusionment.[15]

Was this then a Pyrrhic victory? However the term Pyrrhic victory has been applied in the history of warfare, it has retained a paradoxical meaning.

In the case of the Great Fatherland War, the contrasting elements emerge with striking clarity. There was no viable alternative to winning the war; losing it meant the dismemberment of the state and enslavement if not annihilation of the Russian people. But Stalin's leadership in preparing for the war, fighting it and rebuilding the country exacted a terrible price with serious long-term damage to the economy, population growth and, ultimately, the territorial integrity of the Soviet Union and the political system it had imposed on Eastern Europe. Moreover, as the war drew to a close, a plethora of serious problems added to the burden of recovering the human and material losses.

CIVIL WAR IN THE BORDERLANDS

The fruits of victory began to spoil even before they had been picked. The first crisis erupted in the form of resistance to the re-Sovietization of the territories occupied by the Axis powers. Civil war had broken out in the Baltic republics, Belarus and Western Ukraine, where nationalist bands fought the partisans and assassinated returning Soviet officials.[16] In former Soviet Western Ukraine and the newly annexed territories, the re-Sovietization took the form of a brutal mobilization. After the passage of the Red Army, three repressive agencies, NKVD border forces, blocking detachments and Soviet partisans, swarmed through the region. Only then did party officials begin to appear in the form of operative groups to re-establish the obkom, kraikom and gorkom structures (regional, district and city committees). Defectors from nationalist bands were organized into fake detachments of the Ukrainian Insurgent Army, dressed and equipped like the insurgents. Punitive detachments of special NKVD units called operative groups of militia conducted sweeps through the villages, arresting and deporting without much discrimination. At the same time, teams of judicial officials were sent in to mobilize, register and screen the local population. Clearly these punitive measures were not well co-ordinated and the population was repeatedly subjected to arbitrary and cruel treatment. Khrushchev with Stalin's approval set up a troika of the local party secretary, head of the regional NKVD and regional prosecutor to better co-ordinate these measures. But criticism from the Central Committee continued to focus on the poor performance of local party officials. Periodically Moscow resorted to amnesties and in February 1946 elections to the Supreme Soviet were held in what still amounted to a war zone.[17] Although the large bands were broken up in Ukraine by the end of the war, six months later Moscow still considered it necessary to deploy 20,000 NKVD troops, 10,000 supply troops and 26,000 locally recruited militia against the insurgents.[18]

Elsewhere, the fighting against the nationalist bands also lasted for months, even years in the case of the Lithuanian 'forest brothers'. This term for partisans was first applied in 1905 to bands fighting against the tsarist government and it was revived in 1945 by the anti-Soviet underground partisans opposing the reoccupation of Lithuania by the Red Army after the Germans surrendered. Even before the end of the war Beria was already raising the old bugbear of foreign intervention, writing to Stalin that although the Lithuanian Liberation Army had been 'partially destroyed, it is counting on a new war of the USSR against England and the US and is preparing for a rising in the rear of the Red Army'.[19]

Problems had arisen also in the southern borderlands. There Stalin resorted to the most brutal measures. He imposed a verdict of collective guilt on those nationalities which had shown signs of defection or else where it was anticipated. At Beria's instigation he ordered the deportation to Central Asia of 180,000 Crimean Tatars from their autonomous republic in the Crimea. In rapid order the same measure was carried out against the entire population of the Kabardino-Balkarian Autonomous Republic and the entire Chechen and Ingush peoples from the North Caucasus.[20] In these three cases archival documents reveal split loyalties and fighters on both sides, though the proportions show an advantage for the Soviet side.[21] However, there was no evidence of 'bandit activity' at all to justify the mass deportation of 90,000–100,000 Meskhetian Turks (Islamicized Georgians) or the smaller numbers of Turks, Kurds and Khemshins (Armenian Muslims), none of whom had been occupied by the German army.[22] Beria initiated most of these operations in order to enhance his own power in the region by discrediting local party and Komsomol cadres under his control by playing on Stalin's fears over the potential defection of Soviet nationalities sharing a common frontier with the same or similar ethnic and religious societies. Stalin's nationality policy expressed in the brotherhood of nations was left in shambles.

The war uprooted vast numbers of Soviet citizens, producing what Lewis Siegelbaum has called the migratory 'flood' of 1945. He counts five streams

in the process of dislocation that 'paradoxically afforded a degree of manoeu-
vrability, if not freedom of movement, that well-nigh overwhelmed the state
and its functioning'. First, there were the resettlers, deportees and returnees,
including half a million Ukrainian deportees and large numbers of Crimean
Tatars and North Caucasus nationalities; second, there were the demobilized soldiers and amnestied prisoners, who numbered about 7.5 million by
1947; third, there were the returning prisoners of war, about 2 million, and
3 million *Ostarbeiter*, forced labourers sent to Germany to work. Fourth,
10 million–17 million Soviet citizens who had been evacuated to the east
sought to return home, often to devastated towns, villages and heavily
damaged cities like Kiev. Finally, there were the 'itinerants' living on the
margins of a war-torn society. They had always been a familiar phenomenon in pre-revolutionary Russia, where they were known as 'wanderers',
and then reappeared in the early Soviet years, slipping through the nets of
state control and registration.[23] Stalin's prewar population policies set in
motion a mass movement of peasants and workers in the construction of a
socialist order, while at the same time striving to fix in place millions of
others to prevent disorder and to guarantee a steady flow of food supplies
into the cities. The flood of the postwar years was wholly disruptive and
required a different set of controls, involving untold numbers of party
members, bureaucrats and police in sorting out the productive from the
potentially asocial or pernicious elements and re-assimilating them into a
socialist system.

In addition to restoring order, Stalin and his associates faced problems
not unlike those which during the civil war and intervention of a generation
earlier had bedevilled the nascent Soviet regime. But the difference lay in
re-establishing rather than creating the major props holding up the entire
system. The party was in disarray; the schools in a parlous condition; the
collective farm system in a shambles; wayward tendencies in the intelligentsia abounded; the industrial plan was in need of conversion from military exigencies to a civilian economy. All these problems cried out for
immediate solution from a leader who was worn out by the extreme demands
of war and brooding over real and imaginary conspiracies and the question
of his succession.

At the end of the war Stalin was at the peak of his power and international reputation. But his health was precarious and the problems he faced

were multiple and ultimately intractable. His private life showed the signs of
the wear and tear of wartime. His relations with his children had deteriorated to the point where they were alienated, and close personal relations
with his oldest comrades were frayed or broken.[24] Contemporary accounts
portray him as worn out by the exigencies of supreme command. During
the war, he had worked tirelessly, often sixteen hours a day. He had devoted
his attention to every major aspect of governance as well as the conduct of
military operations, for better or worse; at first worse, but increasingly for
better as the war went on. He had personally supervised negotiations first
with Nazi Germany and Japan, and then at meetings with representatives of
the Western powers. He had abolished the Comintern as a policy-making
body in 1943, preferring to deal separately with the leaders of each communist party, advising, correcting, lecturing and intimidating them as he saw
fit. These meetings placed an additional strain on his energy.

Stalin may have suffered a slight stroke at the end of the war. In any case, in
October 1945 he took his first vacation to the Black Sea in several years. From
then on, the vacations grew longer and his temper grew shorter. He appears to
have reverted to his prewar mental state, yet, as we shall see, there is a danger
in placing exclusive emphasis on his destructive impulses. To be sure, he
displayed dark suspicions that the leading elements in society, who had
devoted themselves so wholeheartedly to winning the war, might endeavour
to expand the relative autonomy they had enjoyed during the war, and he was
concerned about rebuilding his own cult. At the same time, he did not revert
completely to the mass repression of the thirties. As Kaganovich suggested,
there were many Stalins, and the postwar period revealed another one.

Stalin quickly dashed hopes nurtured by wide sections of the population,
especially the elites, that he might institute reforms based on a greater
participation in the process of governance by those groups which had proven
their loyalty. Instead, he reverted to prewar methods of centralization and
mobilization, though he modified their application to fit the new circumstances. Stalin's first organizational moves suggested a thorough overhauling
of the emergency wartime administration. The GOKO was abolished, but
fundamental changes in the wartime structure of governance did not follow.
The centralization of power remained intact. The Council of People's
Commissars – or rather its Orgburo – virtually reproduced the membership
of GOKO. The marshals were dropped; in retrospect the first move in

reducing the political role of the military. Periodic meetings of the Politburo were reintroduced and then allowed to peter out. On domestic policy, he relied on an informal inner circle of close associates as well as a secondary layer of administrators, generals and former Comintern officials.[25] His personal style of governing hardly changed at all, except that intra-party rivalries grew sharper. He encouraged this institutional instability by moving around members of his inner circle from position to position, promoting, demoting and restoring them to their former posts seemingly at random. If there was any rhyme or reason to these moves, it was to prevent any one of them from assuming that he was the heir apparent.[26]

MANAGING THE MILITARY

During the war, Stalin had generously recognized and rewarded his military commanders, lavishing praise, medals and promotions on them; by 1943 he had given his marshals increasing freedom of planning and executing operations while not surrendering his monopoly of making final decisions. But he was quick to reproach or remove those generals who had failed at the front, especially during the disasters of 1941. The senior officers liberated at the end of the war, often by the Americans because of the location of their camps, were forced to undergo intensive interrogation and often torture at the hands of Viktor Abakumov and the agents of his SMERSH (the Counterintelligence Section of the Commissariat of Defence, its name a portmanteau of 'Death to Spies'). Those who could demonstrate that they had surrendered only after being surrounded or wounded were allowed to return to the army after strenuous retraining. The others, including General Vlasov, were condemned and shot. About one half of the returning rank-and-file soldiers were incarcerated.[27] Was it any wonder that Stalin did not permit the formation of any veterans' associations? One was finally formed in 1956.

The bigger question was to what extent was Stalin willing to share the accolades of victory? When it became apparent that he was not physically able to lead the victory parade on horseback, he entrusted the honour to Zhukov who was portrayed everywhere as the man on the white horse. As the conqueror of Berlin, the commander of the most powerful army in Europe, and the Soviet representative on the Allied Control Council of Germany with Eisenhower and Montgomery, he enjoyed enormous popularity at home and great international prestige. Unfortunately, he could not resist adopting a posture in Berlin which aroused Stalin's suspicion. Zhukov appeared to have been acting in ways that may have reminded Stalin, who often thought in terms of historical analogies, of the officers in the Russian army of occupation in Paris in 1815, who returned home to become the leaders of the Decembrist Uprising against the tsar.[28] There was plenty of evidence available to him from the military censors of the discontent among the veterans with the mismanagement and corruption accompanying demobilization and relocation after the war, which they blamed on the 'rear-line rats' in the bureaucracy and party.[29]

With this background in mind, Stalin called Zhukov when he returned to Berlin from a meeting of the Supreme Soviet in March 1946 suggesting that, since Eisenhower and Montgomery were being called back home from Berlin, wasn't it also time for Zhukov to leave? Stalin called again a few days later to inform him that the Politburo had decided to replace him in Berlin with Marshal Vasily Sokolovsky, to abolish Zhukov's position as first deputy minister of defence and supreme commander and to appoint General Nikolai Bulganin as deputy minister, with fewer responsibilities. Despite his rank, Bulganin had never served as a front-line commander, knew little about military affairs and was regarded with disdain by the officer corps. Marshal A.M. Vasilevsky, meanwhile, was named chief of staff. What was left for Zhukov? Stalin offered him the new position of commander of ground forces, a clear demotion, the first in a series of steps to whittle down his prestige and influence. His new duties were limited to administrative matters and he soon clashed with Bulganin over defining the dispositions of the top military posts. Reporting to Stalin, Bulganin distorted Zhukov's proposals to make them appear to increase his own authority.

The next cut came with the sudden arrest of the brilliant minister of the Soviet Air Forces, Marshal Aleksandr Novikov, a close friend and associate of Zhukov during the war. This signalled the commencement of the Aviators Affair, concocted by Abakumov, the rising star of the security services. Originally a protégé of Beria, Abakumov had been rapidly promoted during the war. He became head of SMERSH, with agents stationed down to the regimental level including the activities of Red Army officers. By 1943 he had already placed thirty-five generals under arrest; by the end of the war the list grew to over 100, of whom at least seventy-six were condemned by military tribunals. Egged on by Stalin, he reported that Novikov had given evidence of Zhukov's disloyal attitude.[30] On the basis of this testimony, Stalin summoned the Supreme Military Council with the participation of the Soviet marshals and members of the Politburo to review a document accusing Zhukov of the most serious crimes. At the same time, arrests were made of top military and civilian officers associated with Zhukov. Stalin showed up wearing his prewar military tunic, a sign that he was in a belligerent mood. Accounts differ on specific details of the meeting. But there is no disagreement on the reaction of the main speakers. Stalin called first on the marshals, who with one exception denied that Zhukov had at any time behaved unpatriotically or disloyally to Stalin, although they criticized certain personal characteristics. Members of the Politburo, mentioned differently in different accounts, supported the accusations.[31] Never before had such a clear divide opened up between the top military and party leaders. Stalin then issued an order listing Zhukov's many errors: his personal ambition; his dissatisfaction with insufficient government appreciation of his military achievements and personal worth; his false and immodest claims to have planned and carried out the entire major victorious operations in the Great Fatherland War; his protection of disaffected officers under his command. By a unanimous verdict of the Supreme Military Council, Stalin concluded, Zhukov was relieved of his position as commander of ground forces and named commander of the Odessa military district. In light of the seriousness of the accusations and the arrest of other officers, the fact that Zhukov was not arrested is striking.[32]

It is most likely that Stalin was unwilling to ignore – still less challenge – the united front of the marshals. Moreover, Zhukov's popularity at home and status abroad offered some protection. Although Abakumov considered Zhukov 'a dangerous man', a second Tukhachevsky, he could not provide evidence that linked Zhukov to a foreign conspiracy. Stalin was not about to decapitate the officer corps as in 1937. The marshals had demonstrated their loyalty and there was no evidence that they nourished secret ambitions. What was different then, as would become increasingly clear in other such 'affairs', was that Stalin's vindictiveness was selective – paradoxical, unjust and vicious as it was. Abakumov continued to pursue Zhukov, sending Stalin material revealing Zhukov's extensive looting of valuables from Germany, which he shipped home in seven railway carriages. After another investigation, Zhukov was re-assigned to the even more remote

Urals military district. Then, suddenly, in 1953, Stalin recalled him to Moscow. Presumably Stalin was by this time confident that Zhukov, having been relegated to years of obscurity, was no longer a threat; now it was the turn of the security services. Abakumov had already been arrested in 1951 and now even Beria was under suspicion.[33]

In contrast to the military, the Communist Party had suffered a serious loss of effectiveness and prestige during the war. Rebuilding it ranked high in Stalin's agenda to restore the balance among Soviet institutions upset by the war. The party's controls over propaganda had slackened during the war. Theoretical training had been weakened by substituting for the classics the study on a massive scale from the end of 1943 of Stalin's *On the Great Fatherland War of the Soviet Union*, which was taught in a mechanical and dogmatic way.[34] At the end of the war, Zhdanov admitted that the leadership recognized that 'there were serious shortcomings and serious failures' in the ideological sphere.[35] Reflecting on the postwar years, Dmitry Shepilov, deputy head of the Agitprop Department at the time, later wrote that under conditions where an aureole of glory surrounded 'the triumphal victory of the USSR in the Second World War, it became all too clear that in the field of ideology there was a series of sectors which did not correspond to the victorious era and its glory'.[36] To correct the situation, the party poured forth a stream of documents on the need to sustain Soviet patriotism.[37] This campaign was bolstered by another aimed at improving the level and range of Soviet propaganda in the country and abroad.[38] All these instructions came as the direct result of 'the orders of Comrade Stalin on the improvement of propaganda and agitation'.[39] According to Shepilov, these were edited by Stalin at meetings of the Politburo or the secretariat of the Central Committee or by telephone and frequently in unofficial conversations.[40] Stalin also took an active part in initiating harsh censorship of the foreign press and literature.[41] It was not surprising, then, that the Agitprop Department routinely rejected requests of Soviet scholars for access to the closed funds of libraries and institutes containing 'banned' books and periodicals.[42] Stalin went to great lengths to conceal his instructions from the public.

On the international level the quality of party propaganda had also suffered with the need to shift from advocating capitalist encirclement to linking defence of the fatherland to the alliance with the West. Here too a paradoxical situation prevailed at the very moment of victory. As the chief representative of the Sovinform wrote from London: 'During the war, the chief Soviet propagandist in England was the Red Army on whose tanks the Soviet word was carried forward loud and clear'. But peace turned the asset into a major liability as stories circulated in the Western press about the brutalities and rapes committed by the same heroic Red Army. The situation deteriorated rapidly. In October 1945, Solomon Lozovsky, head of Sovinformburo, sent a special memorandum – 'The Allied Campaign to Discredit the Red Army' – to his chief, Molotov, and to Malenkov, in which he criticized the passive Soviet response to what had become a worldwide campaign of abuse.[43] It was more than passive: 'it was inept, confused and fragmented'. But the leadership had no good advice on how to combat the Western propaganda offensive. One problem was Stalin's unwillingness to reveal the true extent of the Soviet losses for fear this would convey a picture of weakness, instead of demonstrating the disproportionate sacrifice of the Soviet people in the Allied cause of defeating Nazism.

The heavy war losses among the party cadres due to casualties and purges of those who had spent any time in the occupied territories were made up numerically by a vast influx of youth, many of whom were peasants, hastily recruited, without the normal course of prewar instruction in Marxism-Leninism.[44] The leadership faced a situation similar to that after the civil war, when revolutionary cadres drawn from the working class had been much reduced, forcing them to create a virtually new party composed initially of inexperienced and badly educated activists. Problems of recruiting and training a new generation after 1945 were compounded by the massive destabilizing effects of the war on Soviet youth.[45] Rapid promotion during the war to fill losses at the front thrust men into positions for which they were inadequately prepared. After the war, obkom secretaries were routinely removed if they did not measure up to the educational standards expected of them, and then sent to the Higher Party School in Moscow for further instruction. Reforms were drafted to raise the ideological awareness of the leading party officials in the national and autonomous republics, including reorganization of the curricula in the party schools preparing future cadres.[46] Along similar lines, Stalin issued instructions to introduce greater specialization into the party organs in the Soviet republics.[47] Substantial efforts were also made to improve the standard of living of party members by introducing substantial increases in their pay, food allotments and health benefits.[48] To cope with the new demands, Stalin expanded the number of official positions within the party hierarchy to over 45,000 by the end of his life and loaded them down with additional duties. Although he remained highly suspicious and arbitrarily intervened in party affairs, he refrained from returning to massive repression as a means of imposing his will. With a few notable exceptions, to be recounted later in this chapter, discipline was generally maintained by reprimands, demotions or dismissal from office rather than arrests, trials, imprisonment and shootings.

Evidence of Stalin's attempts to establish stability within the party can be drawn from the pattern of longevity in office of the first secretaries of the national and autonomous republics, again with the notable exception of the Russian Republic. In Armenia Gregor Arutinov occupied the post of first secretary of the republic from 1937 to 1954; in Latvia it was Jānis Kalnbērziņš from 1940 to 1959; in Lithuania, Antanas Sniečkus from 1940 to 1974; in Kazakhstan, Zhumbai Shaiakhmetov, from 1946 to 1954; in Tajikistan, Bobojon Ghafurov from 1946 to 1956; in Uzbekistan, U.Iu. Iusupov served from 1937 until 1950 when he was appointed minister of cotton production of the USSR and was replaced by A.I. Niiazov, who had worked closely with Iusupov in the Council of Ministers and Presidium of the Supreme Soviet of Uzbekistan. A large number of first secretaries of the autonomous republics – including the North Ossetian, Tatar, Bashkir, Tuvan, Chuvash and Dagestan – held their posts up to the death of Stalin.[49]

Two of Stalin's favourites, Nicolae Coval and Leonid Brezhnev, served as first secretary of the Moldavian party from 1946 to 1950 and from 1950 to 1952 respectively, despite upheavals caused by deportation and re-Sovietization.[50] Two striking examples illustrate how survival was achieved in the face of serious attacks from within the system. In Armenia, Arutiunov refuted a number of serious accusations, issuing from the Orgburo and signed by Zhdanov, including shortcomings in the ideological training of party cadres and the study of Russian.[51] Mir Jafar Baghirov, the first secretary of the Azerbaijan party from 1933 to 1953, withstood the onslaught of none other than Lev Mekhlis, the commissar of state control, by invoking Stalin's intervention and a review by a high-level group of party stalwarts. Not only was Baghirov exonerated, but the Politburo imposed new limitations on the rights of the commissariat and its local representatives to investigate the activities of central and regional departments.[52]

The situation in Georgia was more complicated. A Stalin favourite, Kandid Charkviani, was first secretary of the Georgian party from 1938 to 1952, consorting with Beria until he was caught up in the so-called Mingrelian Affair. Although accused of tolerating criminal activity, he was demoted but never arrested and assigned to a minor post in the Central Committee. Akaki Mgeladze, another Stalin favourite, was first secretary of the Abkhazian Communist Party from 1943 to 1951 and then succeeded Charkviani in Georgia from 1952 to 1953. He turned Stalin against Charkviani but was dismissed by Beria after Stalin's death. He was never arrested, retained his party membership and occupied a minor position in Abkhazia after Beria was purged.[53]

Running parallel to his policy of restoring and even enhancing the role of the party, Stalin introduced what amounted to countervailing changes which had the result of reducing its effectiveness. First and foremost were his decisions to increase surveillance over the activities of the party down to the lowest level. He expanded the network of reporting agencies, including roving inspectors of the Central Committee, representatives of the procurator's office and local committees of party control. The security services represent another and, alas, less well-documented channel of communication; indirect evidence suggests their surveillance was extensive and growing over time. Finally, to provide a recurring source of self-criticism, the first secretaries of the obkoms and kraikoms were expected to submit periodic reports as well.[54] This massive system of surveillance generated a flood of information which was used to expose abuses in the system.[55] One of the most prominent themes to emerge from the available documentation was the denunciation of widespread failings by local party organizations to maintain 'Bolshevik' standards of behaviour, including arbitrary interference in local life, drunkenness, absenteeism, licentiousness, corruption, dereliction of duty and similar peccadilloes. The inadvertent – indeed paradoxical – effect was a reflex action in the form of the growth and strengthening of clientele networks.[56]

Clientelism had been an integral part of the Soviet system since the civil war.[57] The system had evolved from the early days of that conflict, deriving from the nature of party work and personal interests operating in an environment of deprivation. Stalin hijacked the system by making provincial party secretaries his personal appointees as a means of consolidating power. Yet, paradoxically, the system began to act as a form of insulating local party cliques against pressure from the centre. Stalin reacted strongly. At the March plenum of the Central Committee in 1937 he denounced the practice of selecting workers, 'not by objective criteria, but by accidental, subjective, narrow and provincial criteria. Most frequently so-called acquaintances are chosen, personal friends, fellow countrymen ... [who] eulogize each other and from time to time send empty, nauseating reports to the centre about success'. In citing examples, Stalin ominously declared that 'such practices sought to create for themselves conditions of a certain independence both toward local people and the Central Committee of the Party'.[58] Nevertheless, the practice continued and spread under the pressure of wartime conditions.[59]

A second major factor in diminishing the leading role of the party in Soviet society was indirectly related to Stalin's policy of mobilizing the economy to meet the demands of war. As Moshe Lewin has stressed, these emergency measures introduced deep structural changes that persisted in the postwar period. During the war, the directors of enterprises tended to deal directly with the appropriate ministries (formerly commissariats) which were managing the battle for production. This shift accelerated the division of labour already under way in the prewar period between the economic bureaucrats in the ministries and the party cadres. The overall effect was twofold. First, the party was turned more and more into an appendix of the ministries, leading to its loss of power. Second, the bureaucracy expanded to swollen proportions, deprived of a central co-ordinating body and increasingly impervious to reform.[60] To facilitate rapid fulfilment of orders and access to raw materials, the ministries resorted to the practice of *premirovanie*, variously translated as 'payoff' or 'bonus', but sometimes closer to a bribe.[61] Whatever the definition, the practice was illegal and in the postwar period the leading party organs made strenuous efforts to eliminate it. The Central Committee denounced such rewards as reducing party officials to the 'playthings' of the enterprises, 'shameful and ruinous', depriving them of their independence.[62] It was partly in response to these examples of malfeasance that a new scale of payment for party secretaries was introduced.[63]

THE COLLECTIVE FARMS IN CRISIS

Possibly the most flagrant shortcoming of the party came to light in the failure to restore the collective farm system, which had been devastated by the war. In the immediate postwar years, the collective farm system throughout the Soviet Union showed signs of being in grave danger of collapse. During the war a moral rot had set in and persisted in the postwar years. The crisis was fully documented in a wide-ranging survey of sixty regions and 288 collective farms prepared by Lev Mekhlis for Beria in August 1945. It painted a grim picture of frequent violations of social norms and regulations, the squandering and plundering of socialist property and the failure of the responsible party and state agencies to correct the abuses. Mekhlis stated at the outset that in some regions 'anti-governmental prac-tices' had reached the point where they represented a threat to the future development of the socialist system and the well-being of the collective farmers. He blamed the local authorities for having failed in their duties to educate the kolkhozniki in the collective spirit of the Kolkhoz Statute of 1935, and, worse, for having themselves flagrantly violated the policies of the party and the government. He selected four areas where abuses appeared most frequently: the arbitrary requisition of kolkhoz resources for all kinds of enterprises that had nothing to do with the operation of the farms, including outright embezzlement of funds and the construction of build-ings for other agencies; confiscation of kolkhoz buildings without compen-sation for other uses; seizure of cattle by local officials for their own use; expropriation of kolkhoz labour for other purposes. The kolkhoz accounts were often in such disarray that these rip-offs were easily concealed.[64]

At the same time, Andreev, the president of the Council on Kolkhoz Affairs and a Politburo member, received a flood of letters from individual members of collective farms throughout the Soviet Union, many of them disabled veterans of the war, relating the most poignant details of their exploitation or mistreatment.[65] The situation reached such crisis propor-tions that the council reported to Malenkov in June 1949 that a mass of letters had been received from individual members of kolkhozes docu-menting their persecution for having complained in writing about viola-tions of the Kolkhoz Statute. Investigations had determined that the overwhelming number of these violations had been confirmed. Punishment of these whistleblowers extended from confiscation of livestock to fines, sentences of corrective labour and even exclusion from the kolkhozes. Despite instructions from the council, the Ministry of Justice and the chief procurator, the abuses had not been corrected, and Malenkov was requested to intervene personally.[66] These appeals apparently went unheeded: the complaints by individuals citing flagrant violations of the law on collectives continued into the 1950s.[67]

The decay of the kolkhoz system was also due in no small measure to the resistance of the peasantry to collective labour and their stubborn but rational adherence to archaic practices.[68] During the war, when surveillance over the countryside had diminished, the peasantry began to under-report the amount of land under collective cultivation in order to reduce taxes and to cut out land from the collective and join it to their individual plots. This led to a decrease in the time the peasants spent on the collective as well as reducing its productivity.[69] As late as 1952 the government was still trying to recover this land.[70] An equally venerable tradition shows up in the persistent retention and defence of small kolkhozes in the face of pressures to join larger ones in the interests of efficiency. The rationale behind this was, of course, the preservation of the enlarged family or *dvor* wherein members of the kolkhoz were all related, thus defeating the basic 'spirit' of the law and the socialist ideal.[71] Thus from above and below the collective ideal was being subverted.

Agriculture was struggling to recover prewar levels of production when natural disaster struck. The famine of 1946–47 condemned 1 million–1.5 million people to death. During the war, famine conditions had occurred in widely scattered localities from Siberia in the north to the Kazakh and Uzbek republics. A good harvest in 1945 promised a modest recovery. But a severe drought in 1946 plunged the entire country into a devastating famine which reached a peak in 1947 and did not abate in some regions until several years later.[72] Caused by a severe drought in the western regions, it struck an already hungry and highly vulnerable population, weakened by the effects of the war years.

The situation in the recently annexed territories and throughout Western Ukraine was especially dire. In his reports to Stalin in 1948, Khrushchev, the first secretary of the Ukrainian Soviet Republic, identified three major problems facing the introduction or restoration of the collective farm system. There still existed, three to four years after the Germans had been cleared from Soviet territory, widespread instances of dissolution, corruption and shirking on the part of kolkhoz members, dating back to the prewar period. Khrushchev provided vivid details of how the war allowed these elements to survive and even flourish. In the recently annexed territories, 'banditry' (that is, nationalist resistance) continued to hamper the organization of collectives, spreading fear and confusion among the peasantry. Finally, the soviet, party, police and Komsomol organizations had been weakened during the war and had not sufficiently recovered to pursue vigorously the establishment of order, provide inspiration and guidance in reconstituting the kolkhozes.

Khrushchev proposed to Stalin several major initiatives. First, to provide better security for the collectives, he recommended that the penal battalions be transferred from the army to the security organs so that they could be stationed permanently in the villages where there were collectives and in places where it was necessary to set up kolkhozes, while at the same time thoroughly purging the organs and militia of incompetents and shirkers. He expressed his intention, when next in Moscow, of requesting from Stalin armoured cars and radio equipment for the security organs (and even large numbers of guard dogs) to improve their fighting capability. Finally, he proposed the creation of what later became known as 'courts of honour' to supplement the judicial procedures for crimes committed under the law codes and generate greater local initiative in overcoming lax and morally reprehensible behaviour by peasants.[73]

Stalin's response to these multiple threats to the well-being of the peasantry was, characteristically, to impose ever-tighter controls, and to impose on the agricultural sector what Alec Nove has called 'an extraordinary administrative mish-mash'.[74] In light of the unrelieved suffering inflicted on the peasantry by wartime sacrifices and the postwar re-imposition of a morally bankrupt collective farm system, Stalin's words of praise for the Russian people in his victory speech ring hollow indeed. He had already warned the population in his February 1946 election speech that war was inevitable as long as capitalism survived; this was a transparent hint to prepare for the next war. Sacrifice would continue to be the lot of the people. The paradox remained in place. The postwar reconstruction of the ship of state was like the prewar model – undermined by the means employed.

Stalin's policy toward the disastrous situation in the countryside was to mount a campaign of coercion aimed at restoring discipline. The law of 2 June 1948, 'On the expulsion of those who deliberately refuse to work and lead a parasitic way of life', inspired by Khrushchev's memo, empowered the commune to expel individuals who were regarded as socially harmful. Over the next five years, according to the Ministry of Internal Affairs, 33,266 members of kolkhozes and 12,598 family members were expelled by the action of village courts with local officials presiding over members of the kolkhozes.[75] This measure was designed to supplement the activities of the legal authorities prosecuting violations of the Kolkhoz Statute law of 1935. The number of convictions of collective farm chairmen and team leaders had already reached alarming proportions in the first postwar year.[76]

The war also had a devastating effect on the school system which had played a major role in shaping the values of the first Soviet generation. The requisitioning of school buildings for hospitals and other pressing needs accelerated a prewar trend. As a result, the number of children attending school decreased sharply. The Ministry of Education lacked political clout to reclaim many of the buildings after the war, especially those under army control. Budgetary allocations to education were shifted to meet defence priorities, creating severe shortages of materials and teachers. In the occupied territories, the schools system virtually collapsed; 43 per cent of the schools in the country were destroyed. The rural school network suffered the most. Eight years after the war, the majority of schools in the countryside remained in converted peasant huts.[77] The diminution of a crucial transmission belt for training rural youth added to an already irreparable decline of the collective farm system.

THE RETURN TO PLANNING

Stalin's economic policy in the postwar era gave priority to the mobilization of resources for the rapid repair of wartime damage to the industrial sector and the immediate return to planning. His hopes for substantial financial assistance from the West were already fading several years before the death knell sounded by the Marshall Plan. Lend-Lease was abruptly terminated by Truman at the end of the war. Stalin's repeated requests for a long-term and low-interest $6 billion loan from the United States were tied to conditions (on repayment, return of unused goods and requirements to join a more liberalized international economic order) that the Soviet Union found difficult to accept.[78] The expected delivery of reparations from Germany also fizzled out. The policy of stripping industrial plants of all movable equipment was imposed on the defeated enemy in East Germany, Romania and Manchuria. It was substantial, but often carried out hastily and haphazardly, resulting in unnecessary waste and loss.[79] The Soviet Union would have to rely primarily on its own resources.

During the war, Stalin had patronized leading representatives of two schools of Marxist economic thinking led by Voznesensky and Varga, whose views of the postwar world differed, leading to an open conflict. Paradoxically, the more theoretically original and deviant Varga survived, although disciplined, while the orthodox Voznesensky did not. The reasons for this, however, were more political than economic. In the first postwar year, Voznesensky was also entrusted with drafting the fourth five-year plan, which achieved notable success. According to the most optimistic estimates, the militarization of the Soviet wartime economy had produced impressive results in individual branches such as labour productivity in military industry and aviation industry compared to Germany, even if the quality lagged behind. The organization and production experience of military industry were of little use in the postwar economy and many of its achievements were lost. Nevertheless, the fourth five-year plan designed by Voznesensky and his deputies benefited from the high level of skill and efficiency of the senior levels of managers and administrators whom he had helped to recruit during the war.[80] Recovery was rapid in gross outputs. Although there was a reduction in the size of the conventional armed forces, due to the postwar need for manpower to repair the damage, the plan maintained high levels of defence spending and investment in the nuclear programme.[81] Voznesensky's promotion to a full Politburo membership in 1947 followed the publication of his celebrated book, *The Military Economy of the USSR during the Fatherland War*. Written shortly after the war, it sat on Stalin's desk for a year before he returned it with annotations, corrections and his initials of approval. Voznesensky re-affirmed the basic principles of the Soviet economic system, with the law-governed plan regulated by a scientific determination of production costs and the utilization of outputs, but he also admitted that peacetime norms had been violated under the pressures of wartime emergency.[82] To return to peacetime regularities he stressed the need for a more extensive role for economic levers such as money, prices, credit and incentives and private trade in the form of co-operatives to compete with state stores. To control inflation and restore financial discipline, a currency reform was introduced and rationing was abolished.[83]

Encouragement in that direction would have to have come from Stalin. In his election speech of February 1946, he reminded the people that the inevitability of war remained as long as capitalism survived; but this placed the threat on a distant horizon. He balanced this by insisting on the importance of immediately improving the material condition of the population and the means of production to achieve it. These views were further developed by a special commission entrusted with the drafting of a new party programme in 1947, in which Zhdanov and Voznesensky played the leading roles.[84] The committee set as its main task to design for the economic development of the country for the next twenty to thirty years. While maintaining the emphasis on the increase of heavy industry, the planners envisaged a dramatic leap in consumer production, including provisions for making available individual apartments for the working class, free distribution of basic food products (bread and meat) to the population and the production of private automobiles. These utopian aspirations foreshadowed subsequent proposed reforms by Khrushchev and Aleksei Kosygin, an associate of Voznesensky in Leningrad and minister of light industry after the war, who went on to be a major figure in the planning of reforms in the Soviet economy.[85] These ideas could be distorted to appear to challenge the growing authority of the military-industrial complex that was increasingly dominated by Beria and Malenkov.[86] But given Voznesensky's record during the war, his role in drafting the fourth five-year plan and membership of the Secret Committee on the Atomic Project, something more concrete was necessary to undermine his authority in the economic sphere. A conspiracy to destroy him was already under way, and culminated in what came to be known as the Leningrad Affair (see below, pp. 254–61).

REINING IN THE INTELLIGENTSIA

Even before the end of hostilities, Stalin demonstrated his determination to cut back or eliminate the relative autonomy of groups among the intelligentsia which expected to benefit from their contributions to the war effort to improve their standing in Soviet society relative to the party. His suspicious nature, ever receptive to conspiracies, tempered in the revolutionary underground and struggle for power, did not, however, operate in a random fashion. His gaze fell on specific targets that had emerged during the war behind the façade of patriotism. In seeking the sources of new forms of anti-party activity, he turned more frequently to the tried-and-tested tactic of organizing 'discussions' on a wide range of topics, mainly cultural and intellectual but also in such varied fields as genetics and the economy. Sometimes the agendas were fixed, but not always. They also served as a way of revealing the dimensions of opinion, which could then be used to support desired outcomes or denounce unacceptable ones.

Almost immediately after peace was declared, Stalin turned his attention once more to the cultural front, which required a thorough overhaul. By devising their own methods of demonstrating patriotism, writers had acquired a greater degree of freedom of expression and scientists had claimed an autonomous sphere for their work. Could this spontaneous flowering of independent thought and action on the fringes of *partiinost'* be allowed to continue? A new challenge complicated his task. Despite his best efforts to limit direct contacts with the West, his embrace of the Grand Alliance, his celebration of the second front and the influx of Lend-Lease products – from canned meat to Studebaker trucks – created widespread sympathy for Britain and the US among the population in general and the intelligentsia in particular. How could the financial and political advantages of good relations for postwar reconstruction be maintained without admitting greater influence and perhaps even pressure from the West on the evolution of the Soviet system? Much depended on how serious he regarded that threat to be. It quickly became clear that he intended to re-impose controls on the intelligentsia, but his methods were not always direct and were often masked. Discussion was only one method for exploring differences among his subordinates on questions he had not resolved in his own mind. On other issues he set one member of his inner circle against another. On still others he intervened directly and brutally. His major ideological task was to adjust the balance between two potentially contradictory themes of russo-centrism and Soviet patriotism with its emphasis on the brotherhood of nations. In his efforts to mobilize the population of the entire country, Stalin had contributed himself to the gap opening up between the two visions of the socialist state by allowing and indeed encouraging each tendency to push beyond the limits set by *partiinost'*.

What is in need of serious revision, however, is the well-entrenched interpretation that the re-imposition of controls over the creative intelligentsia began with A.A. Zhdanov's attack in August 1946 on the Leningrad writers Mikhail Zoshchenko and Anna Akhmatova, inaugurating the campaign known as *Zhdanovshchina*. From mid-1943, the security services began to report on 'anti-Soviet manifestations and negative political moods among writers and journalists'. The results were stunning. Based on what must have been information from informers, a number of leading writers were quoted as having expressed views that were far more subversive than anything Zoshchenko or Akhmatova ever wrote. Prominent among these opinions were harsh criticisms of Stalin personally and denunciation of the entire arts bureaucracy for killing independent thought. Hope was expressed for help from the West. Yet no arrests followed.[87]

After Zoshchenko was attacked publicly by critics, he wrote to Stalin in November 1943 defending himself. Instead of recanting as was the normal procedure, he asked Stalin to read his work and judge for himself. Not having received an answer, he wrote to Shcherbakov, this time apologizing for his errors.[88] But Zhdanov was not satisfied and urged the critics to redouble their criticisms. Zoshchenko was still not cowed. Questioned by police agents, he continued to defend himself. Writing in *Bol'shevik*, he accused members of the Writers' Union – and in particular the deputy head of the Central Committee's Agitprop Department, the academician Aleksandr Egolin – of hypocrisy in reversing their opinion of his work. Then, Zoshchenko threw down the gauntlet: 'It is easier to guide industry and railroads than it is art', he declared. 'Our leaders frequently do not have a deep understanding of the goals of the arts.'[89] Zoshchenko was not alone in taking this position but only a few others were willing to back him up.

The persistent demands of the Agitprop Department of the Central Committee to exercise 'oversight' over editorial boards did not stem the tide of 'harmful works'.[90] Vsevolod Merkulov, Beria's deputy, complained to Zhdanov in October 1944 that the writers who had been criticized by the Central Committee remained defiant.[91] Throughout the next months, Malenkov's deputies in the Agitprop Department continued to submit similar reports, focusing on the Leningrad writers.[92] Yet still nothing was done. Stalin became annoyed with the failure to discipline the Leningrad journals. In April 1946, the Politburo instructed Zhdanov and Aleksandrov to submit proposals to improve propaganda and agitation. The following month, Stalin took steps to reduce the authority of Malenkov and Beria, balancing them with Zhdanov, who was given the task of overseeing the

Central Committee apparatus and setting the tone for ideological and cultural policy.[93]

The choice of Zhdanov as Stalin's chief spokesman on the restored cultural front poses a number of questions that remain puzzling. In some ways, he appeared well suited to the role. He considered himself highly educated and culturally sensitive, having studied the piano. Yet his perform-ance as a political figure was patchy, not to say unimpressive. In 1937, he had co-signed with Stalin the notorious order to speed up the terror. His debut in foreign policy had been disastrous. In 1940, he had advocated a 'forward' policy, coming close to the doctrine of an offensive war. He had supported the attack on Finland and misjudged Hitler's intentions.[94] As party boss in Leningrad, he was responsible for defending the city. He repulsed the efforts of his rivals Malenkov and Beria in December 1941 to withdraw all forces from the city in order to defend Moscow. But then conflicting reports circulated about his leadership.[95] At the end of the siege of Leningrad, Stalin appointed him chair of the Allied Control Commission in Finland. Zhdanov dutifully carried out instructions from Molotov and Stalin to adhere strictly to the terms of the armistice. He warned his staff not to get mixed up in Finnish politics, not to bring pressure on the Finnish government or even give advice to the Finnish communists. Of all the Soviet proconsuls in Eastern Europe, he appeared to be the most willing to follow the rules of co-operation with the West.[96] Stalin appeared satisfied with his performance and brought him back to the Central Committee. Whatever Zhdanov's weaknesses, Stalin was, according to Molotov, very fond of Zhdanov and willing to forgive his sins.[97] Having received Zhdanov back into the inner circle, was Stalin continuing to test his loyalty by giving him the unpleasant assignment of attacking the literary culture of his own city?

Zhdanov's response to the criticism of the Leningrad writers and the thick literary journals by Malenkov's men in the Agitprop Department is worth discussing in detail. The documents strongly suggest that Zhdanov had decided to cover himself by taking charge of the ideological campaign himself. By this tactic he was able to avoid a wholesale 'massacre' of leading writers and intellectuals and absolve himself of the blame for having allowed them to flourish in his bailiwick.[98] He diligently adopted Stalin's language and took the offensive by singling out Zoshchenko, Akhmatova and the editors of *Zvezda* and *Leningrad* as the chief culprits in the unsatisfactory state of affairs in Leningrad and by implication elsewhere in the literary community.[99] In the week of 7–13 August, three events led up to this outcome. First, the report of Aleksandrov and Egolin to Zhdanov strongly condemned the Leningrad writers and poets. There was nothing new here that had not formed part of past criticisms, except for one serious accusation directed at the Leningrad party committee for 'missing ideological errors'. Then, at a meeting of the Orgburo with members of the Agitprop Department, the Leningrad party organization, the Leningrad journals and the Writers' Union, Stalin set the tone. There was none of the harsh accusatory language one might have expected from him. Instead, he expressed annoyance at Zoshchenko's 'Adventures of a Monkey', calling it a 'silly story', a 'trivial puppet show piece'. More seriously, he criticized the editor of *Leningrad* for having 'tiptoed in front of foreign writers'. He urged the editor to speak more 'firmly' in admitting his mistakes. What he wanted, he said, was 'better works published, we want to emphasize quality'. He made no blanket condemnation: 'Sometimes *Zvezda* publishes remarkable pieces, absolute diamonds, and alongside diamonds – manure'. There was no mention of socialist realism in the entire discussion of several hours.[100]

Zhdanov's report, written a few days later on 14 August, and later highly praised by Stalin, employed much harsher language. Yet, for all its invective, there was little that was new. Akhmatova had been denounced as far back as 1940 and with some of the very same language. As we have seen, Zoshchenko was under attack from 1943. Moreover, he continued to defend himself before Stalin even after the meeting of the Orgburo.[101] Despite Zhdanov's famous report, which was then published in *Pravda* in September, no arrests followed. The major consequence was the reorganization of the Writers' Union and a shake-up of its leadership. Two Leningrad journals were closed and personnel changes were made in the editorial boards of two others.

While tightening the lines on the literary sector of the cultural front occupied most of the attention of the guardians of ideological conformity, music did not escape their gaze. The postwar revival of the 'musical uproar' of the 1930s exhibited some paradoxical features that shed further light on Stalin's methods of reining in creative autonomy among the Soviet intelligentsia. In the first two years after the end of the war, Stalin continued to reward – lavishly, one is tempted to add – the contributions made by the composers to the war effort. Then he reversed course and permitted or incited attacks against them. Once he concluded that they were sufficiently chastised by a rap or two on the knuckles, he allowed them to return gradually to their eminent position in Soviet music.

In 1946, Shostakovich took personal advantage of a successful performance of one of his songs by the ensemble of the song and dance group of the NKVD, which had been salvaged by Beria after the changes in the state security organs that had removed him from his previous position. In a letter to Beria, Shostakovich requested assistance for a substantial improvement in his living conditions, which Beria passed on to Stalin. Stalin approved the allocation to the composer of a five-bedroom apartment and 60,000 rubles to repair his dacha. Shostakovich had acted without going through the normal channels of the Composers' Union and the Committee on the Arts, which did not have the resources to satisfy his needs; he wrote to Stalin through the special organs.[102] The soon-to-be-condemned composers were meanwhile strongly represented, highly praised and decorated in the celebration of the eightieth anniversary of the Moscow Conservatory.[103] In the competition for a new national hymn, the works of Prokofiev and Shostakovich were singled out for praise.[104] Another group of composers – including Aram Khachaturian, Reinhold Glière and Vano Muradeli – appealed to Voroshilov for a revision of the 1934 pay rates for musical works by Soviet composers. Opposed by the Finance Ministry, the proposal led to a quarrel among representatives of different musical organizations over the compensation for vocal works, a hint of the conflict to come over serious and light music. But for the moment the pre-eminence and prestige of the leading Soviet composers and especially the Leningraders was not seriously challenged.[105] But this was soon to change.

In March 1947 one of the first sustained criticisms reached Stalin from the ranks of performing musicians on the failure of such leading lights as Prokofiev, Shostakovich and Shebalin to write music that was comprehensible to the majority of Soviet citizens. The writer, a violinist, attributed the problem to the absence of folk songs and dances in their music. The situation was bad in chamber music, he wrote, but worse in opera where the vocal parts could not even be sung. He requested Stalin to point out the errors of their ways.[106] This and similar complaints from below were still being gathered and preserved in the confidential reports (*svodky*) to Stalin, when in May 1947 Prokofiev's opera *War and Peace* was awarded a Stalin Prize 1st Class for the composition and the performance.[107] As late as November 1947, Prokofiev, Shostakovich and Khachaturian were awarded the title of people's artist of the Russian Soviet Republic, which was confirmed in February 1948 at the very time when the Central Committee was preparing the bombshell to explode beneath Muradeli's opera.[108]

Meanwhile, a sharp reversal on the cultural front was gaining momentum. Once again Zhdanov spearheaded the assault by carefully preparing the ground. In reviewing the work of the committee on Stalin Prizes in mid-summer, he made the startling comment that though he was not a fan of cacophonic music, having been brought up on the 'mighty handful' of Russian composers and Mozart, Beethoven, Chopin and Verdi, 'perhaps I have lagged behind the newest tendencies in the musical world and am unable now to value cacophonic music?' He went on to criticize E.K. Golubev's oratorio *Immortal Heroes* for being cacophonic, among other sins. A work on the theme of the Great Fatherland War, he concluded, was 'important and should be well developed'. Despite some good points, then, the work did not deserve the Stalin Prize.[109]

By December, Zhdanov had moved to a general offensive. He entrusted the attack to Shepilov, a new figure in his entourage, who can be described as a survivor of the factional in-fighting that characterized the immediate postwar years. In his memoirs, Shepilov described himself as a member of the heroic 'revolutionary romanticists', the generation of *Komsomoltsy*, born of proletarian parents, steeped in the classics of Marxist-Leninist literature, hardened by years of physical labour and tempered by military service as a political commissar in the Second World War, a role that took him from the defence of Moscow to Stalingrad, Bucharest and Vienna. Contemptuous of the 'petty bourgeois careerists' in the Agitprop Department of the Central Committee, who were 'neither revolutionaries nor Marxists' (as represented by Malenkov's client, Aleksandrov and his minions), Shepilov responded with enthusiasm to Zhdanov's invitation to join him in restoring the ideological defences of the cultural front. He was appointed deputy head of the Agitprop Department under another rising star, Mikhail Suslov.[110] But it was Stalin who provided the occasion for a wholesale review and condemnation of deviant tendencies in Soviet music when he reacted negatively to the first performance of Muradeli's new opera *The Great Friendship*.

In 1941 the young Georgian composer had first mooted writing an opera on the exploits of Sergo Ordzhonikidze in the Russian Civil War; it had then been included in the work plan of the Bolshoi Theatre. Originally entitled *The Extraordinary Commissar*, it was rebaptized *The Great Friendship* in 1947. Zhdanov first reacted to Stalin's remarks by attempting unsuccessfully to persuade the performers to disassociate themselves from the work. He then decided the opera afforded an opportunity to set down some general principles on the production of music.[111] Shepilov was entrusted with the task of reviewing the achievements and shortcomings of Soviet composers in preparation for the first All-Union Congress of Soviet Composers, scheduled to meet in February 1948.

Although in his lengthy and repetitive report Shepilov praised symphonic compositions by Prokofiev, Shostakovich, Myaskovsky and Khachaturian for having raised Soviet symphonic music to the 'first rank in the world', Shepilov then turned 180 degrees to condemn symphonic music for having failed to reach the vast mass of the Soviet people by virtue of its difficulty, formalistic tendencies and lack of realistic portrayal of life, in contrast to 'opera and other democratic genres'. But the review also portrayed Soviet opera as a complete disaster: 'for thirty years composers had failed to produce a single opera that occupied a firm place in the permanent repertoire.' While praising specific works by Shostakovich, Prokofiev and Myaskovsky, particularly their vocal compositions, such as Shostakovich's cantata *Motherland* and his oratorio *Song of the Forest*, and Prokofiev's cantata *Dawn of a Mighty Region*, the report went on to criticize much of their 'abstract instrumental' work: the very same work which, according to an earlier part of the report, had gained Soviet music its worldwide reputation. Much of the blame was laid at the door of the Committee on the Arts and the Orgburo of the Union of Soviet Composers for commissioning works lacking popular appeal. These organizations were also taken to task for ignoring the needs of composers in the union republics while committing their resources to the Leningrad and Moscow composers. He held up as the ideal the Russian romantic tradition of Glinka, Tchaikovsky and Rimsky-Korsakov. The words 'socialist realism' did not appear in the text.[112] The implication of this paradoxical diatribe was clear. Soviet music was expected to perform two functions by appealing to two audiences: first and foremost to meet the tastes of the popular masses at home, primarily among Russians but also among the nationalities, and second to meet the standards of world-class music.

Muradeli's opera was mentioned as one of those containing serious political errors, but was not singled out for special critical treatment. For reasons
that are not entirely clear, but might be due to Stalin's personal involvement,
the opera became the focus for a major propaganda campaign on the themes
of *partiinost'*. Russo-centrism and nationality policy, which had dominated
the cultural front in the 1930s, had been allowed to lose some of their ideological force during the war. Underlying these themes was the issue of the
autonomy of the intelligentsia which had come to the fore during the war, as
it had for the scientific community.[113]

Armed with this report, the Politburo – or, more accurately, Stalin –
ordered a thorough purge of the leadership of the Committee on the Arts
of the Central Committee, the Orgburo of the Union of Soviet Composers
and the Musical Section of the Stalin Prize Committee.[114] The Central
Committee then inaugurated a campaign against Muradeli's opera as
emblematic of the parlous state of Soviet music, declaring that 'in his desire
to achieve a falsely conceived originality, Muradeli ignored and disregarded
the finest traditions and experience of classical opera and particularly of
Russian classical opera'. This lack of melodic, artistic and refined music
which had made Russian opera 'the best in the world' prevented Muradeli's
creation from reaching a wide section of the public. The resolution also criticized Muradeli for having 'failed to draw on the wealth of folk melodies,
songs, tunes and dance motifs so abundant in the folk creations of the peoples
of the USSR and in particular among the peoples of the North Caucasus'. The
Central Committee seized on the occasion to reflect on the 'present unsatisfactory state of Soviet music' in general, characterizing it as dominated by a
formalist trend. The harsh wording of the resolution traced the errors of
Soviet composers going back to Shostakovich's *Lady Macbeth*, insisting that
the situation was particularly unsatisfactory with respect to opera and
symphonic music. The leading composers of the Soviet Union, Shostakovich,
Prokofiev, Aram Khachaturian, Vissarion Shebalin and Nikolai Myaskovsky
were singled out for having filled their music with 'atonality, dissonance and
discord' and for preferring 'neuropathological combinations' to melody. The
resolution ended on an ominous note: 'This music smacks very much of the
spirit of the contemporary modernist bourgeois music of Europe and
America, which is a reflection of the decay of bourgeois culture and signifies
complete negation of musical art, its impasse.'[115] Determined to ram home

the lessons of the Central Committee, Zhdanov summoned a general assembly of Soviet composers aimed at forcing them to recant their errors. His critical opening remarks were mild compared to what followed.

The composer Tikhon Khrennikov took up the cudgels of denunciation, assailing many of the major works of twentieth-century musicians, not only Russian and Soviet but also American, French and German. He named specifically wartime compositions by Shostakovich, Prokofiev, Khachaturian and Myaskovsky. He denounced the Committee on the Arts, all the major musical organizations and the journal *Sovetskaia muzyka* for tolerating and rewarding formalist trends in Soviet music. Khrennikov appeared to understand that this was an occasion to re-affirm the correctness of Stalin's nationality policy, with its delicate balance between russo-centrism and national traditions which only the *vozhd* could calibrate.[116] In 1948 he was rewarded by Stalin, who personally appointed him the new head of the Composers' Union, where he remained ensconced until its abolition in 1991 at the end of the Soviet Union.

The paradoxical position of Khrennikov in this unpredictable world of music was as a guardian of Stalinist orthodoxy and a protector of what Shostakovich called intrinsic musical values. As the strict taskmaster of the Union of Soviet Composers, Khrennikov took responsibility for issuing reprimands, handing out demotions and other forms of punishment, even participating in the campaign against cosmopolitanism with its strong anti-Semitic and russifying (but not russo-centric) themes. He counter-attacked when criticized by writing directly to Stalin and he also shielded the leading composers whom he had previously denounced from the worst of the effects of the campaign, and after Stalin's death returned most of them to positions of honour with appropriate awards and financial entitlements.[117]

The major targets of Zhdanov's attack performed the required ritual of self-criticism, but in a selective manner that blunted the ideological edge of the denunciations. While they admitted to allowing aspects of (undefined) formalism to slip into their work, they attributed this to 'snobbishness' (Muradeli), 'certain negative characteristics peculiar to my musical thought' (Shostakovich), 'an overemphasis on technique' (Khachaturian) and 'self-complacency' (Prokofiev). All of them claimed to have employed folk songs and melodic elements in their work, if not sufficiently.[118] The group sent a sycophantic letter to Stalin in praise of his inspiring leadership in setting the proper course for the direction of Soviet music. But there was more to this incident than stoking Stalin's *amour-propre*. Nothing in the Central Committee resolution or the recantations had anything to do with socialist realism. It was part and parcel of the postwar policy of attempting to revoke the elements of autonomy gained by the intelligentsia during the fighting. It was in many ways a return to the thirties, but at a higher level, one soon to be defined as moving from building 'socialism in one country' to building communism. The effort was only partially successful. The position won by the creative intelligentsia during the war could not be easily liquidated without inflicting serious damage to the new-found prestige of the Soviet Union as a world power. Moreover, in asserting its cultural hegemony in the popular democracies and claiming to have achieved a level of civilization superior to that of the West, the export of cultural products performed important political tasks.

As the possibilities for the Soviet Union to spread its influence increased as a result of its great victory over fascism, the party faced difficult decisions which forced compromises in its basic principles and produced controversies among the guardians of orthodoxy over which performers and which performances should be sent abroad. The success of the Moiseev ballet company provides one of the most striking examples of resolving a contradiction between ideological orthodoxy and practical results. The company had been vetted as a loyal ensemble and outstanding representative of the Soviet policy of peace and friendship, before touring Bulgaria, Romania, Yugoslavia and Hungary, 'territory where Soviet troops were stationed'. Visits to Finland and Poland followed. Despite a confidential review by the Ministry of State Security (MGB) that turned up some unsettling details linking Igor Moiseev and his wife to dubious Western contacts, the troupe continued to enjoy Stalin's protection.[119]

During the last years of Stalin's life, Soviet musicians visited the West, but each one had to be personally vetted by him, and not all passed the test. However, with his approval the Moiseev ballet company flourished, becoming the most widely travelled and celebrated international representative of Soviet culture, continuing after his death to gather accolades. Ironically, the foreign critics couched their praise in a language that matched Stalin's expressed desire to have Soviet music combine folk traditions with the refined technique of the classical dance form. Stalin's personal intervention at every level of musical life was not so much a victory for centralized control as an overture to a greater entanglement of the administrative lines of authority in the creative life of the Soviet intelligentsia and ideological confusion over the meaning of such catchwords as *partiinost'* and *narodnost'* while socialist realism faded as a guiding theme. As several accounts make clear, he took decisions on appointments, prizes and celebrations of anniversaries of institutions on the basis of his personal taste, to which he might or might not attach an ideological significance.[120] In an unexpected result of this 'brouhaha', as Kiril Tomoff calls it, the musicians rebuffed the clumsy intervention of the Central Committee and regained some control over their profession. At the same time, there were changes in the leadership of the main musical organizations including the Union of Soviet Composers and demotions of leading composers from positions of influence in the union, the Moscow Conservatory and other musical organizations.

A related challenge facing the new leadership was how to stimulate the development of musical forms in the national republics that would emulate the achievements in the Russian romantic tradition with the addition of indigenous folk songs or dances. One response was to address the complaint that the central leadership was inattentive to the needs of composers outside Moscow. The new leadership created a committee to facilitate links between Moscow and the musical unions of the national republics with the awkward name 'Committee for the Direction and of the Creativity of the Composers of the USSR'. This did not, however, solve the basic problem of creating a national operatic tradition in places like Uzbekistan.[121]

To illustrate by analogy what the party might have expected from the intelligentsia in rebuilding the war-damaged foundations of socialism, one may turn to the exceptionally successful reconstruction of the main thoroughfare of Kiev, the Khreshchatik. The great buildings lining the street were mined by Soviet forces and then blown up while the Germans were in occupation of the city. As soon as Kiev was liberated in 1944 a competition for reconstruction was announced. Twenty-two proposals showed a renewed enthusiasm for the Cossack Baroque style as well as Ukrainian folk motifs. The winning plan, submitted by the famous Russian architects Aleksei Shchusev and Aleksandr Vlasov, combined a modern rendition of folk ornament with a monumental urban ensemble characteristic of the Soviet Russian architecture preferred by Stalin.[122] Such a combination was much more attainable in architecture which lacked the anthropomorphic element. In painting, literature and operatic music the problem of arriving at an acceptable ideological fit between aesthetic technique, creative spirit and *partiinost'* was much more difficult to attain once the overriding theme of defence of the motherland had lost its force.

Stalin's determination to restore controls over the creative work of the scientific and creative intelligentsia was not accompanied by arrests and executions. These areas had assumed too much importance in promoting the image and reality of an enhanced Soviet position in the world, and the few concessions that he allowed to enhance their self-defined functions and value as semi-autonomous bodies did not in any way endanger his power. The situation was quite different in his postwar assault on the Jews and the group of party leaders in Leningrad. Their contributions to victory were very quickly reduced to ashes because he perceived them in a different light.

POLITICAL PURGES: THE JEWISH ANTI-FASCIST COMMITTEE

The Jews suffered most severely from Stalin's determination to correct what he regarded as the excess zeal of the nationalities during the war in assuming an autonomous role within the Soviet system. His decision to downplay the patriotic role and unique ordeal of Soviet Jews undercut the widespread sympathy that his wartime policy toward them had gained, not only among the Jewish diaspora but the Western allies as well. Related to these short-comings was the failure of the Soviet leadership in Stalin's fierce grip to recognize the persuasive power of an orchestrated appeal to the humanistic and moral supremacy of Soviet civilization over Nazism that had been a mainstay of propaganda during the popular front and which was revived and continued in wartime by such popular figures among the Soviet front-line troops as the Jewish war correspondents Ilia Ehrenburg and Vasily Grossman and the Jewish war photographers Emmanuil Evzerkhin, Roman Karmen and Evgeny Khaldei.[123]

From the beginning, however, doubts were raised in the higher ranks of the party and security services about international contacts with Jewish organizations, especially those stressing the victimization of the Jewish population of the Soviet Union by the Nazis. They were also suspicious of any form of nationalist tendencies (Zionism) which were identified after the war with the establishment of the state of Israel. The party sought to discourage the idea that the Jewish population was somehow different and had endured greater suffering than the rest of the Soviet population. One notorious example was the fate of *The Black Book of Soviet Jewry: The Ruthless Murder of Jews by German-Fascist Invaders throughout the Temporarily Occupied Regions of the Soviet Union and in the Death Camps of Poland during the War 1941–1945*. A collection of eye-witness accounts and documents, it had been compiled in 1943 and 1944 by Ehrenburg, Grossman and other writers, Jewish and non-Jewish, under the auspices of the Jewish Anti-Fascist Committee. Soviet censors ordered changes in the text to conceal the exclusively anti-Jewish character of the killings and to downplay the role of Ukrainian police, who had worked with the Nazis. But these changes were not sufficient to alter the picture of the Jews as exceptional victims of Nazism. In 1948, the Soviet edition of the book was scrapped completely. By this time, the JAFC was falling into disfavour over a range of issues. The government twice turned down the request made by Mikhoels and his deputy, Itsik Fefer, that funds raised abroad by Jewish organizations be mailed directly to the JAFC. Molotov justified the decision by claiming that the proposal would enable 'financial organizations to exploit the opportunity to spread bourgeois ideology in our country'. Moreover, the proposal would 'separate the Jews from the mass of the Soviet population and create the grounds for anti-Semitism'.[124] Another sign of the coming reaction was the fate of a proposal made by the JAFC, with Solomon Lozovsky's support, for the creation of a Soviet Jewish Republic in the Crimea; the peninsula had been depopulated by Stalin's order to deport the Crimean Tatars for having exhibited disloyalty during the war. After a discussion by Stalin and a few associates, the plan was turned down. Lozovsky also supported the idea of a postwar transformation of the JAFC into a permanent organization with its own newspaper. This too came to naught. Right after the war, the JAFC began to take precautions to defend itself against accusations of nationalism. The journal *Eynigkayt* began to publish articles denouncing Jewish nationalism. Any mention of Jewish suffering or heroism disappeared from its pages.[125]

These efforts did not prevent Mikhail Suslov, who had taken over the Agitprop Department of the Central Committee, from taking the lead in preparing denunciations of the Zionist and Bundist character of the JAFC's publications. This was followed by strong recommendations to redefine its work in order to promote the achievements of the Soviet Union abroad and discontinue *Eynigkayt* as a newspaper.[126] But the JAFC leadership continued to press for a leading role in representing Jewish interests in the Soviet Union and abroad. Then, in February 1948, the classic pattern of a purely propaganda campaign against 'bourgeois nationalism' was violently broken by Stalin's personal order to have Mikhoels murdered. The circumstances of his killing were bizarre. The killers were two high-ranking members of the MGB operating under the direction of Abakumov; one of the pair, Sergei Ogol'tsov, had in 1942 given the order to execute Wiktor Alter in prison. The assassination had all the hallmarks of a gangland killing: the body of Mikhoels and his companion were given the appearance of having been accidentally run over by a truck. Stalin commended and decorated the killers secretly. The cover-up was elaborate; *Pravda* printed a laudatory obituary and Mikhoels was given a state funeral.[127] A month later Abakumov, whom Stalin increasingly employed to dilute Beria's control over the security services, submitted to the top Soviet leadership the most extensive denunciation of the JAFC as a pro-American, nationalist and anti-Soviet organization with extensive ties to international Jewry and infiltrated by foreign intelligence services.[128]

Reverting to practice, Stalin proceeded more systematically to prepare the ground for the abolition of the JAFC while at the same time moving ahead with plans to support the creation of the state of Israel. Before leaving for his annual vacation, he instructed Malenkov to commission Ehrenburg to write an article on Israel.[129] Ehrenburg had been in touch with members of the JAFC in his efforts to publish the *Black Book*. But he knew what was expected of him. His letter, published in *Pravda* on 21 September 1948, attempted to draw a parallel between anti-Semitism and Zionism. He denounced both as two sides of the same coin, inspired by a racist concept of what it meant to be a Jew; the one – fascist – leading to murderous atrocities; the other – Zionist – also obscurantist, portraying the Jews as a chosen people linked in some mysterious way and seeking to solve the Jewish question by a return to the promised land of Israel. While Ehrenburg affirmed his support for the state of Israel in its struggle to free itself from colonialism and repulse its Arab aggressors, he insisted that the solution to anti-Semitism lay in the victory of the progressive forces of mankind in every country including Israel, as demonstrated by the Soviet Union and the people's democracies of Eastern Europe.[130] Within a month, the Politburo ordered the closure of the JAFC as a centre of anti-Soviet propaganda 'regularly providing anti-Soviet information to organs of foreign intelligence'. The order ended with the words: 'No one should be arrested yet.'[131]

'Yet' proved to be a short-lived interim. Within a few months most of the members of the JAFC including Lozovsky were arrested and preparations were under way for their trial. Although tortured in prison, Lozovsky refused to admit his guilt and skilfully demolished the prosecution's case at his trial. Nevertheless, he was found guilty and, after his appeal to Stalin for clemency was rejected, he was shot in 1952, together with thirteen other members of the JAFC. Grossman survived but died in poverty; Ehrenburg outlived Stalin and with his novel *The Thaw*, published in 1954, he gave a name to Khrushchev's postwar policy of liberalization.

The arrests of members of the JAFC had broad implications for internal Soviet politics. The fate of Jews with ties or strong sympathies with the state of Israel now became deeply entangled in a struggle over control of the security services, which Stalin manipulated as part of his Byzantine manoeuvres in his last years to maintain his monopoly of power and forestall any co-ordinated effort to settle the problem of his succession.[132]

Throughout these months of mounting internal crisis, Stalin approved a strong, apparently paradoxical campaign to support the creation of a Jewish state in Palestine, in contrast to the British and Americans, who initially favoured various forms of trusteeship.[133] The Soviet Union was the first country to recognize the state of Israel and to send an ambassador to Tel Aviv. When Golda Meir arrived in Moscow in September 1948 as the Israeli ambassador, she received a warm welcome from Molotov, Vyshinsky and other high-ranking officials of the Foreign Ministry. Upon her arrival she was greeted spontaneously by a delirious crowd of Jews, estimated at 20,000, at the Central Synagogue in Moscow. A similar popular outpouring accompanied her delegation to the Central Synagogue on Rosh Hashanah.[134] The only cloud on the horizon of official contacts with Israel was the Soviet reluctance to entertain Israeli requests to assist in the emigration of Jews from the Soviet Union.[135] The war had revived the unresolved paradox of the Jewish question in Soviet society. Jews had played a role second only to the Russians in building the Soviet state, and they had been the only nationality in the war zone that had not furnished the enemy with collaborators or defectors.[136] But they were also the nationality with the best-organized and most affluent diaspora in the West and the only nationality to have created an independent state outside the Soviet Union. They were also the only nationality with a separate organizing committee that had ties outside the Soviet Union. The creation of the state of Israel offered the Soviet Union a unique opportunity to penetrate the Middle East. But the shadow of Zionism – or rather its ghost from the early days of the socialism movement in Russia – haunted Stalin with renewed fears about dual loyalties. And despite their contribution to the war effort, Jewish patriots were turned into traitors.

POLITICAL PURGES: THE LENINGRAD AFFAIR

A very different group of celebrated wartime figures converted into victims of cooked-up conspiracies in the early postwar years were leading members of the Leningrad party organization, who were protégés of Andrei Zhdanov. For all its cross-currents and murky details, the so-called Leningrad Affair can be described as a phase in the struggle for succession. It also fits into the paradoxical pattern of Stalin's postwar policies at its extreme expression: the destruction of a group which had contributed to one of the most celebrated victories of the war, the defence of Leningrad during its 900-day siege. A revival of the blood-letting that had stained the party in the thirties after a victorious war under the banner of unity can only be explained as a consequence of the high stakes involved. By the end of the war, it was clear to his inner circle that Stalin was in physical decline and the question of who would succeed him loomed large. Zhdanov's star was again in the ascendance after a brief period of disfavour. He was welcomed back to Moscow's inner circle in 1944 and even acquired a reputation abroad as a potential successor to Stalin.[137] This possibility acquired increasing weight as Stalin reshuffled the older generation of leaders – including Molotov, Beria and Malenkov – in order to reduce their authority in the Central Committee and the security services.[138]

The signs of a factional struggle between Zhdanov and Malenkov together with Beria dated back to the late thirties.[139] Although the incidence and prominence of their clashes diminished during the war, they came to the surface again soon after the end of hostilities. There were clear signs that the factional struggle was growing in intensity as the stakes increased.[140]

After the war, Stalin made several changes in the top leadership of the party. Zhdanov's return to the centre as secretary of the Central Committee and member of the Politburo signalled the rise to prominence within the leading cadres of the party and government of his protégés, most of them from the Leningrad organization. Most prominent among them was Voznesensky, who emerged from the war with a heightened reputation. Rewarded for his distinguished wartime service, he was promoted to full member of the Politiburo in 1947. At the same time, his book, *The Military Economy of the USSR during the Fatherland War*, was published to great acclaim and received the Stalin Prize in 1948.

As the head of Gosplan, he was in charge of drafting the fourth five-year plan, which, as we have seen (above, p. 237), achieved impressive results in restoring the command economy and providing for a higher standard of living. Moreover, in August 1945 he was appointed to the high-powered Special Committee on the Atomic Bomb of GOKO (subsequently of the Sovnarkom) together with Beria, Malenkov, the industrial managers Vannikov, Avraamii Zaveniagin and Mikhail Pervukhin, one of Beria's men, general Vasily Makhnev, and the scientists Kapitsa and Kurchatov. Voznesensky and Zaveniagin were assigned the tasks of supervising the construction and management of factories and laboratories, responding to bottlenecks in production and providing material and financial resources for the many enterprises involved in the project. The full committee reviewed the proposals of Vannikov and Kurchatov and drafted documents for Stalin's signature. Meetings of the committee invariably involved a large number of engineers, scientists and industrial managers who received instructions on a myriad of tasks devolving from their decisions. Voznesensky participated in all seventy-three meetings of the committee up to his removal.[141]

Another Leningrader who had risen to prominence as a result of his wartime service was Aleksei Kuznetsov. Originally recruited by Sergei Kirov, he had performed heroic service during the war as deputy secretary of the Leningrad city organization in organizing the city's defences. In 1946 Kuznetsov had earned Malenkov's enmity by exposing the serious errors he had permitted in the administration of the Ministry of Aviation.[142] He was promoted as Central Committee secretary and head of the key cadres department, replacing Malenkov. He was also placed in charge of overseeing the newly created Ministry of State Security run by Abakumov, a former associate of Beria. Subsequently, a resentful Abakumov became a central figure in purging the Leningraders.

Stalin reportedly expressed in a private conversation his preference for Voznesensky and Kuznetsov as his successors, in state policy and party policy respectively, greatly enhancing their authority.[143] Doubtless this comment or rumour could only have alarmed Malenkov and Beria. There is also evidence that Stalin instructed Kuznetsov as head of cadres to promote younger men with outstanding wartime records to positions of greater responsibility.[144] Here is where the contradictory or obscure elements of the affair begin to surface. Kuznetsov proceeded to increase the appointment of Leningraders throughout the Soviet Union following Zhdanov's example of appointing his men to head the Novgorod and Pskov oblasts. But Zhdanov now came out against the over-centralization of appointments made by the Central Committee, that is against Kuznetsov.[145] Moreover, Stalin had made it clear as early as 1937 that appointments should not be made on the basis of personal relations; this was anti-Bolshevik and 'should end before it is too late'.[146] Kuznetsov ignored these warning signs and continued to appoint or promote his men in regional party organizations throughout the Russian Republic and to key positions in the Central Committee.

A third key figure in the Leningrad Affair was Mikhail Rodionov, brought in by Zhdanov from Gorky before the war. He had also participated in the defence of Leningrad and was appointed chairman of the Council of Ministers of the Russian Republic and member of the Orgburo of the party. Other important appointments of Zhdanov clients included Voznesensky's brother, the rector of Leningrad University during the siege, who was raised to the post of minister of education of the Russian Republic during the wartime educational reform. Aleksei Kosygin, born and educated in Leningrad, had worked closely with Rodionov during the war to sustain the city during the siege. He had organized the colossal tasks of transporting over 1,500 factories to the Urals and supervising the construction of the famous ice road across Lake Ladoga during the siege, which enabled the evacuation of half a million Leningraders and kept the city supplied with food and fuel. In 1943 he was appointed chief of the Sovnarkom of the Russian Republic, and after the war minister of finance (1946) and then light industry (1948–53). In this post he was associated with the rise in living standards, a reputation he was to parley into a leading role in the post-Stalin government for the following thirty years. According to his grandson, Malenkov and Beria wrote to Stalin urging him to eliminate Kosygin as part of the Leningrad conspiracy. During this period he feared for his life. But Stalin valued his administrative skill and his independence from factional politics; he also had the support of Anastas Mikoian.[147]

Shepilov was not a Leningrader by birth or service, but he was very much a Zhdanov protégé. His distinguished wartime record as a political commissar with the southwestern front from Stalingrad to Vienna had earned him an influential position as head of the Agitprop Department of the Central Committee, where, under Zhdanov's supervision, as we have seen (above p. 244), he had drafted the attack on the Soviet composers. But he also fell under the shadow of Malenkov, who told him 'We have been after you for a long time'. Shortly after Voznesensky's arrest he was denounced by a Politburo resolution for having failed to exercise control over the journal *Bol'shevik* and for having recommended Voznesensky's book to regional secretaries as a text. He was dismissed from his position. But Stalin spared him. Considering him 'an educated Marxist', Stalin not only had him appointed an inspector of the Central Committee, but also discussed with him the editing of a new textbook on economics.[148] Although these men were the most influential of Zhdanov's protégés, the Leningrad party organization, Gosplan and numerous second-level figures in industry, cultural affairs and education were indebted to him for his patronage. Once Zhdanov had died in August 1948 of a heart attack, possibly as the result of a misdiagnosis, his erstwhile rivals rapidly set about to destroy his patronage network.

The conspirators were headed by Malenkov, with Beria standing in the background, and Matvei Shkiriatov, the dreaded deputy of the Party Control Commission, and Abakumov, the wartime head of SMERSH and from 1946 minister of state security, as point men.[149] They moved along two converging lines. The first directed against Kuznetsov, for his activities as virtual boss of Leningrad and as head of the cadres department of the Central Committee engaged in colonizing other local party organizations in the Russian Republic; and the second against Voznesensky, for errors in the economic sector and then as the alleged real patron of the Leningraders. The conspiracy was put together gradually from October 1948 to August 1949, although, as we have seen, its origins went back to the war and even earlier. Straws in the winds of war were reassembled by the conspirators to provide evidence of widespread corruption – or 'politically improper conduct by second-level party members in Leningrad' – covered up by their superiors.[150] After the war, the accusations focused on the self-promotion of the top Leningrad party members, including Kuznetsov. They had organized commemorations of the defence of the city and renamed public spaces for the purpose of enhancing and inflating their role in what was later denounced as behaviour completely at odds with Bolshevik morality, that is *partiinost'*.[151]

Meanwhile, Malenkov launched his campaign on a minor key. In late 1948, he accused the Leningrad party organization of failing to obtain approval from the Council of Ministers for a trade fair in Leningrad, although the organizers had followed the normal procedures. Further discredit was heaped on the Leningrad party for not reporting accurately the results of elections to the local party positions. Malenkov stepped up the level of accusations in February 1949, when he identified Kuznetsov, Rodionov and, as yet, an unknown but small number of their Leningrad associates of being an anti-party group, although no evidence was supplied.

Beria, who was fully cognizant of the obsessions of the *vozhd*, kept feeding Stalin information that the Leningrad party leaders were strongly considering and even moving toward the creation of their own Central Committee and government of the Russian Federation to counterbalance the Central Committee of the All-Union Communist Party (b) and the Soviet government.[152] Stalin had opposed the formation of a Russian Communist Party since the early 1920s. That this idea was again being discussed infuriated him. At a Politburo meeting on 15 February 1949, he lashed out at a member of the Leningrad group who suggested that 'the Russian people need their own advocates'. He furiously denounced the sentiment; it 'smacked of Russian ethnic self-interest and incipient nationalism'.[153] Voznesensky and Kuznetsov among others were denounced for aiming to convert the Leningrad organization into a regional fiefdom; an ominous resolution compared their activity to that of Zinoviev in the 1920s, when he had 'attempted to turn the Leningrad organization into a power base for his anti-Leninist faction'.[154] In Stalin's eyes, Leningrad had continued to represent a centre of opposition even after the defeat of Zinoviev and the purge of his network. In order to rebuild the party organization, Stalin had appointed as party secretary Sergei Kirov, a client and friend of his from the days of the civil war in Transcaucasia, far removed from the lure of local Leningrad politics. When Kirov was assassinated in 1934, Stalin ordered NKVD chief

Iagoda to 'Look for the murderers among the Zinovievites.'[155] Two years later, Zinoviev was tried and executed on the basis of fabricated evidence linking him to the Kirov murder. Zhdanov was brought in from Nizhny Novgorod to re-establish order. Under his aegis, the war had restored an aura of uniqueness to Leningrad. The heroic 900-day resistance of the city, organized mainly by members of the local organization, earned the city of Lenin a place in the pantheon of 'hero cities' comparable only to the city of Stalin on the Volga. Could the symbolism have gone unnoticed by the *vozhd*?

At the same time that the Leningraders were being accused of ambitious political aims, their position on the cultural front was again brought under fire. The party organization was reproached for not having learned their lesson from the criticism of the literary journals in 1946. A resolution published in January 1949 denounced the journal *Znamia* for 'several grave errors', touching off a renewal of the campaign 'to fight cosmopolitan critics'.[156] It is instructive to recall at this point that in 1946 when Stalin cross-examined the Leningraders in an Orgburo meeting, he had declared that the city was following a different line on culture, influenced by the city intelligentsia; this showed a willingness to bow and scrape before foreigners. 'Cosmopolitanism' was another formulaic way of describing the same phenomena.

In the summer, Abakumov was enlisted to write to Stalin, accusing the former secretaries of the Leningrad city and party organizations of being English spies. Under torture they then implicated all the top officials in the Leningrad organization, including Kuznetsov and Rodionov. In August, the accused were arrested and denounced as 'demagogic' defenders of the interests of Leningrad, having conducted 'dubious secret self-seeking combinations'.[157] Meanwhile, the conspirators were preparing to pull Voznesensky into the net.

Already in March Voznesensky had been accused of having juggled the figures for gross industrial output in the first quarter of the plan for 1949 to accommodate Stalin's unrealistic demand for increased level of production, thereby creating a discrepancy between the level of investment and the published figures. On the basis of Stalin's hallowed statement that any attempt to alter the figures for Gosplan was a criminal offence, Voznesensky was removed as the body's president. Although Voznesensky made a correction, Beria followed up on his previous accusations that he had made similar errors in drafting the fourth five-year plan. Having acquired the compromising document from one of Voznesensky's deputies, Beria returned to the attack with the serious allegation, which was incorporated into a Politburo resolution, that 'Gosplan has followed a biased and dishonest approach to planning and above all to evaluating the fulfilment of plans'.[158] In July, a recently appointed head of cadres of Gosplan reported that from 1944 to 1949 a number of documents had disappeared from the Gosplan offices. Malenkov forwarded the note to Stalin. It was now the turn of Shkiriatov, acting for the Party Control Commission, to draw up a bill of indictment against Voznesensky, which for the first time linked him to the 'anti-party' Leningrad group. He recommended that Voznesensky be excluded from the Central Committee and put on trial for the loss of the documents. This opinion was confirmed by a plenum of the Central Committee, but there was a month's delay when Stalin apparently was unwilling, as in the cases of Zhukov and Kapitsa, to sacrifice Voznesensky to Beria; instead, he may have considered making him head of the State Bank. In the interim, Shkiriatov prepared another memo outlining in great detail all the peccadilloes of Leningrad party members dating back to 1938 and increasing during and after the war. A heavy emphasis was placed on corruption, embezzlement of party funds, drunkenness, favouritism and licentious behaviour. Voznesensky was not named in connection with these anti-party activities, but rather as the alleged 'patron of the group'.[159] For unclear reasons, it took a month after Voznesensky was denounced and excluded from the Central Committee before the plenum ordered his arrest along with a number of leading Leningrad party officials including Kuznetzov and Rodionov. With Abakumov in charge, they were interrogated and tortured, revealing other names in an alleged conspiracy. The preparations for a trial extended over a year as Abakumov compiled a list of those to be punished. Although the outcome appeared to be predetermined, a public trial was never held. In September 1950 the Military College of the Supreme Court met in secret and condemned the accused. A few days later Voznesensky, Kuznetsov, Rodionov Kapustin, Popkov and Lazutin were executed with Stalin's approval.[160]

With the loss of their patron, the Leningrad organization was vulnerable to a devastating purge. Malenkov led the charge, with Beria once again providing the foot soldiers. In Leningrad in the period from 1949 to 1952 all five regional party secretaries, the four most senior city soviet officials and several high-level regional officials were purged, and as many as 2,000 from the party, Komsomol and trade unions were dismissed for 'hostile actions of an anti-party group', including some outside Leningrad in Zhdanov's former bailiwick of Gorky.[161] Many had performed heroically during the siege, a factor that played no part in determining their fate. Among those tried and shot were Voznesensky's brother, the former head of Leningrad University and minister of education of the Russian Republic and his sister. Almost all Voznesensky's deputies in Gosplan were dismissed. The wave of arrests reached a climax in 1952 with the trial and sentencing to long prison terms of fifty persons occupying responsible positions in the Leningrad region during the siege in Leningrad.[162]

A number of puzzling and unresolved elements in the affair remain, perhaps never to be explained fully. Later, when he was in turn accused of being a member of an anti-party group, Malenkov confessed that he had destroyed many documents relating to the case.[163] Full access to relevant documents in the archives has never been granted. Popular histories abound, most of them offering explanations that are based on one or another of the accusations of the conspirators.[164]

The unique murderous character of the Leningrad Affair in the postwar purges can be further illustrated by contrasting it with the Affair of Georgy Popov, the first secretary of the Moscow party committee. In 1949 Stalin received an anonymous letter accusing the Moscow party leadership of organizing a conspiracy to seize power. The results of the investigation he ordered were presented by Malenkov to the Moscow organization. But there was no mention of a conspiracy. Popov and the top leadership of the Moscow party were found culpable of various sins, including attempts to bring pressure on ministers of state to accede to their demands and interests, breaking party discipline and even ignoring Stalin's personal warning. Popov and his group were relieved of their positions. But there were no arrests and there is no evidence they were dismissed from the party.[165] Yet this is the very time the Leningraders were being crushed.

Stalin's postwar treatment of the party, the military and the technical and creative intelligentsia was scored with deep lines of suspicion, reflecting long-embedded personal characteristics but appearing to grow ever more irrational. Yet it would be a mistake to ignore or neglect shades of difference in his imposition of punishments on those he perceived as miscreants. They

ranged from harsh criticism, demotion and expulsion from official positions to arrest, prison terms and shooting. The following hypothesis is
advanced to move beyond the simple verdict of paranoia and to shed light
on the murky crevices of his mindset. The evidence is largely circumstantial
but highly suggestive, if not compelling.

The one denominator common to almost all the cases was the extent to
which the offending individual or group was engaged in political activity
that, as Stalin perceived it, challenged his monopoly of ideology and power,
including relations with a foreign state. Deviations from what he considered
at any moment to be the correct interpretation of Marxism-Leninism, though
serious, required a lesser punishment than 'anti-state' behaviour, and carried
less heavy penalties. In the postwar period, the miscreants never committed
political crimes as a primary cause for imprisonment or execution. But even
these distinctions are not without exceptions, to be duly noted.

In the cases of Zhukov and his generals, the Jewish Anti-Fascist Committee
and the Leningrad group, their alleged political challenge to Stalin's monopoly
of power disrupted a pattern of promoting stability in the party and state
agencies. Stalin's methods of controlling the ambitions of his inner circle
normally took the form of diluting or reducing their authority. But he did not
break up their patronage-client networks; still less did he have their patrons
shot. Moreover, he also resisted the attempts of members of the inner circle
to destroy their opponents, restraining Beria's plotting against Zhukov or
Kapitsa, resisting Zhdanov's efforts to eliminate Varga. By contrast, only the
assault on the JAFC matched the brutal and extensive purge of the
Leningraders. And how to explain Stalin's decision to spare some prominent
figures, like Kosygin and Shepilov, who were closely associated with
Voznesensky? Given his penchant for secrecy and the absence of reliable
sources on his state of mind, his motivations remain obscure. One can only
guess at the various combinations that might have influenced him: their
proven value during the war, their administrative skills, but mainly their
perceived lack of political ambition. Or was it simply a matter of demonstrating his power to decide men's fate, or just personal amity or enmity?

SOCIALIST ENCIRCLEMENT

In international politics, Stalin's policies veered from a welcome alliance
with the West against fascism which ended the virtual isolation of the Soviet

Union, to a break with the West after their shared ordeal in the Second World War. The result was a return to the idea of capitalist encirclement, tempered by the creation of a socialist bloc that expanded the frontier defences of the Soviet citadel. The victorious Soviet advance into Central Europe and support for the establishment of various forms of popular democracy in Poland, Hungary, Romania, Bulgaria, East Germany, Albania, Czechoslovakia and Yugoslavia laid the foundations for a socialist bloc or commonwealth, although this term was not used at the time. In the early postwar years, Stalin gave serious consideration to the idea of separate roads to socialism.[166] But Stalin was concerned about the internal stability of these governments. Except for Czechoslovakia and Yugoslavia, the local communist parties were in a distinct minority; their leaders inexperienced in governing; the opposition strongly anti-Soviet. He was quick to criticize their mistakes in the areas of politics and economics.

The year 1948 witnessed the confluence of three trends in international politics that had a pronounced and disturbing – not to say disastrous – impact on Stalin's decision to intervene more brusquely, even violently, in the affairs of the local communist parties along parallel lines with his domestic policies. The first was the growing involvement of the United States in Europe, culminating in the Marshall Plan, but already foreshadowed by the Truman Doctrine and the formation of the Organization for Economic Co-operation. At the same time, the US government embarked on an unprecedented commitment to overseas intelligence activities which, though clandestine, did not go unnoticed by the Soviet security services. The second was the rupture with Tito, which Stalin interpreted as a nationalist deviation, a dangerous detour on the path to socialism. The third was the creation of the state of Israel, which initially he supported to enhance Soviet and diminish Western influence in the Middle East. Soon disillusioned on that score, he distrusted the sympathy Israel engendered in the Soviet Union and Eastern Europe. He suspected it of reviving the spectre of Zionism with its threat of dual loyalty, which he thought had long before been put to rest. Stalin interpreted these developments as intertwined in a hostile combination that threatened Soviet domination of Eastern Europe and the recovery and security of the Soviet Union.

The accusations were employed like a spiked club to discipline the East European communist parties, which had been allowed to stray during the war along their national paths to socialism. In identifying the miscreants, Soviet diplomats, country specialists and above all the security services were actively involved at all stages, from denunciations to interrogations and torture. They were able to exploit factional and personal rivalries among the local parties that had developed during the war. Involved in their own struggles for power, local communist leaders provided fabricated information and invited Soviet security personnel to assist them in destroying their colleagues and even the leaders of other national parties. Most of the victims were loyal Stalinists who had undergone severe tests of their dedication during the war.[167] Thus, the effect of the purges was to eliminate many of the 'best people', whose contribution to building socialism was thereby lost. Like many of the condemnations at home, so too in the foreign communist parties, rehabilitations followed Stalin's death. But not in all cases; the miasma of falsifications hung heavily over the parties down to the collapse of communist rule.

EPILOGUE
REMEMBERING THE WAR

From 1946 to 1950, every 9 May – Victory Day – the front page of *Pravda* carried a huge portrait of Stalin, reinstating him in his proper role as the architect of victory. But there was a paradox here too, which the cult of Stalin was unable to resolve after the death of the *vozhd* in 1953. By assuming the role of victor, Stalin unwillingly exposed himself, post mortem, to blame – and even ridicule – for all the mistakes committed in the course of the war. This was Khrushchev's ploy from the very beginning of his de-Stalinization campaign when he took over as first secretary in 1953, culminating at the Twenty-Second Party Congress in 1961. It was also a convenient way to absolve himself of actions he had carried out as Stalin's loyal cupbearer. Already on Victory Day in 1953, two months after Stalin's death, the tributes to the *vozhd* were missing from the banner headlines; there was no military parade. It had been shifted to 1 May, a more traditional date. Victory Day was instead preceded by two organized events. One, on 7 May in the Bolshoi Theatre, celebrated the two hundredth anniversary of the founding of Moscow University. It was timed to coincide with a mass meeting of Soviet youth on Lenin Hills, greeted by the press with an enthusiasm previously reserved for Victory Day. But both had had nothing to do with the war. A second official celebration was held on the eve of Victory Day, 8 May, also in the Bolshoi Theatre, for the top civil and military leaders. The main speaker was General Ivan Konev, a hero of the war but without the stature of a Zhukov or a Rokossovsky. Konev's speech dealt only with the military side of the war and mentioned Stalin only once.[1] The process of what has been called the 'expansion of memory' had begun.[2] Before Khrushchev's removal in 1964, he played the key role in denouncing and eliminating his potential rivals – first Beria, then Malenkov and Molotov – from positions of power, sidelining Zhukov for a second time. If all the wartime leaders were discredited, who then, one could legitimately ask, had led the country to victory?[3]

In a search for answers one turns to the celebrations of the war. The war was in many ways a formative period for the Soviet population as the revolution of 1917 never was, yet Stalin had to 'devaluate' its memory, treating it as a passing moment in the building of socialism. To have done otherwise would have been to celebrate the sense of liberation and self-valuation that came with the themes of mobilization. The arc of the pendulum between russo-centrism and Soviet patriotism had swung dangerously far in each direction; it had to be brought back to a central position. At first, the ritual of Victory Day was exploited by Stalin to reconcile the inherent contradictions between the two positions. The *vozhd* alone possessed the wisdom and far-sightedness to lead the country from victory to a new stage in the development of socialism. Without his close surveillance, guidance and – when necessary – brutal intervention, the building of socialism would lose its momentum and direction. During the early years of the war, Stalin himself had placed restraints on the cult of leadership, briefly fading into the background before he began to burnish his image again.[4] During most of the war, centre stage was occupied by the people, with the Russians in the forefront. The celebrations of Victory Day with Stalin at the centre of his associates on the reviewing platform above Lenin's mausoleum restored the balance. But the celebration of Victory Day was terminated two years after the war and not revived again until 1964 under Brezhnev.

With the restoration of Victory Day in 1964, Stalin's reputation, which had reached its nadir under Khrushchev's withering – often fantastical – recital, gradually recovered. And then, in the Russian Federation, it soared to a 50 per cent approval rating in 2004, where it has hovered ever since. One of the most contested recent battles over Stalin's reputation as warlord centred on a topographical dispute over the naming of the most famous battle of the Second World War in the east; the city of Stalingrad had been renamed Volgograd, but what about the battle? Surely it too would lose its symbolic meaning if it were also renamed.[5]

While Vladimir Putin has embraced the idea that the Soviet Union made the greatest sacrifices and contributed the most to winning the war, he has been more restrained in associating himself with Stalin as the architect of victory.[6] In his brief remarks at Red Square celebrating the seventy-fifth anniversary of Victory Day in 2020, Putin did not mention Stalin at all. In his long article prepared for a Western audience on the anniversary, he briefly acknowledged Stalin's 'crimes' against his own people and 'the horrors of mass repression'. He then went on to praise Stalin's role in foreign policy, first in the course of justifying the Nazi-Soviet Pact as part of a defensive strategy and then at the Tehran and Yalta conferences as a founder of the postwar international system, in other words as a diplomat, not as a warlord. Putin attributed victory in the war to the courage and sacrifices of the people whom he has called variously Soviet and Russian under a collective leadership.[7] This fits the anthropologist Serguei Oushakine's concept of 'patriotic despair', which by evoking the traumatic memories of loss and suffering in war feeds into a powerful myth. This – and not the revolution – is the tradition with which Putin identifies himself.[8] Meanwhile, similar representations of the war have steadily emerged from below in the Russian provinces, suggesting how closely Putin's myth-making replicates the mood of the population.[9]

In the former republics the pattern varied. In Ukraine, Stalin's general popularity was considerably greater in the eastern than the western regions, where it was virtually non-existent. The celebrations of his achievements in war and peace were often marked by extreme demonstrations. In Zaporozhe, in southeastern Ukraine, the Stalin monument erected by the local communists was blown up in December 2010. It was quickly replaced with a bust that linked him even more closely to the Great Fatherland War. In Western Ukraine the memory of Stepan Bandera, the most celebrated anti-Stalinist in Ukrainian memory wars, underwent similar permutations. As of early 2014 there were forty-six full-sized statues or busts of Bandera in Western Ukraine, plus fourteen plaques, all located in L'viv; in addition more than 100 streets have been renamed after him in the same region, and five museums commemorating him were constructed between 1990 and 2010. But, as was the case with Stalin, memory wars can be fought with real weapons. The first two monuments erected in Bandera's home town were blown up in the early 1990s and plaques dedicated to him were desecrated with swastikas.[10] The fight in Ukraine goes on; truly this was 'the war that failed to end'.[11]

Stalin's conduct of the war will remain mired in controversy; its long-term consequences may never be fully grasped. Such are the fruits of paradox. His wartime policies were on one level a continuation at higher levels of prewar trends towards centralization and control; on another level they deviated from those trends. Just how radically they deviated may be judged from the fate of the major innovations and improvisations introduced in the postwar period. Simply put, most of them were discarded or repressed. Changes were marginal: a modified flexible definition of the professional autonomy of the technical and creative intelligentsia, however still monitored by party and police surveillance. The new postwar campaigns of mobilization – reminiscent of the thirties – restored the more punitive aspects. Various reform schemes failed to prevent a further decline in the viability of the collective farm system in the post-Stalin years. Attempts to shift resources to the material needs of the population were not permitted to diminish traditional investments in heavy industry, which, with the exception of defence needs, became increasingly outmoded in the decades that followed.[12] An increase in the level of educational standards was notable in physics and mathematics, but biology and especially genetics took years to recover.[13] The social sciences and humanities were heavily burdened by ideological considerations until the end of the Soviet period. Training and performance standards in music, the theatre and ballet remained high, but for a long time the repertoire – with few exceptions – was drawn from pre-revolutionary works.

Stalin's record as a warlord was paradoxical on a gigantic scale. His leadership – steady, ruthless, tireless and remarkably flexible, given the prewar evidence – was a major factor in winning the war, but then after the war he took measures which suppressed or stifled the most creative elements in the country that he had barely unfettered for four years. His successors failed to break the dead hand of Stalinism on the country. His legacy was to burden the Soviet Union and its successor to our own days.

CHRONOLOGY

1878 (79?)	Ioseb Dzhugashvili (Stalin) born in Gori, Georgia, Russian Empire
1894–99	Stalin educated at Tiflis Orthodox Seminary, first contact with Marxist literature
1899–1905	Stalin's revolutionary activity in Georgia
1906–17	Stalin suffers arrests and Siberian exile
1917	Stalin's participation in Bolshevik Revolution
1918–21	Stalin as political commissar in civil war and commissar of nationalities
1919	First Congress of Comintern
1921–27	New Economic Policy
1922	Stalin becomes general secretary of the Communist Party
1928	Shakhty Trial
1929	Beginning of collectivization; first five-year plan launched
1932	Creation of Union of Soviet Writers
1934 (December)	Assassination of Kirov
1936	Beginning of show trials of leading Bolsheviks
1936–38	Great Terror
1939 (August)	Nazi-Soviet Pact

1939–40	Soviet-Finnish War; occupation of Baltic states and Bessarabia
1941 (April)	Soviet-Japanese Neutrality Pact
1941 (22 June)	Nazi invasion of Soviet Union (Operation Barbarossa)
1941 (December)	Germans stopped at Moscow
1942 (June)	Major German offensive in Ukraine
1942–43	Battle of Stalingrad
1943 (May)	Dissolution of Comintern
1943 (July)	Battle of Kursk
1943 (September)	Stalin gives permission for a Church Council
1943 (November)	Tehran Conference
1943–44	Deportation of peoples of North Caucasus and Crimea
1944 (August–October)	Warsaw Uprising
1945 (February)	Election of Patriarch Aleksei; Yalta Conference
1945 (May)	Surrender of Nazi Germany
1945 (July–August)	Potsdam Conference
1946 (February)	Stalin's election speech on inevitability of war
1946 (August)	Central Committee attack on Zoshchenko and Akhmatova
1946–47	Famine in Ukraine
1947	Creation of Cominform; currency reform in USSR
1948 (January)	Murder of Mikhoels
1948 (February)	Central Committee denunciation of decadence in music
1948 (June)	Cominform expels Yugoslavia
1948 (November)	Dissolution of Jewish Anti-Fascist Committee
1949	Leningrad Affair
1953 (March)	Death of Stalin

GLOSSARY

Agitprop	Agitation and Propaganda Department of the Central Committee of the Communist Party of the Soviet Union
aktiv	party rank and file
ASSR	Autonomous Soviet Socialist Republic: administrative division of nationalities within USSR
GOKO	(Gosudarstvennyi komitet oborony) State Defence Committee
Gosplan	(Gosudarstvennyi plan) State Planning Committee
Gulag	Main Administration of the Labour Camps
Komsomol	Communist Youth League
krai	an administrative region, used without a clear distinction from oblast
kraikom	the party committee of the krai
NKVD	People's Commissariat of Internal Affairs: the secret police; successor to the OGPU, renamed the Ministry of Internal Affairs in 1946 (when commissariats became ministries)
obkom	regional committee of the Communist Party
oblast	an administrative region; cf. krai above
OUN	Organization of Ukrainian Nationalists (anti-Soviet)
partiinost'	method of analyzing literature and the arts that defines the position of the party; carries the sense of being imbued with Bolshevik values

polpred	abbreviation of *polnomochnyi predstavitel'*, meaning plenipotentiary, the equivalent of ambassador
praktiki	men with practical training in education, as opposed to theoretical; also applied to type of work
raikom	district committee of the Communist Party
RSFSR	Russian Soviet Federated Socialist Republic; from 1937 the name of the largest of the Soviet republics, inhabited mainly by ethnic Russians
SMERSH	Counterintelligence section of the Red Army
Sovnarkom	Council of People's Commissars
SSR	Soviet Socialist Republic
Stavka	General Headquarters of the Supreme Command

ABBREVIATIONS

AVP	Arkhiv Vneshnei Politiki Rossiiskoi Federatsii, Moscow
GARF	Gosudarstvennyi Arkhiv Rossiisskoi Federatsii, Moscow
KI	*Kommunisticheskii internatsional*
KPSS	Communist Party of the Soviet Union
Perkins et al., *FRUS*	E.R. Perkins, R.P. Churchill and J.G. Reid (eds), *Foreign Relations of the United States: The Soviet Union, 1933–1939* (Washington, DC: US Government Printing Office, 1952)
RGASPI	Rossiiskii gosudarstvennyi arkhiv sotsial'no-politicheskoi istorii, Moscow
TsK	Central Committee
VIZh	*Voenno-istoricheskii zhurnal*
Volokitina et al., *VE*	T.V. Volokitina et al. (eds), *Vostochnaia Evropa v dokumentakh Rossiiskikh arkhivov, 1944–1953 gg.*, 2 vols (Moscow and Novosibirsk: Sibirskii khronograf, 1997).

NOTES

INTRODUCTION: THE PARADOX OF POWER

1. In Russia Stalin's reputation has shifted from a low point in the 1990s to a much more positive level, in part due to state-sponsored propaganda. In 2010, 60 per cent of Russians polled supported legislation to protect the memory of Stalin's state and the Soviet Army during the Second World War. By 2015 a slight majority of Russians polled by Levada expressed a favourable view of Stalin generally. D. Khapaeva, 'Triumphant Memory of the Perpetrators in Putin's Policy of Re-Stalinization', *Communist and Post-Communist Studies* 49:1 (March 2016), pp. 61–73; pp. 7–8. See also T.H. Nelson, *Bringing Stalin Back In: Memory Politics and the Creation of a Useable Past in Putin's Russia* (Lanham, MD: Lexington Books, 2019).
2. Cf. M. Edle, *Stalinism at War: The Soviet Union in World War II* (London: Bloomsbury Academic, 2021).
3. R.G. Suny, *Stalin: Passage to Revolution* (Princeton, NJ: Princeton University Press, 2020) is the most convincing portrait of these years. See also S. Kotkin, *Stalin: Paradoxes of Power, 1878–1928* (New York: Penguin, 2016), who employs the paradoxical motif in different ways. My use of the term, which I first employed with respect to foreign policy, differs from his. See A.J. Rieber, 'Stalin as Foreign Policy Maker: Avoiding War, 1927–1953', in S. Davies and J.R. Harris (eds), *Stalin: A New History* (Cambridge: Cambridge University Press, 2005), pp. 140–59, and editors' introduction, 'Joseph Stalin: Power and Ideas', pp. 1–18; p. 9. I expanded upon this theme in my *Stalin and the Struggle for Supremacy in Eurasia* (Cambridge: Cambridge University Press, 2015).
4. A.J. Rieber, 'Stalin: Man of the Borderlands', *American Historical Review* 5 (December 2001), pp. 1,683–96.
5. I.V. Stalin, *Sochineniia*, 13 vols (Moscow: Gospolitizdat, 1946–52), vol. 4, pp. 74–81, vol. 6, p. 399, vol. 8, pp. 14, 173 and 263. For an extended analysis see Rieber, *Stalin and the Struggle*, pp. 93–6.
6. Historians have tended to place different emphases on the modern and the so-called neo-traditional character of the emerging Soviet society. See a summary in M. David-Fox, 'Multiple Modernities vs Neo-Traditionalism: On Recent Debates in Russian and Soviet History', *Jahrbücher für Geschichte Osteuropas* 54:4 (2006), pp. 535–55. My book seeks to reconcile these two perspectives through the agency of paradox.
7. S. Rosefielde, 'Documented Homicides and Excess Deaths: New Insights into the Scale of Killing in the USSR during the 1930s', *Communist and Postcommunist Studies* 30:3

(September 1997), pp. 321–31 distinguishes among six different categories of excess deaths. By combining losses attributed directly to collectivization (about 800,000) and those within Gulag camps, he arrives at a figure of over 1 million peasants killed, based on NKVD sources; see chart, ibid., p. 327.

8. The coercive measures employed to eliminate the peasant property-owners (kulaks) and force the remainder into kolkhozes or collective farms triggered mass resistance verging on civil war. A. Graziosi, *The Great Soviet Peasant War: Bolsheviks and Peasants, 1918–1933* (Cambridge, MA: Harvard University Press, 1996) and L. Viola, *Peasant Rebels under Stalin: Collectivization and the Culture of Peasant Resistance* (New York: Oxford University Press, 1999).

9. R.W. Davies, O.V. Naumov and S.G. Wheatcroft, *The Years of Progress: The Soviet Economy, 1934–1936* (New York: Palgrave Macmillan, 2014).

10. This was the verdict of a review by a commission of the Soviet Academy of Sciences in 1966 on the initiative of Aleksei Kosygin, one of the leading economists in Leningrad during the war years. But his proposed reforms of the Stalinist system failed to take hold. M. Lewin, *Le Siècle soviétique* (Paris: Fayard, 2003), pp. 413–15.

11. K.E. Bailes, *Technology and Society under Lenin and Stalin: Origins of the Soviet Technical Intelligentsia* (Princeton, NJ: Princeton University Press, 1978), chap. 3.

12. M.J. Payne, *Stalin's Railroad: Turksib and the Building of Socialism* (Pittsburgh, PA: University of Pittsburgh Press, 2001), pp. 255–85.

13. From a large literature see J.A. Getty and O.V. Naumov, *The Road to Terror: Stalin and the Self-Destruction of the Bolsheviks, 1932–1939*, updated and abridged edn (New Haven, CT: Yale University Press, 2010) and W.Z. Goldman, *Terror and Democracy in the Age of Stalin: The Social Dynamics of Repression* (Cambridge: Cambridge University Press, 2007) with extensive bibliographical commentary, pp. 1–6.

14. According to the International Red Cross the number was 3.8 million. *Argumenty i fakty* 6 (1990), p. 8.

15. For a brief survey of the Soviet historiography of the Second World War see V.M. Kulish, 'Sovetskaia istoriografiia Velikoi Otechestvennoi voiny', in Iu.N. Afanasev (ed.), *Sovetskaia istoriografiia* (Moscow: Rossiiskii gosudarstvennyi gumanitarnyi universitet, 1996), pp. 274–311. On the Western side the revisionist works of G. Gorodetsky, *Grand Illusion: Stalin and the German Invasion of Russia* (New Haven, CT: Yale University Press, 2016) and G. Roberts, *Stalin's Wars: From World War to Cold War, 1939–1953* (New Haven, CT: Yale University Press, 2006) present Stalin as a rational statesman, pragmatic and realistic in both his preparation for war and his conduct of it.

16. The most celebrated and extreme example of this aspect was the Stakhanovite (shock workers) movement, which – as L.H. Siegelbaum pointed out in his *Stakhanovism and the Politics of Productivity in the USSR, 1935–1941* (Cambridge: Cambridge University Press, 1988) – was intense but short-lived. R. Thurston, 'The Stakhanovite Movement: The Background to the Great Terror in the Factories, 1935–1938', in J.A. Getty and R.T. Manning (eds), *Stalinist Terror: New Perspectives* (Cambridge: Cambridge University Press, 1993), pp. 142–62 focuses on tensions on the factory floor created by the movement, leading to denunciations for 'wrecking'. For a more positive interpretation of an emerging Soviet working class, see K.M. Straus, *Factory and Community in Stalin's Russia: The Making of an Industrial Working Class* (Pittsburgh, PA: University of Pittsburgh Press, 1997).

CHAPTER 1: MOBILIZATION AND REPRESSION AT THE CENTRE

1. Moshe Lewin described the process as an emerging 'system of orderly bureaucracy' undermined by 'extralegal' means. 'The Social Background of Stalinism', in R.C. Tucker (ed.), *Stalinism: Essays in Historical Interpretation* (New York: Norton, 1977), pp. 111–36; p. 135.

2. Samples of the most important works are P. Holquist, '"Information Is the Alpha and Omega of Our Work": Bolshevik Surveillance in Its Pan-European Context', *Journal of*

Modern History 69:3 (1997), pp. 415–50; P. Holquist, *Making War, Forging Revolution: Russia's Continuum of Crisis, 1914–1921* (Cambridge, MA: Harvard University Press, 2002); P. Holquist, 'Violent Russia: Deadly Marxism? Russia in the Epoch of Violence, 1905–1921', *Kritika* 4:3 (spring 2003), pp. 627–52; E. Lohr, *Nationalizing the Russian Empire: The Campaign against Enemy Aliens during World War I* (Cambridge, MA: Harvard University Press, 2003); A. Weiner, 'Introduction: Landscaping the Human Garden', in Weiner, *Landscaping the Human Garden: Twentieth-Century Population Management in a Comparative Framework* (Palo Alto, CA: Stanford University Press, 2003), pp. 1–10.

3. The title of chap. 10 in J. Erickson, *The Soviet High Command: A Military-Political History, 1918–1941* (London: Macmillan, 1984).

4. R.J. Brody, 'Ideology and Political Mobilization: The Soviet Home Front during World War Two', *Carl Beck Papers in Russian and East European Studies* 1,104 (October 1994) gives a comprehensive picture of the institutional basis, while documenting the shortcomings in the Agitprop work admitted by party stalwarts on the eve of and during the war.

5. R. Tucker, 'On Revolutionary Mass-Movement Regimes', in *The Soviet Political Mind: Studies in Stalinism and Post-Stalinist Change*, rev. edn (New York: Norton, 1972), pp. 3–19; pp. 7, 16, 18.

6. P. Kenez, *The Birth of the Propaganda State: Soviet Methods of Mass Mobilization 1917–1929* (Cambridge: Cambridge University Press, 1985); V. Bonnell, *Iconography of Power: Soviet Political Posters under Lenin and Stalin* (Berkeley, CA: University of California Press, 1997) for the important role of one aspect of visual art.

7. Viola, *Peasant Rebels under Stalin*; Graziosi, *The Great Soviet Peasant War*.

8. War scares are a recurrent if understated theme in Soviet history, beginning with the tense situation in 1923 reaching one climax in 1927 and another in 1930 and remaining thereafter as a touch-point for army reform and mobilization of the civilian population under the banner of patriotism. See M. von Hagen, *Soldiers in the Proletarian Dictatorship: The Red Army and the Soviet Socialist State, 1917–1930* (Ithaca, NY: Cornell University Press, 1990), pp. 184, 196–7, 291–2, 336–7.

9. For the conflicting views within the Comintern see A. Di Biagio, 'Moscow, the Comintern and the War Scare', in S. Pons and A. Romano (eds), *Russia in the Age of Wars, 1914–1945* (Milan: Feltrinelli, 2000), pp. 83–102.

10. J.P. Sontag, 'The Soviet War Scare of 1926–27', *Russian Review* 34:1 (January 1975), pp. 66–77.

11. A. Nove, *An Economic History of the USSR* (London: Penguin, 1969), pp. 228–9 cites Soviet statistics showing an increase in defence spending by 286 per cent from 1937 to 1938 and a decrease in the quantity of machine tools imported from abroad from 78 to 10 per cent.

12. L.S. Komarov, *Rossiia tankov ne imela. Dokumental'no-khudozhestvennoe povestvovanie* (Chelyabinsk: L.S. Komarov, 1994).

13. L. Samuelson, 'Wartime Perspectives and Economic Planning: Tukhachevsky and the Military Industrial Complex', in Pons and Romano (eds), *Russia in the Age of Wars*, pp. 186–214; pp. 206–9 (quotation p. 206, with italics in original).

14. Von Hagen, *Soldiers in the Proletarian Dictatorship*, pp. 244–7 and W.E. Odom, *Soviet Volunteers: Modernization and Bureaucracy in a Public Mass Organization* (Princeton, NJ: Princeton University Press, 1973).

15. A. Romano, 'Permanent War Scare: Mobilization, Militarization and Peasant War', in Pons and Romano (eds), *Russia in the Age of Wars*, pp. 103–19; pp. 103–8.

16. N.S. Simonov, '"Strengthen the Defence of the Land of the Soviets": The 1927 "War Alarm" and Its Consequences', *Europe-Asia Studies* 48:8 (1996), pp. 355–64: p. 357.

17. Romano, 'Permanent War Scare', pp. 108–10.

18. Rieber, *Stalin and the Struggle*, pp. 113–15; A. Graziosi, 'Collectivisation, révoltes paysannes et politiques gouvernementales à travers les rapports du GPU d'Ukraine de février–mars 1930', *Cahiers du monde russe* 35:3 (1994), pp. 437–72.

19. Throughout the crisis, Stalin hammered away at the distinction between Bukharin's abstract formula on the *inevitability* of war and the specific prediction of Zinoviev and Kamenev on the *imminent* possibility of war. Stalin, *Sochineniia*, vol. 10, pp. 47–8, 53–4, 59, 81–2, 86–7, 199–200. Over the following months, his verbal manipulations of 'dangers' and 'threats' proliferated wildly. See the full record in N.V. Nagladin, *Istoriia uspekhov i neudach sovetskoi diplomatii. Politologicheskii aspekt* (Moscow: Mezhdunarodnye otnosheniia, 1990), pp. 84–6.

20. Voroshilov's letter to the head of the Main Political Directorate of the Red Army, Jan Gamarnik, on 17 March in RGASPI, f. 74, op. 2, d. 93, listy 39–39b as cited in Romano, 'Permanent War Scare', p. 118.

21. RGASPI, f. 17, op. 162, d. 7, listy 102–3 as cited in Simonov, '"Strengthen the Defence"', p. 362.

22. 'I.V. Stalin, pis'ma', in V.S. Lel'chuk (ed.), *Sovetskoe obshchestvo. Vozniknovenie, razvitie, istoricheskii final*, 2 vols (Moscow: Rossiiskii gosudarstvennnyi gumanitarnyi universitet, 1997), vol. 1, p. 427 ff.; L.T. Lih, O.V. Naumov and O.V. Khlevniuk (eds), *Stalin's Letters to Molotov, 1925–1936* (New Haven, CT: Yale University Press, 1995), letter 56, pp. 190–6; for a reprint of the trial see S.A. Krasil'nikov et al. (eds), *Sudebnii protsess 'Prompartii' 1930 g. Podgotovka, provedenie, itogi*, 2 vols (Moscow: ROSSPEN, 2016). A printed brochure, *Materialy po delu kontrrevoliutsionnoy 'Trudovoy krestianskoy partii' i gruppirovki Sukhanova-Gromana (Iz materialov sledstvennogo proizvodstva OGPU)* was widely distributed among party and state directors on Stalin's orders. Stalin to Molotov, 2 August 1930 in Lih, Naumov and Khlevniuk (eds), *Stalin's Letters*, letter 56, pp. 199–200. See also T.H. Ostashko, 'Vlast' i intelligentsia. Dinamik vzaimootnoshenii na rubezhe 1920–1930-kh godov', *Otechestvennaia istoriia* 2 (1998), pp. 19–24.

23. Bailes, *Technology and Society*, pp. 122–40. The purges were aimed mainly at oppositionists and many of the leading engineers were spared, helping to restore standards of quality with less emphasis on the class origins of students and more on preparation in maths and science. Ibid., pp. 223–9 et passim; quotation on p. 242. This remains the standard work, though published before the archives were open.

24. R.W. Davies, *Crisis and Progress in the Soviet Economy, 1931–1933* (London: Macmillan, 1996), pp. 164–76; p. 176.

25. Ibid., p. 475.

26. A. Livschiz, 'Pre-Revolutionary in Form, Soviet in Content? Wartime Educational Reforms and the Post War Quest for Normality', *History of Education* 35:4–5 (July–September, 2006), pp. 541–60; pp. 543–7. For the general problem of hooliganism before the war see S. Fitzpatrick, *Everyday Stalinism: Ordinary Life in Extraordinary Times – Soviet Russia in the 1930s* (Oxford: Oxford University Press, 1999), pp. 152–3.

27. E.T. Ewing, *Separate Schools: Gender, Policy and Practice in Postwar Soviet Education* (DeKalb, IL: Northern Illinois University Press, 2010), pp. 82, 184. The end of the war sparked a new debate in which the proponents of a return to co-education rejected the idea that separate educational classes offered any substantive arguments in favour. But the controversy only ended with Stalin's death. Ibid., p. 191.

28. J. Dunstan, *Soviet Schooling in the Second World War* (Basingstoke: Macmillan and Centre for Russian and East European Studies, University of Birmingham, 1997), chap. 5.

29. G. Dimitrov, *The Diary of Georgi Dimitrov, 1933–1949*, ed. I. Banac and trans. J.T. Hedges, T.D. Sergay and I. Faion (New Haven, CT: Yale University Press, 2003), entry for 11 November 1937, pp. 69–70. Years later Molotov resorted to the same explanation for the terror. F.I. Chuev, *Sto sorok besed s Molotovym. Iz dnevnika F. Chueva* (Moscow: Terra, 1991), p. 254.

30. W. Hedeler, 'Ezhov's Scenario for the Great Terror and the Falsified Record of the Third Moscow Show Trial', in B. McLoughlin and K. McDermott (eds), *Stalin's Terror: High Politics and Mass Repression in the Soviet Union* (New York: Palgrave Macmillan, 2003),

pp. 34–55; p. 52. See also Getty and Naumov, *The Road to Terror*, pp. 422–5 and B. McLoughlin, 'Mass Operations of the NKVD, 1937–8: A Survey', in McLoughlin and McDermott (eds), *Stalin's Terror*, pp. 118–52; pp. 122–3 and 142.

31. O.V. Khlevniuk, 'The Reasons for the Great Terror: The Foreign-Political Aspect', in Pons and Romano (eds), *Russia in the Age of Wars*, pp. 159–69.

32. Terror was a defining characteristic of the Socialist Revolutionaries. O.H. Radkey, *The Agrarian Foes of Bolshevism: Promise and Default of the Russian Socialist Revolutionaries, February to October 1917* (New York: Columbia University Press, 1958), pp. 67–74. Trotsky was responsible for the most complete theoretical justification of terror in constructing the socialist state. L. Trotsky, *The Defence of Terrorism and Communism: A Reply to Karl Kautsky* (London: Allen and Unwin, 1935).

33. The multiple causation of the purges has been well documented although its roots in pre-revolutionary Russia are less well explored. For recent representative examples see J.A. Getty, *The Origins of the Great Purges: The Soviet Communist Party Reconsidered, 1933–1938* (New York: Cambridge University Press, 1985); G.T. Rittersporn, *Stalinist Simplifications and Soviet Complications: Social Tensions and Political Conflicts in the USSR, 1933–1953* (Chur and New York: Harwood Academic Publishers, 1991); Getty and Manning (eds), *Stalinist Terror*; O.V. Khlevniuk, *1937. Stalin, NKVD i sovetskoe obshchestvo* (Moscow: Respublika, 1992); H. Kuromiya, *Freedom and Terror in the Donbas: A Ukrainian-Russian Borderland, 1870s–1990s* (New York: Cambridge University Press, 1998); Getty and Naumov, *The Road to Terror* and D. Priestland, *Stalinism and the Politics of Mobilization: Ideas, Power and Terror in Interwar Russia* (Oxford: Oxford University Press, 2007). See the bibliography in McLoughlin and McDermott (eds), *Stalin's Terror*, pp. 14–18. A great deal of evidence suggests widespread participation, not only by the NKVD and party organs, but by 'ordinary people' as well. For the vast and devastating effect of the purges on the private lives of Russians see O. Figes, *The Whisperers: Private Life in Stalin's Russia* (London: Allen Lane, 2007), especially chap. 4.

34. O.V. Khlevniuk et al. (ed.), *Politbiuro. Mekhanizmy politicheskoi vlasti v 1930-e gody* (Moscow: ROSSPEN, 1996) and Khlevniuk, 'Stalin as Dictator', in Davies and Harris (eds), *Stalin*, pp. 108–20, especially pp. 110–11.

35. Paul Hagenloh has argued that by 1937 the purges lost every semblance of popular participation and utopian visions. See his *Stalin's Police: Public Order and Mass Repression in the USSR, 1926–1941* (Washington, DC and Baltimore, MD: Woodrow Wilson Center Press and Johns Hopkins University Press, 2009).

36. See the suggestive comments in R. Service, *Stalin: A Biography* (London: Macmillan, 2004), pp. 286–7.

37. I. Deutscher, *The Prophet Unarmed: Trotsky, 1921–1929* (Oxford: Oxford University Press, 1959), pp. 349–51. Tukhachevsky, however, did not sign the statement.

38. The preferences of Stalin and Trotsky constituted a reversal of their ideas at the outset of the civil war. For the history of these debates see R.L. Garthoff, *How Russia Makes War: Soviet Military Doctrine* (London: Allen and Unwin, 1954); Erickson, *The Soviet High Command*, chap. 7; and for the Frunze reforms, von Hagen, *Soldiers in the Proletarian Dictatorship*, especially chap. 5.

39. P.A. Zaionchkovsky, *Samoderzhavie i russkaia armiia na rubezhe XIX–XX stoletii* (Moscow: Mysl', 1973), chap. 6; W. Fuller, *Civil-Military Conflict in Imperial Russia, 1881–1914* (Princeton, NJ: Princeton University Press, 1985), pp. 29–36, 260–2. Solzhenitsyn's fictional account of Colonel Vorotyntsev captures the spirit of the 'young Turks' in his *August 1914* (New York: Farrar, Straus and Giroux, 1972), see especially pp. 112–13.

40. See, among others, S. Naveh, 'Mikhail Nikolayevich Tukhachevsky', in H. Shukman (ed.), *Stalin and His Generals* (London: Phoenix Press, 1997), pp. 255–74, and Samuelson, 'Wartime Perspectives and Economic Planning', pp. 187–214. Cf. S.W. Stoecker, *Forging Stalin's Army: Marshal Tukhachevsky and the Politics of Military Innovation* (Boulder, CO:

Westview Press, 1998), especially pp. 164–8, who minimizes Tukhachevsky's clashes with Voroshilov and his differences with Stalin.

41. A.S. Bubnov, S.S. Kamenev and M.N. Tukhachevsky, *Grazhdanskaia voina*, 2 vols (Moscow and Leningrad: Voennyi vestnik, 1930), B.M. Shaposhnikov, *Na Visle. K istorii kampanii 1920 goda* (Moscow: Voennyi vestnik, 1928). The entire dispute is thoroughly reviewed in N. Kuzmin, 'Ob odnoi nevypolnennoi direktiva Glavkoma', *VIZh* (September 1962), pp. 49–52.

42. Erickson, *The Soviet High Command*, appendix I, Tukhachevsky's letter to Zinoviev, 18 July 1920, pp. 784–5.

43. G.K. Zhukov, *Vospominaniia i razmyshleniia* (Moscow: Novosti, 1969), pp. 115–16; S. Biriuzov, 'Predislovie', in M.N. Tukhachevsky, *Izbrannye proizvedeniia* (Moscow: Voenizdat 1964), vol. 1, pp. 1–11; and *Marshal Tukhachevsky. Vospominaniia druzei i soratnikov*, N.I. Koritskii et al. (comp.) (Moscow: Voenizdat, 1997).

44. P.A. Zhilin (ed.), *Zarozhdenie i razvitie sovetskoi voennoi istoriografii. 1917–1941* (Moscow: Nauka, 1985), pp. 11–13, 17–19.

45. V.M. Ivanov, *Marshal M.N. Tukhachevsky* (Moscow: Voenizdat, 1990), pp. 234–5.

46. L. Samuelson, 'Mikhail Tukhachevsky and War-Economic Planning: Reconsiderations on the Pre-War Soviet Military Build-up', *Journal of Slavic Military Studies* 9:4 (1996), pp. 804–47.

47. Biriuzov, 'Predislovie', p. 8.

48. For Stalin's political difficulties see R. Conquest, *The Great Terror* (New York: Macmillan, 1968), pp. 27–31; for Zhukov's estimation, see K.I. Simonov, 'Zametki k biografii G.K. Zhukova', *VIZh* 12 (December 1987), pp. 42–57; p. 42.

49. M.N. Tukhachevsky, 'Novye voprosy voiny', *VIZh* (February 1962), pp. 62–77; pp. 66–7, 70–5.

50. Ivanov, *Marshal Tukhachevsky*, pp. 253–4.

51. Ibid., pp. 255–6, 273.

52. A.P. Romanov, *Raketam pokoriaetsia prostranstvo* (Moscow: Politizdat, 1976), pp. 31–4; Iu.A. Pobedonostsev and K.M. Kuznetsov, *Pervye starty* (Moscow: DOSAFF, 1972), p. 24.

53. Zhilin, *Zarozhdenie*, pp. 74–4, 152–4; M.N. Tukhachevsky, 'O novom polevom ustave RKKR', in M.N. Tukhachevsky, *Izbrannye sochineniia*, 2 vols (Moscow: Krasnaia zvezda, 1937), vol. 2, pp. 245–9. See also Erickson, *The Soviet High Command*, p. 390.

54. M.N. Tukhachevsky, 'Voprosy sovremmenoi strategii', in Tukhachevsky, *Izbrannye sochineniia*, vol. 1, pp. 244–61; p. 246.

55. Tukhachevsky, 'Voennye plany nyneshnei Germanii', in ibid., vol. 2, pp. 233–9. There was perhaps a touch of wistfulness in Tukhachevsky's regret that France had failed to implement the innovative ideas of de Gaulle on armoured warfare. The two men were old friends, having been prisoners of war together in Ingolstadt, then rivals on opposite sides of the battle lines in Warsaw in 1920, only to meet again in France in 1935. There was a striking similarity in their strategic thinking. When de Gaulle made his last visit to the Soviet Union in 1966, he asked to meet the survivors of Tukhachevsky's family. The request was denied. Ivanov, *Marshal Tukhachevsky*, pp. 3–5.

56. M.N. Tukhachevsky, 'Kharakter pogranichnykh operatsii', in Tukhachevsky, *Izbrannye sochineniia*, vol. 2, pp. 217–21.

57. Ivanov, *Marshal Tukhachevsky*, pp. 285–6.

58. In 1933 he wrote to Voroshilov that his adherence to old-fashioned tactics was 'sowing confusion in the minds of the commanders'. Biriuzov, 'Predislovie', p. 18.

59. Simonov, 'Zametki', p. 44.

60. D.A. Volkogonov, *Triumf i tragediia. Politicheskii portret I.V. Stalina*, 2 vols (Moscow: Novosti, 1989), vol. 1, pt 2, p. 261.

61. O.F. Suvenirov, 'Represii v partorganizatsii RKKA v 1937–1938 gg', *Voprosy istorii KPSS* 6 (1990), pp. 37–49; 'Delo o tak nazyvaemoi "anti-sovetskoi trotskistskoi voennoi organizatsii v Krasnoi armii"', *Izvestiia TsK KPSS* 4 (1989), pp. 44–80; pp. 42–61. For the argument that Stalin's repression of the army leaders was based on an exaggerated concern

over security and his long-term suspicion of professional officers, see P. Whitewood, 'Stalin's Purge of the Red Army and the Misperception of Security Threats', in J. Ryan and S. Grant (eds), *Revisioning Stalin and Stalinism: Contradictions and Complexities* (London: Bloomsbury Academic, 2021), pp. 38–51; pp. 40–50.

62. A.A. Kokoshin, *Armiia i politika. Sovetskaia voenno-politicheskaia i voenno-strategicheskaia mysl', 1918–1991 gody* (Moscow: Mezhdunarodnye otnosheniia, 1995), pp. 50–1.

63. G.A. Stefanovsky, 'Politicheskie organy armii i flota', *Voprosy istorii KPSS* 6 (1989), pp. 18–32; p. 24 citing military archives.

64. 'Zapiska M.P. Kirponosa i N.N. Vashugina k N.S. Khrushchevu, 16/18 apreliia 1941' and 'Zapiska A.I. Zaporozhetsa v Sektretariat TsK VKP(b), 25 apreliia 1941', in *Izvestiia TsK KPSS* 5 (May 1990), pp. 195–7.

65. Stefanovsky, 'Politicheskie organy', p. 27.

66. Conquest, *The Great Terror*, especially pp. 228, 485, and Erickson, *The Soviet High Command*, pp. 449–52.

67. R.R. Reese, 'The Red Army and the Great Purges', in Getty and Manning (eds), *Stalinist Terror*, pp. 198–214; p. 213. Soviet sources estimated the number of repressed at 40,000. Institut marksizma-leninizma, *Velikaia Otechestvennaia voina Sovetskogo Soiuza, 1941–1945. Kratkaia istoriia* (Moscow: Voenizdat, 1965), pp. 39–40; *VIZh* 4 (1963), p. 65; *Pravda*, 29 April 1988. In certain frontier military districts like Kiev, the replacement of the top officers was extremely high, including 100 per cent of corps commanders and 96 per cent of divisional commanders. O.F. Suvenirov, 'Vsearmeiskaia tragediia', *VIZh* 3 (1989), pp. 39–48; pp. 47–8.

68. R.A. Medvedev, *Let History Judge: The Origins and Consequences of Stalinism* (New York: Knopf, 1971), p. 213.

69. B.A. Starkov, 'Narkom Ezhov', in Getty and Manning (eds), *Stalinist Terror*, pp. 21–39; p. 37.

70. G. Roberts, *Stalin's Library: A Dictator and His Books* (New Haven, CT, and London: Yale University Press, 2022), pp. 154–64.

71. H. Shukman, 'Introduction', in Shukman (ed.), *Stalin and His Generals*, pp. 1–9; pp. 3–4.

72. One of the reasons for Stalin's angry dismissal of Voroshilov from command of the Leningrad front in the early months of the war was his reliance on workers' battalions instead of conventional defences for the city. D. Volkogonov, 'Klimenty Yefremovich Voroshilov', in Shukman (ed.), *Stalin and His Generals*, pp. 313–26; p. 318.

73. Pospelov et al., *Istoriia Velikoi Otechestvennoi voiny Sovetskogo Soiuza 1941–1945*, 6 vols (Moscow: Institut marksizma-leninizma pri TsK KPSS, 1960–65), vol. 3, pp. 419–21.

74. The following relies heavily on Iu.A. Gorkov, *Kreml'. Stavka. Genshtab* (Tver': RIF LTD, 1995), pp. 55–65.

75. M. Zakharov, *General'nyi shtab v predvoennye gody* (Moscow: Voenizdat, 1989), pp. 219–20.

76. V.P. Naumov et al. (eds), *Rossiia XX vek. Dokumenty. 1941 god*, 2 vols (Moscow: Mezhdunarodnyi fond Demokratiia, 1998), vol. 1, doc. 134, p. 289.

77. Gorkov, *Kreml'*, pp. 61–2.

78. The idea of a pre-emptive strike was initiated by V. Suvorov (Rezun), *Icebreaker: Who Started the Second World War?* (London: Hamish Hamilton, 1990) with a Russian edition in 1992. The book gave rise to an extensive debate in Russia. See G. Gorodetsky, *Mif 'Ledokhoda'. Nakanune voiny* (Moscow: Progress-Akademiia, 1995). For Western refutations of the central thesis see G. Gorodetsky, 'Was Stalin Planning to Attack Hitler in June 1941?', *RUSI Journal* 131:2 (1986), pp. 69–72; D.M. Glantz, *Stumbling Colossus: The Red Army on the Eve of World War* (Lawrence, KS: University Press of Kansas, 1998), pp. 1–8; T.J. Uldricks, 'The Icebreaker Controversy: Did Stalin Plan to Attack Hitler?', *Slavic Review* 58:3 (autumn 1999), pp. 626–43; and J. Erickson, 'Barbarossa June 1941: Who Attacked Whom?', *History Today* 51:7 (July 2001), pp. 11–17. A recent revised view of Icebreaker that finds 'the circumstantial evidence [for a pre-emptive strike] compelling' is C. Bellamy, 'Brute Force and Genius: Stalin as War Leader', in Ryan and Grant (eds), *Revisioning Stalin*, pp. 63–78; p. 72.

79. Among the various strategic plans worked out on the eve of the war, one signed by Timoshenko and K.A. Meretskov stood out by emphasizing the offensive. See B.N. Petrov, 'O strategicheskom razvertyvanii Krasnoi Armii nakanune voiny', in G.A. Bordiugov (ed.), *Gotovil li Stalin nastupitel'nuiu voinu protiv Gitlera? Nezaplanirovannaia diskussiia. Sbornik materialov* (Moscow: Airo-XX, 1995), p. 66. Under Zhdanov's instructions the Political Section of the Red Army launched a major campaign to justify any war fought by the Soviet Union as just and to inspire the Red Army with the offensive spirit. V.A. Nevezhin, 'Vystuplenie Stalin 5 maia 1941 g. in povorot v propaganda. Analiz direktivnykh materialov', in ibid., pp. 150–8.

80. K.A. Meretskov, *Na sluzhbe narodu*, 5th rev. edn (Moscow: Veche, 1988), pp. 100–5, 170–9, 193–200, 214; Iu.Ia. Kirshin, 'Kontseptsiia mirovoi sotsialisticheskoi revoliutsii i sovetskaia voennaia doktrina', *Soviet Union/Union Soviétique* 18:1–3 (1991), pp. 80–99. For more details see A.J. Rieber, 'Zhdanov in Finland', *Carl Beck Papers in Russian and East European Studies* 1,107 (February 1995), pp. 8–12.

81. Gorkov, *Kreml'*, p. 65, quoting A. Vasilevsky, *Nakanune*, Arkhiv presidenta Rossiisskoi Federatsiia, f. 73, op. 2, d. 3.

82. V.A. Anfilov, *Doroga k tragedii sorok pervogo goda* (Moscow: Akopov, 1997), pp. 201–7.

83. G.K. Zhukov, 'Iz neopublikovannykh vospominanii', *Kommunist* 14 (September 1988), pp. 87–101; pp. 97–9.

84. S.V. Stepashin and V.P. Iampol'sky (eds.), *Organy gosudarstvennoi bezopasnosti SSSR v Velikoi Otechestvennoi Voine. Sbornik Dokumentov, Nakanune (noiabr' 1938 g.–dekabr' 1940 g.)*, 2 vols (Moscow: A/O Kniga i biznes, 1995), vol. 1, bk 1, docs 4 and 5, pp. 22–5, 26–8. That it was taken seriously by the commander of the Kiev military district and first secretary of the Communist Party of Ukraine, N.S. Khrushchev, is clear from the letter of the latter to Timoshenko requesting confirmation and discussion in the Military Council. The decree creating the special departments (ibid., doc. 6, pp. 29–30), signed by Voroshilov and Beria, represented a tactical victory for Beria in his campaign to gain ascendency over the army, which the commissar of defence was obliged to endorse. This was another occasion on which Beria and Zhdanov were on opposing sides.

85. Ibid., p. 35.

86. Glantz, *Stumbling Colossus*, pp. 149–50. Colonel Glantz has provided the most devastating picture of the unpreparedness of the Soviet Union for war. See also Iu.A. Gor'kov and Iu.N. Semin, 'Konets global'noi lzhi. Operativnye plany zapadnykh pogranichnykh voennykh okrugov 1941 sviditel'svuiut – SSSR ne gotovilsiia k napadeniiu Germaniiu', *VIZh* 2 (March–April 1996), pp. 5–17, and *VIZh* 4 (July–August 1996), pp. 3–17, translated into English in Glantz, *Stumbling Colossus*, pp. 270–88.

87. Ibid., pp. 178–80.

88. The rapid and deep penetration of the German forces gave rise to a postwar controversy between Zhukov and Vasilevsky. Vasilevsky maintained that the 'main strength' of the Red Army should have been mobilized, placed on full military alert and deployed on the frontiers in order to repulse the German attack. Zhukov countered that the Red Army's concentration of 'all its strength' on the frontiers would have played into the strategic plans of the Germans, led to the annihilation of the frontier forces and increased the chances of German success; 'Moscow and Leningrad would have been occupied in 1941.' Gorkov, *Kreml'*, pp. 66–7.

89. Two very large collections of documents contain intelligence reports: V.P. Naumov et al. (eds), *Dokumenty 1941*, and *Organy gosudarstvennoi bezopasnosti*, the official publication of the security services (FSB), which seeks to justify its predecessor by arguing that the intelligence was ample and accurate enough to predict the time and scope of the attack, but that the information was disregarded by Stalin and the Supreme Command.

90. V. Lota, *Sekretnyi front General'nogo shtaba* (Moscow: Molodaia gvardiia, 2005), pp. 36, 46–7, 60–8.

91. D. Holloway, 'Stalin and Intelligence: Two Cases'. I am grateful to Professor Holloway for sharing his unpublished manuscript with me.

92. Ibid. See also Gorodetsky, *Grand Illusion*, pp. 222–6 and Roberts, *Stalin's Wars*, pp. 64–70. Stalin was not alone in holding this view. Meretskov later wrote: 'we could not stay out of the war until 1943, of course … but it was not inconceivable (*ne iskliucheno*) that we could stay out of the war until 1942'. *Na sluzhbe*, pp. 195–6. It is not clear to what degree Stalin was influenced in this view by Zhdanov or Beria.

93. Pospelov et al., *IVOV*, vol. 1, p. 65; M. von Boetticher, *Industrialisierungspolitik und Verteidigungskonzeption der UdSSR 1926–1930: Herausbildung des Stalinismus und 'äussere Bedrohung'* (Düsseldorf: Drostel, 1976).

94. M.Iu. Mukhin, 'Evoliutsiia sistemy upravleniia sovetskoi oboronoi promyshlennost'iu v 1921–1941 godakh i smena prioritetov "oboronki"', in G.B. Nabatov et al. (comp.), *Velikaia Otechestvennaia voina. Voprosy istorii. Materialy mezhdunarodnoi nauchno-metodicheskoi konferentsii 18–20 aprelia 2000 g. k 55-letiu Pobedy v Velikoi Otechestvennoi voine* (Nizhny Novgorod: Nizhegorodskii gos. universitet, 2000), pp. 9–14.

95. J.R. Azrael, *Managerial Power and Soviet Politics* (Cambridge, MA: Harvard University Press, 1966), p. 100 and note 88; p. 228.

96. Bailes, *Technology and Society*, pp. 353, 366–8.

97. A.F. Khavin, 'Razvitie tiazheloi promyshlennosti v tretei piatiletke (1938–iiun' 1941 gg.)', *Istoriia SSSR* 1 (1959), pp. 10–35.

98. Medvedev, *Let History Judge*, pp. 228–30; P.K. Oshchepov, *Zhizn' i mechta. Zapiski inzhenera-izobretatelia, konstruktora i uchenego* (Moscow: Moskovskii rabochii, 1967); G.S. Isserson, 'Zapiski sovremennika o M.N. Tukhachevskom', *VIZh* 4 (April 1963), pp. 64–78; pp. 67–8; 'Speeches of B.P. Beschev and N.M. Shvernik at the XXII Party Congress', *Current Digest of the Soviet Press* 14:2 (7 February 1962), pp. 24–5, and 14:5 (28 February 1962), pp. 25–6.

99. B.L. Vannikov, 'Iz zapisok Narkoma vooruzheniia', *VIZh* (February 1962), pp. 78–86.

100. R.W. Davies, M. Harrison, O.V. Khlevniuk and S.G. Wheatcroft, *The Industrialisation of Soviet Russia*, vol. 7: *The Soviet Economy and the Approach of War, 1937–1939* (London: Palgrave Macmillan, 2018), pp. 165–7.

101. M. Harrison, *Accounting for War: Soviet Production, Employment and the Defence Burden, 1940–1945* (New York: Cambridge University Press, 1996), p. 23 citing M.V. Terpilovsky (ed.), *Finansovaia sluzhba Vooruzhennykh sil SSSR v period Voiny. Organizatsia finansirovaniia Sovetskoi armii i Voenno-morskogo flota vo vremia Velikoi Otechestvennoi voiny 1941–1945 gg.* (Moscow: Voenizdat, 1967), p. 29. The following figures represent the increase in industrial production as cited in Harrison, p. 68, with sources in appendices, table B1, ibid. p. 180.

Increase in Industrial Production, 1940–41

	1940	1941
Combat aircraft	8,331	12,377
Armoured vehicles	2,794	6,590
Guns	15,343	40,547
Shells	43,000,000	83,000,000
Small arms	1,916,000	2,956,000
Cartridges	3,006,000,000	4,335,000,000

102. A.M. Nekrich, *1941. 22 iuniia*, 2nd edn (Moscow: Pamiatniki istoricheskoi mysli, 1995), pp. 74–6; M. Mukhin, 'The Market for Labor in the 1930s: The Aircraft Industry', in M. Harrison (ed.), *Guns and Rubles: The Defense Industry in the Stalinist State* (New Haven, CT: Yale University Press, 2008), pp. 180–209; pp. 196–206.

103. M. Harrison, *Soviet Planning in Peace and War, 1938–1945* (Cambridge: Cambridge University Press, 1988).

104. Khavin, 'Razvitie tiazheloi promyshlennosti', pp. 11–15.

105. Volkogonov, *Triumf i tragediia*, vol. 2, pt 2, pp. 73, 78.

106. B.L. Vannikov, 'Oboronnaia promyshlennost'. SSSR nakanune voiny. Iz zapisok Narkoma', *Voprosy istorii*, vol. 10 (1968), pp. 116–23; p. 123 for aviation; see Bailes, *Technology and Society*, chap. 14.

107. Pospelov et al., *IVOV*, vol. 3, pp. 421–5; D.N. Bolotin and A.A. Bumagin, *Sovetskoe strelkovoe oruzhie za 50 let. Katalog* (Moscow: Voenizdat, 1983), p. 314; Volkogonov, *Triumf i tragediia*, vol. 2, pt 2, p. 74.

108. M. Harrison, 'N.A. Voznesensky (1 December 1903–30 September 1950): A Soviet Commander of the Economic Front', Warwick Economics Research Paper Series no. 242, University of Warwick, Department of Economics, 1983, p. 336. I am grateful to Professor Harrison for permission to cite his paper.

109. Associated with the diplomacy and embodied in the alliances with France and Czechoslovakia in 1935 endorsed by the Comintern the same year, collective security signified co-operation with anti-fascist forces against the rise of Nazi Germany.

110. Ministerstvo inostrannykh del SSSR, *Dokumenty vneshnei politiki SSSR. 1939*, 2 vols (Moscow: Mezhdunarodnye otnosheniia, 1992), vol. 1, doc. 2, pp. 10–12. See also V.V. Sokolov, 'Na postu zamestitelia Narkoma inostrannykh del SSSR (O zhizni i deiatel'nosti B.S. Stomoniakova)', *Novaia i noveishaia istoriia* 5 (1988), pp. 111–26, and A.A. Roshchin, 'V Narkomindele nakanune voiny', *Mezhdunarodnaia zhizn'* 4 (1988), pp. 120–6; pp. 122–3.

111. Perkins et al., *FRUS*, pp. 318, 398, 449–50, 517, 645; Z. Sheinis, *Maksim Maksimovich Litvinov. Revoliutsioner, diplomat, chelovek* (Moscow: Politizdat, 1989), p. 348; *Documents on German Foreign Policy, 1918–1945*, Series C, 6 vols (London: HMSO, 1949–83), vol. 6, p. 1,003; R. Coulondre, *De Staline à Hitler. Souvenirs de deux ambassades, 1936–1939* (Paris: Hachette, 1950), chaps 8 and 10.

112. Sheinis, *Maksim Maksimovich Litvinov*, p. 350. Litvinov refused to participate in any of the sessions organized by the party within the Foreign Commissariat to denounce enemies of the people in its ranks.

113. Sokolov, 'Na postu', pp. 148–50.

114. Z. Shtein, 'Sud'ba diplomata. Shtrikhi k portretu Borisa Shteina', in N.V. Popov (comp.), *Arkhivy raskryvaiut tainy ... Mezhdunarodnye voprosy. Sobytiia i liudi* (Moscow: Gospolitizdat, 1991), pp. 286–306.

115. The committee to select new cadres for the Commissariat was composed of Molotov, Beria, Malenkov, Dekanozov – and Litvinov! Even those who were newly recruited experienced moments of frightening insecurity before being finally vetted. V.V. Sokolov, 'Posol SSSR F.T. Gusev v Londone v 1943–1947 godakh', *Novaia i noveishaia istoriia* 4 (2005), pp. 102–28; p. 103.

116. Chuev, *Sto sorok besed s Molotovym*, p. 98.

117. G. Gorodetsky (ed.), *The Maisky Diaries: The Wartime Revelations of Stalin's Ambassador in London* (New Haven, CT: Yale University Press, 2016), pp. 171, 218 and 267. In defending himself to Gusev, Maisky pointed out that the embassy staff in London was composed of insufficiently prepared men without experience; one intern, a former tractor driver, had no English. Ibid., pp. 268–9.

118. For the fate of the *Litvinovtsy*, see S. Dullin, *Men of Influence: Stalin's Diplomats in Europe, 1930–1939* (Edinburgh: Edinburgh University Press, 2008) and A. Kocho-Williams, 'The Soviet Diplomatic Corps and Stalin's Purges', *Slavonic and East European Review* 86:1 (2008), pp. 90–110; pp. 90–102.

119. J. Haslam, *The Soviet Union and the Struggle for Collective Security in Europe, 1933–1939* (London: St Martin's Press, 1984), pp. 234–5 on the press; Sheinis, *Maksim Maksimovich Litvinov*, pp. 368–70.

120. V. Mastny, 'The Cassandra in the Foreign Commissariat: Maxim Litvinov and the Cold War', *Foreign Affairs* 54:2 (1976), pp. 366–76; G. Roberts, 'Litvinov's Lost Peace, 1941–1946', *Journal of Cold War Studies* 4:2 (spring 2002), pp. 23–54; for Molotov's behind-the-back

dealings with Stalin's consent, Perkins et al., *FRUS*, pp. 579–80; on Vyshinsky, Sheinis, *Maksim Maksimovich Litvinov*, p. 419; on Dekanozov, Conquest, *The Great Terror*, pp. 455, 472 and A. Werth, *Russia at War, 1941–1945* (New York: Dutton, 1964), p. 94.

121. Perkins et al., *FRUS*, pp. 567–8; for his meeting with the British ambassador see E. Estorick, *Stafford Cripps* (London: Heinemann, 1949), pp. 253–7. Others included Ribbentrop, of course, on 19 August 1939 to negotiate the Nazi-Soviet Pact, the Turkish foreign minister Şükrü Saraçoğlu in October 1939 and the Japanese foreign minister Y. Matsuoka (twice) in 1941 to negotiate the neutrality treaty. M. Beloff, *The Foreign Policy of Soviet Russia, 1936–1941*, 2 vols (New York: Oxford University Press, 1949), vol. 2, pp. 371–4.

122. Perkins et al., *FRUS*, pp. 515–16.

123. Chuev, *Sto sorok besed s Molotovym*, pp. 98–9.

124. A. Gromyko, *Memoirs* (New York: Doubleday, 1991), p. 24. By and large this is an extremely disappointing and uninformative memoir.

125. Having succeeded Maisky in London, Gusev was regarded as something of a non-entity by top British officials. Gorodetsky (ed.), *The Maisky Diaries*, pp. 538–9.

126. Ibid., pp. 339 and 360.

127. A.A. Gromyko et al. (eds), *Diplomaticheskii slovar'*, 3 vols (Moscow: Gospolitizdat, 1960–64), vol. 1, pp. 328, 413–14, 417; vol. 2, p. 412; vol. 3, p. 449; N.V. Novikov, *Put' i pereputia sovetskogo diplomata. Zapiski, 1943–1944* (Moscow: Nauka, 1975) and V.M. Berezhkov, *Stranitsy ot diplomaticheskoi istorii* (Moscow: Partizdat, 1984), p. 129.

128. N.V. Novikov, *Vospominaniia diplomata. Zapiski, 1938–1947* (Moscow: Politizdat, 1989), pp. 4–25. By this time Novikov was important enough to be included among the very few top officials, mainly members of the Politburo, who received copies of diplomatic dispatches of major importance.

129. AVP, fond Molotova, op. 5, por. 383, papka 32, listy 1–2 (undated).

130. Ibid., listy 7–22.

131. Ibid., listy 40–1.

132. V.V. Aldoshin and Iu.V. Ivanov (comps), *Sovetsko-amerikanskie otnosheniia. 1945–1948* (Moscow: Mezhdunarodnyi fond Demokratiia, 2004), doc. 138, pp. 12–21. A translation with commentary is in 'The Novikov Telegram, Washington, September 27, 1946', *Diplomatic History* 15:4 (autumn 1991), pp. 527–38. See also K.M. Jensen (ed.), *Origins of the Cold War: The Novikov, Kennan and Roberts 'Long Telegrams' of 1946* (Washington, DC: US Institute of Peace, 1991) and Roberts, *Stalin's Wars*, pp. 305–6.

133. Aldoshin and Ivanov, *Sovetsko-amerikanskie otnosheniia. 1945–1948*, doc. 198, p. 430.

134. Volokitina et al., *VE*, vol. 1, doc. 227, p. 673.

135. I.S. Kulikova, 'Zavetnye tetrady A.M. Kollontai', *Voprosy istorii KPSS* (8 August 1989), pp. 106–7.

136. R. Dennett and J.E. Johnson (eds), *Negotiating with the Russians* (Boston, MA: World Peace Foundation, 1951), especially P.E. Mosely, 'Techniques of Negotiation', pp. 210–28.

137. This was particularly true of Loy Henderson and George Kennan. In a long dispatch dated 16 November 1936, Henderson compared the practice of 'isolating members of foreign missions [which was] borrowed by the Soviet government from the old tsarist government'. Perkins et al., *FRUS*, p. 318. See also Kennan's memo of 24 November 1937, in which he reported 'an anti-foreign campaign of almost unparalleled intensity' that made little distinction between 'neutral' states like the USA and Germany and Japan. Ibid., p. 398. Even Joseph Davies was repelled by the tendency towards isolationism in the Soviet government. Ibid., p. 548. See also D. Yergin, *Shattered Peace: The Origins of the Cold War and the National Security State* (Boston, MA: Houghton Mifflin, 1977), the fullest account, though it is not necessary to accept his somewhat artificial division between the Riga and Yalta axioms. There is nothing so good for similar reactions among academics who later entered government service during the war.

138. Sir Stafford Cripps was particularly sensitive to these currents. Estorick, *Stafford Cripps*, p. 257. See also M. Hughes, *Inside the Enigma: British Officials in Russia, 1900–1939* (London: Hambledon Press, 1997), pp. 211–21.

139. For a revised interpretation see G. Roberts, *Molotov: Stalin's Cold Warrior* (Washington, DC: Potomac Books, 2012) which argues for a more independent role for Molotov.

140. S. Fitzpatrick, 'Stalin and the Making of a New Elite, 1928–1939', *Slavic Review* 38:3 (September 1979), pp. 377–402, and Straus, *Factory and Community*.

CHAPTER 2: MOBILIZATION AND PURGES ON THE PERIPHERIES

1. T. Martin, *The Affirmative Action Empire: Nations and Nationalism in the Soviet Union, 1923–1939* (Ithaca, NY: Cornell University Press, 2001), pp. 8–9, 317, 312–18, 351.

2. Medvedev, *Let History Judge*, p. 207.

3. T.H. Rigby, *Communist Party Membership in the USSR, 1917–1967* (Princeton, NJ: Princeton University Press, 1968), pp. 369, 371, 373.

4. Martin, *Affirmative Action*, pp. 329–32; see also G. Simon, *Nationalism and Policy toward the Nationalities in the Soviet Union* (Boulder, CO: Westview Press, 1991), especially pp. 60–2.

5. V.N. Khaustov et al. (eds), *Lubianka. Stalin i VCHK-GPU-OGPU-NKVD. Ianvar' 1922– dekabr' 1936* (Moscow: ROSSPEN, 2002), doc. 227, pp. 235–6. See also doc. 537, p. 682 for Postyshev's report on the frontier districts of Kiev region.

6. Martin, *Affirmative Action*, pp. 332–3.

7. M. Gelb, 'An Early Soviet Ethnic Deportation: The Far-Eastern Koreans', *Russian Review* 54:3 (July 1995), pp. 389–412; pp. 389–92; P. Polian, *Ne po svoei vole . . . Istoriia i geografiia prinuditel'nykh migratsii v SSSR* (Moscow: Memorial, 2001), pp. 91–3. Terry Martin, who concurs with Gelb that this was the first case of 'ethnic cleansing', estimates that in 1922 only a third of the deported Koreans held Soviet passports. T. Martin, 'The Origins of Soviet Ethnic Cleansing', *Journal of Modern History* 70:4 (December 1998), pp. 813–61; pp. 833–5.

8. Hagenloh, *Stalin's Police*, pp. 277–81. To be sure, the police were not too discriminating in identifying ethnic groups caught up in their operational sweeps.

9. M. Jansen and N.V. Petrov, *Stalin's Loyal Executioner: People's Commissar Nikolai Ezhov, 1895–1940* (Stanford, CA: Hoover Institution Press, 2002), pp. 93–8.

10. McLoughlin, 'Mass Operations', p. 123. By the time the national operations were terminated in the autumn of 1938, a total of about 350,000 people had been swept up, of whom 247,157 had been condemned to death. Jansen and Petrov, *Stalin's Loyal Executioner*, p. 99.

11. A.V. Kvashonkin, *Sovetskoe rukovodstvo. Perepiska, 1928–1941* (Moscow: ROSSPEN, 1999), docs 235, 236, pp. 393–5.

12. KPSS, *Dvenadtsatyi s'ezd RKP(b). Stenograficheskii otchet, 17–25 aprelia 1923 goda* (Moscow: Politizdat, 1968), pp. 503–5 (Grinko); pp. 569–74 (Skrypnyk); pp. 576–82 (Rakovski); pp. 612–13 (Bukharin); pp. 648–61 (votes on amendments).

13. R.S. Sullivant, *Soviet Politics and the Ukraine, 1917–1957* (New York: Columbia University Press, 1962), pp. 82–3.

14. E.H. Carr and R.W. Davies, *Foundations of a Planned Economy, 1926–1929*, 2 vols (New York: Macmillan, 1971), vol. 2, p. 195.

15. Stalin, *Sochineniia*, vol. 5, pp. 244–7, 329–30.

16. Sullivant, *Soviet Politics*, chaps 3 and 4.

17. Martin, *Affirmative Action*, p. 360 lists this as one of several errors, including weakening cultural ties between Ukraine and Russia and threatening the status of Russians in Ukraine through forced Ukrainianization. Ibid., pp. 352–4.

18. Ibid., p. 361.

19. I.D. Nazarenko (ed.), *Ocherki po istorii Kommunisticheskoi partii Ukrainy* , 3rd edn (Kyiv: Institut istorii partii TsK KP Ukrainy, 1972). See also Conquest, *The Great Terror*, pp. 251–9.

20. P.N. Wexler, *Purism and Language: A Study in Modern Ukrainian and Belarus Nationalism (1840–1967)* (Bloomington, IN: Indiana University Press, 1974), pp. 158–65, records the

attack on Ukrainian linguistic specialists as favouring dialecticism and archaisms in order to render the language different from Russian.

21. J.A. Armstrong, *Ukrainian Nationalism*, 2nd edn (New York: Columbia University Press, 1963), chaps 2 and 3.

22. T. Snyder, *Sketches from a Secret War: A Polish Artist's Mission to Liberate Soviet Ukraine* (New Haven, CT: Yale University Press, 2005), pp. 162-7.

23. M.S. Totoev, *Istoriia Severo-Ossetinskoi ASSR* (Ordzhonikidze: Severo-Ossetinskoe knizhnoe izd., 1966), p. 247; B.E. Kalmykov, *Stat'i i rechi* (Nal'chik: Kabardino-Balkarskoe knizhnoe idz., 1961); M.O. Kosvena and B.A. Gardanov, *Narody Kavkaza*, 2 vols (Moscow: Insititut etnografiia imeni Miklukhno-Makala 1960-62); Conquest, *The Great Terror*, p. 287.

24. N.F. Bugai and A.M. Gonov, *Kavkaz. Narody v eshelonakh (20-60-e gody)* (Moscow: INSAN, 1998), pt 3.

25. Conquest, *The Great Terror*, pp. 249-50; D.M. Lang, 'A Century of Russian Impact on Georgia', in W.S. Vucinich (ed.), *Russia and Asia: Essays on the Influence of Russia on the Asian Peoples* (Palo Alto, CA: Stanford University Press, 1972), pp. 219-47; pp. 238-9. R.G. Suny, *The Making of the Georgian Nation* (Bloomington, IN: Indiana University Press, 1994); S. Gazarian, 'Eto ne dolzhno povtoritsa', *Zvezda* 2 (1989).

26. *Organy gosudarstvennoi bezopasnosti*, vol. 1, bk 1, doc. 133, pp. 270-8. French intelligence interpreted the connection between Georgian émigrés and German espionage in Iran as a means of promoting internal disturbances in the Soviet Union in order to detach the oil region of Azerbaijan, initially to unite it to Turkey then, as in 1918, to join it to a government which would give the Germans economic control. Ibid., appendix, 'Captured Material', doc. 5, pp. 333-4.

27. Ts.P. Agaian, *Ocherki istorii Kommunisticheskoi partii Armenii* (Yerevan: Alestan, 1967), pp. 365-66; *Aktivnye bortsy za Sovetskuiu vlast v Azerbaidzhana* (Baku: Azerbaidzhanskoe gosudarstvennoe izd., 1957).

28. M.S. Iskenderov, *Ocherki istorii Kommunisticheskoi partii Azerbaidzhana* (Baku: Azerbaidzhanskoe gosudarstvennoe izd., 1962), pp. 540-3 with extensive lists of purged leaders; Medvedev, *Let History Judge*, p. 344.

29. *Organy gosudarstvennoi bezopastnosti*, vol. 1, bk 1, doc. 41, pp. 94-5.

30. S.B. Baishev, *Ocherki istorii Kommunisticheskoi partii Kazakhstana* (Alma Ata: Kazakhskoe gosudarstvennoe izd., 1963), pp. 376-7; S. Tashiliev, *Ocherki istorii Kommunisticheskoi partii Turkmenistana* (Ashkabad: Turkmenistanskoe gosudarstvennoe izd., 1965), pp. 494-6; A.K. Kazakbaev, *Ocherki istorii Kommunisticheskoi partii Kirgizii* (Frunze: Izd. Kyrgyzstan, 1966), pp. 284-9; E.V. Vasil'ev et al. (eds), *Ocherki istorii Kommunisticheskoi partii Tadzhikistana* (Dushanbe: Institut tarikhi partiia, 1964), pp. 177-9; E.Iu. Iusupov et al. (eds), *Ocherki istorii Kommunisticheskoi partii Uzbekistana* (Tashkent: Izd. Uzbekistan, 1964), pp. 373-7; *Report of the Court Proceedings in the Case of the Anti-Soviet 'Block of Rights and Trotskyites' Heard before the Military Collegium of the Supreme Court of the USSR, Moscow, March 2-13, 1938* (Moscow: People's Commissariat of Justice of the USSR, 1938), pp. 217-25, 348; Kvashonkin, *Sovetskoe rukovodstvo*, docs 216, 217, 218 and 219, pp. 372-5.

31. Ibid., docs 221, 222, 223, pp. 377-9.

32. There were, to be sure, numerous non-Russian Slavic commanders of exceptional talent like Konstantin Rokossovsky, Sergei Shtemenko, Sergei Rudenko, Kirill Moskalenko, to mention only the leading commanders. See the essays in Shukman (ed.), *Stalin and His Generals*.

33. E.H. Carr, *Twilight of the Comintern, 1930-1935* (New York: Pantheon, 1982) and for a Soviet anti-Stalinist critique, B.M. Leibzon and K.K. Shirinia, *Povorot v politike Kominterna. K 30-letiiu VII Kongressa* (Moscow: Mysl', 1965).

34. J. Humbert-Droz, *La Crise de croissance de l'Internationale communiste* (Milan: Instituto Giangiacomo Feltrinelli, 1968), pp. 33-4, 40 et passim; N.E. Rosenfeldt, *Stalin's Secret Chancellery and the Comintern: Evidence about the Organizational Patterns* (Copenhagen: C.A. Reitzels, 1991), pp. 49, 59, 62-3 et passim.

35. B. Lazitch, 'Two Instruments of Control by the Comintern: The Emissaries of the ECCI and the Party Representatives in Moscow', in M.M. Drachkovitch and B. Lazitch (eds),

The Comintern: Historical Highlights. Essays, Recollections, Documents (Palo Alto, CA: Stanford University Press, 1966), pp. 45–65, and Lazitch, 'Stalin's Massacre of the Foreign Communist Leaders', in ibid., pp. 167–9, 173; pp. 139–74.

36. *La Correspondance internationale* 2 (9 January 1929), 23 (13 March 1929), 37 (4 May 1929), 38 (8 May 1929), 49 (12 June 1929), and *X plenum IKKI. Mezhdunarodnoe polozhenie i zadachi Kommunisticheskogo internatsionala*, vol. 1 (Moscow: Politizdat, 1929), pp. 235–7 (Ulbricht), pp. 16–20 (Kuusinen), pp. 62–4 (Manuilsky); Stalin, *Sochineniia*, vol. 1, pp. 306–9.

37. F.I. Firsov and I.S. Iazhborovskaia, 'Komintern i Kommunisticheskaia partiia Pol'shi', *Voprosy istorii KPSS* 12 (December 1988), pp. 20–35; pp. 31–3.

38. 'Novye dokumenty G. Dimitrova', *Voprosy istorii KPSS* 8 (August 1989), pp. 53–79; pp. 75–7.

39. *Report of the Court Proceedings in the Case of the Anti-Soviet Trotskyite Centre* (Moscow: People's Commissariat of Justice of the USSR, 1937), pp. 6–18, 574–5. See also H. Kuromiya, 'Accounting for the Great Terror', *Jahrbücher für Geschichte Osteuropas* 53:1 (2005), pp. 86–101; p. 91.

40. *The Case of the Anti-Soviet Trotskyite Centre*, pp. 159–61, 192, 196.

41. 'Materialy fevral'sko–martovskogo plenuma TsK VKP(b), 1937 goda', *Voprosy istorii* (1995), pp. 3–26; pp. 11–14.

42. Dimitrov, *Diary*, entries for 20 and 25 June 1937, pp. 62, 65–6. See also F.I. Firsov, 'Dimitrov, the Comintern and Stalinist Repression', in McLoughlin and McDermott (eds), *Stalin's Terror*, pp. 56–81.

43. W.J. Chase, *Enemies within the Gates? The Comintern and Stalinist Repression, 1934–1939* (New Haven, CT: Yale University Press, 2001), pp. 116–19, quotation on p. 116. The resolution of the Comintern Executive on the Polish question in January 1936 accused the party of every sin in the book: left sectarianism, right nationalist deviation, factional struggles and infiltration by Polish intelligence. Ibid., pp. 121–4.

44. Snyder, *Sketches*, pp. 117–19. Snyder casts serious doubt on the Polish spy mania of the NKVD. Ibid., pp. 120–6.

45. N. Petrov and A. Roginsky, 'The "Polish Operation" of the NKVD, 1937–8', in McLoughlin and McDermott (eds), *Stalin's Terror*, pp. 153–72.

46. Ibid., pp. 170–1; Snyder, *Sketches*, pp. 119–21.

47. Firsov and Iazhborovskaia, 'Komintern', pp. 48–51.

48. Chase, *Enemies*, pp. 287–9. The formal dissolution came only nine months later, reflecting Stalin's preference to delay publication of the resolution in order to avoid demoralizing other parties.

49. Snyder, *Sketches*, pp. 143–4.

50. A. Burmeister, *Dissolution and Aftermath of the Comintern: Experiences and Observations, 1937–1947* (New York: Research Program on the USSR, 1955), pp. 1–2; I. Banac, *With Stalin against Tito: Cominformist Splits in Yugoslav Communism* (Ithaca, NY: Cornell University Press, 1988), pp. 67–8; G. Ionescu, *Communism in Romania, 1944–1962* (Oxford: Oxford University Press, 1964), pp. 43, 352, 355; *Sovetskaia istoricheskaia entsiklopediia*, 16 vols (Moscow: Sovetskaia entsiklopediia, 1969–76), vol. 13, p. 951; C. Chaqueri, 'Sultanzade: The Forgotten Revolutionary Theoretician of Iran – A Biographical Sketch', *Iranian Studies* 17:2/3 (spring–summer 1984), pp. 215–35; pp. 226, 234. T. Atabaki, 'Incommodious Hosts, Invidious Guests. The Life and Time of Iranian Revolutionaries in Soviet Union (1921–1929)', in S. Cronin (ed.), *Reformers and Revolutionaries in Modern Iran: New Perspectives on the Iranian Left* (London: RoutledgeCurzon, 2004), pp. 147–64; p. 160. K. McDermott and J. Agnew, *The Comintern: A History of International Communism from Lenin to Stalin* (London: Macmillan, 1995), pp. 148–9.

51. 'Za pravil'noe osveshchenie istorii kompartii Latvii', *Kommunist* 12 (1964), pp. 65–9; pp. 67–8; G. Zvimach, *Latyshskie revoliutsionnye deiateli* (Riga: Latyshskoe gosudarstvennoe izd., 1958), pp. 87–93; V. Mishke, *Ocherki istorii Kommunisticheskoi partii Latvii*, 2 vols (Riga: Latyshskoe gosudarstvennoe izd., 1966), vol. 2, pp. 369–74, 378, 444;

A. Trapāns, 'The Latvian Communist Party and the Purge of 1937', *Journal of Baltic Studies* 11:1 (1980), pp. 25–38.

52. A. Pankseev and A. Liban, *Ocherki istorii Kommunisticheskoi partii Estonii*, 3 vols (Tallin: Estonskoe gos. izd-stvo, 1961–1970), vol. 3, pp. 39–41. According to one report, a leading Estonian communist imported in the baggage trains of the Red Army had lived in Russia since childhood and was a railway substation master when he was lifted to prominence. J.A. Armstrong, *The Politics of Totalitarianism: The Communist Party of the Soviet Union from 1934 to the Present* (New York: Random House, 1961), p. 125.

53. P.D. Grishchenko and G.A. Gurin (eds.), *Bor'ba za Sovetskuiu pribaltiku v Velikoi Otechestvennoi voine, 1941–1945*, 2 vols (Riga: Liesma, 1966), vol. 1, p. 24.

54. Burmeister, *Dissolution*, pp. 5–12.

55. 'Muzhestvo protiv bezzakoniia', *Problemy mira i sotsializma* 7 (1989), pp. 89–92; p. 91.

56. Firsov, 'Dimitrov, the Comintern and Stalinist Repression', pp. 75–7.

57. Dimitrov to Andreev, 3 January 1939, in Chase, *Enemies*, doc. 44, pp. 307–8.

58. Haslam, *The Soviet Union and the Struggle for Collective Security*, pp. 222–3.

59. D.L. Brandenberger, 'The Fate of Interwar Soviet Internationalism: A Case Study of the Editing of Stalin's 1938 *Short Course on the History of the ACP(b)*', *Revolutionary Russia* 29:1 (2016), pp. 1–23; pp. 10–14 emphasizes the domestic, replacing international aspects of the revolution by the construction of 'socialism in one country' as the key to the history of the party.

60. Ibid., p. 10.

61. Grishchenko and Gurin (eds.), *Bor'ba za Sovetskuiu pribaltiku*, vol. 1, pp. 22–3; K. Tazva, 'Poet-borets', in S. Tashliev (ed.), *Ob estonskoi literature. Sbornik literaturno-kriticheskikh stat'ei* (Tallinn: Estonskoe gosudarstvennoe izd., 1956).

62. For insights into the attitudes and rationalizations of sympathetic Western visitors to the Soviet Union in these years which have parallels with the behaviour of embattled communists see M. David-Fox, *Showcasing the Great Experiment: Cultural Diplomacy and Western Visitors to the Soviet Union, 1921–1941* (New York: Oxford University Press, 2012).

CHAPTER 3: FORGING THE SINEWS OF WAR

1. C. Streit, *Keine Kameraden. Die Wehrmacht und die sowjetischen Kriegsgefangenen, 1941–1945* (Stuttgart: Deutsche Verlags-Anstalt, 1978), pp. 127–37 and A. Streim, *Die Behandlung sowjetischer Kriegsgefangener im 'Fall Barbarossa'* (Heidelberg: C.F. Mueller, 1981).

2. D.M. Glantz, *Before Stalingrad: Barbarossa – Hitler's Invasion of Russia 1941* (Stroud: Tempus, 2003), pp. 50–60. See also A.I. Kruglov, 'O nekotorykh prichinakh bol'shoi poter' Sovetskikh Vooruzhennykh sil v pervom periode Velikoi Otechestvennoi voiny', in *Liudskie poteri SSSR v period Vtoroi mirovoi voiny. Sbornik statei* (Saint Petersburg: Izd-vo Russko-Baltiski informatsionnyi tsentr Blits, 1995), pp. 71–123; pp. 97–9. A.A. Grechko et al. (eds), *Istoriia Vtoroi mirovoi voiny 1939–1945*, 12 vols (Moscow: Voenizdat, 1982 edn), vol. 4, pp. 35, 137–9.

3. P.N. Knyshevsky et al. (eds), *Skrytaia pravda. 1941 god. Neizvestnye dokumenty* (Moscow: Russkaia kniga, 1992), pp. 77–98.

4. N.S. Khrushchev, *Memoirs of Nikita Khrushchev*, vol. 1, *Commissar, 1918–1945*, ed. S. Khrushchev (University Park, PA: Penn State University Press, 2004), p. 304.

5. 'Dokumenty russkoi istorii', *Istochnik* 2:15 (1995), pp. 112–13.

6. For accounts of individuals who met with him see T.B. Toman, 'Partiia v pervye mesiatsy voiny', *Voprosy istorii KPSS* 7 (July 1991), pp. 36–49; pp. 37–8.

7. Chuev, *Sto sorok besed s Molotovym*, pp. 51–3.

8. F. Chuev, *Tak govoril Kaganovich. Ispoved' stalinskogo apostola* (Moscow: Otechestvo, 1992), p. 88.

9. 'Iz tetriadi zapisi lits I.V. Stalinym 21–28 iiunia 1941', *Izvestiia TsK KPSS* 6 (1990), pp. 196–222; pp. 216–20.

10. *KPSS v rezoliutsiiakh i resheniiakh s'ezdov konferentsii i plenum TsK 1938-1945*, 9th edn (Moscow: Politizdat, 1985), pp. 211, 212 and 213. See also Roberts, *Stalin's Wars*, pp. 89–91, who argues in general for Stalin's vigorous response to the attack.

11. 'Otvety P.K. Ponomarenko na voprosy professora G.A. Kumaneva (2/11/1978)', in G.A. Kumanev, *Riadom so Stalinym. Otkrovennye svidetel'stva* (Moscow: Bylina, 1999), pp. 93–144; p. 121.

12. Dimitrov, *Diary*, entry for 22 June 1941, pp. 166–7.

13. A.I. Mikoian, *Tak bylo. Razmyshleniia o minuvshem* (Moscow: Vagrius, 1999), p. 389. C. Pleshakov, *Stalin's Folly. The Tragic First Ten Days of World War II on the Eastern Front* (Boston, MA: Houghton Mifflin, 2005) portrays Stalin as a distraught nervous wreck, and then is hard put to explain his recovery or that of the Soviet Union.

14. Service, *Stalin*, p. 414 suggests the intriguing possibility that Stalin might have staged this scenario, imitating Ivan IV's well-known withdrawal to a monastery in order to test the loyalty of the boyars.

15. Mikoian, *Tak bylo*, pp. 390–2.

16. *Voprosy istorii KPSS* 9 (1990), p. 95; ibid. 6 (1991), pp. 217–18.

17. E. Zubkova, *Obshchestvo i reform, 1945-1964* (Moscow: Rossiia molodaia, 1993), p. 17.

18. W. Anders, *An Army in Exile: The Story of the Second Polish Corps* (London: Macmillan, 1949). For a vivid eyewitness account see J. Czapski, *Inhuman Land: Searching for the Truth in Soviet Russia, 1941-1942*, trans. A. Lloyd-Jones (New York: New York Review of Books, 2018). The search was too late for the 22,000 Polish officers massacred at Katyn.

19. N.F. Bugai, *L. Beriia–I.Stalinu. 'Soglasno vashemu ukazaniiu'* (Moscow: Airo-XX, 1995), pp. 36–9. Beria's agents hunted down Volga Germans in the ranks of the Red Army and by 1945 had expelled and re-settled in labour camps 33,625 Volga German veterans.

20. 'Deportatsiia Nemtsev (sentiabr' 1941–fevral' 1942 g.)', in *Deportatsiia Narodov SSSR (1930-1950-e gody)*, pt 2, comp. O.I. Milov (Moscow: Institut etnologiia, 1995) comp. O.L. Milov (Moscow: Institut etnologiia 1995), pp. 118–19; *Organy gosudarstvennoi bezopastnosti*, vol. 2, bk 1, pp. 559–6; N.F. Bugai (comp.), *Iosif Stalin–Lavrentiu Beriia. 'Ikh nado deportirovat'. . .' Dokumenty, fakty, kommentarii* (Moscow: Druzhba narodov, 1992), pp. 62–3. By an order of GOKO over 100,00 of the deportees between the ages of seventeen and fifty were mobilized for railway construction and timbering for the duration of the war. V.A. Auman and V.G. Chebotareva (eds), *Istoriia rossiiskikh nemtsev v dokumentakh 1763-1992 gg.*, 2 vols (Moscow: Mezhdunarodnyi institut gumanitarnykh programm, 1993), vol. 1, pp. 168–9.

21. *Organy gosudarstvennoi bezopastnosti*, vol. 2, bk 1, doc. 505, appendix, p. 528.

22. Grishchenko and Gurin (eds), *Bor'ba za Sovetskuiu pribaltiku*, vol. 1, pp. 112–14; A.M. Budreckis, *The Lithuanian National Revolt of 1941* (Boston, MA: Lithuanian Encyclopedia Press, 1968).

23. Grishchenko and Gurin (eds), *Bor'ba za Sovetskuiu pribaltiku*, vol. 2, pp. 191, 239–43, 291 ff.; A.S. Chaikovs'kyi, *Nevidoma viina. Partizans'kyi rukh Ukraïni 1941-1944 rr. Movoiu dokumentiv, ochyma istoryka* (Kyiv: Ukraina, 1994), pp. 16–25, 173–5.

24. Grishchenko and Gurin (eds), *Bor'ba za Sovetskuiu pribaltiku*, vol. 2, pp. 191, 239–43, 291 ff.

25. 'Telegramma iz Gomela' (29 June 1941), *Izvestiia TsK KPSS* 6 (1990), pp. 214–15 and '"Polozhenie na Pinskom napravlenii", ne pozdnee 30 iiunia 1941', *Izvestiia TsK KPSS* 6 (1990), pp. 214–16. An occasional marginal comment by Stalin, 'Clarify', proves he was reading these reports. On the eve of the war, the lack of preparedness in air defence was particularly serious with many projected airfields in an incomplete state, lacking aircraft to prevent German reconnaissance. 'Telegramma iz Murmanska' (19 June 1941), *Izvestiia TsK KPSS* 5 (1990), pp. 155–214; p. 206.

26. According to German field reports the local population greeted the invaders with bread and salt, but the local Communist Party representatives praised the Belarusian peasantry's high level of patriotism. For the German reports, see N. Vakar, *Belorussia: The*

Making of a Nation (Cambridge, MA: Harvard University Press, 1956), chap. 13; for the party reports, see 'Polozhenie v raione El'nia', pp. 193-95, and 'O razvitii partizanskogo dvizheniia', *Izvestiia TsK KPSS* 7 (1990), pp. 193-216; p. 210.

27. L. Rein, *The Kings and the Pawns: Collaboration in Byelorussia during World War II* (New York and Oxford: Berghahn Books, 2011), pp. 263-72. For the involvement of the local police in the murder of Jews, see also M. Dean, *Collaboration in the Holocaust: Crimes of the Local Police in Belorussia and Ukraine, 1941-44* (New York: Palgrave Macmillan, 2000), pp. 38, 46, 60, 65 et passim.

28. Sheptyts'kyi had a long history of opposing pro-Russian Orthodox priests and secret proselytizing in Habsburg Galicia before the First World War. His reputation earned him the hostility of the top tsarist military commanders who personally supervised his arrest and deportation to Kiev during their occupation of Galicia in September 1914. M. von Hagen, *War in a European Borderland: Occupations and Occupation Plans in Galicia and Ukraine, 1914-1918* (Seattle, WA: University of Washington Press, 2007), pp. 37-40.

29. H.J. Stehle, 'Sheptyts'kyi and the German Regime', in P.R. Magocsi (ed.), *Morality and Reality: The Life and Times of Andrei Sheptyts'kyi* (Edmonton: Canadian Institute of Ukrainian Studies, 1989), pp. 125-144; p. 129.

30. Toman, 'Partiia v pervye mesiatsy voiny', p. 43.

31. N.G. Tomilina et al. (eds), *Nikita Sergeevich Khrushchev. Dva tsveta vremeni. Dokumenty lichnogo fonda N.S. Khrushchev*, 2 vols (Moscow: Mezhdunarodnyi fond Demokratiia, 2009), vol. 1, doc. 1, p. 15. This collection gives a positive picture of Khrushchev's realistic and hard-hitting reporting to Stalin on the shortcomings and successes of the southwestern front during the war.

32. 'Dokumenty russkoi istorii', *Istochnik* 2:15 (1995), p. 114. These accusations were contained in a letter by 'an ordinary party member' to Stalin on 18 August 1941.

33. The following is based on the perceptive article by E.S. Seniavskaia, 'Dukhovnyi oblik frontovogo pokoleniia. Istoriko-psikhologicheskii ocherk', *Vestnik Moskovskogo univer-siteta* 8:4 (1992), pp. 39-51.

34. Simonov, 'Zametki', *VIZh* 12 (December 1987), p. 51.

35. For the campaign of 1940 see K.-H. Frieser, *Blitzkreig-Legende. Der Westfeldzug, 1940* (Munich: R. Oldenbourg, 1995) and the exceptional account of the German operational victories in France and the Soviet Union in 1941 in A. Tooze, *The Wages of Destruction: The Making and Breaking of the Nazi Economy* (New York: Viking, 2007), pp. 368-80 and 486-506.

36. Rieber, Stalin and the Struggle, pp. 170-3.

37. Volkogonov, *Triumf i tragediia*, vol. 2, pt 1, pp. 191-2, 198-9.

38. *Organy gosudarstvennoi bezopastnosti*, vol. 2, docs 277-329 are a sample covering the first five days of the war.

39. 'Spetsvodka UNKGB po g. Moskve i Moskovskoi oblasti 1-mu sekretariu MK i MGK VKP(b). A.S. Shcherbakovu o reagirovanii naseleniia na vystuplenie I.V. Stalina, 3 iiulia 1941', in ibid., doc. 356, pp. 161-9.

40. 'Moskovskie chekhisty v oborone stolitsy, 1941-1944', *VIZh* 1 (1991), p. 10.

41. 'Prikaz NKGB SSSR, NKVD SSSR i Prokuratury SSSR ... o poriadke privlecheniia k otvetstvennosti izmennikov rodiny i chlenov ikh semei, 28 iuniia 1941', *Organy gosudarst-vennoi bezopastnosti*, vol. 2, doc. 332 and notes, pp. 114-15.

42. Ibid., pp. 37-8, 42-3. Later, they were credited with an important contribution to the rapid advance of the Red Army in Manchuria in 1945.

43. I.I. Petrov, 'Iz istorii partiinogo rukovodstva pogranichnymi voiskami (1941-1944 gg.)', *Voprosy istorii KPSS* 1 (January 1985), pp. 36-41.

44. A.J. Rieber, 'Civil Wars in the Soviet Union', *Kritika* 4:1 (2003), pp. 129-60.

45. *Organy gosudarstvennoi bezopastnosti*, vol. 1, bk 2, note, p. 179. This massive under-taking created a security nightmare as 'hostile elements' concealed themselves among the evacuated. Ibid., doc. 362, p. 178.

46. Iu.L. D'iakov and G.A. Kumanev, *Kapital'noe stroitel'stvo v SSSR, 1941–1945* (Moscow: Nauka, 1988), pp. 5–20.
47. Volkogonov, *Triumf i tragediia*, vol. 2, pt 1, pp. 176–7.
48. The following is based on Harrison, 'N.A. Voznesensky', the best treatment of Voznesensky's early career – although the author now considers his view of Voznesensky's 'moderation' overly optimistic. Personal correspondence, 26 January 2021.
49. Its purpose was 'to concentrate the full panoply of power in the government' in its hands; it ordered 'all citizens, party members, soviet, Komsomol and military organizations to obey its decisions and decrees'. L.P. Kosheleva, L.A. Rogovaia and O.V. Khlevniuk (eds), *Sovetskoe Voenno-Politicheskoe Rukovodstvo v Gody Velikoi Otechestvennoi Voiny. Gosudarstvennyi Komitet Oborony SSSR. Politbiuro TsK VKP(b). Sovet Narodnykh Komissarov SSSR* (Moscow: Kuchkovo pole Muzeon, 2020), doc. 1, p. 43.
50. One illustrative example was Mikoian's whirlwind tour of the grain-surplus provinces in November–December 1942 which revealed startling shortfalls in production. Ibid., docs 174–7, pp. 255–70.
51. Ibid., pp. 34–8.
52. Reports on the failure of the party organizations to take emergency measures in key areas like the Donbas stressed the need for greater centralization of decision-making in a single person at every level. 'Iz istorii Velikoi Otechestvennoi voiny; Zapiska P.F. Iudina I.V. Stalinu, 4 oktiabria 1941', *Izvestiia TsK KPSS* 12 (1990), pp. 208–9.
53. Volkogonov, *Triumf i tragediia*, vol. 2, pt 1, pp. 176–7.
54. Toman, 'Partiia v pervye mesiatsy voiny', pp. 37–9.
55. Simonov, 'Zametki', *VIZh* 10 (October 1987), p. 63.
56. The protocols of the bureau occupy pp. 361–659 in Kosheleva, Rogovaia and Khlevniuk (eds), *Sovetskoe Voenno-Politicheskoe Rukovodstvo*. Its creation in December 1942 signalled an attempt to introduce more rational and co-ordinated decisions in transportation and military production. Ibid., p. 28.
57. D'iakov, *Kapital'noe stroitel'stvo*, pp. 20–3.
58. Harrison, *Soviet Planning*, pp. 94–102. The Bureau of the Sovnarkom routinely brought in specialists to deal with urgent problems. Among the more active members were A.I. Mikoian, A.N. Kosygin, the GOKO plenipotentiary in Leningrad, and Nikolai Shvernik, dealing mainly with evacuation and the assignment and distribution of workers. Kosheleva, Rogovaia and Khlevniuk (eds), *Sovetskoe Voenno-Politicheskoe Rukovodstvo*.
59. Harrison, *Soviet Planning*, pp. 167, 193–204; A.V. Vasilevsky, *Delo vsei zhizni*, 4th edn (Moscow: Voenizdat, 1983), pp. 482–3. Voznesensky published his *Voennaia ekonomika SSSR v period Otechestvennoi voiny* (Moscow: Gospolitizdat, 1948), in which he summarized some of these achievements. For the controversy over the work see pp. 254–60.
60. Mikoian, *Tak bylo*, pp. 422–5.
61. D'iakov, *Kapital'noe stroitel'stvo*, pp. 46–7, 120–30. See Bailes, *Technology and Society* for prewar problems with delays between research and development due to their separate organization.
62. Vannikov, 'Oboronnaia promyshlennost'', pp. 127–8; Mikoian, *Tak bylo*, p. 424.
63. Vannikov, 'Oboronnaia promyshlennost'', pp. 131–4.
64. Mikoian, *Tak bylo*, pp. 394–401 shows his tough negotiating stance as well; J. Sapir, 'The Economics of War in the Soviet Union During World War II', in Ian Kershaw and Moshe Lewin (eds), *Stalinism and Nazism: Dictatorships in Comparison* (Cambridge: Cambridge University Press, 1997), pp. 208–36; pp. 232–3; G.A. Kumanev and L.M. Chuvakov, 'Sovetskii Soiuz i Lend-Liz, 1941–1945', in G.N. Sevost'ianov (ed.), *Voina i obshchestvo, 1941–1945*, 2 vols (Moscow: Nauka, 2004), vol. 1, pp. 60–87. Lend-Lease supplied 100 per cent of Soviet requests for radios, 83.5 per cent for steel, 70 per cent for railway flat wagons, and 70 per cent for grain, though only 44 per cent for aluminium and 42.3 per cent for aircraft, in addition to 100,000 trucks and 10,200 motorcycles. Ibid., pp. 366–7.
65. Stalin's telephone instructions to Zhdanov and Kuznetsov, 4 October 1941, *Izvestiia Tsk KPSS* 12 (1990), p. 208.

66. Harrison, *Soviet Planning*, pp. 63–79, gives the more positive side. His work is based mainly on A.M. Belikov, 'Transfert de l'industrie soviétique vers l'est (juin 1941–1942)', *Revue de l'histoire de la Deuxième Guerre mondiale* 43 (1961), pp. 35–50, and A.M. Belikov, 'Tiazhelaia promyshlennost' – v glubokii tyl', in I.Ia. Poliakov (ed.), *Eshelony idut na Vostok. Iz istorii perebazirovaniia proizvoditel'nykh sil SSSR v 1941–1942 gg. Sbornik statei i dokumentov* (Moscow: Nauka, 1966); cf. T. Dunmore, *The Stalinist Command Economy: The Soviet State Apparatus and Economic Policy, 1945–1953* (London: Macmillan, 1980), p. 34, which suggests that the economic importance of the evacuation has been exaggerated.

67. Vannikov, 'Oboronnaia promyshlenost'', pp. 133–4; A.V. Mitrofanova et al. (eds), *Rabochii klass SSSR nakanune i v gody Velikoi Otechestvennoi voiny, 1938–1945 gg.*, 3 vols (Moscow: Nauka, 1984), vol. 3, pp. 206–11; V.A. Vinogradov et al. (eds), *Sovetskaia ekonomika na kanune i v pervoi period Velikoi Otechestvennoi voiny, 1938–1945 gg.*, 5 vols (Moscow: Nauka, 1978), vol. 5, pp. 172–9, 188.

68. Sapir, 'The Economics of War', pp. 221–2, 229 and 232–3.

69. H. Hunter, 'Successful Spatial Management', in S.J. Linz (ed.), *The Impact of World War II on the Soviet Union* (Totowa, NJ: Rowman & Allanheld, 1985), pp. 47–58; pp. 50–4.

70. A.V. Khrulev, 'Stanovlenie strategicheskogo tyla v Velikoi Otechestvennoi voine', *VIZh* 6 (June 1961), pp. 64–86; pp. 78–80.

71. G.A. Kumanev, 'Sovetskie zheleznodorozhniki v pervyi period Velikoi Otechestvennoi voiny (1941–1942)', *Istoriia SSSR* 1 (1959), pp. 36–52.

72. Vinogradov et al. (eds), *Sovetskaia ekonomika*, vol. 5, pp. 425–8; Hunter, 'Successful Spatial Management', p. 55.

73. Pospelov et al., *IVOV*, vol. 3, p. 376; vol. 4, p. 157; vol. 6, p. 341; vol. 7, p. 49; *Strana sovetov za 50 let. Sbornik statisticheskikh materialov* (Moscow: Statistika, 1967), p. 53.

74. Harrison, *Accounting for War*, p. 262.

75. Iu.V. Arutiunian, *Sovetskoe krest'ianstvo v gody Velikoi Otechestvennoi voiny* (Moscow: Akademiia nauk, 1970), pp. 75, 118, 183.

76. Ibid., pp. 45–60.

77. W. Moskoff, *The Bread of Affliction: The Food Supply in the USSR during World War II* (New York: Cambridge University Press, 1990), pp. 127–45.

78. Ibid., pp. 98–111.

79. The contribution of Lend-Lease deliveries in feeding the Russian population was relatively modest. Most importantly, shipments of canned meat, animal fats and vegetable oils supplemented the diet of the Red Army soldiers. The total grain deliveries amounted only to about one month's supply for the Red Army. Ibid., pp. 119–22.

80. A.M. Volkov, 'Kolkhoznoe krest'ianstvo SSSR v pervye poslevoennyi gody', *Voprosy istorii* 6 (1970), pp. 3–19.

81. Zhukov, 'Iz neopublikovannykh vospominanii', p. 97.

82. Vasilevsky, *Delo*, pp. 466–7; S.M. Shtemenko, *The Soviet General Staff at War, 1941–1945* (Moscow: Progress Publishers, 1985), chap. 7.

83. Ibid., pp. 114, 344; G.K. Zhukov, *The Memoirs of Marshal Zhukov* (New York: Delacorte Press, 1971), p. 267.

84. Khrulev, 'Stanovlenie strategicheskogo tyla', pp. 64–9, 76–80.

85. 'Istoriia Velikoi Otechestvennoi voiny. Delo marshala G.I. Kulika (ianvar'–mart 1942 g.)', *Izvestiia TsK KPSS* 4 (August 1991), pp. 197–210.

86. O.V. Khlevniuk, 'Stalin and the General: Reconstructing Trust during World War II', *Europe-Asia Studies* (October 2021), pp. 1–22.

87. Simonov, 'Zametki', *VIZh* (October 1987), pp. 60–1.

88. Vasilevsky, *Delo*, pp. 242, 486–7 and 492–3; Zhukov, *Memoirs*, pp. 281–4; Shtemenko, *The Soviet General Staff*, pp. 184–5, 241–2.

89. Simonov, 'Zametki', *VIZh* (October 1987), p. 62.

90. Zhukov, *Memoirs*, p. 237; Simonov, 'Zametki', *VIZh* (December 1987), p. 44. But after the Kharkov disaster, Stalin angrily removed him from his post and never again allowed him to command a front.
91. Volkogonov, *Triumf i tragediia*, vol. 2, pt 1, pp. 326-8.
92. Simonov, 'Zametki', *VIZh* (December 1987), p. 42.
93. N.I. Savinkin and K.M. Bogoliubov (comps), *KPSS o Vooruzhenykh sil Sovetskogo Soiuza. Dokumenty, 1917-1981. Sbornik* (Moscow: Voenizdat, 1981), pp. 358-61; Erickson, *The Soviet High Command*, p. 603.
94. Zhukov, *Memoirs*, p. 361.
95. J. Erickson, *The Road to Stalingrad* (New York: Harper and Row, 1975), pp. 47-54, 57-66 for a summary of the literature on Stalin's role at Moscow.
96. Vasilevsky, *Delo*, pp. 130-1, 180-1; Zhukov, *Memoirs*, pp. 288-9.
97. The Politburo harshly criticized Voroshilov's conduct during his tenure as minister of defence during the Finnish War and as commander of the northwestern front in the first year of the Fatherland War, sending him to the rear for 'military work'. Kosheleva, Rogovaia and Khlevniuk (eds), *Sovetskoe Voenno-Politicheskoe Rukovodstvo*, doc. 167, pp. 226-31.
98. Fresh light on the relations of Zhukov, Vasilevsky and Antonov with Stalin can be found in Volkogonov, *Triumf i tragediia*, vol. 2, pt 1, pp. 329-43.
99. E.F. Ziemke and M.E. Bauer III, *Moscow to Stalingrad: Decision in the East* (Washington, DC: Center of Military History, United States Army, 1987), pp. 506-8. See also Pospelov et al., *IVOV*, vol. 5, p. 236 and Erickson, *The Road to Stalingrad*, p. 403.
100. The rush to the front created an immediate problem of finding replacements for the 47,000 leaders of the party, Komsomol and trade union organizations, not to speak of the over 500,000 regular party members. I.M. Shliapin, M.A. Shvarev and I.Ia. Fomichenko, *Kommunisticheskaia partiia v period Velikoi Otechestvenoi voiny* (Moscow: Voenizdat, 1958), p. 48.
101. A. Statiev, 'Penal Units in the Red Army', *Europe-Asia Studies* 62:5 (2010), pp. 730-9.
102. S.A. Tiushkevich, *Sovetskie Vooruzhennye sily. Istoriia stroitel'stva* (Moscow: Voenizdat, 1978), pp. 20-82, 314-28 and 344-52.
103. Ibid., pp. 295-8.
104. R.H. McNeal (ed.), *I.V. Stalin, Works*, 3 vols (Stanford, CA: Hoover Institution Press, 1967), vol. 1, pp. 91, 132.
105. Garthoff, *How Russia Makes War*, pp. 103-5, 108-9; Ziemke and Bauer, *Moscow to Stalingrad*, p. 512; Ivanov, *Marshal Tukhachevsky*, p. 289.
106. Simonov, 'Zametki', *VIZh* (October 1987), p. 61.
107. Tiushkevich, *Sovetskie Vooruzhennye sily*, pp. 293-4, 329-30.
108. R.R. Reese, *The Soviet Military Experience* (London: Routledge, 2000), pp. 124-5.
109. J. Erickson, *The Road to Berlin* (New Haven, CT: Yale University Press, 1999), pp. 80, 134, 214.
110. D.M. Glantz and J.M. House, *The Battle of Kursk* (Lawrence, KS: University Press of Kansas, 1999).
111. Mikoian, *Tak bylo*, pp. 452-61 for the formation of the Reserve Front; Shtemenko, *The Soviet General Staff*, pp. 219-26 and Vasilevsky, *Delo*, pp. 298, 301 for the military planning. Figures differ on the total forces engaged if not the results. Cf. ibid., pp. 306-10 and Erickson, *The Road to Berlin*, pp. 80, 134, 214.
112. Zhukov, *Memoirs*, p. 542; Vasilevsky, *Delo*, p. 346.
113. Zhukov, *Memoirs*, p. 542.
114. Shtemenko, *The Soviet General Staff*, p. 401. Shtemenko's account should dispel the myth that Stalin was playing Zhukov against Konev in order to provoke rivalries among the generals.
115. Quoted in Werth, *Russia at War*, p. 739.
116. Shtemenko, *The Soviet General Staff*, pp. 456-64.
117. Ibid., pp. 446-50.

118. K. Slepyan, *Stalin's Guerrillas: Soviet Partisans in World War II* (Lawrence, KS: University Press of Kansas, 2006), p. 24.
119. This is one firm conclusion that emerges from the debate over whether Stalin was planning a 'preventative' attack. See for example M.I. Mel'tiukhov, 'Spory vokrug 1941 goda. Opyt kriticheskogo osmysleniia odnoi diskussii', *Otechestvennaia istoriia* 3 (1994), pp. 4–22.
120. 'Partorg rotu N.L. Sheshenina I.V. Stalinu, ne pozdnee 22 avgusta, 1941', *Izvestiia TsK KPSS* 9 (1990), pp. 193–215; pp. 204–6.
121. 'Ponomarenko I.V. Stalinu' (telegrams 2 July and undated 1941, from Ponomarenko to Stalin), ibid. 7 (1990), pp. 158–216; p. 196.
122. Beria to Stalin, 8 August 1941, in ibid., pp. 197–8; 'Ob organizatsii bor'by v tylu germanskikh voisk', ibid., p. 217.
123. L.D. Grenkevich, *The Soviet Partisan Movement, 1941–1944: A Critical Historiographical Analysis*, ed. D. Glantz (London: Frank Cass, 1999), pp. 6–7 and 84–6.
124. P. Ponomarenko, 'Idet beshenaia natsionalisticheskaia propaganda tovarishchu Stalinu, I.V. 21 June 1943', in 'Dokumenty russkoi istorii', *Istochnik* 2:15 (1995), pp. 120–2; includes a condemnation of the commander of the Bryansk partisan detachments.
125. I.G. Starinov, 'Podrivniki na kommunikatsiia agressora', *Voprosy istorii* 2 (1988), pp. 97–110; p. 109, gives the important testimony of a participant.
126. N.I. Epoletov, 'Iz opyta raboty kompartii po razvitiiu partizanskogo dvizheniia (1941–1944)', *Voprosy istorii KPSS* 5 (May 1987), pp. 99–109; pp. 106–8.
127. The party made strenuous efforts to provide new cadres to work with the partisans. For example, by the end of the war in Belarus, 3,900 activists were trained and sent behind the lines. Most of these, however, arrived after 1943 and never exceeded 1 per cent of the total number of partisans. Ibid., p. 108.
128. C. Chatterjee, *Celebrating Women: Gender, Festival Culture and Bolshevik Ideology 1910–1939* (Pittsburgh, PA: University of Pittsburgh Press, 2001), pp. 135–6; S. Fitzpatrick and Y. Slezkine (eds), *In the Shadow of Revolution: Life Stories of Russian Women from 1917 to the Second World War* (Princeton, NJ: Princeton University Press, 2000), p. 9; W.Z. Goldman, *Women at the Gates: Gender and Industry in Stalin's Russia* (Cambridge: Cambridge University Press, 2002).
129. R.D. Markwick and E. Charon Cardona, *Soviet Women on the Frontline in the Second World War* (Basingstoke: Palgrave Macmillan, 2012), pp. 84, 149, 151–3.
130. Ibid., p. 229.
131. Slepyan, *Stalin's Guerrillas*, pp. 186–8, 199–201.
132. RGASPI, f. 69, op. 10, d. 160, 3 June 1943, as cited in Markwick and Charon Cardona, *Soviet Women*, pp. 141–2.
133. Ibid., p. 245.
134. A.J. Rieber, 'Persistent Factors in Russian Foreign Policy: An Interpretive Essay', in H. Ragsdale (ed.), *Imperial Russian Foreign Policy* (Cambridge and Washington, DC: Cambridge University Press and Woodrow Wilson Center, 1993), pp. 315–59.

CHAPTER 4: THE SCIENTIFIC AND TECHNICAL INTELLIGENTSIA

1. For analysis of the shifting meanings of the term 'intelligentsia' as applied to the Russian and Soviet scientific community see M.D. Gordin and K. Hall, 'Introduction: Intelligentsia Science inside and outside Russia', *Osiris* 23:1 (2008), pp. 1–19.
2. S. Fitzpatrick, *The Commissariat of Enlightenment: Soviet Organization of Education and the Arts under Lunacharsky* (Cambridge: Cambridge University Press, 1970).
3. L.R. Graham, *Science in Russia and the Soviet Union: A Short History* (Cambridge: Cambridge University Press, 1993), pp. 160–4; H.D. Balzer, 'The Engineering Profession', in Balzer (ed.), *Russia's Missing Middle Class: The Professions in Russian History* (Armonk, NY: M.E. Sharpe, 1995), pp. 55–88, and 'Conclusion', ibid., pp. 293–319; pp. 297–8; for the early origins of the technocratic approach in Russia see A.J. Rieber, *The Imperial*

Russian Project: Autocratic Politics, Economic Development and Social Fragmentation (Toronto: University of Toronto Press, 2017), chap. 5; for a comprehensive analysis of technocracy see Bailes, *Technology and Society*, pp. 95–121.

4. A.A. Baikov, 'Zadachi AN SSSR', *Vestnik Akademiia nauk* 1–2 (1944), pp. 24–30, and 'Iosifu Vissarionovichu Stalinu', ibid., pp. 20–1, expressing delight at Stalin's praise of the academy.

5. McNeal (ed.), *I.V. Stalin, Works*, vol. 2, pp. 60, 116, 160.

6. V.P. Gar'kin and G.A. Shirokov, *Otechestvennaia voina i vyshaia shkola 1941–1945. Sbornik materialov* (Samara: Samarskii Universitet, 2008); Shirokov, *Nauka. Tretii front 1941–1945. Sbornik materialov* (Samara: Samarskii universitet, 2008); and Shirokov, *Otechestvennaia voina i nauka 1941–1945. Sbornik materialov* (Samara: Samarskii Universitet, 2008). See also L.S. Leonova, 'Deiatel'nost' vyshei shkoly i Akademicheskikh uchrezhdenii v gody Velikoi Otechestvennoi voiny', *Novaia i noveishaia istoriiia* 6 (November–December 2010), pp. 73–87.

7. For the unique aspects of the Soviet institute as an organizing structure for research and development see L.R. Graham, 'The Formation of Soviet Research Institutions: A Combination of Revolutionary Innovation and International Borrowing', in D.K. Rowney and G.E. Orchard (eds), *Russian and Slavic History* (Columbus, OH: Slavica, 1977), pp. 49–75 and M.B. Adams, 'Science, Ideology and Structure: the Kol'tsov Institute, 1900–1970', in L. Lubrano and S.G. Solomon (eds), *The Social Context of Soviet Science* (Boulder, CO: Westview Press, 1980), pp. 173–204.

8. V.E. Gromov et al. (eds), 'Vklad uchenykh v oborone strany (1941–1945 gg.)', in G.D. Komkov et al. (eds), *Akademiia nauk SSSR. Kratkii istoricheskii ocherk* (first edition), 2 vols (Moscow: Nauka, 1974), p. 341.

9. N. Krementsov, *Stalinist Science* (Princeton, NJ: Princeton University Press, 1997), pp. 97–8.

10. The following is based mainly on Gromov et al. (eds), 'Vklad uchenykh v oborone', pp. 344–52.

11. Ibid., p. 347. Fersman was an established geologist before the revolution.

12. D.J.B. Shaw and J.D. Oldfield, 'Soviet Geographers and the Great Patriotic War, 1941–1945: Lev Berg and Andrei Grigorev', *Journal of Historical Geography* 47 (January 2015), pp. 40–9; pp. 40–5. After the closure of Fersman's Commission for Geological-Geographical Services to the Red Army in the second half of 1943, much of its work transferred to departments of the military. Geographers in the institute turned their attention to assisting in the rehabilitation of war-ravaged regions.

13. In a telegram sent to Komarov, Shvernik, the chairman of the Supreme Soviet, welcomed 'your initiative in mobilizing the resources of the Ural'. Cited in Gromov et al. (eds), 'Vklad uchenykh v oborone', p. 349. The party organs in the region were instructed to co-operate.

14. Ibid., pp. 368–75. In the exploration and development of the 'New Baku', the local party organization was credited with contributing transport and physical labourers, illustrating indirectly the disparity between the abilities of the scientists and the party organizations to meeting the challenge of providing new sources of energy and raising levels of productivity.

15. S. Kaftanov, *Sovetskaia intelligentsia v Velikoi Otechestvennoi voine* (Moscow: Ogiz, 1945), pp. 60–80 et passim.

16. Mitrofanova et al. (eds), *Rabochii klass SSSR*, vol. 3, p. 261.

17. V.D. Esakov (comp.), *Akademiia nauk v resheniiakh Politbiuro TsRKP(b)–VKP(b), 1922–1952* (Moscow: ROSSPEN, 2000), docs 250, 259, 261 and 273, pp. 274–5, 282–3, 284–5 and 291.

18. Leonova, 'Deiatel'nost' vysshei shkoly', p. 86.

19. Gromov et al. (eds), 'Vklad uchenykh v oborone', p. 361.

20. M. Mirsky, *Istseliaiushii skal'pel'. Akademik N.N. Burdenko* (Moscow: Znanie, 1983), pp. 57–67 and 131–60.

21. A.M. Cienciala, N.S. Lebedeva and W. Materski (eds), *Katyn: A Crime without Punishment* (New Haven, CT: Yale University Press, 2007), pp. 262–4.

22. Gromov et al. (eds), 'Vklad uchenykh v oborone', pp. 355–60, 366, 367.

23. Sapir, 'The Economics of War', pp. 215, 228–9.

24. On 23 June an enlarged plenum of the Presidium of the Academy of Sciences outlined its commitment to war-related work. B.I. Kozlov, 'Akademiia nauk SSSR v gody voiny. Urok istorii', *Vestnik RAN* 75:5 (2005), pp. 387–92.

25. 'Iosifu Vissarionovichu Stalinu', *Vestnik Akademiia nauk* 1–2 (1944), pp. 20–1 and Baikov, 'Zadachi AN SSSR', pp. 24–30.

26. *Pravda*, 24 September 1943.

27. RGASPI, f. 17, op. 175, d. 302, the reference provided to me courtesy of Karl Hall. Landau continued to do brilliant work and to cover himself politically, contributing on the theoretical side to the development of the atomic and hydrogen bombs, for which he received Stalin Prizes in the dictator's final years of 1949 and again in 1953. R. Rhodes, *Dark Sun: The Making of the Hydrogen Bomb* (New York: Simon and Schuster, 2005), p. 33.

28. G. Gorelik, 'The Top-Secret Life of Lev Landau', *Scientific American* 277:2 (August 1997), pp. 72–7. Gorelik was briefly permitted access to the files of the KGB in 1991.

29. D. Holloway, *Stalin and the Bomb: The Soviet Union and Atomic Energy, 1939–1956* (New Haven, CT: Yale University Press, 1995), pp. 10–11; for the early career of Vernadsky see ibid., pp. 29–34; for his organization of the Uranium Commission in 1940, see ibid., pp. 60–2; for its difficulties in obtaining governmental support in the early years of the war, see ibid., pp. 88–102.

30. Ibid., p. 112 and K.E. Bailes, *Science and Russian Culture in an Age of Revolutions: V.I. Vernadsky and His Scientific School, 1863–1945* (Bloomington, IN: Indiana University Press, 1990), p. 177. Vernadsky's essay was only published in *Piroda* in 1975. The reasons for the delay may be imagined.

31. O.V. Khlevniuk et al. (eds), *Stalin i Kaganovich. Perepiska 1931–1936 gg.* (Moscow: ROSSPEN, 2001), doc. 533, pp. 486–7. Kuibyshev and Kaganovich recommended the detainment of Kapitsa, whose work they insisted had 'military significance'. Stalin concurred with the reservation that Kapitsa should not be formally arrested. Stalin to Kaganovich and Kuibyshev, 21 September 1936, ibid., doc. 540, p. 492; Esakov (comp.), *Akademiia nauk*, doc. 169, pp. 195–6; doc. 272, p. 290.

32. Gromov et al. (eds), 'Vklad uchenykh v oborone', p. 363. One of his collaborators was Lev Landau. *Akademiia nauk v resheniiakh Politbiuro TsK RKP-VKP(b)-KPSS 1922–1991*, vol. 1 (Moscow: ROSSPEN, 2000), doc. 272, p. 290.

33. Kapitsa to Beria, 26 April 1939 and to Stalin, 14 June 1940, in J.W. Boag, P.E. Rubinin and D. Shoenberg (eds), *Kapitza in Cambridge and Moscow: Life and Letters of a Russian Physicist* (Amsterdam: North-Holland, 1990), pp. 350–1. Migdal later recalled that when he became an academician Kapitsa told him, 'Well now you really have got a Stalin Studentship'. Ibid., p. 351.

34. Kapitsa to V.M. Molotov, 14 October 1943 and to Niels Bohr, 28 October 1943, in ibid., pp. 353–5 and communication (by radio?) to Paul Langevin, 23 January 1945, in ibid., p. 361.

35. Kapitsa to G.M. Malenkov, 3 March 1944, in ibid., p. 360.

36. Kapitsa to G.M. Malenkov, 23 March 1944, in ibid., p. 361.

37. Kapitsa to Stalin, 19 April 1943, 13 October 1944, 14 March 1945 and 13 April 1945, in ibid., pp. 349, 361, 363–5 and 366–7.

38. P.L. Kapitsa, 'Ob organizatsii nauchnoi raboty v Institute fizicheskikh problem', *Vestnik Akademiia nauk* 6 (1943), pp. 75–89; pp. 79–82.

39. V. Soifer, *Vlast' i nauka. Istoriia razgroma genetiki v SSSR* (Saint Petersburg: Ermitazh, 1989), pp. 364–7.

40. Ibid., p. 97 and T.D. Lysenko, 'O nekotorykh osnovnykh zadachakh sel'skokhozaistvennoi nauki', *Vestnik Akademiia nauk* 5–6 (1942), pp. 49–59.

41. Kaftanov to *Pravda*, 1 April 1942 and 18 June 1944 quoted in Leonova, 'Deiatel'nost' vysshei shkoly', pp. 78 and 81.

42. Soifer, *Vlast' i nauka*, p. 370.
43. Kapitsa, 'Ob organizatsii', pp. 90–4 for comments of Ioffe and Shtern; A.F. Ioffe, 'Fizika i voina', *Vestnik Akademiia nauk* 5–6 (1942), pp. 66–76; see also L.A. Orbeli, 'Biologiia i voina', ibid., pp. 76–85; P.L. Pevsner, 'Kharakteristika sovremennogo sostoianiia silikatnoi promyshlennosti Urala', *Vestnik Akademiia nauk* 7–8 (1942), pp. 84–90; I.A. Dobrosev, 'Ural-Stanovoi khrebet oborony', *Vestnik Akademiia nauk* 4–5 (1943), pp. 26–35.
44. A. Sakharov, *Memoirs* (New York: Knopf, 1990), chap. 4 especially pp. 96–7 and 100. The phrase was Enrico Fermi's.
45. G.A. Kumanev (ed.), *Tragicheskie sud'by. Repressirovannye uchenye Akademii nauk SSSR. Sbornik statei* (Moscow: Nauka, 1995) and D.A. Sobolev, 'Istoriia Samoletov 1919–1945', *Repressii v Sovetskoi aviapromyshlennosti* (Moscow: ROSSPEN, 1997). A.L. Kiselev and E.S. Levina, *Lev Aleksandrovich Zil'ber (1894–1966). Zhizn' i nauka* (Moscow: Nauka, 2005), who discovered a means of curing pellagra in subzero environments.
46. G.A. Ozerov, *Tupolevskaia sharaga*, 2nd edn (Frankfurt am Main: Possev, 1973), p. 37; S. Gerovitch, 'Stalin's Rocket Designers' Leap into Space: The Technical Intelligentsia Faces the Thaw', *Osiris* 23:1 (2008), pp. 189–209; pp. 189–90. Korolev luckily was removed at the last moment from a list of seventy-four military specialists and defence engineers sentenced to death by Stalin in September 1938.
47. A.I. Shakhurin, *Kryl'ia pobedy*, 3rd edn (Moscow: Politizdat, 1990), pp. 247–8 and V.P. Naumov and Iu. Sichagev (comps), *Lavrentii Beriia: Stenogramma iul'skogo plenuma TsK KPSS i drugie dokumenty* (Moscow: Mezhdunarodnyi fond Demokratiia, 1999), p. 175.
48. Naumov and Sichagev, *Lavrentii Beriia*, pp. 145–7.
49. Holloway, *Stalin and the Bomb*, p. 144. True to his word Stalin dismissed Kapitsa from his post but allowed him to continue his research at a small laboratory. Stalin's action closely resembles his response to Beria's request to arrest Zhukov.
50. V.P. Kozlov et al. (eds), *Istoriia stalinskogo gulaga. Konets 1920–pervaia polovina 1950-kh godov. Sobranie dokumentov v semi tomakh* (Moscow: ROSSPEN, 2004), doc. 169, pp. 445–6.
51. Ibid., pp. 446–50. After the war, the imprisoned specialists continued to contribute to the design of turbo-jet engines and the organization of a construction bureau to manufacture them. Ibid., doc. 170, pp. 450–51 and note 324, pp. 584–5.
52. A.I. Kokurin and N.V. Petrov (comps), *GULAG (Glavnoe upravlenie lagerei). 1918–1960* (Moscow: ROSSPEN, 2002), p. 276.
53. The following is based mainly on Holloway's classic study, *Stalin and the Bomb*.
54. Ibid., pp. 46, 54 and 58.
55. Ibid., p. 69 quoting Vernadsky's diary.
56. Zhukov, *Vospominaniia*, p. 334.
57. In a long conversation with Kurchatov, Stalin made both these points, proposing to increase the rewards and raise the living standards of scientists, yet expressing reservations about the devotion of leading figures like Kapitsa, Sergei Vavilov and Ioffe. Kurchatov's notes, cited in Holloway, *Stalin and the Bomb*, pp. 147–9. He made even more sweeping comments on the 'insufficiently educated feelings of Soviet patriotism' of the scientific as well as the entire intelligentsia to the writer Konstantin Simonov. W.G. Hahn, *Postwar Soviet Politics* (Ithaca, NY: Cornell University Press, 1982), p. 126. By putting Beria in charge of the atomic project Stalin made clear his belief that scientists had to be kept under surveillance even while working for the motherland.
58. V.S. Gott (ed.), *Filosovskie voprosy sovremennoi fiziki* (Moscow: Vysshaia shkola, 1988), pp. 22–5, 64–5, 297 and 406.
59. Holloway, *Stalin and the Bomb*, pp. 146–7, 245–50; V.P. Glushko, *Rocket Engines GDL-OKB* (Moscow: Novosti, 1975); Glushko, *Razvitie raketostroeniia i kosmonavtiki v SSSR* (Moscow: Nauka, 1987); J. Harford, *Korolev: How One Man Masterminded the Soviet Drive to Beat America to the Moon* (Hoboken, NJ: Wiley and Sons, 1997); B.N. Malinovskii, *Akademik V. Glushkov. Stranitsy zhizni i tvorchestva* (Kiev: Anukova

Dumka, 1993); T.A. Grichenko and A.A. Stognii, 'Viktor Mikhailovich Grichenko i ego shkola', *Matematichni mashin i sysmemu* 4 (2006), pp. 3–14.

60. Soifer, *Vlast' i nauka*, p. 370–1; D. Joravsky, *The Lysenko Affair* (Cambridge, MA: Harvard University Press, 1970), pp. 152–8.

61. Graham, *Science in Russia*, p. 167.

62. H.D. Balzer, 'Conclusion', in Balzer (ed.), *Russia's Missing Middle Class*, pp. 298–300; pp. 298–99.

63. M.J. Berry, 'Science, Technology and Innovation', in M. McCauley (ed.), *Khrushchev and Khrushchevism* (Bloomington, IN: Indiana University Press, 1987), pp. 71–94; pp. 81–92.

64. A term which literally means braking or slowing down of the mechanism of state as an integrated hierarchical system. M. Lewin, *Russia/USSR/Russia: The Drift and Drive of a Superstate* (New York: New Press, 1995), p. 313.

65. R.B. Day, *Cold War Capitalism: The View from Moscow, 1945–1975* (London: Routledge, 2016), chap. 1, pt 4.

66. 'Izuchenie ekonomiki i politiki zarubezhnykh stran', *Mirovoe khoziastvo i mirovaia politika* 5 (1945), pp. 77–84.

67. There is some evidence that Varga gave testimony against Kun during his trial. B. Kovrig, *Communism in Hungary: From Kun to Kádár* (Stanford, CA: Hoover Institution Press, 1979), p. 128; W.J. Chase, 'Microhistory and Mass Repression: Politics, Personalities and Revenge in the Fall of Béla Kun', *Russian Review* 67:3 (2008), pp. 454–83; p. 477.

68. Dimitrov, *Diary*, entries for 16 September 1938 and 13 May 1943, p. 273, italics in original.

69. E. Varga, 'Reshaiushchaia rol' gosudarstva v voennom khozaistve kapitalisticheskikh stran', *Mirovaia khoziastvo i mirovaia politika* 1 (1945), pp. 11–21. There is an eerie foreshadowing here of what President Eisenhower would later call the 'military-industrial complex'.

70. 'Problema promyshlennogo tsikla posle voiny. (Doklad akad. E.S. Varga i preniia)', *Mirovoe khoziastvo i mirovaia politika* 2–3 (1945), pp. 79–87.

71. I. Lemin, 'Vsemirno-istoricheskaia pobeda', *Mirovoe khoziastvo i mirovaia politika* 5 (1945), pp. 6–22. In an earlier work, I had erroneously placed Lemin among the advocates of 'the Western threat' camp, not having had access to this article. He corrected my mistake when I was his host at Northwestern University in 1964 during his visit to the United States. He told me then that 'Stalin understood nothing of the economic situation after the war'.

72. For example, I. Trakhtenberg, 'Finansirovanie voiny i infliatsiia', *Mirovoe khoziastvo i mirovoe politika* 2–3 (1945), pp. 3–21; L. Frei, 'Poslevoennye voprosy vneshnei torgovoi politiki', *Mirovoe khoziastvo i mirovaia politika* 1 (1945), pp. 55–66; p. 65, who praises Litvinov's views on international trade in 1933; A. Troianovsky, 'Pamiati velikogo presidenta', *Mirovoe khoziastvo i mirovaia politika* 5 (1945), pp. 46–53, commemorating Roosevelt on the occasion of the president's death and stressing the need for postwar co-operation. M Bokshinitsky, 'Vtoraia mirovaia voina i izmeneniia v promyshlennosti SShA', *Mirovoe khoziastvo i mirovaia politika* 4 (1945), pp. 30–45; pp. 43–4. I. Dreizenshtok, 'Zheleznodorozhnyi transport SShA i ego poslevoennye perspektivy', *Mirovoe khoziastvo i mirovaia politika* 3 (1945), pp. 58–70; pp. 68–9. S. Vishnev, 'Razvitie vooruzhennykh sil derzhav v khode Vtoroi mirovoi voiny', *Mirovoe khoziastvo i mirovaia politika* 5 (1945), pp. 35–45. S. Zakharov, 'Mirovaia profsoiuznaia konferentsiia v Londone', *Mirovaia khoziastvo i mirovaia politika* 4 (1945), pp. 3–7; despite differences between left and right unions the author perceived hope for the ending of the historic split in the working class. Iu. Vintser, 'Poslevoennye plany natsionalizatsii v Anglii i SShA', *Mirovoe khoziastvo i mirovaia politika* 2–3 (1945), pp. 54–60.

73. P. Lisovsky, 'Krymskaia konferentsiia', *Mirovoe khoziastvo i mirovaia politika* 2–3 (1945), pp. 22–32; p. 32.

74. S. Sladovskoi, 'Polozhenie v Italii', *Mirovoe khoziastvo i mirovaia politika* 4 (1945), pp. 14–15, and K. Dimitrov, 'Agrarnyi vopros i agrarnaia reforma v Rumynii', *Mirovaia*

khoziastvo i mirovaia politika 6 (1945), pp. 13–20. They also welcomed as another sign of unity the international support for the position of a Soviet trade union delegation in London by radical unions in France (the CGT), the US (the CIO) and Italy ranged against the old reformist unions of the Amsterdam group, the AFL in the US and certain British unions. Zakharov, 'Mirovaia profsoiuznaia konferentsiia v Londone', pp. 3–7.

CHAPTER 5: ON THE CULTURAL FRONT

1. To describe this process, the term cultural revolution was introduced into the literature and most fully developed by S. Fitzpatrick, *The Cultural Front: Power and Culture in Revolutionary Russia* (Ithaca, NY: Cornell University Press, 1992). It generated an extensive debate summarized by M. David-Fox, 'What is Cultural Revolution?', *Russian Review* 58:2 (April 1999), pp. 181–201. See aso Fitzpatrick's reply, 'Cultural Revolution Revisited', *Russian Review* 58:2 (April 1999), pp. 202–9.
2. Fitzpatrick, *The Cultural Front*, pp. 248–50.
3. I.M. Gronsky and V.N. Perel'man (comps), *Assotsiatsiia khudozhnikov revoliutsionnoi Rossii. Sbornik vospominanii, statei, dokumentov* (Moscow: Izabratel'noe iskusstvo, 1973), doc. 69, p. 166. The author was reporting on a meeting of a Politburo commission in Stalin's study and lasting six to seven hours, held sometime in April–May 1932. Gronsky subsequently became the secretary for the organizing committee of the First Congress of Soviet Writers.
4. Zhdanov's optimistic letter to Stalin on the results was refuted by reports of the Secret Political Department of the NKVD based on informers at the congress. Babel called it 'a literary requiem'. A. Novikov-Priboi listened 'in pain; orders in literature are the end'. Valerian Pravdukhin denounced it as 'a servile gathering', and so forth. Ibid., docs 70, 71, 72, 73, pp. 167–71. Even Gorky was disillusioned; he deplored the appointments to the Union Executive Committee as 'ignorant people who will be directing people who are significantly more literate than they are'. Ibid., doc. 74, p. 172. Once the congress disbanded, the criticisms multiplied. Ibid., doc. 75, p. 176. The police reports also denounced 'hostile, great power chauvinistic moods' among the poet-translators from the national languages. Ibid., doc. 76, p. 177.
5. M. Zezina, 'Crisis in the Union of Soviet Writers in the early 1950s', *Europe-Asia Studies* 46:4 (1996), pp. 649–61; p. 649 describes the First Congress in the words of one of its participants as being conducted in 'a vicious atmosphere'. Despite its protocols, the congress had not been summoned after its founding meeting in 1934 until after the war. The plenums were held irregularly instead of three times a year. Ibid., p. 650.
6. M. Friedberg, 'Literary Culture: "The New Soviet Man" in the Mirror of Literature', in D.N. Shalin (ed.), *Russian Culture at the Crossroads: Paradoxes of Postcommunist Consciousness* (New York: Routledge, 2018), pp. 239–58.
7. J. Förster, 'Das Unternehmen "Barbarossa" als Eroberungs- und Vernichtungs-Krieg', in H. Boog et al. (eds), *Das deutsche Reich und der Zweite Weltkrieg*, 4 vols (Stuttgart: Deutsche Verlags-Anstalt, 1983), vol. 4, *Der Angriff auf die Sowjetunion*, pp. 413–50 and O. Bartov, *Hitler's Army: Soldiers, Nazis and War in the Third Reich* (New York: Oxford University Press, 1991). For the Soviet reaction see 'Nota narodnogo komissara inostrannykh del V.M. Molotova o chudovishchnykh zlodeianiiakh zverstvakh i nasiliiakh nemetsko-fashistskikh zakhvatchikov v okkupirovannykh sovetskikh raionakh i ob otvetstvennosti Germanskogo pravitel'stva i komandovaniia za eti prestupleniia' (Moscow, 27 April 1942), documenting the atrocities and sent to all embassies having relations with the Soviet Union.
8. M. Gefter, 'Stalin umer vchera . . ', in A.A. Protashchik (ed.), *Inogo ne dano* (Moscow: Progress, 1988), p. 305, and the essays in Gefter (ed.), *Iz tekh i etikh let* (Moscow: Progress, 1991).
9. G. Bordiugov, 'Ukradennaia politika', *Komsomolskaia pravda*, 5 May 1990, as quoted in Zubkova, *Obshchestvo*, p. 14.

10. K.C. Berkhoff, *Motherland in Danger: Soviet Propaganda during World War II* (Cambridge, MA: Harvard University Press, 2012), pp. 12–20 gives extensive statistics on the press. For the 'paradoxical' outcome, see p. 14.

11. J. von Geldern, 'Radio Moscow: The Voice from the Center', in R. Stites (ed.), *Culture and Entertainment in Wartime Russia* (Bloomington, IN: Indiana University Press, 1995), pp. 44–61; pp. 51–4.

12. C.D. Shaw, 'Making Ivan-Uzbek: War, Friendship of the Peoples, and the Creation of Soviet Uzbekistan, 1941-1945', doctoral thesis, University of California, Berkeley, 2015.

13. E.M. Malysheva, 'Sovetskaia publitsistika i SMI v gody Velikoi Otechestvennoi voiny. Opyt aktualizatsii', in I.I. Gorlova et al. (eds), *Kulturnoe nasledie severnogo Kavkaza kak resurs mezhnatsional'nogo soglasiia. Sbornik nauchnykh statei* (Moscow-Krasnodar: Institut naslediia and Iuzhnyi filial, 2015), pp. 364–5. It is estimated that Ehrenburg alone published 1,500 pieces during the war.

14. *Partiinost'* or party-mindedness was the ideal of Bolsheviks; russo-centrism was a theme stressing the Russian component of the Soviet Union; Soviet patriotism was invented to encompass all the nationalities. These were already being combined in 1938 by the party propagandists. See B. Volin, 'Velikii russkii narod', *Bol'shevik* 9 (1 May 1938), pp. 26–36; V. Kirpomin, 'Russkaia kultura', *Bol'shevik* 12 (June 1938), pp. 47–63; and Editorial, 'Velikaia druzhba narodov SSSR', *Bol'shevik* 13 (13 July 1938), pp. 1–7.

15. A. Weiner, *Making Sense of War: The Second World War and the Fate of the Bolshevik Revolution* (Princeton, NJ: Princeton University Press, 2001).

16. Cf. K. Clark, *The Soviet Novel: History as Ritual* (Chicago, IL: University of Chicago Press, 1981), especially chaps 1 and 6, which are suggestive in dealing with the same phenomenon in a literary context.

17. For party membership drawn from archives, see Pospelov et al., *IVOV*, vol. 6, pp. 342 and 365; for concern over new recruits, see Shliapin, Shvarev and Fomichenko, *Kommunisticheskaia partiia*, pp. 47–8; M.E. Brodskaia, *Verolomnoe napadenie fashistskoi Germanii o Sovetskii Soiuz. Mobilizatsiia partiei sovetskogo naroda na otpor vragu* (Chardzhou: 1957), p. 13; E.I. Iaroslavsky, *Chego trebuet partiia ot kommunistov v dni Otechestvennoi voiny* (Leningrad: Partizdat, 1945), pp. 8–9.

18. For a content analysis in 1942 and 1943 see D.J. Dallin, *The Changing World of Soviet Russia* (New Haven, CT: Yale University Press, 1956).

19. Pospelov et al., *IVOV*, vol. 6, pp. 369–70.

20. Ibid., pp. 344, 355–7.

21. E. Razin, 'Lenin o sushchnosti voiny', *Bol'shevik* 1 (January 1943), pp. 46–54 quoting Lenin on p. 48. Stalin's contribution was emphasized in M. Leonov, 'Lenin o voine i roli moral'nogo faktora v nei', *Agitator i propagandist Krasnoi armii* 6 (March 1945), pp. 19–32.

22. V. Chuvikov, 'Uchenie Lenina–Stalina o voinakh spravedlivykh i nespravedlivykh', *Bol'shevik* 7–8 (April 1945), pp. 14–26; pp. 25–6.

23. For the contemporary debate during the 'Fatherland War of 1812' among conservatives over the nature of patriotism see A.M. Martin, *Romantics, Reformers and Reactionaries: Russian Conservative Thought and Politics in the Reign of Alexander I* (DeKalb, IL: Northern Illinois University Press, 1997), pp. 123–42.

24. Stalin revived the use of the term *rodina* for the first time in 1933 when he praised the pilots who had dramatically rescued the crew of an ice breaker that had sunk in the Arctic Ocean; it was then incorporated into May Day slogans and anti-fascist fiction. D.L. Brandenberger, *Propaganda State in Crisis: Soviet Ideology, Indoctrination and Terror under Stalin, 1927-1941* (New Haven, CT: Yale University Press, 2011), pp. 99, 101–2, 116–18. *Rodina* can mean 'native land', as distinct from *otechestvo*, which may mean 'state'.

25. I.V. Stalin, *On the Great Patriotic War of the Soviet Union* (London: Hutchinson, 1943), p. 5–9. Roberts, *Stalin's Wars*, p. 94, calls it a 'bravura performance'.

26. D.L. Brandenberger, *National Bolshevism: Stalinist Mass Culture and the Formation of Modern Russian National Identity, 1931-1956* (Cambridge, MA: Harvard University Press, 2002).

27. I. Vinogradov, 'Zhizn' i smert' sovetskogo poniatiia "druzhba narodov"', *Cahiers du monde russe* 36:4 (December 1995), pp. 455-62; p. 460. Martin, *Affirmative Action*, chap. 11.

28. Brandenberger, *National Bolshevism*, pp. 43-5.

29. McNeal (ed.), *I.V. Stalin, Works*, vol. 2, pp. 8, 9. Cf. N.K. Shil'der, *Imperator Aleksandr Pervyi*, 3 vols (Saint Petersburg: Surovin, 1904), vol. 3, p. 83 and especially Alexander's letter to Baron Shtein, 27 March 1812, ibid., p. 497. Isaac Deutscher was the first to remark on the close historical parallels between the two campaigns: Deutscher, *Stalin: A Political Biography* (New York: Oxford University Press, 1949), p. 463.

30. O. Budnitskii, 'Istoriia voiny s Napoleonom v sovetskoi propagande, 1941-1945', *Rossiiskaia istoriia* 6 (2012), pp. 157-69. See also L. Yaresh, 'The Campaign of 1812', in C.E. Black (ed.), *Rewriting Russian History*, 2nd edn (New York: Vintage Books, 1962), pp. 268-75.

31. S. Morrison, *The People's Artist: Prokofiev's Soviet Years* (Oxford: Oxford University Press, 2009), pp. 176, 179.

32. McNeal (ed.), *I.V. Stalin, Works*, vol. 2, p. 203.

33. Ibid., p. 35; L.R. Tillett, *The Great Friendship: Soviet Historians on the Non-Russian Nationalities* (Chapel Hill, NC: North Carolina University Press, 1969), p. 77; Brandenberger, *National Bolshevism*, pp. 116-24, 145-57.

34. The rehabilitation of Ivan served many purposes. M. Perrie, *The Cult of Ivan the Terrible in Stalin's Russia* (London: Palgrave Macmillan, 2001) points out his usefulness in justifying Soviet expansion into the Baltic states in 1939 and 1940. D.L. Brandenberger, 'Terribly Romantic, Terribly Progressive, or Terribly Tragic: Rehabilitating Ivan IV under I.V. Stalin', *Russian Review* 58:4 (1999), pp. 635-54. For Peter see N.V. Riasanovsky, *The Image of Peter the Great in Russian History and Thought* (New York: Oxford University Press, 1985), pp. 280-2.

35. G. Reavey, *Soviet Literature Today* (London: L. Drummond, 1946), pp. 49-56; C. Corbet, *Une Littérature aux fers. Le pseudo-réalisme soviétique* (Paris: La Pensée universelle, 1975), p. 187; L. Yaresh, 'Ivan the Terrible and the Oprichnina', in Black (ed.), *Rewriting Russian History*, pp. 220-9.

36. See A. Miller, 'The Romanov Empire and the Russian Nation', in S. Berger and A. Miller (eds), *Nationalizing Empires* (Budapest: Central European University Press, 2015), pp. 309-68, and for the army A.J. Rieber, 'Nationalizing Imperial Armies: A Comparative and Transnational Study of Three Empires', in ibid., pp. 595-605.

37. 'Istoricheskie korni nemetskogo fashizma. Stat'ia akademika R.Iu. Vippera. Avgust, 1941', *Istoricheskii arkhiv* 4 (2000), pp. 187-204; pp. 187-8. It is striking that Vipper not only endorsed the *longue durée* approach of the *Annales* school but foreshadowed the *Sonderweg* concept of postwar German historians.

38. D.L. Brandenberger and A.M. Dubrovsky, '"The People Need a Tsar": The Emergence of National Bolshevism as Stalinist Ideology, 1931-1941', *Europe-Asia Studies* 50:5 (July 1998), pp. 873-92.

39. J. Plamper, *The Stalin Cult: A Study in the Alchemy of Power* (New Haven, CT: Yale University Press, 2012) stresses the visual representations. For film see P. Kenez, *Cinema and Soviet Society, 1917-53* (London: I.B. Tauris, 2001).

40. Compare the views of S. Kotkin, *Magnetic Mountain: Stalinism as a Civilization* (Berkeley, CA: University of California Press, 1997) and J. Hellbeck, 'Working, Struggling, Becoming: Stalin-Era Autobiographies and Text', in I. Halfin (ed.), *Language and Revolution: Making Political Identities* (London: Frank Cass, 2002), pp. 135-60, who both stress the internalization by the population of 'Bolshevik speak', to the sceptical perspective of S. Davies, *Popular Opinion in Stalin's Russia: Terror, Propaganda, and Dissent, 1934-1941* (Cambridge: Cambridge University Press, 1997) and S.A. Shinkarchuk, *Obshchestvennoe mnenie v Sovetskoi Rossii v 30-e gody. Po materialam Severozapada*

(Saint Petersburg: Iz Sankt-Peterburgskogo universiteta ekonomiki i finansova, 1995). The collection of documents, K. Bukov et al. (comps), *Moskva voennaia, 1941-1945. Memuary i arkhivnye dokumenty* (Moscow: Mosgoarkhiv, 1995), based on official and unofficial sources, also presents a variegated picture; the memoirs stressing patriotic sentiments, the diaries and secret police reports revealing complaints and even anti-Soviet views. All these works are based on local or regional archives and raise the same problem of how representative their findings are of different strata of the population and of the country as a whole.

41. 'Materialy plenuma TsK VKP(b) (1944)', *Istoricheskii arkhiv* 1 (1992), pp. 61–5; p. 62. This was the only plenum of the Central Committee held during the war and it merely rubber-stamped Stalin's proposals.

42. Quoted in Werth, *Russia at War*, p. 743.

43. Communist activists sought to resuscitate the cult of heroes and apply it to the common soldier in the trenches of Stalingrad. J. Hellbeck, *Die Stalingrad Protokolle. Sowjetische Augenzeugen berichten aus der Schlacht* (Frankfurt am Main: S. Fischer, 2012).

44. F.J. Miller, *Folklore for Stalin: Russian Folklore and Pseudo-folklore of the Stalin Era* (Armonk, NY: M.E. Sharpe, 1990), pp. 7–10, Gorky quote on p. 7. The tale of Ilia Muromets also provided the structure for the symphonic tone poem of the same name by the head of the Musicians' Union, Reinhold Glière. *Bogatyri* had been famously portrayed on canvas in 1898 by Viktor Vasnetsov and hung in the Tretiakov Gallery.

45. Ibid., pp. 20, 25–7.

46. A collection of folk tales on the war is Institut russkoi literatury (Pushkinskii dom), *Ocherki russkogo narodnopoeticheskogo tvorchestva sovetskoi epokhi* (Moscow: Akademiia nauk, 1952), pp. 459–523.

47. Miller, *Folklore for Stalin*, pp. 36 and 75 ff.

48. K. Tomoff, *Creative Union: The Professional Organization of Soviet Composers, 1939-1953* (Ithaca, NY: Cornell University Press, 2006), pp. 80–1.

49. E. Polyudova, *Soviet War Songs in the Context of Russian Culture* (Cambridge: Cambridge Scholars Publishing, 2016), pp. 8, 23, 26, 28.

50. A. Tvardovsky, 'Vasily Tyorkin', in J. von Geldern and R. Stites (eds), *Mass Culture in Soviet Russia: Tales, Poems, Songs, Movies, Plays and Folklore, 1917-1953* (Bloomington, IN: Indiana University Press, 1995), pp. 371–7; p. 371.

51. V.S. Dunham, *In Stalin's Time: Middle-Class Values in Soviet Fiction* (Cambridge: Cambridge University Press, 1976), pp. 4–7, with excerpts from several poets; J. Brooks, 'Pravda Goes to War', in Stites (ed.), *Culture and Entertainment*, pp. 9–27; pp. 17–19, and R. Sartorti, 'On the Making of Heroes, Heroines and Saints', in ibid., pp. 176–93; pp. 176–80.

52. See for example R.P. Shaw and Y. Wong, *Genetic Seeds of Warfare: Evaluating Nationalism and Patriotism* (Boston, MA: Unwin Hyman, 1989) and D. Bar-Tal and E. Staub (eds), *Patriotism: In the Lives of Individuals and Nations* (Chicago, IL: Nelson-Hall, 1997).

53. Cf. Martin, *Affirmative Action* and F. Hirsch, *Empire of Nations: Ethnographic Knowledge and the Making of the Soviet Union* (Ithaca, NY: Cornell University Press, 2005).

54. *Pravda*, 28 November 1941, 21 January 1942, 5 September 1942 and *Izvestiia*, 2 April 1942 to the Ukrainians; *Pravda*, 20 January 1942, 1 October 1942 to the Belarusians; ibid., 1 October 1942 to the Latvians; ibid., 3 March 1942 to the Estonians; and *Izvestiia*, 29 April 1942 to the Lithuanians.

55. Tomoff, *Creative Union*, pp. 24, 27, 66–7.

56. V. Orlov, 'Prokofiev and the Myth of the Father of Nations: The Cantata *Zdravitsa*', *Journal of Musicology* 30:4 (autumn 2013), pp. 577–620; p. 583.

57. Morrison, *The People's Artist*, p. 178. His colleague Myaskovsky described it as 'fantastical, monstrously, even yet mainly interesting'. Ibid., p. 179. Morrison in a rare slip misnumbers the quartet as the first.

58. 'Rech' I.V. Stalina na devnadtsatogo godovshchina oktiabrskoi revoliutsii', *Bol'shevik* 21 (November 1944), pp 1–8; p. 8. In the monthly review of events, 'Mezhdunarodnyi obzor', as well as individual articles, the phrases 'Soviet land' and 'Soviet people' were frequently

employed to suggest the multi-national character of the country. *Bol'shevik* 22 (December 1944), pp. 23–4; *Bol'shevik* 2 (January 1945), p. 14.

59. An early example of this was the speech of Politburo member A.S. Shcherbakov, *Pod znamenem Lenina, 22 ianvariia 1942* (Gorky: Gorkovskoe obl. kn-vo, 1942), pp. 3–31, p. 10.

60. The most comprehensive treatment is Tillett, *The Great Friendship*, chap. 4. See also K.F. Shteppa, 'The "Lesser Evil" Formula', in Black (ed.), *Rewriting Russian History*, pp. 107–19.

61. I. Vlasov, 'O sovetskom patriotizme', *Propagandist i agitator Krasnoi armii* 5 (March 1945), pp. 17–18.

62. A.Ia. Vyshinsky, *Sovetskoe Gosudarstvo – Gosudarstvo novogo tipa. Doklad, pochitannyi na sessii Akademii nauk SSSR, 20 noiabria 1942 g.* (Moscow: Gospolitizdat, 1943), pp. 15–19, 28 and 37–8; Vyshinsky, *Sovetskoe Gosudarstvo v Otechestvennoi voine* (Moscow: Gospolitizdat, 1944), pp. 2, 10, 16, 41.

63. M.I. Kalinin, *Stat'i i rechi. 1941–1946* (Moscow: Politizdat, 1975), especially 'Chto nachit byt' sovetskim patriotom v nashi dni', pp. 36–9 and 'Edinaia boevaia sem'ia', pp. 289–94.

64. B. Schechter, ' "The People's Instructions": Indigenizing the Great Patriotic War among "Non-Russians" ', *Ab Imperio* 3 (2012), pp. 109–33; p. 110.

65. N.A. Kirsanov, *Partiinye mobilizatsii na front v gody Velikoi Otechestvennoi voiny* (Moscow: Izd. Moskovskogo universiteta, 1972), pp. 155–82.

66. In addition a campaign of letter-writing between soldiers and the home front was inaugurated to provide an emotional link to their defence of their motherland. Schechter, ' "The People's Instructions" ', pp. 114–22.

67. E.M. Malysheva, *Ispytanie. Sotsium vlast'. Problem vzaimodeistviia v gody Velikoi Otechestvennoi voiny* (Maikop: Adygeia, 2000), pp. 211 and 216.

68. Volkogonov, *Triumf i tragediia*, vol. 2, pt 1, p. 256. Three and a half thousand Chechen and Ingush women had already been decorated with the medal for factory production, 'For the Defence of the Caucasus'. Malysheva, *Ispytanie*, p. 216.

69. 'Materialy plenuma', *Istoricheskii arkhiv*, p. 62.

70. E.A. Beliaev and N.S. Pyshkova, *Formirovanie i razvitie seti nauchnykh uchrezhdenii SSSR. Istoricheskii ocherk* (Moscow: Nauka, 1979). The Ukrainian and Belarusian Academies had existed since the early years of the Soviet state. A. Vucinich, *Empire of Knowledge: The Academy of Sciences of the USSR (1917–1970)* (Berkeley, CA: University of California Press, 1985), pp. 90, 203–6.

71. *KPSS v rezoliutsiiakh*, pp. 114, 119, 125–9, 131.

72. Brandenberger, *National Bolshevism*, pp. 123–9. Pankratova had been a student of M.N. Pokrovsky, the dean of Soviet historians in the early period and a favourite of Lenin who had denounced tsarist imperialism as having created a 'prison of nations'. Under party pressure she participated in a denunciation of her teacher. See B.D. Grekov et al. (eds), *Protiv istoricheskoi kontseptsii M.N. Pokrovskogo. Sbornik statei*, 2 vols (Moscow: Akademiia nauk, 1939–40). But clearly she continued to cherish part of his legacy. See R.E. Zelnik, *The Perils of Pankratova: Some Stories from the Annals of Soviet Historiography* (Seattle, WA: University of Washington Press, 2005), pp. 27–35.

73. S. Yekelchyk, 'Stalinist Patriotism as Imperial Discourse: Reconciling the Ukrainian and Russian "Heroic Pasts", 1941–1945', *Kritika* 3:1 (2002), pp. 51–80; pp. 68–77.

74. Schechter, ' "The People's Instructions" ', pp. 130–1; Tillett, *The Great Friendship*, pp. 159, 84–100; and Brandenberger, *National Bolshevism*, pp. 123–6.

75. L.L. Mininberg, *Sovetskie evrei v nauke i promyshlennosti SSSR v period Vtoroi mirovoi voiny, 1941–1945 gg. Ocherki* (Moscow: ITS-Garant, 1996), pp. 136, 189, 378; for the above statistics, pp. 12–14 and 18.

76. S. Redlich, 'Jews in General Anders' Army in the Soviet Union, 1941–42', *Soviet Jewish Affairs* 1:2 (1971), pp. 90–8.

77. The following is based on S. Redlich, 'The Jewish Antifascist Committee in the Soviet Union', *Jewish Social Studies* 31:1 (January 1969), pp. 25–36.

78. G. Estraikh, 'The Life, Death and Afterlife of the Jewish Anti-Fascist Committee', *East European Jewish Affairs* 48:2 (2018), pp. 139–48; pp. 140–2.

79. M. Lewin, *The Making of the Soviet System: Essays in the Social History of Interwar Russia* (New York: Pantheon, 1985), pp. 281-3, 309-10.
80. *The Case of the Anti-Soviet Trotskyite Centre*, p. 482 et passim.
81. Bonnell, *Iconography of Power*, pp. 220-4.
82. Kukryniksy, *Sobranie proizvedenii v 4-kh tomakh*, 4 vols (Moscow: Izobrazitel'noe iskusstvo, 1982-88), vol. 2, fig. 41; see also figs 9, 13, 26, 34, 46, 57 (1942); 26, 82, 92, 109, 115 (1943); Kukryniksy, *Vtroem* (Moscow: Khudozhnik, 1975), pp. 118, 156.
83. McNeal (ed.), *I.V. Stalin, Works*, vol. 2, p. 162; Kukryniksy, *Sobranie*, vol. 2, fig. 39. For other examples see A.K. Pisiotis, 'Images of Hate in the Art of War', in von Geldern and Stites (eds), *Mass Culture in Soviet Russia*, pp. 141-56.
84. Berkhoff, *Motherland in Danger*, pp. 174-5.
85. H. Ermolaev, *Mikhail Sholokhov and His Art* (Princeton, NJ: Princeton University Press, 1982), pp. 46-6. The story was translated and widely circulated in the West. See for example M. Sholokhov, B. Gorbatov, W. Wassilewska, K. Simonov and F. Panferov, *Soviet War Stories* (London: Hutchinson, n.d. [1944?]).
86. For some examples see Malysheva, 'Sovetskaia publitsistika', pp. 367-70. Ehrenburg made effective use too of captured diaries and letters received by German soldiers. J. Hellbeck, '"The Diaries of Fritzes and the Letters of Gretchens": Personal Writings from the German–Soviet War and Their Readers', *Kritika* 10:3 (summer 2009), pp. 571-606; see especially pp. 585-604. According to front folklore, instructions were given to reuse newspaper as necessary, 'except for the articles of Ehrenburg'.
87. The wartime articles are conveniently assembled and translated in I. Ehrenburg and K. Simonov, *In One Newspaper: A Chronicle of Unforgettable Years*, trans. A. Kagan (New York: Sphinx Press, 1985); see pp. 143-50 for 'The Science of Hatred'.
88. Berkhoff, *Motherland in Danger*, pp. 177-9. The author questions the effectiveness of this propaganda compared to reports of German atrocities. Ibid., pp. 197-201.
89. D.J. Youngblood, 'A War Remembered: Soviet Films of the Great Patriotic War', *American Historical Review* 106:3 (June 2001), pp. 839-56; pp. 841-4; Sartorti, 'On the Making of Heroes, Heroines and Saints', pp. 176-93; pp. 185-6. P. Kenez, 'Black and White: The War on Film', in Stites (ed.) *Culture and Entertainment*, pp. 167-8; pp. 157-75.
90. V. Kepley, *In the Service of the State: The Cinema of Alexander Dovzhenko* (Madison, WI: University of Wisconsin Press, 1986).
91. L.A. Kirschenbaum, '"Our City, Our Hearths, Our Families": Local Loyalties and Private Life in Soviet World War II Propaganda', *Slavic Review* 59:4 (winter 2000), pp. 825-47; J. Brooks, *Thank You, Comrade Stalin! Soviet Public Culture from Revolution to Cold War* (Princeton, NJ: Princeton University Press, 2000). It seems to be the case, as with other campaigns based on letters to the editor, that the official propaganda apparatus manipulated genuine expressions of emotions and opinions arising spontaneously from the population. To what extent remains unclear.
92. For an early invocation of the lyrical theme in literature, see A. Miasnikaia, 'Otechestvennaia voina i sovetskaia literatura', *KI* 7 (1942), pp. 68-75.
93. The following is based on K. Clark, 'Shostakovich's Turn to the String Quartet and the Debates about Socialist Realism in Music', *Slavic Review* 72:3 (autumn 2013), pp. 573-89 and more generally her book, *The Soviet Novel*.
94. Clark, 'Shostakovich's Turn', p. 299.
95. As early as February 1942, Stalin sought to deflect criticism in the Western press on the cult of hatred by denying that the Red Army had any intention of annihilating the German people and destroying a German state. *Pravda*, 23 February 1942.
96. Even his orders, however, could not immediately bring to a halt the mass rapes of German women and pillaging of German homes that were concealed at the time but amply documented since. O. Budnitskii, 'The Intelligentsia Meets the Enemy: Educated Soviet Officers in Defeated Germany, 1945', trans. S. Rupp, *Kritika* 10:3 (summer 2009), pp. 629-82; pp. 637-47, 662-7.

97. I. Ehrenburg, *The War: 1941–1945*, trans. T. Shebunina in collaboration with Y. Knapp (Cleveland: World Publishing Co., 1964), pp. 19, 29–33, 176. Ehrenburg did not resent so much the politics of the thing as the distortion of his views, which were more nuanced than Goebbels – or Aleksandrov – had painted them. But then again, the Soviet leadership had never appreciated his individual approach. As Shcherbakov put it early in the war, when Ehrenburg complained that his pieces were being cut: 'You shouldn't try to be original.' Ibid., p. 13.

98. Sergius had been acting patriarch from Tikhon's death in 1924 to his arrest and imprisonment in 1927. Freed in 1934 and restored as acting patriarch, he was elected patriarch of Moscow and All Russia in 1943.

99. D. Pospielovsky, *The Russian Church under the Soviet Regime, 1917–1982* (Crestwood, NY: St Vladimir's Seminary Press, 1984) and P. Walters, 'The Russian Orthodox Church and the Soviet State', *Annals of the American Academy of Political and Social Science* 483 (January 1986), pp. 135–45.

100. A. Dickinson, 'Quantifying Religious Oppression: Russian Orthodox Church Closures and Repression of Priests, 1917–1941', *Religion, State and Society* 28:4 (2000), pp. 327–35. E.P. Titkov, *Dukhovnyi mech Velikoi pobedy. Russkaia pravoslavnaia tserkov' v gody Velikoi Otechestvennoi voiny* (Arzamas: AGPI, 2010), pp. 15–16.

101. R.R. Reese, 'The Russian Orthodox Church and "Patriotic" Support for the Stalinist Regime during the Great Patriotic War', *War and Society* 35:2 (May 2014), pp. 131–53; pp. 135, 137. Reese concludes that the contributions of the Orthodox Church in patriotic giving and charitable activities was 'a conscious means to challenge state policies' and mobilize 'support for itself at Stalin's expense'. Ibid., p. 153.

102. Ibid., pp. 138–9, 145–6, 150–1. This does not include additional, more modest funds raised by the Renovationist and even the Josephite churches.

103. Ibid., p. 141.

104. 'Proshu vashikh ukazanii', Dokladnye zapiski predsedatelia Soveta po delam Russkoi pravoslavnoi tserkvi G.G. Karpov v TsK VKP (b) i SNK SSSR, 1943', *Istoricheskii arkhiv* 2 (2000), doc. 17, pp. 153–86; pp. 176–8, Karpov to Stalin and Molotov.

105. T.A. Chumachenko, *Church and State in Soviet Russia: Russian Orthodoxy from World War II to the Khrushchev Years*, ed. and trans. E.E. Roslof (Armonk, NY: M.E. Sharpe, 2002), pp. 28 and 38–9. Local soviet, communist and Komsomol authorities engaged in anti-religious propaganda before the war were unhappy and often offered resistance to reopening. There were still a few Renovationist churches open until 1948.

106. M.V. Shkarovsky, 'Russkaia pravoslavnaia tserkov' v 1943–1957 godakh', *Voprosy istorii* 8 (1995), pp. 36–56, and Shkarovsky, *Tserkov' zovet k zashchite rodiny: Religioznaia zhizn' Leningrada i Severo-Zapada v gody Velikoi Otechestvennoi voiny* (Saint Petersburg: Satis derzhava, 2005), pp. 78–9.

107. W.C. Fletcher, 'The Soviet Bible Belt', in Linz (ed.), *The Impact*, pp. 91–106, emphasizes the rapid increase in the underground schismatic churches but indicates that the defections would have been far greater if there had been no patriarch in Moscow.

108. O.Iu. Vasil'eva, 'Russkaia pravoslavnaia tserkov', 1927–1943', *Voprosy istorii* 4 (1994), pp. 35–46; p. 41.

109. M.V. Shkarovsky (ed.), 'V ogne voiny. Russkaia pravoslavnaia tserkov' v 1941–1945 gg. (Po materialam Leningradskoi eparkhii)', *Russkoe proshloe* 5 (1994), pp. 259–316; pp. 264–6. For a picture of the widespread anti-communist and pro-German sentiments among the local clergy and the 'mission' in the western borderlands see the letter of an emissary of the Leningrad and Novgorod eparchy to Metropolitan Aleksei in ibid., doc. 14, pp. 290–5. In April 1944, Metropolitan Sergius (Voskresensky) wrote to the Reichskommissar of Ostland that 'the Orthodox bishopric too wishes the fall of the Soviet regime, but possibly and even more definitively, its hopes are no longer tied to a German victory'. Z. Balevits, *Pravoslavnaia tserkov' Latvii pod sen'iu svastiki (1941–1944)* (Riga: Zinatne, 1967), p. 80.

110. B. Bociurkiw, *The Ukrainian Greek Catholic Church and the Soviet State: 1939–1950* (Edmonton: Canadian Institute of Ukrainian Studies, 1996), pp. 103.

111. 'Proshu vashikh ukazanii', doc. 18, p. 178.

112. Ibid., p. 179; Iu. Shapoval, 'The Ukrainian Years, 1894–1949', in W. Taubman et al. (eds), *Nikita Khrushchev* (New Haven, CT: Yale University Press, 2000), pp. 8–43.

113. Bociurkiw, *The Ukrainian Greek Catholic Church*, pp. 137–8, 146.

114. Sovnarkom to Stalin and Beria, 30 April 1945, in 'Proshu vashikh ukazanii', doc. 19, pp. 179–82. For the American response see *Foreign Relations of the United States. Diplomatic Papers, 1945*, vol. 5 (Washington, DC: US Government Printing Office, 1967), pp. 111–23. A TASS reporter told Charles Bohlen that the Soviet Union fully intended to use the Orthodox Church in the Balkans as an instrument of struggle against the Roman Catholics. Ibid., 1944, vol. 4, p. 1,214 ff.

115. 'Proshu vashikh ukazanii', doc. 20, p. 183.

116. D. Kalkandjieva, *The Russian Orthodox Church, 1917–1948: From Decline to Resurrection* (Budapest: Central European University Press, 2015), pp. 311–38. The 'Democratic' churches in Eastern Europe did have their canonical status raised, including the establishment of the first Bulgarian patriarchate since the fourteenth century. Ibid., p. 337

117. Chumachenko, *Church and State*, pp. 87–103.

118. R.J. Sontag and J.S. Beddie (eds), *Nazi-Soviet Relations 1939–1941: Documents from the Archives of the German Foreign Office as Released by the Dept of State* (Washington, DC: US Government Printing Office, 1948), pp. 91–4, 96.

119. S. Plokhy, 'The Call of Blood: Government Propaganda and Public Response to the Soviet Entry into World War II', *Cahiers du monde russe* 53:2/3 (2012), pp. 293–319; pp. 301–2.

120. Sontag and Beddie (eds), *Nazi-Soviet Relations*, pp. 105–6.

121. Plokhy, 'The Call of Blood', uses the NKVD reports on the mood of the Ukrainian population to indicate the positive reception to annexation, especially among Ukrainian academics, but based on the ethnic rather than the class principle emphasized in the official media.

122. Dimitrov, *Diary*, entry for 27 February 1941, p. 150.

123. Joking with his associates in a bomb shelter in September 1941, Stalin remarked that 'If we win we'll give East Prussia back to Slavdom, where it belongs. We'll settle the whole place with Slavs'. Ibid., entry for 8 September 1941, p. 193. Of course, in this case, he wasn't joking.

124. *KI* 5 (1942), p. 16; see also ibid. 3–4 (1942), pp. 98–9.

125. RGASPI, f. 17, op. 163, d. 1,338, listy 2–3, Shcherbakov to Stalin with Stalin's signature of approval.

126. Dimitrov, *Diary*, entry for 1 September 1941, p. 192; M. Djilas, *Conversations with Stalin* (New York: Harcourt, Brace and World, 1962), p. 26; H. Kohn, *Pan-Slavism: Its History and Ideology* (Notre Dame, IL: Notre Dame University Press, 1953), pp. 231–2.

127. 'Vozvanie k slavianam vsego mira uchastnikov vtorogo Vseslavianskogo mitinga sostoiavshevosia v g. Moskve 4–5 aprelia 1942', *Vestnik AN SSSR* 4 (1942), pp. 26–30; G.F. Aleksandrov, 'Otechestvennaia voina sovetskogo naroda i zadachi obshchestvennykh nauk', *Vestnik AN SSSR* 5–6 (1942), pp. 22–37.

128. E.V. Tarle, 'Tevtonskie rytsari i ikh "nasledniki"', *Vestnik AN SSSR* 5–6 (1942), pp. 38–48.

129. Notes on the conversation of I.V. Stalin with Orlemanski, 28 April 1944, in Volokitina et al., *VE*, vol. 1, doc. 3, pp. 36–42; see also Roberts, *Stalin's Wars*, pp. 210–11.

130. W.M. Franklin and W. Gerber (eds), *Foreign Relations of the United States: Diplomatic Papers, The Conferences at Cairo and Tehran, 1943* (Washington, DC: US Government Printing Office, 1961), pp. 532, 604; T. Sharp, 'The Russian Annexation of the Koenigsberg Area, 1941–45', *Survey* 23:4 (1977), pp. 156–62; McNeal (ed.), *I.V. Stalin, Works*, vol. 2, pp. 184–6; D. Anishev, 'Pol'skii narod na puti k svobode i nezavisimosti', *Svobodnaia mysl'* 5 (2010), pp. 57–70, reprinting article from *Bol'shevik* 13–14 (July 1944), pp. 49–61.

131. E. Taborsky, 'Beneš and Stalin: Moscow, 1943 and 1945', *Journal of Central European Affairs* 13 (1953), pp. 154–81; pp. 167, 178–9.

132. Volokitina et al., *VE*, vol. 1, doc. 37, p. 132. Stalin later dropped this idea but it suggests how uncertain he was about the postwar organization of the Balkans.

133. P.E. Mosely, 'Soviet Policy and Nationality Conflicts in East Central Europe', in Mosely, *The Kremlin and World Politics: Studies in Soviet Policy and Action* (New York: Vintage Books, 1960), pp. 221–46.

134. I. Deutscher, *The Prophet Outcast: Trotsky, 1929–1940* (Oxford: Oxford University Press, 1963), pp. 459–61. American Trotskyists composed a piquant ditty at the time, 'My Darling Party Line' (to the tune of 'My Darling Clementine'), with the stanza, 'Leon Trotsky was a Nazi/ We knew it for a fact/ *Pravda* said it, we all read it/ Before the Nazi-Soviet Pact.' The last verse ended 'Volga boatmen sail the Rhine'. Recording in possession of author.

135. N.S. Lebedeva and M.M. Narinsky (eds), *Komintern i Vtoraia mirovaia voina*, pt 1, *do 22 iiunia 1941 g.* (Moscow: Pamiatniki istoricheskoi mysli, 1994), docs 5 and 6, pp. 73–6, 85–6. The Italian party was also firm in its denunciation of fascism, asserting that if war did break out it would lead to a destruction of fascism 'as one of the conditions opening up before the peoples of capitalist Europe a new future which will promise freedom, peace and social progress'. Ibid., doc. 5, p. 80. This was followed by a stringent prohibition against communists volunteering for national legions (in the spirit of the Spanish Civil War) to fight against Nazi Germany. Ibid., doc. 13, pp. 96–8.

136. Ibid., doc. 27, pp. 156–7; doc. 28, pp. 164–5; doc. 34, p. 183; doc. 35, pp. 185; doc. 36, p. 188. Meanwhile, confusion was rampant among the Austrian and German rank and file. Ibid., doc. 23, pp. 138–9; doc. 26, pp. 154–5; doc. 39, pp. 143–7.

137. T. Judt (ed.), *Resistance and Revolution in Mediterranean Europe, 1939–1948* (London: Routledge, 1989), especially the essays by G. Swain, 'The Comintern and Southern Europe, 1938–43', pp. 34–41; L. Tayler, 'Le Parti Communiste Français and the French Resistance in the Second World War', pp. 53–70; and M. Wheeler, 'Pariahs to Partisans to Power: The Communist Party of Yugoslavia', pp. 119–29. See also P. Spriano, *Stalin and the European Communists* (London: Verso, 1985), pp. 90–126 and M. Adereth, *The French Communist Party: A Critical History (1920–1984)* (Manchester: University of Manchester Press, 1984), p. 92 ff.

138. W. Gomułka, *Izbrannye stat'i i rechi, 1964–1967* (Moscow: Izd-vo polit. lit-ry, 1968), p. 368; A. Lecœur, *Le Parti communiste français et la résistance, août 1939–juin 1941* (Paris: Plon, 1968), pp. 61–2, 78–80.

139. Dimitrov, *Diary*, entries for 20 and 21 April 1941, pp. 155 and 156, emphasis in original.

140. E. Fisher, 'Ot narodnogo fronta k obshchenatsional'nomu frontu', *KI* 8–9 (1942), pp. 26–30.

141. A.J. Rieber, *Stalin and the French Communist Party, 1941–1947* (New York: Columbia University Press, 1962), chap. 6 explores the communist use of the term 'insurrection' to indicate a rising against the occupier and not a seizure of power.

142. J. Tomasevich, *The Chetniks: War and Revolution in Yugoslavia, 1941–1945: Occupation and Collaboration* (Palo Alto, CA: Stanford University Press, 1975); I. Banac, *The National Question in Yugoslavia: Origins, History, Politics* (Ithaca, NY: Cornell University Press, 1984); A. Djilas, *The Contested Country: Yugoslav Unity and Communist Revolution, 1919–1953* (Cambridge, MA: Harvard University Press, 1991); B. Petranović, *Srbija u drugom svetskom ratu, 1939–1945* (Belgrade: Vojnoizdavački i novinski centar, 1992).

143. C. de Gaulle, *Mémoires de guerre*, 3 vols (Paris: Plon, 1954–60), vol. 2, p. 353.

144. *KI* 8 (1942), docs 3–4, pp. 93–5; doc. 5, pp. 60–3; doc. 7, pp. 57–60; docs 8–9, pp. 70–6; docs 10–11, pp. 70–3; doc. 12, pp. 59–60; *KI* 9 (1943), doc. 1, pp. 48–51; docs 2–3, pp. 57–61; doc. 4, pp. 49–52.

145. *KI* 8 (1942), doc. 7, pp. 28–37.

146. Ibid., docs 3–4, p. 98; doc. 6, pp. 59–60.

147. Ibid., doc. 5, pp. 24–30; doc. 6, pp. 42–44. Articles on the 'German resistance' ceased to appear after mid-1942.

148. Ibid., doc. 12, pp. 24–4, 63–4; *KI* 9 (1943), doc. 4, pp. 19–20; J.B. Urban, *Moscow and the Italian Communist Party, from Togliatti to Berlinguer* (Ithaca, NY: Cornell University Press, 1986), pp. 160–8.

149. *KI* 8 (1942), docs 3–4, pp. 59–66; docs 10–11, pp. 51–6.

150. *KI* 9 (1943), doc. 1, pp. 30–3. See also A.J. Rieber, 'The Crack in the Plaster: Crisis in Romania and the Origins of the Cold War', *Journal of Modern History* 76 (March 2004), pp. 62–106.

151. Dimitrov, *Diary*, entry for 11 May 1943, p. 272.

152. Ibid., entry for 21 May 1943, p. 276.

153. For differing estimates of the dissolution see Armstrong, *Politics of Totalitarianism*, pp. 155–6, who states that 'the Soviet rulers had by no means abandoned the aim of expansion through revolution and subversion'; and Fernand Claudín, who believes that 'the dissolution symbolized the abandonment . . . of any idea of bringing the terrible crisis through which the capitalist system was passing to a revolutionary conclusion'. F. Claudín, *The Communist Movement: From Comintern to Cominform*, 2 vols (London: Monthly Review Press, 1975), vol. 2, pp. 401 and vol. 1, pp. 15–33 for the full analysis.

154. Dimitrov appeared greatly relieved that the constituent parties unanimously approved the decision to dissolve. Dimitrov, *Diary*, entries for 4 and 8 June 1943, pp. 278–9. Did he really expect reservations or opposition?

155. *KI* 9 (1943), docs 5–6, 9, 13, 17–18.

156. A.J. Rieber, 'Popular Democracy: An Illusion?', in V. Tismaneanu (ed.), *Stalinism Revisited: The Establishment of Communist Regimes in East-Central Europe* (Budapest: Central European University Press, 2008), pp. 103–30.

157. Dimitrov, *Diary*, entries for 5 March 1944, 20 June 1944 and especially 19 November 1944, pp. 304, 322–3 and 342–3. 'Anglichane i Amerikantsy khotiat vezde sozdat' reaktionnnye pravitel'stva', *Istochnik* 3:4 (1995), pp. 152–8. S. Pons, 'Stalin, Togliatti, and the Origins of the Cold War in Europe', *Journal of Cold War Studies* 3:2 (spring 2001), pp. 3–27; pp. 6–9, and M.M. Narinsky, 'I.V. Stalin i M. Thorez, 1944–1947. Novye materiali', *Novaia i noveishaia istoriia* 1 (1996), pp. 19–28; p. 19.

158. B. Lazitch, *Les Partis communistes d'Europe, 1917–1955* (Paris: Îles d'or, 1956) and N.D. Bogoliubov et al. (eds), *Istoriia mezhdunarodnogo rabochego i natsional'no-osvobozhditel'nogo dvizheniia. Uchebnoe posobie*, 3 vols (Moscow: Vysshaia partiinaia shkola pri TsK KPSS, 1962–66), vol. 2.

CHAPTER 6: A PYRRHIC VICTORY?

1. It is estimated that nearly 200,000 death sentences were carried out on the orders of military tribunals and the NKVD. These numbers do not include death sentences imposed by civilian courts or arbitrary shootings by partisan forces. O. Budnitskii, 'The Great Patriotic War and Soviet Society: Defeatism, 1941–42', *Kritika* 15:4 (autumn 2014), pp. 747–97; pp. 792–4. In the view of the author, the contributions of the consensualist and the oppositionist schools of interpretation should be supplemented by what he terms the most important factor: the recognition that the goal of Nazi policies was the destruction of the country and the extermination of its inhabitants. Ibid., pp. 795–7.

2. Harrison, *Accounting for War*, and G.V. Kirilenko, 'Ekonomicheskoe protivoborstvo storon', in Sevost'ianov (ed.), *Voina i obshchestvo*, vol. 1, pp. 333–59.

3. Tooze, *Wages of Destruction*, pp. 611–22.

4. Harrison, *Accounting for War*, pp. 157–61. Cf. the statistical analysis of wartime losses broken down into regional, national and civil-military categories in *Liudskie poteri SSSR*, section 2, 'Losses of Armed Forces of the USSR', pp. 71–123, and section 3, 'Losses of the Civilian Population', pp. 124–88.

5. V.B. Konasov and A.V. Tereshchuk, 'Novyi podkhod k uchetu bezvozvratnykh poter' v gody Velikoi Otechestvennoi voiny', *Voprosy istorii* 6 (1990), pp. 185–8.

6. B.V. Sokolov, 'Sootnoshenii poter' v liudakh i boevoi tekhnike na sovetsko-germanskom fronte v khode Velikoi Otechestvennoi voiny', *Voprosy istorii* 9 (1988), pp. 116–26; p. 117, 'based on official sources'. The figure of death from wounds was exaggerated according to R.A. Stepanov, 'Nel'zia igrat' tsiframi', *VIZh* 6 (1989), pp. 38–42; p. 39, but he gives no precise figures of his own. The most complete account is G.F. Krivosheev, 'Poteri Vooruzhenykh sil SSSR', in *Liudskie poteri SSSR*, pp. 71–123; pp. 75–6, calculating the permanent military losses at 11,944,100.

7. T. Sosnovy, 'The Soviet Military Budget', *Foreign Affairs* 42:3 (April 1964), pp. 487–94; p. 492.

8. Harrison, *Accounting for War*, p. 165. His calculations are based on the conventional theory that 'a postwar demographic deficit should be accompanied by accelerated population growth'. But this did not occur in the Soviet Union. 'On the contrary, fertility rates (which had been declining in the 1930s) continued to decline and never regained their prewar levels.' Ibid., p. 165.

9. E. Zubkova, *Russia after the War: Hopes, Illusions and Disappointments, 1945–1959* (London: Routledge, 1998), chap. 2. The English edition of Zubkova's *Obshchestvo* is much enlarged. For a general picture of the depressed standard of living among the kolkhoz peasantry see Arutiunian, *Sovetskoe krest'ianstvo*.

10. D. Filtzer, 'Standard of Living versus Quality of Life: Struggling with the Urban Environment in Russia during the Early Years of Post-War Reconstruction', in J. Fürst (ed.), *Late Stalinist Russia: Society between Reconstruction and Reinvention* (London: Routledge, 2006), pp. 81–102; p. 83.

11. Ibid., pp. 82–3.

12. N. Ganson, *The Soviet Famine of 1946–47 in Global and Historical Perspective* (New York: Palgrave Macmillan, 1999), pp. 6, 10–11.

13. S.G. Wheatcroft, 'The Soviet Famine of 1946–1947, the Weather and Human Agency in Historical Perspective', *Europe-Asia Studies* 64:6 (2012), pp. 987–1,005; p. 997.

14. Zubkova, *Russia after the War*, pp. 22–3.

15. J. Fürst, *Stalin's Last Generation: Soviet Post-War Youth and the Emergence of Mature Socialism* (London: Oxford University Press, 2010), especially pp. 15–29. After having demonstrated the specific impact on youth, she concludes: 'in many ways, and in particular when taking the example of youth allegiance and socialization, the Soviet Union won a pyrrhic victory over fascist Germany – a victory whose multiple ripple effects ultimately destroyed its very foundations'. For the western borderlands see Weiner, *Making Sense of War*.

16. For a full account see Rieber, *Stalin and the Struggle*, pp. 256–82.

17. Z. Polova, 'Collaboration and Resistance in Western Ukraine (1941–1947)', doctoral thesis, Central European University, 2006, pp. 181–215, 239–42, 258. See also A. Statiev, *The Soviet Counterinsurgency in the Western Borderlands* (Cambridge: Cambridge University Press, 2010), p. 201 ff.

18. GARF, f. 9401, op. 2, d. 102, listy 101–10, 116–18.

19. Ibid., d. 96, listy 306, 310–14; d. 102, listy 290–1. Beria sent fortnightly reports to Stalin on the numbers and types of treasonable activities of those arrested. Rieber, *Stalin and the Struggle*, pp. 277–9.

20. O.V. Roman'ko, 'Krymsko-Tatarskie formirovaniia. Dokumenty tret'ego reikha svidetel'svuiut', *VIZh* 3 (1991), pp. 89–95. The documents show small numbers of defectors, hardly justifying the massive deportation.

21. The main problem facing the Soviet regime in Chechnya was desertion or failure to show up for induction into the army. J. Burds, 'The Soviet War against "Fifth Columnists": The Case of Chechnya, 1942–4', *Journal of Contemporary History* 42:2 (April 2007), pp. 267–314; p. 292.

22. GARF, f. 9401, op. 2, d. 64, list 2, pp. 162–7. The episode is analyzed in Bugai and Gonov, *Kavkaz*, pp. 120–33, 153–73 and Burds, 'The Soviet War', pp. 303–7.

23. L.H. Siegelbaum, 'The "Flood" of 1945: Regimes and Repertoires of Migration in the Soviet Union at the War's End', *Social History* 42:1 (2017), pp. 52–72, quotation on p. 55.

24. O.V. Khlevniuk, *Stalin: New Biography of a Dictator*, trans. N. Seligman Favorov (New Haven, CT: Yale University Press, 2015), pp. 195–7; S. Fitzpatrick, *On Stalin's Team: The Years of Living Dangerously in Soviet Politics* (Princeton, NJ: Princeton University Press, 2017), pp. 175–6 and 197–9.

25. Scholars have used numerous terms to identify the men closest to Stalin during these years, including 'gang', 'inner circle' and 'oligarchy'. Each has its own special meaning. I prefer to use the more neutral term 'inner circle'. This term also implies, correctly, that there were outer circles of individuals at a remove from top positions in the hierarchy. Stalin could call upon them to avoid relying too heavily on those in the inner circle, thus giving him greater freedom of action.

26. See Iu.N. Zhukov, 'Bor'ba za vlast' v rukovodstve SSSR v 1945–1952 godakh', *Voprosy istorii* 2 (1995), pp. 1–8.

27. A.A. Maslov, *Captured Soviet Generals: The Fate of Soviet Generals Captured by the Germans, 1941–1945*, ed. and trans. D.M. Glantz and H.S. Orenstein (London: Frank Cass, 2001), on the survivors pp. 93–107, and the condemned, pp. 13–51. From 1945 to 1952, 101 generals and admirals were arrested and seventy-six condemned. Ibid., p. 156. See also A.A. Maslov, 'Forgiven by Stalin: Soviet Generals Who Returned from German Prisons in 1941–45 and Who Were Rehabilitated', *Journal of Slavic Military Studies* 12:2 (1999), pp. 173–219 for poignant details on individual cases, which varied greatly.

28. Cf. E.S. Seniavskaia, *Frontovoe pokolenie. Istoriko-psikhologicheskie issledovanie* (Moscow: Institut rossiiskoi istorii RAN, 1995), p. 91; E. Zubkova, *Poslevoennoe sovetskoe obshchestvo. Politika i povsednevnost' 1945–1953* (Moscow: ROSSPEN, 2000), p. 32.

29. R. Dale, 'Rats and Resentment: The Demobilization of the Red Army in Postwar Leningrad, 1945–50', *Journal of Contemporary History* 45:1 (January 2010), pp. 113–33; especially pp. 124–33. For the tactics used to defuse possible collective action by veterans see M. Edele, 'Soviet Veterans as an Entitlement Group, 1945–1955', *Slavic Review* 65:1 (spring 2006), pp. 111–37.

30. I.I. Kuznetsov, 'Stalin's Minister V.S. Abakumov 1908–54', *Journal of Slavic Military Studies* 12:4 (March 1999), pp. 149–65; pp. 152–8, 161, based on a series of articles in *VIZh* by I.N. Kostenko, October, November and December 1992, May and June 1993 and June 1994.

31. B.V. Sokolov, *Neizvestnyi Zhukov. Portret bez retusha v zerkale epokhi* (Moscow: Rodiolaplius, 2000), pp. 515–17 summarizes the alternative versions.

32. As with other postwar 'affairs', as we shall see, much remains obscure. For a summary of Abakumov's persecution of Zhukov during and after these events see M. Parrish, *The Lesser Terror: Soviet State Security, 1939–1953* (Westport, CT: Praeger, 1996), pp. 179–83.

33. Stalin's machinations through the Mingrelian Affair and the Doctors' Plot to undermine Beria fall outside the scope of this book.

34. A.P. Kriukovskikh, *Vo imia pobedy. Ideologicheskaia rabota Leningradskoi partinoi organizatsii v gody Velikoi Otechesvtennoi voiny* (Leningrad: Lenizdat, 1988), p. 142.

35. A.N. Iakovlev (gen. ed.), *Stalin i kosmopolitizm, 1945–1953. Dokumenty Agitpropa TsK KPSS, 1945–1953*, D.G. Nadzafov and Z.S. Belousova (comps) (Moscow: Mezhdunarodnyi fond Demokratiia, 2005), doc. 13, pp. 46–8.

36. D.T. Shepilov, *I primknuvshii k nim Shepilov. Pravda o cheloveke, uchenom, voine, politike*, ed. T. Tolchanova and M. Lozhnikov (Moscow: Zvonnitsa-Mg, 1998), p. 143.

37. Iakovlev (gen. ed.), *Stalin i kosmopolitizm*, docs 38, 43, 51, 100, 102, 108, pp. 110–14, 123–8, 140–1, 232–41, 250–8.

38. Ibid., docs 3, 16, 18, 28, 42, 128, pp. 26–7, 55, 60–5, 88–92, 121–3, 321–4.

39. Ibid., doc. 50, p. 139.

40. D.T. Shepilov, 'Vospominaniia', *Voprosy istorii* 5 (1998), pp. 3–27; pp. 13, 14.

41. Iakovlev (gen. ed.), *Stalin i kosmopolitizm*, docs 6, 29 and 258, pp. 31–2, 93–5, 665–6.

42. Ibid., doc. 244, pp. 617–18.

43. V. Pechatnov, 'Exercise in Frustration: Soviet Foreign Propaganda in the Early Cold War 1945–1947', *Cold War History* 1:2 (January 2001), pp. 1–27; pp. 3–8, and D.G. Nadzhafov, 'The Beginning of the Cold War between East and West: The Aggravation of Ideological Confrontation', *Cold War History* 4:2 (January 2004), pp. 140–74.

44. Iaroslavsky, *Chego trebuet partiia ot kommunistov*, pp. 8–9 admitted that wartime conditions gave little opportunity to study the Marxist classics, and insisted that this be rectified. See also C.S. Kaplan, 'The Impact of World War II on the Party', in Linz (ed.), *The Impact*, pp. 157–87; pp. 160–1.

45. Fürst, *Stalin's Last Generation*, pp. 50–2.

46. V.V. Denisov et al. (eds), *TsK VKP(b) i regional'nye partinye komitety, 1945–1953* (Moscow: ROSSPEN, 2004), doc. 56, p. 134 cites the case of the first secretary of Kostroma obkom as an example; for the reforms in the national and autonomous republics, which were clearly a major cause of concern, see ibid., docs 57 and 58, pp. 135–9.

47. Ibid., docs 4, 8, 10, 11, 12, 13, 14, 15, 17, pp. 25–44.

48. Ibid., docs 62 and 63, pp. 143–54.

49. Ibid., pp. 9–10.

50. C. King, *The Moldovans: Romania, Russia, and the Politics of Culture* (Stanford, CA: Hoover Institution Press, 1999), pp. 96–100.

51. Denisov et al. (eds), *TsK VKP(b) i regional'nye partinye komitety*, doc. 26, pp. 84–5.

52. Ibid., pp. 8–9, and doc. 46, pp. 118–20.

53. Ibid., pp. 8–10 and G. Mamoulia, 'The First Cracks in the Imperial Base of the Post-War USSR: Georgia and the South Caucasus, 1946–1956', 6th Silk Road International Conference: 'Globalization and Security in Black and Caspian Seas Regions' (Tbilisi and Batumi, 27–29 May 2011), pp. 63–72.

54. Denisov et al. (eds), *TsK VKP(b) i regional'nye partinye komitety*, pp. 6–7 and doc. 106, p. 199. One example of the extensive reporting of the MGB was the 300 confidential communications of the local MGB agent to Abakumov in the three-year period 1946–49, which contributed to the fabrication of the Leningrad Affair. B.I. Berezhkov, *Piterskie prokuratory. Rukovoditeli BChK-MGB, 1918–1954* (Saint Petersburg: Russo-Baltiskii informatsionyi tsentr, 1998), p. 235.

55. In the period 1948–51, the control commission agencies removed 183,284 party members for such abuses. B. Tromly, 'The Leningrad Affair and Soviet Patronage Politics, 1949–1950', *Europe-Asia Studies* 56:5 (July 2004), pp. 707–29; p. 727, note 86.

56. T.N. Nikonorova, 'Konstruiruia roskosh'. Bytovoe prostranstvo Sovetskoi nomenklatury, 1940–1952 gody', *Soviet and Post-Soviet Review* 43 (2016), pp. 219–42.

57. T.H. Rigby, 'Early Provincial Cliques and the Rise of Stalin', *Soviet Studies* 33:1 (January 1981), pp. 3–28 is the fundamental work. C.H. Fairbanks Jr, 'Clientelism and the Roots of the Post-Soviet Disorder', in R. Suny (ed.), *Transcaucasia, Nationalism and Social Change: Essays in the History of Armenia, Azerbaijan and Georgia*, rev. edn (Ann Arbor, MI: University of Michigan Press, 1996), pp. 341–76 focuses on Georgia but with wide-ranging implications for the development of the Soviet system. The role of clientelism is central to Tromly's analysis of the Leningrad Affair.

58. McNeal (ed.), *I.V. Stalin, Works*, vol. 3, pp. 230–1.

59. Kaplan, 'The Impact of World War II on the Party', pp. 172–5; see especially G.A. Kumanev, *Govoriat stalinskie narkovy* (Smolensk: Rusich, 2005) for interviews with officials in the 1940s.

60. M. Lewin, 'Fin de parti', in Lewin, *Le Siècle soviétique*, pp. 174–80.

61. The Central Committee had first detected the widespread distribution of rewards by the oil, coal and medium machine industries in 1941 on the eve of the war. Denisov et al. (eds), *TsK VKP(b) i regional'nye partinye komitety*, note, p. 150.

62. Ibid., doc. 65, pp. 156–7. In this case, the minister of light industry rewarded the obkom secretary of Udmurtia and chairman of the Council of Ministers of the ASSR with gold watches, hunting rifles, monthly payments and medals. Similar reproaches were levelled at twenty-three party secretaries in Zaporozhe and Vinnytsia in Ukraine, sixteen local

secretaries in Armenia, the Altai region, Karaganda and many others. The perpetrators were removed from office. Ibid., docs 66–72, pp. 156–62.

63. Ibid., docs 73 and 74, pp. 162–3.
64. V.P. Popov (ed.), *Krestianstvo i gosudarstvo (1945–1953)* (Paris: YMCA Press, 1992), doc. 1, pp. 21–40. Particularly shocking was the misuse of funds assigned for the construction of houses destroyed under the German occupation. Ibid., p. 26.
65. Ibid., docs 2, 3, 5, 8 and 9, pp. 41–6, 47–55, 61, 73–4 and 75–83.
66. Ibid., doc. 7, pp. 68–72.
67. Ibid., doc. 61, p. 278.
68. For the view that the application of a socialist realist model to agriculture challenged rational behaviour of the peasantry, see M. Haber, 'Socialist Realist Science: Continuity of Knowledge about Rural Life in the Soviet Union, 1943–1958', doctoral thesis, UCLA, 2013, especially pp. 208 ff.
69. Popov, *Krestianstvo i gosudarstvo*, docs 57–60, pp. 261–77. As the editor notes, citing Leo Tolstoy's diary, the idea that the peasantry regarded his landed property as theirs was a well-established tradition during serfdom in imperial Russia: 'We are yours, but the land is ours.' Ibid., note, p. 260.
70. Ibid., doc. 61, p. 78.
71. Ibid., p. 22 citing archival documents.
72. Ganson, *The Soviet Famine*, and Wheatcroft, 'The Soviet Famine', pp. 987–1,005 offer correctives to previous work by stressing the overriding importance of weather conditions and refuting the idea of Stalin's exploitation of the famine as a means of disciplining and punishing the Ukrainian people.
73. Memo to Stalin, 17 January 1948, in Tomilina et al. (eds), *Nikita Sergeevich Khrushchev*, vol. 1, doc. 20, pp. 216–19 and 'Report to Conference of Obkom Secretaries and MGB Heads of Oblasts of Lvov', ibid., pp. 220–8.
74. A few statistics reveal the depth of the crisis.

Livestock Owned by Kolkhoz Peasantry (per 100 Households)

	1940	1952
Cattle	100	86
of which cows	66	55
Sheep and goats	164	88
Pigs	45	27

Nove, *An Economic History*, pp. 296–301; statistics from *Kommunist* 1 (1954).

75. R.G. Pikhoia, *Sovetskii Soiuz. Istoriia vlasti, 1945–1991* (Moscow: RAGS, 1998), pp. 21–3; and J. Adamec, 'Courts of Honour in the Post-War Soviet Union', *Dvacáté století – The Twentieth Century* 6:1 (2014), pp. 74–84 which includes a case study of a village court. O.V. Khlevniuk et al. (eds), *Politbiuro. TsK VKP(b) i soviet ministrov SSSR, 1945–1963* (Moscow: ROSSPEN, 2002), pp. 229–30.
76. The following figures on annual convictions were compiled by the head of the Legal Section of the Supreme Soviet and sent to A.A. Andreev in the autumn of 1947: 1945 (full year): 5,757; 1946 (first half): 3,322; 1946 (second half): 6,189. Popov, *Krestianstvo i gosudarstvo*, doc. 2, p. 41.
77. Livschiz, 'Pre-Revolutionary in Form', pp. 552–3, 555.
78. *Foreign Relations of the United States. Diplomatic Papers, 1945*, vol. 5, pp. 882–3, 942–3, 945–6, 1,009, 1,015–16, 1,018, 1,026–7, 1,032–3, 1038; L.C. Martel, *Lend-Lease, Loans, and the Coming of the Cold War: A Study of the Implementation of Foreign Policy* (Boulder, CO: Westview Press, 1979), pp. 202–5, 209–21; B.I. Zhiliaev and V.I. Savchenko (comps), *Sovetsko-amerikanskie otnosheniia. 1939–1945. Dokumenty* (Moscow: Mezhdunarodnyi fond Demokratiia, 2004), docs 112, 266 and 334, pp. 229, 602–4 and 716–17.

79. D.G. Gillan and R.H. Myers (eds), *Last Chance in Manchuria: The Diary of Chang Kia-ngau* (Palo Alto, CA: Stanford University Press, 1989), pp. 71, 85, 153–5, 162–3; N.M. Naimark, *The Russians in Germany: A History of the Soviet Zone of Occupation* (Cambridge, MA: Harvard University Press, 1995); Rieber, 'The Crack in the Plaster', pp. 68–9 and 74–5.

80. G.I. Khanin, 'The 1950s: The Triumph of the Soviet Economy', *Europe-Asia Studies* 55:8 (June 2010), pp. 1,187–211; pp. 1,190–3.

81. For problems involved in calculating the real defence expenditures in the published state budget for the two decades after the war see Sosnovy, 'The Soviet Military Budget', pp. 487–94.

82. Voznesensky, *Voennaia ekonomika*. The book was immediately translated into English in the Soviet Union (which is unreliable) and in 1948 by the American Council of Learned Societies in the US.

83. For the argument that this represented an alternative plan B for the Soviet economy that reproduced elements of the New Economic Policy, and that his progressive views contributed to his downfall, see A.A. Danilov and A.V. Pyzhikov, *Rozhdenie sverkhderzhavy. SSSR v pervye poslevoennye gody* (Moscow: ROSSPEN, 2001), pp. 214–20. This view was repeated in the introductory material to a lavish republication of Voznesensky's *Voennaia ekonomika* (Moscow: Iz. dom Ekonomicheskaia gazeta, 2003) with an introduction by Iu. Iakutin and commentary on his life and work by L. Abalkin, E. Ivanov, V. Ivanchenko and A. Pyzhykov, unfortunately without annotated sources. For a critique see Y. Gorlizki and O.V. Khlevniuk, *Cold Peace: Stalin and the Soviet Ruling Circle, 1945–1953* (Oxford: Oxford University Press, 2004), p. 15 and note 61.

84. For fresh insights into Voznesensky's postwar economic policies see G. Cadioli, 'The Politics of Rehabilitation in the USSR under Khrushchev: The Case of Nikolai Alekseevich Voznesensky' (forthcoming).

85. Danilov and Pyzhikov, *Rozhdenie sverkhderzhavy*, pp. 220–4; an appendix to the 2003 edition of *Voennaia ekonomika*, pp. 378–81, lists the posthumous honours periodically awarded to Voznesensky from his rehabilitation in 1953 to 2003, celebrating him as a major figure in Russian economic development.

86. Danilov and Pyzhikov, *Rozhdenie sverkhderzhavy*, p. 238. Beria had been bombarding Stalin with complaints about Voznesensky's trick of underestimating the targets of those branches of the economy under his control, metallurgy and chemical, while overestimating those run by Beria. Volkogonov, *Triumf i tragediia*, vol. 2, pt 2, p. 64

87. K. Clark et al. (eds), *Soviet Culture and Power: A History in Documents, 1917–1953*, trans. M. Schwartz (New Haven, CT: Yale University Press, 2007), doc. 152, pp. 352–64. Individual writers were labelled former Trotskyites, Social Revolutionaries and Kadets.

88. Ibid., doc. 154 (8 January 1944), pp. 367–8.

89. Ibid., doc. 155 (20 July 1944), pp. 369–70.

90. Ibid., docs 156 (10 February 1944), 157 (2 December 1943), 158 (3 December 1943), 159 (7 August 1944), pp. 374–6.

91. Ibid., doc. 160 (31 October 1944), pp. 380–91. Even Ehrenburg expressed deep dissatisfaction. 'True literature is scarcely possible right now; it is all structured in the style of salutes, whereas truth is blood and tears.' He added that the attacks on writers like Zoshchenko, Selvinsky, Fedin and Chukovsky were examples of 'administrative tyranny'. Ibid., p. 388.

92. Ibid., doc. 161 (3 August 1945), pp. 393–8.

93. Ibid., editor's comments, p. 398 and Khlevniuk, *Stalin: New Biography*, p. 273.

94. Rieber, 'Zhdanov in Finland', pp. 112–13.

95. Mikoian considered him a drunkard and coward. Mikoian, *Tak bylo*, p. 562; Molotov thought him to be a good comrade, but not a strong leader, who was confused at the beginning of the siege. Chuev, *Sto sorok besed s Molotovym*, p. 55.

96. RGASPI, f. 77, op. 3, d. 39, listy 19, 21, 22. This did not prevent him from adopting the role for himself of a stern and often impatient mentor of the Finnish communists. But he never sought to violate the legal framework of the armistice. This was in line with Stalin's policy at the time. Rieber, 'Zhdanov in Finland', pp. 27–40; Rieber, *Stalin and the Struggle*, pp. 352–4.

97. Chuev, *Sto sorok besed s Molotovym*, p. 322.

98. Clark et al. (eds), *Soviet Culture*, doc. XXX, p. 401.

99. Ibid., doc. 165, pp. 421–4 and doc. 166, p. 424, Stalin to Zhdanov, praising his report as having come out 'superbly'.

100. Ibid., doc. 164, pp. 407–20. Akhmatova was only dismissed briefly by the head of the Writers' Union, Nikolai Tikhonov. Ibid., p. 417.

101. 'I have never been an anti-Soviet person', wrote Zoshchenko. And while apologizing for some errors, he called the 'Adventurers of a Monkey' a children's story without any 'Aesopian language or sub-text'. Zoshchenko to Stalin, 27 August 1946, ibid., doc. 167, pp. 425–7.

102. L. Maksimenkov (comp.), *Muzyka vmesto sumbura. Kompozitory i muzykanty v strane sovetov, 1917–1991* (Moscow: Mezhdunarodnyi fond Demokratiia, 2013), Shostakovich to Stalin, 17 May 1946, doc. 199 and editorial note, pp. 245–6. At the same time, Beria submitted to Stalin, at the latter's request, a proposal for constructing an apartment dwelling for members of the orchestra of the Bolshoi Theatre. Ibid., doc. 202, pp. 248–9. Shostakovich, Glière, Myaskovsky, Prokofiev and Khachaturian followed up this signal success by writing to Stalin as 'Moscow composers', requesting the assignment of a 'living co-operative' of sixty-four rooms and over 4,700 square metres for composers living and working in straitened physical conditions. Ibid., doc. 203, pp. 249–50.

103. One hundred and thirty-nine professors were awarded medals and orders and even those who had emigrated – like Rachmaninov – were honoured. Ibid., doc. 205, pp. 251–2.

104. Ibid., doc. 206, p. 252.

105. Having demonstrated their vigilance in the case of the Leningrad writers, Zhdanov and Kuznetsov proceeded to strengthen the position of the Leningraders in the field of art and literature by packing the committee on Stalin Prizes and replacing the popular song composer I.O. Dunaevsky as head of the Leningrad Union of Soviet Composers by Shostakovich. Ibid., doc. 207, p. 253. They also placed their candidate as the incoming head of the department of Marxism-Leninism of the Leningrad Conservatory, a veteran teacher during the war in the Military Engineering School in Leningrad and the author of a thesis on 'The Problem of Nationality [*Narodnost'*] in the Russian Musical Aesthetic of the Nineteenth Century'. Ibid., doc. 224, p. 275.

106. Ibid., doc. 210, pp. 256–7.

107. Ibid., doc. 212, pp. 259–60. Three times decorated during the war, in 1946 and 1947 Prokofiev garnered four Stalin Prizes 1st Class (ballet *Zolushka*; Fifth Symphony and Eighth Piano Sonata; film score for *Ivan the Terrible*; and sonata for violin and piano) and one Stalin Prize 2nd Class for the piano trio. Ibid., doc. 223, p. 274.

108. Ibid., doc. 223, editorial comment, pp. 274–5.

109. Zhdanov's review of opera ('there is no Soviet opera'), ballet, literature, theatre and film followed similar lines, stressing the theme of patriotism. Ibid., doc. 214, pp. 261–2.

110. J. Brent and V.P. Naumov, *Stalin's Last Crime: The Plot against the Jewish Doctors, 1948–1953* (New York: Harper Collins, 2003); Shepilov, 'Vospomianiia', pp. 3–27; pp. 3–7 and 12–13.

111. E. Vlasova, *1948 god v sovetskoi muzyki. Dokumentirovannoe issledovanie* (Moscow: Klassika, 2010), pp. 223–30.

112. Maksimenkov (comp.), *Muzyka vmesto sumbura*, doc. 225, pp. 276–82. Cf. Shepilov, *I primknuvshii k nim Shepilov*, pp. 101–2, in which he seeks to absolve himself of criticizing Shostakovich and others.

113. Maksimenkov (comp.), *Muzyka vmesto sumbura*, pp. 11–12.

114. Ibid., doc. 229, p. 288. All the leading composers were removed from these bodies and representatives of the Belarusian, Latvian, Georgian, Armenian and Uzbek national republics were to be included in the Musical Section of the Stalin Prize Committee.

115. Ibid., doc. 230, pp. 289–90. Myaskovsky came in tears to a noted pianist pedagogue, who later told me, 'He cried out, "Me! Me! Boris! Writing formalist music!?"' Discrimination in aesthetic matters was not a strong point of the Central Committee or else something else was at play here.

116. T. Khrennikov, 'O muzyke i muzykal'noi kritike', *Oktiabr'* 4 (1948), p. 163.

117. Maksimenkov (comp.), *Muzyka vmesto sumbura,* docs 247, 259 and note, 280, pp. 329–30, 360–1, 391–2, and in general Tomoff, *Creative Union.*

118. Making only a passing reference to his formalist errors, Muradeli focused his apology on his failure to use Georgian folk music, despite the fact that, as he stated, 'I grew up in the atmosphere of folk music. My first compositions hardly differed from simple songs of the people. In my later works – Four Georgian Songs, Symphonic Dance and Ten Heroic Songs – I again turned for inspiration to these sources of people's music.' *Vsesoiuznye s'ezd sovetskikh kompositorov. Stenograficheskii otchet* (Moscow: Izvestiia, 1948). I have used the complete text in N. Slonimsky (ed.), *Music since 1900* (New York: Norton, 1971), pp. 1,362–76. Muradeli's opera was rehabilitated by a Central Committee decree of 28 May 1958 as part of the post-Stalin refutation of 'the unjust and unfounded' attacks on Soviet music and musicians. Maksimenkov (comp.), *Muzyka vmesto sumbura,* doc. 366, pp. 502–3.

119. Ibid., doc. 216, pp. 265–6. This kind of review normally would have destroyed any possibility of travelling to the West.

120. This working style was vividly illustrated by Dmitry Shepilov in his eye-witness account of Stalin's participation in the selection of the prize bearing his name in all fields of the visual and literary arts. Shepilov, *The Kremlin's Scholar: A Memoir of Soviet Politics under Stalin and Khrushchev,* ed. S.V. Bittner and trans. A. Austin (New Haven, CT and London: Yale University Press, 2007), pp. 104–14.

121. K. Tomoff, 'Uzbek Music's Separate Path: Interpreting "Anticosmopolitanism" in Stalinist Central Asia, 1949–52', *Russian Review* 63:2 (April 2004), pp. 212–40; p. 221 ff.

122. G. Castillo, 'Peoples at an Exhibition: Soviet Architecture and the National Question', in T. Lahusen and E. Dobrenko (eds), *Socialist Realism without Shores* (Durham, NC: Duke University Press, 1997), pp. 91–119; pp. 113–14

123. K. Clark, 'Ehrenburg and Grossman: Two Cosmopolitan Jewish Writers Reflect on Nazi Germany at War', *Kritika* 10:3 (summer 2009), pp. 607–28; see also J. Rubenstein, *Tangled Loyalties: The Life and Times of Ilya Ehrenburg* (Tuscaloosa, AL: University of Alabama Press, 1999) and V. Grossman, *A Writer at War: A Soviet Journalist with the Red Army, 1941–1945,* ed. and trans. A. Beevor and L. Vinogradova (London: Pimlico, 2005); the majority of the war photographers were Jewish. See D. Shneer, 'Soviet Jewish Photographers Confront World War II and the Holocaust', in V.A. Kivelson and J. Neuberger (eds), *Picturing Russia: Explorations in Visual Culture* (New Haven, CT: Yale University Press, 2008), pp. 207–13.

124. Aleksandrov to Malenkov, 15 October 1945, Iakovlev (gen. ed.), *Stalin i kosmopolitizm,* doc. 5, pp. 29–30.

125. S. Redlich, *Propaganda and Nationalism in Wartime Russia: The Jewish Anti-Fascist Committee in the USSR, 1941–1948* (Boulder, CO: East European Quarterly, 1982), pp. 35 and 39–65.

126. S. Redlich, *War, Holocaust and Stalinism: A Documented History of the Jewish Anti-Fascist Committee in the USSR* (London: Routledge, 2016), docs 170–2, pp. 423–39. At the same time, high-ranking officials like Shcherbakov and Aleksandrov were criticizing the nationalistic and religio-mystical themes in Soviet Yiddish literature. Ibid., docs 167–8, pp. 414–21.

127. The details of the assassination were relayed by Beria to Malenkov after Stalin's death. Ibid., doc. 179, pp. 448–50. Redlich's account of the circumstances leading up to the killing remains the most complete. Ibid., pp. 126–32. He suggests that Stalin was

motivated to exact personal vengeance on Mikhoels for having participated in a plot, concocted by Abakumov, to pass information on Stalin's private life obtained by members of Stalin's in-laws, the Alliluev family, to US intelligence. Cf. Fitzpatrick, *On Stalin's Team*, pp. 203–4 generally accepts this explanation.

128. Redlich, *War, Holocaust and Stalinism*, doc. 180, pp. 451–64.
129. Ehrenburg agreed to write, but only as a private individual. Ibid., doc. 168, p. 352.
130. Ibid., pp. 352–60.
131. Redlich, *War, Holocaust and Stalinism*, doc. 181, p. 464. *Eynigkayt* was closed down at the same time. Simultaneously efforts were under way to break the ties between the Jewish autonomous oblast of Birobidzhan and the American Birobidzhan Committee, which in the postwar years supplied the republic with the equivalent of 6 million rubles in gifts. The Politburo denounced the leadership of the autonomous republic for promoting 'pro-American and bourgeois nationalist' tendencies among the population, plans to transform the autonomous into a union republic and a host of other administrative errors; as a result a large number of leading party officials of the republic were removed from office. Denisov et al. (eds), *TsK VKP(b) i regional'nye partinye komitety*, doc. 1,009, pp. 208–9.
132. A. Knight, *Beria: Stalin's First Lieutenant* (Princeton, NJ: Princeton University Press, 1993), pp. 146–75; Fitzpatrick, *On Stalin's Team*, pp. 202, 203–5, 207–8; J. Rubenstein and V.P. Naumov (eds), *Stalin's Secret Pogrom: The Postwar Inquisition of the Jewish Anti-Fascist Committee*, trans. L.E. Wolfson (New Haven, CT: Yale University Press, 2001), pp. 59–60, 226–30. See also Estraikh, 'Life, Death and Afterlife'.
133. See the strong letter of Molotov to Stalin, 9 April 1948, rejecting the British and American trusteeship proposal as likely to lead to 'an aggravation of the struggle between Jews and Arabs and in so doing will create a threat to peace and will intensify unrest in the Middle East … [and] leave the country in a semi-colonial position'. E. Bentsur, *Documents on Israeli-Soviet Relations 1941–1953*, (ed.) The Cummings Center for Russian Studies, 2 parts (London: Routledge, 2000), part 1: *May 1941–1949*, doc. 117, pp. 269–70. Two days later Andrei Gromyko elaborated on the Soviet position in a speech to a special session of the UN General Assembly. Ibid., doc. 119, pp. 277–80. Molotov and Vyshinsky continued to support Israeli objections to Count Bernadotte's proposals on depriving Israel of the Negev and other restrictions on Israeli freedom of action. Ibid., docs 184–5, pp. 383–6.
134. Ibid., docs 155–7, 159–60, 167, pp. 332–6, 339, 350–2. At Molotov's reception on the anniversary of the revolution, Meir and the Israeli guests 'were the centre of attention'; Meir had an emotional conversation with Molotov's wife in Yiddish. Ibid., doc. 195, pp. 401–2.
135. Ibid., docs 173, pp. 365–6, and Vyshinsky, friendly but evasive on the question of emigration, ibid., doc. 215, pp. 429–30. In January 1949 the Soviet government officially denounced as illegal Israeli attempts to recruit Soviet citizens for emigration. Ibid., doc. 220, p. 438.
136. During the war, 123,822 Jewish soldiers and officers were awarded military medals and titles, and 105 Jews received the very highest distinction, Hero of the Soviet Union, for their bravery and heroism against the German invaders. Several of these were members of the JAFC. J.N. Porter (ed.), *Jewish Partisans of the Soviet Union during World War II* (Brookline, MA: Cherry Orchard Books, 2021), p. vii.
137. The popular American weekly, *Time*, had featured Zhdanov on its cover.
138. For these see Fitzpatrick, *On Stalin's Team*, chap. 8. See also D. Brandenberger, A. Amosova and N. Pivovarov, 'The Rise and Fall of a Crimean Party Boss: Nikolai Vasil'evich Solov'ev and the Leningrad Affair', *Europe-Asia Studies* 71:6 (July 2019), pp. 951–71; p. 953, who divides the major scholars writing on the Leningrad Affair into three groups, depending on how they perceive Stalin's role and motivations in the affair. The different perceptions are a good illustration of how obscure and secretive Stalin's actions were in these latter years of his life.

139. J. Harris, 'The Origins of the Conflict between Malenkov and Zhdanov: 1939–1941', *Slavic Review* 35:2 (June 1976), pp. 287–303 and W.O. McCagg, *Stalin Embattled, 1943–1948* (Detroit, MI: Wayne State University Press, 1978), pp. 8–9 and 115–46.
140. Zhukov, 'Bor'ba za vlast', pp. 23–40.
141. L.D. Riabev (ed.), *Atomnyi proekt SSSR. Dokumenty i materialy*, 10 vols (Moscow: Izd. Firma fiziko-matematicheskaia literature RAN, 1998–), vol. 2, bk 1 (1999), pp. 11, 12, 15–18, 20, 23, 27, 48, 83–4, 94, 104, 116, 125. On at least one occasion Voznesensky chaired the committee in Beria's absence. Ibid., vol. 2, bk 4, p. 72. Voznesensky's name on the committee masthead appeared for the last time on 18 March 1949 but there is no explanation given in these documents for the reason for his removal. Ibid., vol. 1, bk 1, p. 354.
142. When Stalin re-appointed Malenkov as secretary of the Central Committee their rivalry entered a new phase according to Pikhoia, *Sovetskii Soiuz*, p. 65.
143. 'Protokol no. 3, zasedaniia Komissii Politbiuro, TsK KPSS. "O tak nazyvaemom leningradsom dele"', *Izvestiia TsK KPSS* 2 (1989), pp. 124–37; p. 127. It is not clear whether Stalin made these comments in order to stimulate rivalry among his subordinates.
144. A.N. Iakovlev (ed.), *Reabilitatsiia. Politicheskie protsessy 30–50-kh godov* (Moscow: Politizdat, 1991), p. 313.
145. A.V. Sushkov and A.E. Bedel' (eds), '"Leningradskoe delo". K voprosu o kadrovoi politike Smol'nogo v pervye poslevoennye gody', in *Gramota* 19 (2018), pp. 60–8; p. 62.
146. Stalin singled out the error of L.I. Mirzoian, the first secretary of the Kazakh party, who had appointed his friends from previous posts in Azerbaijan and the Ural organizations. 'Materialy fevral'sko–martovskogo plenuma TsK VKP(b), 1937 goda', *Voprosy istorii* 11–12 (1995), pp. 3–26.
147. O. Anikina, 'Aleksei Gvishiani. Ne nado zhalet' Kosygina', *Pravda*, 19 February 2004; Lewin, *Le Siècle soviétique*, pp. 129–30 and V.I. Andrianov, *Kosygin* (Moscow: Molodaia gvardiia, 2003), pp. 67–78, 99–108.
148. Shepilov, *The Kremlin's Scholar*, pp. 188–91.
149. Shkiriatov was an active prosecutor of numerous purge cases in the 1930s, including the arrest and execution of Jan Ruzutak, A.P. Smirnov, Bukharin and Rykov. After the war, he compiled the dossier on Molotov's wife, Polina Zhemchuzhina. K.A. Zalessky, *Imperiia Stalina. Biograficheskii entsiklopedicheskii slovar'* (Moscow: Veche, 2000); A.Iu. Vaksberg, *Tsaritsa dokazatel'stv. Vyshyinskii i ego zhertvy* (Moscow: AO, 1992), p. 287.
150. Sushkov and Bedel', '"Leningradskoe delo"', pp. 61, 63, 64.
151. Ibid., p. 65.
152. Tomilina et al. (eds), *Nikita Sergeevich Khrushchev*, vol. 1, doc. 11, p. 528. Khrushchev recalled a conversation with Zhdanov who expressed regret that the Russian Federation lacked the republican institutions of the other republics, like Ukraine, with their own councils of ministers and central committees. Ibid.
153. For a summary of Stalin's remarks see D.L. Brandenberger, 'Stalin, the Leningrad Affair, and the Limits of Postwar Russocentrism', *Russian Review* 63:2 (April 2004), pp. 241–55; p. 53 for the quotation. Cf. Tromly, 'The Leningrad Affair', pp. 707–29, who acknowledges that accusations of 'Great Russian chauvinism' did appear in the trials of Voznesensky and Kuznetsov, but discounts their importance. Ibid., p. 722, note 11. For the terse published version see Khlevniuk (ed.), *Politbiuro*, pp. 66–8.
154. Ibid., p. 65.
155. Cited in M.E. Lenoe, *The Kirov Murder and Soviet History* (New Haven, CT: Yale University Press, 2010), p. 291.
156. Clark et al. (eds), *Soviet Culture*, doc. 168, pp. 428–9. This was the prelude to a whole new set of procedures for reprinting works from journals without permission of one of the secretaries of the Central Committee. Ibid., doc. 169, p. 431.
157. Tomilina et al. (eds), *Nikita Sergeevich Khrushchev*, vol. 1, doc. 9, pp. 502 and 506; see also Gorlizki and Khlevniuk, *Cold Peace*, pp. 17–18. In 1956 Khrushchev declared that Beria and Abakumov considered Kuznetsov 'dangerous' because Stalin had appointed

him as secretary of the Central Committee in charge of appointments to the MGB. Tomilina et al. (eds), *Nikita Sergeevich Khrushchev*, vol. 1, doc. 14, p. 562.

158. Gorlizki and Khlevniuk, *Cold Peace*, pp. 12–13 and 16–17.

159. The report is contined in RGASPI, f. 17, op. 118, and is summarized in Sushkov and Bedel', '"Leningradskoe delo"', pp. 60–8. In Stalin's treacherous world of betrayals, Shkiriatov occupies a distinctive place. During the war he wrote a long, extraordinarily intimate letter to Zhdanov praising his defence of Leningrad and concluding by sending special greetings to Kuznetsov. Kosheleva, Rogovaia and Khlevniuk (eds), *Sovetskoe Voenno-Politicheskoe Rukovodstvo*, doc. 171 (27 April 1942), pp. 246–8.

160. Iakovlev (ed.), *Reabilitatsiiia*, pp. 318–19. Gorlizki and Khlevniuk, *Cold Peace*, p. 119.

161. Ibid., p. 319 and V.A. Kutuzov, '"Leningradskoe delo". K voprosu o kolichestve repressirovanykh', in *Peterburgskoe chtenie 98–99. Materialy entsiklopedicheskoi bibliotek 'Sankt Petersburg-2003'* (Saint Petersburg: Peterburgskii institute pechati, 1999), pp. 378–80.

162. After the death of Stalin all the major figures who had been condemned were rehabilitated, but not all the perpetrators were punished. For example, Shkiriatov was never tried or punished.

163. Iakovlev (ed.), *Reabilitatsiia*, p. 321.

164. These are examined and criticized in A.A. Amosova and D. Brandenberger, 'Noveishie podkhody k interpretatsii "Leningradskogo dela" kontsa 1940-kh nachala 1950-kh godov v Rossiiskikh nauchno-populiarnykh izdaniia', *Noveishaia istoriia Rossii* 18:7 (2017), pp. 94–112.

165. Denisov et al. (eds), *TsK VKP(b) i regional'nye partinye komitety*, docs 111–13, pp. 222–8. Popov was replaced by Khrushchev, who wrote little about the affair, although he attributed his appointment to Stalin's desire to balance the influence of Beria and Malenkov. Tomilina et al. (eds), *Nikita Sergeevich Khrushchev*, vol. 1, note 101, p. 641.

166. For more coverage see Rieber, *Stalin and the Struggle* and Roberts, *Stalin's Wars*.

167. The best treatment based on archives now difficult to access remains T.V. Volokitina, *Moskva i vostochnaia Evropa. Stanovlenie politicheskikh rezhimov sovetskogo tipa, 1949–1953. Ocherki istorii* (Moscow: ROSSPEN, 2008).

EPILOGUE: REMEMBERING THE WAR

1. D.A. Andreev and G.A. Bordiugov, *Prostranstvo pamiati. Velikaia pobeda i vlast'* (Moscow: Airo-XX, 2005), pp. 15–19.

2. Ibid.

3. Ibid., pp. 20–51 continues to analyze the celebrations of the war over ten-year periods to demonstrate how the collective memory of Victory Day was 'expanded' to serve the changing needs of the leadership.

4. For Stalin's role in constructing his *Short Biography* see D.L. Brandenberger, 'Stalin as Symbol: A Case Study of the Personality Cult and Its Construction', in Davies and Harris (eds), *Stalin*, pp. 249–270; pp. 264–70.

5. M. Kangaspuro and J. Lassila, 'From the Trauma of Stalinism to the Triumph of Stalingrad: the Toponymic Dispute over Volgograd', in J. Fedor et al. (eds), *War and Memory in Russia, Ukraine and Belarus* (Cham: Palgrave Macmillan, 2017), pp. 141–70.

6. E.A. Wood, 'Performing Memory: Vladimir Putin and the Celebration of WWII in Russia', *Soviet and Post-Soviet Review* 38:2 (2011), pp. 172–200; pp. 175–7; V. Shlapentokh and V. Bondartsova, 'Stalin in Russian Ideology and Public Opinion: Caught in a Conflict between Imperial and Liberal Elements', *Russian History* 36:2 (2009), pp. 302–25.

7. V. Putin, 'The Real Lessons of the 75th Anniversary of World War II', *The National Interest*, 18 June 2020; online at https://nationalinterest.org/feature/vladimir-putin-real-lessons-75th-anniversary-world-war-ii-162982 (accessed 25 November 2021).

8. S.A. Oushakine, *The Patriotism of Despair: Nation, War, and Loss in Russia* (Ithaca, NY: Cornell University Press, 2009).

9. See, for example, on the participants from Krasnodar, P. Ternovsky, *Oni srazhalis' za nas* (Krasnodar: Vol'naia N.N., 2015); on Eastern Siberia, N.A. Iatmanov (comp.), *Pamiatniki pobedy sovetskogo naroda v Velikoi Otechestvennoi voine v Respublike Khakasiia* (Abakan: Brigantina, 2015); on Tver', V.M. Vorobev, *Geroi Sovetskogo Soiuza na Tversloi zemle: biograficheskie ocherki*, 5 vols (Tver': Sed'maia bukva, 2015); on Vyshnyii, V. Volochek, '*S veroi v liubov' i pobedu*' in Iurii Bychkov, *Nasha Liubov* (Tver': Irida-pros, 2015); on Kemerova, Kuznetsk Basin, N. Usol'tseva, *Oni dyshali vozdukhom voiny* (Kemerovo: Kuzbassvuzizdat, 2015). In April 2021 it was widely reported in the Russian press that the local communist party in Bor, Nizhnyi Novgorod Province, had laid the foundation stone for a Stalin Centre Museum.

10. A. Liebich and O. Myshlovska, 'Bandera: Memorialization and Commemoration', *Nationalities Papers* 42:5 (2014), pp. 750–70; pp. 751, 753 and 763.

11. S. Plokhy, 'When Stalin Lost His Head: World War II and Memory Wars in Contemporary Ukraine', in Fedor et al. (eds), *War and Memory*, pp. 171–88. In the former Baltic republics, monuments to Stalin were removed without a fight. The main battles were fought over monuments to the Red Army soldiers. See, for example, in Tallinn, Estonia, K. Brüggemann and A. Kasekamp, 'The Politics of History and the "War of Monuments" in Estonia', *Nationalities Papers* 36:3 (2008), pp. 425–48. In Central Asia, by contrast, monuments to veterans served as a symbol of patriotism in the newly constructed national myth. See for example, K.M. Rees, 'Recasting the Nation: Transforming the Heroes of the Soviet Union into Symbols of Kazakhstani Patriotism', *Nationalities Papers* 39:4 (2020), pp. 445–62.

12. M. Lewin, *Political Undercurrents in Soviet Economic Debates: From Bukharin to the Modern Reformers* (Princeton, NJ: Princeton University Press, 1974), D.A. Dyker, 'Soviet Agriculture since Khrushchev: Decentralisation and Dirigisme', *IDS Bulletin* 13:4 (1982), pp. 29–35, and Dyker, *The Future of the Soviet Economic Planning System* (Armonk, NY: M.E. Sharpe, 1985), chaps 2–3.

13. Graham, *Science in Russia*, pp. 133–4 on biology, and appendices A and B for a summary of developments in all fields; Holloway states that only work on the atomic bomb saved physics for the fate of biology and enabled the physicists among all scientists to enjoy a modicum of autonomy. Holloway, *Stalin and the Bomb*, pp. 211 and 362–3.

BIBLIOGRAPHY

ARCHIVES

Arkhiv vneshnei politiki Rossiiskoi Federatsii (AVP – Foreign Policy Archive of the Russian Federation, Moscow)
f. Molotova
Gosudarstvennyi arkhiv Rossiisskoi Federatsii (GARF – State Archive of the Russian Federation, Moscow)
f. 9, 40 NKVD reports
f. 17   Internal Department Files, Politburo Protocols, Sovinform Files
f. 77   Zhdanov Papers
Rossiiskii Gosudarstvennyi Arkhiv Sotsial'no-Politicheskoi Istorii (RGASPI – Russian State Archive of Social-Political History, Moscow)

PRINTED DOCUMENTS, MEMOIRS AND WORKS

Aldoshin, V.V. and Iu.V. Ivanov (comps). *Sovetsko-amerikanskie otnosheniia. 1945–1948* (Moscow: Mezhdunarodnii fond Demokratiia, 2004).

'Anglichane i Amerikantsy khotiat vezde sozdat' reaktionnnye pravitel'stva', *Istochnik* 3:4 (1995), pp. 152–8.

Antonov-Ovseenko, A. et al. (eds). *Beriia. Konets kar'ery* (Moscow: Politizdat, 1991).

Auman, V.A. and V.G. Chebotareva (eds). *Istoriia rossiiskikh nemtsev v dokumentakh 1763–1992 gg.*, 2 vols (Moscow: Mezhdunarodnyi institut gumanitarnykh programm, 1993).

Belikov, A.M. 'Tiazhelaia promyshlennost' – v glubokii tyl', in I.Ia. Poliakov (ed.), *Eshelony idut na Vostok. Iz istorii perebazirovaniia proizvoditel'nykh sil SSSR v 1941–1942 gg. Sbornik statei i dokumentov* (Moscow: Nauka, 1966).

Berezhkov, B.I. *Piterskie prokuratory. Rukovoditeli BChK-MGB, 1918–1954* (Saint Petersburg: Russo-Baltiskii informatsionyi tsentr, 1998).

Bordiugov, G.A. (ed.) *Gotovil li Stalin nastupitel'nuiu voinu protiv Gitlera? Nezaplanirovannaia diskussiia. Sbornik materialov* (Moscow: Airo-XX, 1995).

Bugai, N.F. *L. Beriia–I. Stalinu. 'Soglasno vashemu ukazaniiu'* (Moscow: Airo-XX, 1995).

— (comp.). *Iosif Stalin–Lavrentiu Beriia. 'Ikh nado deportirovat ...' Dokumenty, fakty, kommentarii* (Moscow: Druzhba narodov, 1992).

Bukov, K. et al. (comps). *Moskva voennaia, 1941–1945. Memuary i arkhivnye dokumenty* (Moscow: Mosgoarkhiv, 1995).

Chaikovs'kyi, A.S. *Nevidoma viina. Partizans'kyi rukh Ukraïni 1941–1944 rr. Movoiu dokumentiv, ochyma istoryka* (Kyiv: Ukraina, 1994).

Chuev, F.I. *Sto sorok besed s Molotovym. Iz dnevnika F. Chueva* (Moscow: Terra, 1991).

De Gaulle, C. *Mémoires de guerre*, 3 vols (Paris: Plon, 1954–60).

Denisov, V.V. et al. (eds). *TsK VKP(b) i regional'nye partinye komitety, 1945–1953* (Moscow: ROSSPEN, 2004).

Documents on German Foreign Policy, 1918–1945, Series C, 6 vols (London: HMSO, 1949–83).

Franklin, W.M. and W. Gerber (eds). *Foreign Relations of the United States: Diplomatic Papers, The Conferences at Cairo and Tehran, 1943* (Washington, DC: US Government Printing Office, 1961).

Gar'kin, V.P. and G.A. Shirokov. *Otechestvennaia voina i vyshaia shkola 1941–1945. Sbornik materialov* (Samara: Samarskii Universitet, 2008).

Gomułka, W. *Izbrannye stat'i i rechi, 1964–1967* (Moscow: Izd-vo polit. lit-ry, 1968).

Gromyko, A. *Memoirs* (New York: Doubleday, 1991).

Gronsky, I.M. and V.N. Perel'man (comps). *Assotsiatsiia khudozhnikov revoliutsionnoi Rossii. Sbornik vospominanii, statei, dokumentov* (Moscow: Izabratel'noe iskusstvo, 1973).

Iakovlev, A.N. (ed.). *Reabilitatsiia. Politicheskie protsessy 30–50-kh godov* (Moscow: Politizdat, 1991).

— *Sovetsko-amerikanskie otnosheniia. 1939–1945. Dokumenty* (Moscow: Materik, 2004).

— (gen. ed.). *Stalin i kosmopolitizm, 1945–1953. Dokumenty Agitpropa TsK KPSS, 1945–1953.* D.G. Nadzafov and Z.S. Belousova (comps) (Moscow: Mezhdunarodnyi fond Demokratiia, 2005).

Iampol'skii, V.P. et al. (eds). *Organy gosudarstvennoi bezopasnosti SSSR v Velikoi Otechestvennoi voine: sbornik dokumentov* (Moscow: Kuchkovo Pole, 2007).

'I.V. Stalin, pis'ma', in V.S. Lel'chuk (ed.). *Sovetskoe obshchestvo. Vozniknovenie, razvitie, istoricheskii final*, 2 vols (Moscow: Rossiiskii gosudarstvennnyi gumanitarnyi universitet, 1997), vol. 1, p. 427 ff.

'Iz istorii Velikoi Otechestvennoi voiny; Zapiska P.F. Iudina I.V. Stalinu, 4 oktiabria 1941', *Izvestiia TsK KPSS* 12 (1990), pp. 203–18; pp. 208–9.

Kalinin, M.I. *Stat'i i rechi. 1941–1946* (Moscow: Politizdat, 1975).

Khaustov, V.N. et al. (eds). *Lubianka. Stalin i VCHK-GPU-OGPU-NKVD. Ianvar' 1922–dekabr' 1936* (Moscow: ROSSPEN, 2002).

Khlevniuk, O.V. et al. (eds). *Politbiuro. Mekhanizmy politicheskoi vlasti v 1930-e gody* (Moscow: ROSSPEN, 1996).

— *Stalin i Kaganovich. Perepiska 1931–1936 gg.* (Moscow: ROSSPEN, 2001).

— *Politbiuro. TsK VKP(b) i soviet ministrov SSSR, 1945–1963* (Moscow: ROSSPEN, 2002).

Khrushchev, N.S. *Memoirs of Nikita Khrushchev*, vol. 1, *Commissar, 1918–1945*, ed. S. Khrushchev (University Park, PA: Penn State University Press, 2004).

Knyshevsky, P.N. et al. (eds). *Skrytaia pravda. 1941 god. Neizvestnye dokumenty* (Moscow: Russkaia kniga, 1992).

Kokurin, A.I and N.V. Petrov (eds). *GULAG (Glavnoe upravlenie lagerei). 1918–1960* (Moscow: ROSSPEN, 2002).

Komarov, L.S. *Rossiia tankov ne imela. Dokumental'no-khudozhestvennoe povestvovanie* (Chelyabinsk: L.S. Komarov, 1994).

Kosheleva, L.P., L.A. Rogovaia and O.V. Khlevniuk (eds). *Sovetskoe Voenno-Politicheskoe Rukovodstvo v Gody Velikoi Otechesvennoi Voiny. Gosudarstvennyi Komitet Oborony SSSR. Politbiuro TsK VKP(b). Sovet Narodnykh Komissarov SSSR* (Moscow: Kuchkovo pole Muzeon, 2020).

Kozlov, V.P. et al. (eds). *Istoriia stalinskogo gulaga. Konets 1920–pervaia polovina 1950-kh godov. Sobranie dokumentov v semi tomakh* (Moscow: ROSSPEN, 2004).

KPSS v rezoliutsiiakh i resheniiakh s'ezdov konferentsii i plenum TsK 1938–1945, 9th edn (Moscow: Politizdat, 1985).

KPSS. *Dvenadtsatyi s'ezd RKP(b). Stenograficheskii otchet, 17–25 aprelia 1923 goda* (Moscow: Politizdat, 1968).

Krasil'nikov, S.A. et al. (eds). *Sudebnii protsess 'Prompartii' 1930 g. Podgotovka, provedenie, itogi*, 2 vols, (Moscow: ROSSPEN, 2016).

Kukryniksy. *Vtroem* (Moscow: Khudozhnik, 1975).

— *Sobranie proizvedenii v 4-kh tomakh*, 4 vols (Moscow: Izobrazitel'noe iskusstvo, 1982–88).

Kulikova, I.S. 'Zavetnye tetrady A.M. Kollontai', *Voprosy istorii KPSS* (8 August 1989), pp. 106–7.

Kvashonkin, A.V. *Sovetskoe rukovodstvo. Perepiska, 1928–1941* (Moscow: ROSSPEN, 1999).

Leningrad v osade. Sbornik dokumentov o geroicheskoi oborone Leningrada v gody Velikoi Otechestvennoi voiny 1941–1945, A.R. Dzeniskevich (comp.) (Saint Petersburg: Liki Rossii, 1995).

Maksimenkov, L. (comp.). *Muzyka vmesto sumbura. Kompozitory i muzykanty v strane sovetov, 1917–1991* (Moscow: Mezhdunarodnyi fond Demokratiia, 2013).

Marshal Tukhachevsky. Vospominaniia druzei i soratnikov, N.I. Koritskii et al. (comp.) (Moscow: Voenizdat, 1997).

Materialy po delu kontrrevoliutsionnoy 'Trudovoy krestianskoy partii' i gruppirovki Sukhanova-Gromana (Iz materialov sledstvennogo proizvodstva OGPU).

Ministerstvo innostrankh del SSSR, *Dokumenty vneshnei politiki SSSR 1939 god*, 2 vols (Moscow: Mezhdunarodnye otnosheniia, 1992).

Mozokhina, O.B. *Organy gosudarstvennoi bezopastnosti: sbornik dokumentov* (Moscow: Kuchkogo Pole, 2017).

Naumov, V.P. et al. (eds). *Rossiia XX vek. Dokumenty. 1941 god*, 2 vols (Moscow: Mezhdunarodnyi fond Demokratiia, 1998).

Naumov, V.P. and Iu. Sichagev (comps). *Lavrentii Beriia. Stenogramma iul'skogo plenuma TsK KPSS i drugie dokumenty* (Moscow: Mezhdunarodnyi fond Demokratiia, 1999).

'Nota narodnogo komissara inostrannykh del V.M. Molotova o chudovishchnykh zlodeiani-iakh zverstvakh i nasiliiakh nemetsko-fashistskikh zakhvatchikov v okkupirovannykh sovetskikh raionakh i ob otvetstvennosti Germanskogo pravitel'stva i komandovaniia za eti prestupleniia' (Moscow, 27 April 1942).

Novikov, N.V. *Put' i pereputia sovetskogo diplomata. Zapiski, 1943–1944* (Moscow: Nauka, 1975).

'Novye dokumenty G. Dimitrova', *Voprosy istorii KPSS* 8 (August 1989), pp. 53–79; pp. 75–7.

Oshchepov, P.K. *Zhizn' i mechta. Zapiski inzhenera-izobretatelia, konstruktora i uchenego* (Moscow: Moskovskii rabochii, 1967).

'Otvety P.K. Ponomarenko na voprosy professora G.A. Kumaneva (2/11/1978)', in G.A. Kumanev, *Riadom so Stalinym. Otkrovennye svidetel'stva* (Moscow: Bylina, 1999), pp. 93–144; pp. 134–5.

'"Polozhenie na Pinskom napravlenii", ne pozdnee 30 iiunia 1941', *Izvestiia TsK KPSS* 6 (1990), pp. 196–222; pp. 215–16.

'Rech' I.V. Stalina na devnadtsatogo godovshchina oktiabrskoi revoliutsii', *Bol'shevik* 21 (November 1944), pp. 1–6.

Report of the Court Proceedings in the Case of the Anti-Soviet 'Block of Rights and Trotskyites' Heard before the Military Collegium of the Supreme Court of the USSR, Moscow, March 2–13, 1938 in re: N.I. Bukharin ... et al ...: Verbatim Report (Moscow: People's Commissariat of Justice of the USSR, 1938).

Report of the Court Proceedings in the Case of the Anti-Soviet Trotskyite Centre (Moscow: People's Commissariat of Justice of the USSR, 1937).

Savinkin, N.I. and K.M. Bogoliubov (comps). *KPSS o Vooruzhenykh sil Sovetskogo Soiuza. Dokumenty, 1917–1981. Sbornik* (Moscow: Voenizdat, 1981).

Shcherbakov, A.S. *Pod znamenem Lenina, 22 ianvariia 1942* (Gorky: Gorkovskoe obl. kn-vo, 1942).

Shepilov, D.T. 'Vospomianiia', *Voprosy istorii* 2–3 (1998), pp. 3–27.

— *The Kremlin's Scholar: A Memoir of Soviet Politics under Stalin and Khrushchev*, ed. S.V. Bittner and trans. A. Austin (New Haven, CT and London: Yale University Press, 2007).

Shirokov, G.A. *Nauka. Tretii front 1941–1945. Sbornik materialov* (Samara: Samarskii universitet, 2008).
Shkarovsky, M.V. (ed.). 'V ogne voiny. Russkaia pravoslavnaia tserkov' v 1941–1945 gg. (Po materialam Leningradskoi eparkhii)', *Russkoe proshloe* 5 (1994), pp. 259–316.
Simonov, K.I. 'Zametki k biografii G.K. Zhukova', *VIZh* 10 (October 1987) pp. 60–72; 12 (December 1987), pp. 48–57.
Sontag, R.J. and J.S. Beddie (eds). *Nazi-Soviet Relations 1939–1941: Documents from the Archives of the German Foreign Office as Released by the Dept of State* (Washington, DC: US Government Printing Office, 1948).
'Speeches of B.P. Beschev and N.M. Shvernik at the XXII Party Congress', *Current Digest of the Soviet Press* 14:2 (7 February 1962), pp. 24–6.
Stalin, I.V. *On the Great Patriotic War of the Soviet Union* (London: Hutchinson, 1943).
— *Sochineniia*, 13 vols (Moscow: Gospolitizdat, 1951–).
Statiev, A. 'Penal Units in the Red Army', *Europe-Asia Studies* 62:5 (2010), pp. 721–47.
Stepashin, S.V. and V.P. Iampol'sky (eds). *Organy gosudarstvennoi bezopasnosti SSSR v Velikoi Otechestvennoi voine. Sbornik dokumentov* (Moscow: A.O. Kniga i biznes, 1995).
Strana Sovetov za 50 let. Sbornik statisticheskikh materialov (Moscow: Statistka, 1967).
Sushkov, A.V. and A.E. Bedel' (eds). '"Leningradskoe delo". K voprosu o kadrovoi politike Smol'nogo v pervye poslevoennye gody', in *Gramota* 19 (2018), pp. 60–8.
'Telegramma iz Gomela' (29 June 1941), *Izvestiia TsK KPSS* 6 (1990), pp. 214–15.
'Telegramma iz Murmanska' (19 June 1941), *Izvestiia TsK KPSS* 5 (1990), p. 206.
Tomilina, N.G. et al. (eds). *Nikita Sergeevich Khrushchev. Dva tsveta vremeni. Dokumenty lichnogo fonda N.S. Khrushchev*, 2 vols (Moscow: Mezhdunarodnyi fond Demokratiia, 2009).
Tukhachevsky, M.N. *Izbrannye sochineniia*, 2 vols (Moscow: Krasnaia zvezda, 1937).
— 'Novye voprosy voiny', *VIZh* (February 1962), pp. 62–77.
'Tukhachevsky's Letter to Zinoviev, July 18, 1920', in J. Erickson, *The Soviet High Command: A Military-Political History, 1918–1941* (New York: St Martin's Press, 1962), pp. 784–5.
Vannikov, B.L. 'Iz zapisok Narkoma vooruzheniia', *VIZh* (February 1962), pp. 78–86.
Varga, E. 'Reshaiushchaia rol' gosudarstva v voennom khozaistve kapitalisticheskikh stran', *Mirovoe khoziastvo i mirovaia politika* 1 (1945), pp. 11–21.
Vasilevsky, A.V. *Delo vsei zhizni*, 4th edn (Moscow: Voenizdat, 1983).
'Vozvanie k slavianam vsego mira uchastnikov vtorogo Vseslavianskogo mitinga sostoiavshevosia v g. Moskve 4–5 aprelia 1942', *Vestnik Akademiia nauk SSSR* 4 (1942), pp. 26–30.
Vsesoiuznye s'ezd sovetskikh kompositorov. Stenograficheskii otchet (Moscow: Izvestiia, 1948).
Vyshinsky, A.Ia. *Sovetskoe Gosudarstvo – Gosudarstvo novogo tipa. Doklad, rechitannyi na sessii Akademii nauk SSSR, 20 noiabria 1942 g.* (Moscow: Gospolitizdat, 1943).
— *Sovetskoe Gosudarstvo v Otechestvennoi voine* (Moscow: Gospolitizdat, 1944).
X plenum IKKI. Mezhdunarodnoe polozhenie i zadachi Kommunisticheskogo internatsionala, vol. 1 (Moscow: Politizdat, 1929).
'Zapiska A.I. Zaporozhetsa v Sekretariat TsK VKP(b), 25 apreliia 1941', *Izvestiia TsK KPSS* 5 (May 1990), pp. 180–219; p. 197.
'Zapiska M.P. Kirponosa i N.N. Vashugina k N.S. Khrushchevu, 16/18 apreliia 1941', *Izvestiia TsK KPSS* 5 (May 1990), pp. 180–219; p. 188.
'Zapiski sovremennika o M.N. Tukhachevskom', *VIZh* (April 1963), pp. 64–78.
Zhiliaev, B.I. and V.I. Savchenko (comps). *Sovetsko-amerikanskie otnosheniia 1939–45. Dokumenty* (Moscow: Mezhdunarodnyi fond Demokratiia, 2004).
Zhukov, G.K. *Vospominaniia i razmyshleniia* (Moscow: Novosti, 1969).
— *The Memoirs of Marshal Zhukov* (New York: Delacorte Press, 1971).
— 'Iz neopublikovannykh vospominanii', *Kommunist* 14 (September 1988), pp. 87–101.

BOOKS

Adereth, M. *The French Communist Party: A Critical History (1920–1984)* (Manchester: University of Manchester Press, 1984).

Agaian, Ts.P. *Ocherki istorii Kommunisticheskoi partii Armenii* (Yerevan: Alestan, 1967).

Akademiia nauk v resheniiakh Politbiuro TsK RKP–VKP(b)–KPSS 1922–1991, vol. 1 (Moscow: ROSSPEN, 2000).

Aktivnye bortsy za Sovetskuiu vlast v Azerbaidzhane (Baku: Azerbaidzhanskoe gosudarst-vennoe izd., 1957).

Anders, W. *An Army in Exile: The Story of the Second Polish Corps* (London: Macmillan, 1949).

Andreev, D.A. and G.A. Bordiugov. *Prostranstvo pamiati. Velikaia pobeda i vlast'* (Moscow: Airo-XX, 2005).

Andrianov, V.I. *Kosygin* (Moscow: Molodaia gvardiia, 2003).

Anfilov, V.A. *Doroga k tragedii sorok pervogo goda* (Moscow: Akopov, 1997).

Armstrong, J.A. *The Politics of Totalitarianism: The Communist Party of the Soviet Union from 1934 to the Present* (New York: Random House, 1961).

— *Ukrainian Nationalism*, 2nd edn (New York: Columbia University Press, 1963).

Arutiunian, Iu.V. *Sovetskoe krest'ianstvo v gody Velikoi Otechestvennoi voiny* (Moscow: Nauka, 1970).

Azrael, J.R. *Managerial Power and Soviet Politics* (Cambridge, MA: Harvard University Press, 1966).

Bailes, K.E. *Technology and Society under Lenin and Stalin: Origins of the Soviet Technical Intelligentsia* (Princeton, NJ: Princeton University Press, 1978).

— *Science and Russian Culture in an Age of Revolutions: V.I. Vernadsky and His Scientific School, 1863–1945* (Bloomington, IN: Indiana University Press, 1990).

Baishev, S.B. *Ocherki istorii Kommunisticheskoi partii Kazakhstana* (Alma Ata: Kazakhskoe gosudarstvennoe izd., 1963).

Balevits, Z. *Pravoslavnaia tserkov' Latvii pod sen'iu svastiki (1941–1944)* (Riga; Zinatne 1967).

Banac, I. *The National Question in Yugoslavia: Origins, History, Politics* (Ithaca, NY: Cornell University Press, 1984).

— *With Stalin against Tito: Cominformist Splits in Yugoslav Communism* (Ithaca, NY: Cornell University Press, 1988).

Bar-Tal, D. and E. Staub (eds). *Patriotism: In the Lives of Individuals and Nations* (Chicago, IL: Nelson-Hall, 1997).

Bartov, O. *Hitler's Army: Soldiers, Nazis and War in the Third Reich* (New York: Oxford University Press, 1991).

Beliaev, E.A. and N.S. Pyshkova. *Formirovanie i razvitie seti nauchnykh uchrezhdenii SSSR. Istoricheskii ocherk* (Moscow: Nauka, 1979).

Beloff, M. *The Foreign Policy of Soviet Russia, 1936–1941*, 2 vols (New York: Oxford University Press, 1949).

Bentsur, E. *Documents on Israeli-Soviet Relations 1941–1953*, The Cummings Center for Russian Studies (ed.), 2 parts (London: Routledge, 2000), part 1: *May 1941–1949*.

Berezhkov, V.M. *Stranitsy ot diplomaticheskoi istorii* (Moscow: Partizdat, 1984).

Berkhoff, K.C. *Motherland in Danger: Soviet Propaganda during World War II* (Cambridge, MA: Harvard University Press, 2012).

Boag, J.W., P.E. Rubinin and D. Shoenberg (eds), *Kapitza in Cambridge and Moscow: Life and Letters of a Russian Physicist* (Amsterdam: North-Holland, 1990).

Bociurkiw, B. *The Ukrainian Greek Catholic Church and the Soviet State: 1939–1950* (Edmonton: Canadian Institute of Ukrainian Studies, 1996).

Boetticher, M. von. *Industrialisierungspolitik und Verteidigungskonzeption der UdSSR 1926–1930: Herausbildung des Stalinismus und 'äussere Bedrohung'* (Düsseldorf: Drostel, 1976).

Bogoliubov, N.D. et al. (eds). *Istoriia mezhdunarodnogo rabochego i natsional'no-osvobozhditel'nogo dvizheniia. Uchebnoe posobie*, 3 vols (Moscow: Vysshaia partiinaia shkola pri TsK KPSS, 1962–66).

Brandenberger, D.L. *National Bolshevism: Stalinist Mass Culture and the Formation of Modern Russian National Identity, 1931–1956* (Cambridge, MA: Harvard University Press, 2002).

— *Propaganda State in Crisis: Soviet Ideology, Indoctrination and Terror under Stalin, 1927–1941* (New Haven, CT: Yale University Press, 2011).

Brent, J. and V.P. Naumov. *Stalin's Last Crime: The Plot against the Jewish Doctors, 1948–1953* (New York: Harper Collins, 2003).

Brodskaia, M.E. *Verolomnoe napadenie fashistskoi Germanii o Sovetskii Soiuz. Mobilizatsiia partiei sovetskogo naroda na otpor vragu* (Chardzhou: 1957)

Brooks, J. *Thank You, Comrade Stalin! Soviet Public Culture from Revolution to Cold War* (Princeton, NJ: Princeton University Press, 2000).

Bubnov, A.S., S.S. Kamenev and M.N. Tukhachevsky. *Grazhdanskaia voina*, 2 vols (Moscow and Leningrad: Voennyi vestnik, 1930).

Budreckis, A.M. *The Lithuanian National Revolt of 1941* (Boston, MA: Lithuanian Encyclopedia Press, 1968).

Bugai, N.F. and A.M. Gonov. *Kavkaz. Narody v eshelonakh (20–60-e gody)* (Moscow: INSAN, 1998).

Burmeister, A. *Dissolution and Aftermath of the Comintern: Experiences and Observations, 1937–1947* (New York: Research Program on the USSR, 1955).

Carr, E.H. *Twilight of the Comintern, 1930–1935* (New York: Pantheon, 1982).

Carr, E.H. and R.W. Davies. *Foundations of a Planned Economy, 1926–1929*, 2 vols (New York: Macmillan, 1971).

Chase, W.J. *Enemies within the Gates? The Comintern and Stalinist Repression, 1934–1939* (New Haven, CT: Yale University Press, 2001).

Chatterjee, C. *Celebrating Women: Gender, Festival Culture and Bolshevik Ideology 1910–1939* (Pittsburgh, PA: University of Pittsburgh Press, 2001).

Chuev, F. *Tak govoril Kaganovich. Ispoved' stalinskogo apostola* (Moscow: Otechestvo, 1992).

Chumachenko, T.A. *Church and State in Soviet Russia: Russian Orthodoxy from World War II to the Khrushchev Years*, ed. and trans. E.E. Roslof (Armonk, NY: M.E. Sharpe, 2002).

Cienciala, A.M., N.S. Lebedeva and W. Materski (eds). *Katyn: A Crime without Punishment* (New Haven, CT: Yale University Press, 2007).

Clark, K. *The Soviet Novel: History as Ritual* (Chicago, IL: University of Chicago Press, 1981).

Clark, K. et al. (eds). *Soviet Culture and Power: A History in Documents, 1917–1953*, trans. M. Schwartz (New Haven, CT: Yale University Press, 2007).

Claudín, F. *The Communist Movement: From Comintern to Cominform*, 2 vols (London: Monthly Review Press, 1975).

Conquest, R. *The Great Terror* (New York: Macmillan, 1968).

Corbet, C. *Une Littérature aux fers. Le pseudo-réalisme soviétique* (Paris: La Pensée universelle, 1975).

Coulondre, R. *De Staline à Hitler. Souvenirs de deux ambassades, 1936–1939* (Paris: Hachette, 1950).

Czapski, J. *Inhuman Land: Searching for the Truth in Soviet Russia, 1941–1942*, trans. A. Lloyd-Jones (New York: New York Review of Books, 2018).

D'iakov, Iu.L. and G.A. Kumanev. *Kapital'noe stroitel'stvo v SSSR, 1941–1945* (Moscow: Nauka, 1988).

Dallin, D.J. *The Changing World of Soviet Russia* (New Haven, CT: Yale University Press, 1956).

Danilov, A.A. and A.V. Pyzhikov. *Rozhdenie sverkhderzhavy. SSSR v pervye poslevoennye gody* (Moscow: ROSSPEN, 2001).

David-Fox, M. *Showcasing the Great Experiment: Cultural Diplomacy and Western Visitors to the Soviet Union, 1921–1941* (New York: Oxford University Press, 2012).

Davies, R.W., M. Harrison, O.V. Khlevniuk and S.G. Wheatcroft. *The Industrialisation of Soviet Russia*, vol. 7, *The Soviet Economy and the Approach of War, 1937–1939* (London: Palgrave Macmillan, 2018).

Davies, R.W., O.V. Khlevniuk and S.G. Wheatcroft. *The Years of Progress: The Soviet Economy, 1934–1936* (New York: Palgrave Macmillan, 2014).

Davies, S. *Popular Opinion in Stalin's Russia: Terror, Propaganda, and Dissent, 1934–1941* (Cambridge: Cambridge University Press, 1997).

Davies, S. and J.R. Harris (eds). *Stalin: A New History* (Cambridge: Cambridge University Press, 2005).

Day, R.B. *Cold War Capitalism: The View from Moscow, 1945–1975* (London: Routledge, 2016).

Dean, M. *Collaboration in the Holocaust: Crimes of the Local Police in Belorussia and Ukraine, 1941–44* (New York: Palgrave Macmillan, 2000).

Dennett, R. and J.E. Johnson (eds). *Negotiating with the Russians* (Boston, MA: World Peace Foundation, 1951).

Deutscher, I. *Stalin: A Political Biography* (New York: Oxford University Press, 1949).

— *The Prophet Unarmed: Trotsky, 1921–1929* (Oxford: Oxford University Press, 1959).

— *The Prophet Outcast: Trotsky, 1929–1940* (Oxford: Oxford University Press, 1963).

Dimitrov, G. *The Diary of Georgi Dimitrov, 1933–1949*, ed. I. Banac and trans. J.T. Hedges, T.D. Sergay and I. Faion (New Haven, CT: Yale University Press, 2003).

Djilas, A. *The Contested Country: Yugoslav Unity and Communist Revolution, 1919–1953* (Cambridge, MA: Harvard University Press, 1991).

Djilas, M. *Conversations with Stalin* (New York: Harcourt, Brace and World, 1962).

Dullin, S. *Men of Influence: Stalin's Diplomats in Europe, 1930–1939* (Edinburgh: Edinburgh University Press, 2008).

Dunham, V.S. *In Stalin's Time: Middle-Class Values in Soviet Fiction* (Cambridge: Cambridge University Press, 1976).

Dunmore, T. *The Stalinist Command Economy: The Soviet State Apparatus and Economic Policy, 1945–1953* (London: Macmillan, 1980).

Dunstan, J. *Soviet Schooling in the Second World War* (Basingstoke: Macmillan and Centre for Russian and East European Studies, University of Birmingham, 1997).

Dyker, D.A. *The Future of the Soviet Economic Planning System* (Armonk, NY: M.E. Sharpe, 1985).

Edele, M. *Stalinism at War: The Soviet Union in World War II* (London: Bloomsbury Academic, 2021).

Erenburg, I. *The War: 1941–1945*, trans. T. Shebunina in collaboration with Y. Knapp (Cleveland, OH: World Publishing Co., 1964).

Erenburg, I. and K. Simonov. *In One Newspaper: A Chronicle of Unforgettable Years*, trans. A. Kagan (New York: Sphinx Press, 1985).

Erickson, J. *The Soviet High Command: A Military-Political History, 1918–1941* (London: Macmillan, 1984), reprint of the 1962 original.

— *The Road to Stalingrad* (New York: Harper and Row, 1975).

— *The Road to Berlin* (New Haven, CT: Yale University Press, 1999).

Ermolaev, H. *Mikhail Sholokhov and His Art* (Princeton, NJ: Princeton University Press, 1982).

Esakov, V.D. (comp.). *Akademiia nauk v resheniiakh Politbiuro TsKRKP(b)–VKP(b), 1922–1952* (Moscow: ROSSPEN, 2000).

Estorick, E. *Stafford Cripps* (London: Heinemann, 1949).

Ewing, E.T. *Separate Schools: Gender, Policy and Practice in Postwar Soviet Education* (DeKalb, IL: Northern Illinois University Press, 2010).

Figes, O. *The Whisperers: Private Life in Stalin's Russia* (London: Allen Lane, 2007).

Fitzpatrick, S. *The Commissariat of Enlightenment: Soviet Organization of Education and the Arts under Lunacharsky* (Cambridge: Cambridge University Press, 1970).

— *The Cultural Front: Power and Culture in Revolutionary Russia* (Ithaca, NY: Cornell University Press, 1992).

— *Everyday Stalinism: Ordinary Life in Extraordinary Times – Soviet Russia in the 1930s* (Oxford: Oxford University Press, 1999).

— *On Stalin's Team: The Years of Living Dangerously in Soviet Politics* (Princeton, NJ: Princeton University Press, 2017).

Fitzpatrick, S. and Y. Slezkine (eds). *In the Shadow of Revolution: Life Stories of Russian Women from 1917 to the Second World War* (Princeton, NJ: Princeton University Press, 2000).

Frieser, K.-H. *Blitzkreig-Legende. Der Westfeldzug, 1940* (Munich: R. Oldenbourg, 1995).

Fuller, W.C. *Civil-Military Conflict in Imperial Russia, 1881–1914* (Princeton, NJ: Princeton University Press, 1985).

Fürst, J. *Stalin's Last Generation: Soviet Post-War Youth and the Emergence of Mature Socialism* (London: Oxford University Press, 2010)

Ganson, N. *The Soviet Famine of 1946–47 in Global and Historical Perspective* (New York: Palgrave Macmillan, 1999).

Garthoff, R.L. *How Russia Makes War: Soviet Military Doctrine* (London: Allen and Unwin, 1954).

Getty, J.A. *The Origins of the Great Purges: The Soviet Communist Party Reconsidered, 1933–1938* (New York: Cambridge University Press, 1985).

Getty, J.A. and R.T. Manning (eds). *Stalinist Terror: New Perspectives* (Cambridge: Cambridge University Press, 1993).

Getty, J.A. and O.V. Naumov. *The Road to Terror: Stalin and the Self-Destruction of the Bolsheviks, 1932–1939*, updated and abridged edn (New Haven, CT: Yale University Press, 2010).

Gillan, D.G. and R.H. Myers (eds). *Last Chance in Manchuria: The Diary of Chang Kia-ngau* (Palo Alto, CA: Stanford University Press, 1989).

Glantz, D.M. *Stumbling Colossus: The Red Army on the Eve of World War* (Lawrence, KS: University Press of Kansas, 1998).

— *Before Stalingrad: Barbarossa – Hitler's Invasion of Russia 1941* (Stroud: Tempus, 2003).

Glantz, D.M. and J.M. House. *The Battle of Kursk* (Lawrence, KS: University Press of Kansas, 1999).

Glushko, V.P. *Rocket Engines GDL-OKB* (Moscow: Novosti, 1975).

— *Razvitie raketostroeniia i kosmonavtiki v SSSR* (Moscow: Nauka, 1987).

Goldman, W.Z. *Terror and Democracy in the Age of Stalin: The Social Dynamics of Repression* (New York: Cambridge University Press, 2007).

Gorkov, Iu.A. *Kreml'. Stavka. Genshtab* (Tver': RIF LTD, 1995).

Gorlizki, Y. and O.V. Khlevniuk. *Cold Peace: Stalin and the Soviet Ruling Circle, 1945–1953* (Oxford: Oxford University Press, 2004).

Gorodetsky, G. *Mif 'Ledokhoda'. Nakanune voiny* (Moscow: Progress-Akademiia, 1995).

— *Grand Illusion: Stalin and the German Invasion of Russia* (New Haven, CT: Yale University Press, 2016).

Gorodetsky, G. (ed.). *The Maisky Diaries: The Wartime Revelations of Stalin's Ambassador in London* (New Haven, CT: Yale University Press, 2016).

Gott, V.S. (ed.). *Filosovskie voprosy sovremennoi fiziki* (Moscow: Vysshaia shkola, 1988).

Graham, L.R. *Science in Russia and the Soviet Union. A Short History* (Cambridge: Cambridge University Press, 1993).

Graziosi, A. *The Great Soviet Peasant War: Bolsheviks and Peasants, 1918–1933* (Cambridge, MA: Harvard University Press, 1996).

Grechko, A.A. et al. (eds). *Istoriia Vtoroi mirovoi voiny 1939–1945*, 12 vols, reprint (Moscow: Voenizdat, 1982).

Grekov, B.D. et al. (eds). *Protiv istoricheskoi kontseptsii M.N. Pokrovskogo. Sbornik statei*, 2 vols (Moscow: Akademiia nauk, 1939–40).

Grenkevich, L.D. *The Soviet Partisan Movement, 1941–1944: A Critical Historiographical Analysis*, ed. D. Glantz (London: Frank Cass, 1999).

Grishchenko, P.D. and G.A. Gurin (eds). *Bor'ba za Sovetskuiu pribaltiku v Velikoi Otechestvennoi voine, 1941–1945*, 2 vols (Riga: Liesma, 1966).

Gromyko, A.A. et al. (eds.). *Diplomaticheskii slovar'*, 3 vols (Moscow: Gospolitizdat, 1960–64).

Grossman, V. *A Writer at War: A Soviet Journalist with the Red Army, 1941–1945*, ed. and trans. A. Beevor and L. Vinogradova (London: Pimlico, 2005).

Hagenloh, P. *Stalin's Police: Public Order and Mass Repression in the USSR, 1926–1941* (Washington, DC and Baltimore, MD: Woodrow Wilson Center Press and Johns Hopkins University Press, 2009).

Hahn, W.G. *Postwar Soviet Politics* (Ithaca, NY: Cornell University Press, 1982).

Harrison, M. *Soviet Planning in Peace and War, 1938–1945* (Cambridge: Cambridge University Press, 1985).

— *Accounting for War: Soviet Production, Employment and the Defence Burden, 1940–1945* (New York: Cambridge University Press, 1996).

Haslam, J. *The Soviet Union and the Struggle for Collective Security in Europe, 1933–1939* (London: St Martin's Press, 1984).

Hirsch, F. *Empire of Nations: Ethnographic Knowledge and the Making of the Soviet Union* (Ithaca, NY: Cornell University Press, 2005).

Holloway, D. *Stalin and the Bomb: The Soviet Union and Atomic Energy, 1939–1956* (New Haven, CT: Yale University Press, 1995).

Holquist, P. *Making War, Forging Revolution: Russia's Continuum of Crisis, 1914–1921* (Cambridge, MA: Harvard University Press, 2002).

Hughes, M. *Inside the Enigma: British Officials in Russia, 1900–1939* (London: Hambledon Press, 1997).

Humbert-Droz, J. *La Crise de croissance de l'Internationale communiste* (Milan: Instituo Giangiacomo Feltrinelli, 1968).

Iaroslavsky, E.I. *Chego trebuet partiia ot kommunistov v dni Otechestvennoi voiny* (Leningrad: Partizdat, 1945).

Iatmanov, N.A. (comp.). *Pamiatniki pobedy sovetskogo naroda v Velikoi Otechestvennoi voine v Respublike Khakasiia* (Abakan: Brigantina, 2015).

Institut marksizma-leninizma. *Velikaia Otechestvennaia voina Sovetskogo Soiuza, 1941–1945. Kratkaia istoriia* (Moscow: Voenizdat, 1965).

Institut russkoi literatury (Pushkinskii dom). *Ocherki russkogo narodnopoeticheskogo tvorchestva sovetskoi epokhi* (Moscow: Akademiia nauk, 1952).

Ionescu, G. *Communism in Romania, 1944–1962* (Oxford: Oxford University Press, 1964).

Iskenderov, M.S. *Ocherki istorii Kommunisticheskoi partii Azerbaidhzana* (Baku: Azerbaidzhanskoe gosudarstvennoe izd., 1962).

Iusupov, E.Iu. et al. (eds). *Ocherki istorii Kommunisticheskoi partii Uzbekistana* (Tashkent: Izd. Uzbekistan, 1964).

Ivanov, V.M. *Marshal M.N. Tukhachevsky* (Moscow: Voenizdat, 1990).

Jansen, M. and N.V. Petrov. *Stalin's Loyal Executioner: People's Commissar Nikolai Ezhov, 1895–1940* (Stanford, CA: Hoover Institution Press, 2002).

Jensen, K.M. (ed.). *Origins of the Cold War: The Novikov, Kennan and Roberts 'Long Telegrams' of 1946* (Washington, DC: US Institute of Peace, 1991).

Joravsky, D. *The Lysenko Affair* (Cambridge, MA: Harvard University Press, 1970).

Judt, T. (ed.). *Resistance and Revolution in Mediterranean Europe, 1939–1948* (London: Routledge, 1989).

Kaftanov, S. *Sovetskaia intelligentsia v Velikoi Otechestvennoi voine* (Moscow: Ogiz, 1945).

Kalkandjieva, D. *The Russian Orthodox Church, 1917–1948: From Decline to Resurrection* (Budapest: Central European University Press, 2015).

Kalmykov, B.E. *Stat'i i rechi* (Nal'chik: Kabardino-Balkarskoe khizhnoe idz., 1961).

Kazakbaev, A.K. *Ocherki istorii Kommunisticheskoi partii Kirgizii* (Frunze: Izd. Kyrgyzstan, 1966).

Kenez, P. *The Birth of the Propaganda State: Soviet Methods of Mass Mobilization 1917–1929* (Cambridge: Cambridge University Press, 1985).

— *Cinema and Soviet Society, 1917–53* (London: I.B. Tauris, 2001).

Kepley, V. *In the Service of the State: The Cinema of Alexander Dovzhenko* (Madison, WI: University of Wisconsin Press, 1986).

Khlevniuk, O.V. *Stalin, NKVD i Sovetskoe obshchestvo* (Moscow: Respublika, 1992).

King, C. *The Moldovans: Romania, Russia, and the Politics of Culture* (Stanford, CA: Hoover Institution Press, 1999).

Kirsanov, N.A. *Partiinye mobilizatsii na front v gody Velikoi Otechestvennoi voiny* (Moscow: Izd. Moskovskogo universiteta, 1972).

Knight, A. *Beria: Stalin's First Lieutenant* (Princeton, NJ: Princeton University Press, 1993).

Kohn, H. *Pan-Slavism: Its History and Ideology* (Notre Dame, IL: Notre Dame University Press, 1953).

Kokoshin, A.A. *Armiia i politika. Sovetskaia voenno-politicheskaia i voenno-strategicheskaia mysl', 1918–1991 gody* (Moscow: Mezhdunarodnye otnosheniia, 1995).

Kosvena, M.O. and B.A. Gardanov. *Narody Kavkaza*, 2 vols (Moscow: Institut etnografii imeni Miklukhno-Makala, 1960–62).

Kotkin, S. *Magnetic Mountain: Stalinism as a Civilization* (Berkeley, CA: University of California Press, 1997).

— *Stalin: Paradoxes of Power, 1878–1928* (New York: Penguin, 2016).

Kovrig, B. *Communism in Hungary: From Kun to Kádár* (Stanford, CA: Hoover Institution Press, 1979).

Krementsov, N. *Stalinist Science* (Princeton, NJ: Princeton University Press, 1997).

Kriukovskikh, A.P. *Vo imia pobedy. Ideologicheskaia rabota Leningradskoi partinoi organizatsii v gody Velikoi Otechesvtennoi voiny* (Leningrad: Lenizdat, 1988).

Kumanev, G.A. (ed.). *Tragicheskie sud'by. Repressirovannye uchenye Akademii nauk SSSR. Sbornik statei* (Moscow: Nauka, 1995).

Kuromiya, H. *Freedom and Terror in the Donbas: A Ukrainian-Russian Borderland, 1870s–1990s* (New York: Cambridge University Press, 1998).

Lazitch, B. *Les Partis communistes d'Europe, 1917–1955* (Paris: Îles d'or, 1956).

Lebedeva, N.S. and M.M. Narinsky (eds). *Komintern i Vtoraia mirovaia voina*, pt 1, *Do 22 iiunia 1941 g.* (Moscow: Pamiatniki istoricheskoi mysli, 1994).

Lecœur, A. *Le Parti communiste français et la résistance, août 1939–juin 1941* (Paris: Plon, 1968).

Leibzon, B.M. and K.K. Shirinia. *Povorot v politike Kominterna. K 30-letiiu VII Kongressa* (Moscow: Mysl', 1965).

Lenoe, M.E. *The Kirov Murder and Soviet History* (New Haven, CT: Yale University Press, 2010).

Lewin, M. *Political Undercurrents in Soviet Economic Debates: From Bukharin to the Modern Reformers* (Princeton, NJ: Princeton University Press, 1974).

— *The Making of the Soviet System: Essays in the Social History of Interwar Russia* (New York: Pantheon, 1985).

— *Russia/USSR/Russia: The Drift and Drive of a Superstate* (New York: New Press, 1995).

Lih, L.T., O.V. Naumov and O.V. Khlevniuk (eds). *Stalin's Letters to Molotov, 1925–1936* (New Haven, CT: Yale University Press, 1995).

Lohr, E. *Nationalizing the Russian Empire: The Campaign against Enemy Aliens during World War I* (Cambridge, MA: Harvard University Press, 2003).

Lota, V. *Sektretnyi front general'nogo shtaba* (Moscow: Molodaia gvardiia, 2005).

Malysheva, E.M. *Ispytanie. Sotsium vlast'. Problem vzaimodeistviia v gody Velikoi Otechestvennoi voiny* (Maikop: Adygeia, 2000).

Markwick, R.D. and E. Charon Cardona. *Soviet Women on the Frontline in the Second World War* (Basingstoke: Palgrave Macmillan, 2012).

Martel, L.C. *Lend-Lease, Loans, and the Coming of the Cold War: A Study of the Implementation of Foreign Policy* (Boulder, CO: Westview Press, 1979).

Martin, A.M. *Romantics, Reformers and Reactionaries: Russian Conservative Thought and Politics in the Reign of Alexander I* (DeKalb, IL: Northern Illinois University Press, 1997).

Martin, T. *The Affirmative Action Empire: Nations and Nationalism in the Soviet Union, 1923–1939* (Ithaca, NY: Cornell University Press, 2001).

Maslov, A.A. *Captured Soviet Generals: The Fate of Soviet Generals Captured by the Germans, 1941–1945*, (ed. and trans.) D.M. Glantz and H.S. Orenstein (London: Frank Cass, 2001).

McCagg, W.O. *Stalin Embattled, 1943–1948* (Detroit, MI: Wayne State University Press, 1978).

McDermott, K. and J. Agnew. *The Comintern: A History of International Communism from Lenin to Stalin* (London: Macmillan, 1995)

McNeal, R.H. (ed.). *I.V. Stalin, Works*, 3 vols (Stanford, CA: Hoover Institution Press, 1967).

Medvedev, R.A. *Let History Judge: The Origins and Consequences of Stalinism* (New York: Knopf, 1971).

Meretskov, K.A. *Na sluzhbe narodu*, 5th rev. edn (Moscow: Veche, 1988).

Mikoian, A.I. *Tak bylo. Razmyshleniia o minuvshem* (Moscow: Vagrius, 1999).

Miller, F.J. *Folklore for Stalin: Russian Folklore and Pseudo-folklore of the Stalin Era* (Armonk, NY: M.E. Sharpe, 1990).

Mininberg, L.L. *Sovetskie evrei v nauke i promyshlennosti SSSR v period Vtoroi mirovoi voiny, 1941–1945 gg. Ocherki* (Moscow: ITS-Garant, 1996).

Mirsky, M. *Istseliaiushii skal'pel'. Akademik N.N. Burdenko* (Moscow: Znanie, 1983).

Mishke, V. *Ocherki istorii Kommunisticheskoi partii Latvii*, 2 vols (Riga: Latyshskoe gosudarst-vennoe izd., 1966).

Mitrofanova, A.V. et al. (eds). *Rabochii klass SSSR nakanune i v gody Velikoi Otechestvennoi voiny, 1938–1945 gg.*, 3 vols (Moscow: Nauka, 1984).

Morrison, S. *The People's Artist: Prokofiev's Soviet Years* (Oxford: Oxford University Press, 2009).

Mosely, P.E. *Some Soviet Techniques of Negotiation* (New York: Columbia University Press, 1960) in R. Dennett and J.E. Johnson (eds.), *Negotiating with the Russians* (Boston, MA: World Peace Foundation, 1951).

Moskoff, W. *The Bread of Affliction: The Food Supply in the USSR during World War II* (New York: Cambridge University Press, 1990).

Naimark, N.M. *The Russians in Germany: A History of the Soviet Zone of Occupation* (Cambridge, MA: Harvard University Press, 1995).

Nazarenko, I.D. (ed.). *Ocherki po istorii Kommunisticheskoi partii Ukrainy*, 3rd edn (Kyiv: Institut istorii partii TSK KP Ukrainy, 1972).

Nekrich, A.M. *1941. 22 iuniia*, 2nd edn (Moscow: Pamiatniki istoricheskoi mysli, 1995).

Nove, A. *An Economic History of the USSR* (London: Penguin, 1969).

Odom, W.E. *Soviet Volunteers: Modernization and Bureaucracy in a Public Mass Organization* (Princeton, NJ: Princeton University Press, 1973).

Oushakine, S.A. *The Patriotism of Despair: Nation, War, and Loss in Russia* (Ithaca, NY: Cornell University Press, 2009).

Ozerov, G.A. *Tupolevskaia sharaga*, 2nd edn (Frankfurt am Main: Possev, 1973).

Pankseev, A. and A. Liban, *Ocherki istorii Kommunisticheskoi partii Estonii*, 3 vols (Tallin: Estonskoe gos. izd-stvo, 1961–1970).

Parrish, M. *The Lesser Terror: Soviet State Security, 1939–1953* (Westport, CT: Praeger, 1996).

Payne, M.J. *Stalin's Railroad: Turksib and the Building of Socialism* (Pittsburgh, PA: University of Pittsburgh Press, 2001).

Perrie, M. *The Cult of Ivan the Terrible in Stalin's Russia* (London: Palgrave Macmillan, 2001).

Peterburgskoe chtenie 98–99. Materialy Entsiklopedicheskoi bibliotek 'Sankt Petersburg-2003' (Saint Petersburg: Peterburgskii institut pechati, 1999).

Petranović, B. *Srbija u drugom svetskom ratu, 1939–1945* (Belgrade: Vojnoizdavački i novinski centar, 1992).

Pikhoia, R.G. *Sovetskii Soiuz. Istoriia vlasti, 1945–1991* (Moscow: RAGS, 1998).

Plamper, J. *The Stalin Cult: A Study in the Alchemy of Power* (New Haven, CT: Yale University Press, 2012).

Pleshakov, C. *Stalin's Folly. The Tragic First Ten Days of World War II on the Eastern Front* (Boston, MA: Houghton Mifflin, 2005).

Pobedonostsev, Iu.A. and K.M. Kuznetsov. *Pervye starty* (Moscow: DOSAAF, 1972).

Polian, P. *Ne po svoei vole . . . Istoriia i geografiia prinuditel'nykh migratsii v SSSR* (Moscow: Memorial, 2001).

Polyudova, E. *Soviet War Songs in the Context of Russian Culture* (Cambridge: Cambridge Scholars Publishing, 2016).

Popov, V.P. (ed.). *Krestianstvo i gosudarstvo (1945–1953)* (Paris: YMCA Press, 1992).

Porter, J.N. (ed.). *Jewish Partisans of the Soviet Union during World War II* (Brookline, MA: Cherry Orchard Books, 2021).

Pospelov, P.N. et al. (eds). *Istoriia Velikoi Otechestvennoi voiny Sovetskogo Soiuza 1941–1945 (IVOV)*, 6 vols (Moscow: Institut marksizma-leninizma pri TsK KPSS, 1960–65).

Pospielovsky, D. *The Russian Church under the Soviet Regime, 1917–1982* (Crestwood, NY: St Vladimir's Seminary Press, 1984).

Priestland, D. *Stalinism and the Politics of Mobilization: Ideas, Power and Terror in Interwar Russia* (Oxford: Oxford University Press, 2007).

Radkey, O.H. *The Agrarian Foes of Bolshevism: Promise and Default of the Russian Socialist Revolutionaries, February to October 1917* (New York: Columbia University Press, 1958).

Reavey, G. *Soviet Literature Today* (London: L. Drummond, 1946).

Redlich, S. *Propaganda and Nationalism in Wartime Russia: The Jewish Anti-Fascist Committee in the USSR, 1941–1948* (Boulder, CO: East European Quarterly, 1982).

— *War, Holocaust and Stalinism: A Documented History of the Jewish Anti-Fascist Committee in the USSR* (London: Routledge, 2016).

Reese, R.R. *The Soviet Military Experience* (London: Routledge, 2000).

— *Red Commanders. A Social History of the Soviet Army Officer Corps, 1918–1991* (Lawrence KS: University Press of Kansas, 2005).

Rein, L. *The Kings and the Pawns: Collaboration in Byelorussia during World War II* (New York and Oxford: Berghahn Books, 2011).

Rhodes, R. *Dark Sun: The Making of the Hydrogen Bomb* (New York: Simon and Schuster, 2005).

Riabev, L.D. (ed.). *Atomnyi proekt SSSR. Dokumenty i materialy*, 10 vols (Moscow: Izd. Firma fiziko-matematicheskaia literatura RAN, 1998).

Riasanovsky, N.V. *The Image of Peter the Great in Russian History and Thought* (New York: Oxford University Press, 1985).

Rieber, A.J. *Stalin and the French Communist Party, 1941–1947* (New York: Columbia University Press, 1962).

— *Stalin and the Struggle for Supremacy in Eurasia* (Cambridge: Cambridge University Press, 2015).

— *The Imperial Russian Project: Autocratic Politics, Economic Development and Social Fragmentation* (Toronto: University of Toronto Press, 2017).

Rigby, T.H. *Communist Party Membership in the USSR, 1917–1967* (Princeton, NJ: Princeton University Press, 1968).

Rittersporn, G.T. *Stalinist Simplifications and Soviet Complications: Social Tensions and Political Conflicts in the USSR, 1933–1953* (Chur and New York: Harwood Academic Publishers, 1991).

Roberts, G. *Stalin's Wars: From World War to Cold War, 1939–1953* (New Haven, CT: Yale University Press, 2006).

— *Molotov: Stalin's Cold Warrior* (Washington, DC: Potomac Books, 2012).

—*Stalin's Library: A Dictator and His Books* (New Haven, CT, and London: Yale University Press, 2022).

Romanov, A.P. *Raketam pokoriaetsia prostranstvo* (Moscow: Politizdat, 1976).

Rosenfeldt, N.E. *Stalin's Secret Chancellery and the Comintern: Evidence about the Organizational Patterns* (Copenhagen: C.A. Reitzels, 1991).

Rubenstein, J. *Tangled Loyalties: The Life and Times of Ilya Ehrenburg* (Tuscaloosa, AL: University of Alabama Press, 1999).

Rubenstein, J. and V.P. Naumov (eds). *Stalin's Secret Pogrom: The Postwar Inquisition of the Jewish Anti-Fascist Committee*, trans. L.E. Wolfson (New Haven, CT: Yale University Press, 2001).

Seniavskaia, E.S. *Frontovoe pokolenie. Istoriko-psikhologicheskie issledovanie* (Moscow: Institut rossiiskoi istorii RAN, 1995).

Service, R. *Stalin: A Biography* (London: Macmillan, 2004).

Shakhurin, A.I. *Kryl'ia pobedy*, 3rd edn (Moscow: Politizdat, 1990).

Shaposhnikov, B.M. *Na Visle. K istorii kampanii 1920 goda* (Moscow: Voennyi vestnik, 1928).

Shaw, R.P. and Y. Wong. *Genetic Seeds of Warfare: Evaluating Nationalism and Patriotism* (Boston, MA: Unwin Hyman, 1989).

Sheinis, Z. *Maksim Maksimovich Litvinov. Revoliutsioner, diplomat, chelovek* (Moscow: Politizdat, 1989).

Shepilov, D.T. *I primknuvshii k nim Shepilov. Pravda o cheloveke, uchenom, voine, politike*, ed. T. Tolchanova and M. Lozhnikov (Moscow: Zvonnitsa-Mg, 1998).

Shil'der, N.K. *Imperator Aleksandr Pervyi*, 3 vols (Saint Petersburg: Surovin, 1904).

Shinkarchuk, S.A. *Obshchestvennoe mnenie v Sovetskoi Rossii v 30-e gody. Po materialam Severozapada* (Saint Petersburg: Sankt-Peterburgskogo universiteta ekonomiki i finansova, 1995).

Shkarovsky, M.V. *Tserkov' zovet k zashchite rodiny: Religioznaia zhizn' Leningrada i Severo-Zapada v gody Velikoi Otechestvennoi voiny* (Saint Petersburg: Satis derzhava, 2005).

Shliapin, I.M., M.A. Shvarev and I.Ia. Fomichenko. *Kommunisticheskaia partiia v period Velikoi Otechestvenoi voiny* (Moscow: Voenizdat, 1958).

Sholokhov, M., B. Gorbatov, W. Wassilewska, K. Simonov and F. Panferov. *Soviet War Stories* (London: Hutchinson, n.d. [1944?]).

Shtemenko, S.M. *The Soviet General Staff at War, 1941–1945* (Moscow: Progress Publishers, 1985).

Shukman, H. (ed.). *Stalin and His Generals* (London: Phoenix Press, 1997).

Siegelbaum, L.H. *Stakhanovism and the Politics of Productivity in the USSR, 1935–1941* (Cambridge: Cambridge University Press, 1988).

Simon, G. *Nationalism and Policy toward the Nationalities in the Soviet Union* (Boulder, CO: Westview Press, 1991).

Slepyan, K. *Stalin's Guerrillas: Soviet Partisans in World War II* (Lawrence, KS: University Press of Kansas, 2006).

Slonimsky, N. *Music since 1900* (New York: Norton, 1971).

Snyder, T. *Sketches from a Secret War: A Polish Artist's Mission to Liberate Soviet Ukraine* (New Haven, CT: Yale University Press, 2005).

Soifer, V. *Vlast' i nauka. Istoriia razgroma genetiki v SSSR* (Saint Petersburg: Ermitazh, 1989).

Sokolov, B.V. *Neizvestnyi Zhukov. Portret bez retusha v zerkale epokhi* (Moscow: Rodiolaplius, 2000).

Sovetskaia istoricheskaia entsiklopediia, ed. E.M. Zhukov, 16 vols (Moscow: Sovetskaia entsiklopediia, 1969–76).

Spriano, P. *Stalin and the European Communists* (London: Verso, 1985).

Statiev, A. *The Soviet Counterinsurgency in the Western Borderlands* (Cambridge: Cambridge University Press, 2010).

Stoecker, S.W. *Forging Stalin's Army: Marshal Tukhachevsky and the Politics of Military Innovation* (Boulder, CO: Westview Press, 1998).

Straus, K.M. *Factory and Community in Stalin's Russia: The Making of an Industrial Working Class* (Pittsburgh, PA: University of Pittsburgh Press, 1997).

Streim, A. *Die Behandlung sowjetischer Kriegsgefangener im 'Fall Barbarossa'* (Heidelberg: C.F. Mueller, 1981).

Streit, C. *Keine Kameraden. Die Wehrmacht und die sowjetischen Kriegsgefangenen, 1941–1945* (Stuttgart: Deutsche Verlags-Anstalt, 1978).

Sullivant, R.S. *Soviet Politics and the Ukraine, 1917–1957* (New York: Columbia University Press, 1962).

Suny, R.G. *The Making of the Georgian Nation* (Bloomington, IN: Indiana University Press, 1994).

— *Stalin: Passage to Revolution* (Princeton, NJ: Princeton University Press, 2020).

Suvorov, V. (Rezun). *Icebreaker: Who Started the Second World War?* (London: Hamish Hamilton, 1990).

Tashiliev, S. (ed.) *Ocherki istorii Kommunisticheskoi partii Turkmenistana* (Ashkabad: Turkmenistanskoe gosudarstvennoe izd., 1965).

Ternovsky, P. *Oni srazhalis' za nas* (Krasnodar: Vol'naia N.N., 2015).

Terpilovsky, M.V. *Finansovaia sluzhba Vooruzhennykh sil SSSR v period Voiny. Organizatsia finansirovaniia Sovetskoi armii i Voenno-morskogo flota vo vremia Velikoi Otechestvennoi voiny 1941–1945 gg.* (Moscow: Voenizdat, 1967).

Tillett, L.R. *The Great Friendship: Soviet Historians on the Non-Russian Nationalities* (Chapel Hill, NC: North Carolina University Press, 1969).

Titkov, E.P. *Dukhovnyi mech Velikoi pobedy. Russkaia pravoslavnaia tserkov' v gody Velikoi Otechestvennoi voiny* (Arzamas: AGPI, 2010).

Tiushkevich, S.A. *Sovetskie Vooruzhennye sily. Istoriia stroitel'stva* (Moscow: Voenizdat, 1978).

Tomasevich, J. *The Chetniks: War and Revolution in Yugoslavia, 1941–1945* (Palo Alto, CA: Stanford University Press, 1975).

Tomoff, K. *Creative Union: The Professional Organization of Soviet Composers, 1939–1953* (Ithaca, NY: Cornell University Press, 2006).

Tooze, A. *The Wages of Destruction: The Making and Breaking of the Nazi Economy* (New York: Viking, 2007).

Totoev, M.S. *Istoriia Severo-Ossetinskoi ASSR* (Ordzhonikidze: Severo-Ossetinskoe khizhnoe izd., 1966).

Trotsky, L. *The Defence of Terrorism and Communism: A Reply to Karl Kautsky* (London: Allen and Unwin, 1935).

Urban, J.B. *Moscow and the Italian Communist Party, from Togliatti to Berlinguer* (Ithaca, NY: Cornell University Press, 1986).

Usol'tseva, N. *Oni dyshali vozdukhom voiny* (Kemerovo: Kuzbassvuzizdat, 2015).

Vakar, N.P. *Belorussia: The Making of a Nation* (Cambridge, MA: Harvard University Press, 1956).

Vaksberg, A.Iu. *Tsaritsa dokazatel'stv. Vyshyinskii i ego zhertvy* (Moscow: AO, 1992).

Vasil'ev, E.V. et al. (eds). *Ocherki istorii Kommunisticheskoi partii Tadzhikistana* (Dushanbe: Institut tarikhi partiia, 1964).

Vasilenko, V.S. and E.D. Orekhova (comps). *Kommunisticheskaia partiia v period Velikoi Otechestvennoi voiny* (Moscow: Gospolitizdat, 1961).

Vinogradov, V.A. et al. (eds). *Sovetskaia ekonomika na kanune i v pervoi period Velikoi Otechestvennoi voiny, 1938–1945 gg.*, 5 vols (Moscow: Nauka, 1978).

Viola, L. *Peasant Rebels under Stalin: Collectivization and the Culture of Peasant Resistance* (New York: Oxford University Press, 1999).

Vlasova, E. *1948 god v sovetskoi muzyki. Dokumentirovannoe issledovanie* (Moscow: Klassika, 2010).

Volkogonov, D.A. *Triumf i tragediia. Politicheskii portret I.V. Stalina, V 2-kh knigakh* (Moscow: Izd-vo APN, 1989).

— *Triumf i tragediia. Politicheskii portret I.V. Stalina*, 4 vols (Moscow: Novosti, 1990).

Volochek, V. *S veroi v liubov' i pobedu* (Tver': Irida-pros, 2015).

Volokitina, T.V. *Moskva i Vostochnaia Evropa. Stanovlenie politicheskikh rezhimov sovetskogo tipa, 1949–1953. Ocherki istorii* (Moscow: ROSSPEN, 2008).

Von Geldern, J. and R. Stites (eds). *Mass Culture in Soviet Russia: Tales, Poems, Songs, Movies, Plays and Folklore, 1917–1953* (Bloomington, IN: Indiana University Press, 1995).

Von Hagen, M. *Soldiers in the Proletarian Dictatorship: The Red Army and the Soviet Socialist State, 1917–1930* (Ithaca, NY: Cornell University Press, 1990).

— *War in a European Borderland: Occupations and Occupation Plans in Galicia and Ukraine, 1914–1918* (Seattle, WA: University of Washington Press, 2007).

Vorobev, V.M. *Geroi Sovetskogo Soiuza na Tversloi zemle: biograficheskie ocherki*, 5 vols (Tver': Sed'maia bukva, 2015).

Voznesensky, N.A. *Voennaia ekonomika SSSR v period Otechestvennoi voiny* (Moscow: Gospolitizdat, 1948).

Vucinich, A. *Empire of Knowledge: The Academy of Sciences of the USSR (1917–1970)* (Berkeley, CA: University of California Press, 1984).

Weiner, A. *Making Sense of War: The Second World War and the Fate of the Bolshevik Revolution* (Princeton, NJ: Princeton University Press, 2001).

Werth, A. *Russia at War, 1941–1945* (New York: Dutton, 1964).

Wexler, P.N. *Purism and Language: A Study in Modern Ukrainian and Belarus Nationalism (1840–1967)* (Bloomington, IN: Indiana University Press, 1974).

Yergin, D. *Shattered Peace: The Origins of the Cold War and the National Security State* (Boston, MA: Houghton Mifflin, 1977).

Zagladin, N.V. *Istoriia uspekhov i neudach sovetskoi diplomatii. Politologicheskii aspekt* (Moscow: Mezhdunarodnye otnosheniia, 1990).

Zaionchkovsky, P.A. *Samoderzhavie i russkaia armiia na rubezhe XIX–XX stoletii* (Moscow: Mysl', 1973).

Zakharov, M. *General'nyi shtab v predvoennye gody* (Moscow: Voenizdat, 1989).

Zalessky, K.A. *Imperiia Stalina. Biograficheskii entsiklopedicheskii slovar'* (Moscow: Veche, 2000).

Zelnik, R.E. *The Perils of Pankratova: Some Stories from the Annals of Soviet Historiography* (Seattle, WA: University of Washington Press, 2005).

Zhilin, P.A (ed.). *Zarozhdenie i razvitie sovetskoi voennoi istoriografii. 1917–1941* (Moscow: Nauka, 1985).

Ziemke, E.F. and M.E. Bauer III. *Moscow to Stalingrad: Decision in the East* (Washington, DC: Center of Military History, United States Army, 1987).

Zubkova, E. *Obshchestvo i reform, 1945–1964* (Moscow: Rossiia molodaia, 1993).

— *Russia after the War: Hopes, Illusions and Disappointments, 1945–1959* (London: Routledge, 1998).

— *Poslevoennoe sovetskoe obshchestvo. Politika i povslednevnost' 1945–1953* (Moscow: ROSSPEN, 2000).

Zvimach, G. *Latyshskie revoliutstionnye deiateli* (Riga: Latyshskoe gosudarstvennoe izd., 1958).

NEWSPAPERS AND PERIODICALS

Argumenty i fakty
Bol'shevik
Izvestiia
Izvestiia TsK KPSS
Krasnaia zvezda
La Correspondance internationale
Mirovoe khozaistvo i mirovaia politika
Novoe vremiia
Pravda
Voina i rabochii klass
Voprosy istorii KPSS
Zvezda

ARTICLES AND BOOK CHAPTERS

Adamec, J. 'Courts of Honour in the Post-War Soviet Union', *Dvacáté století – The Twentieth Century* 6:1 (2014), pp. 74–84.

Adams, M.B. 'Science, Ideology and Structure: the Kol'tsov Institute, 1900–1970', in L. Lubrano and S.G. Solomon (eds), *The Social Context of Soviet Science* (Boulder, CO: Westview Press, 1980), pp. 173–204.

Aleksandrov, G.F. 'Otechestvennaia voina sovetskogo naroda i zadachi obshchestvennykh nauk', *Vestnik AN SSSR* 5–6 (1942), pp. 22–37.

Anikina, O. 'Aleksei Gvishiani. Ne nado zhalet' Kosygina', *Pravda*, 19 February 2004.

Anishev, D. 'Pol'skii narod na puti k svobode i nezavisimosti', *Svobodnaia mysl'* 5 (2010), pp. 57–70, reprint of *Bol'shevik* 13–14 (July 1944).

Amosova A.A. and D. Brandenberger. 'Noveishie podkhody k interpretatsii "Leningradskogo dela" kontsa 1940-kh nachala 1950-kh godov v Rossiiskikh nauchno-populiarnykh izdaniia', *Noveishaia istoriia Rossii* 18:7 (2017), pp. 94–112.

Atabaki, T. 'Incommodious Hosts, Invidious Guests. The Life and Time of Iranian Revolutionaries in Soviet Union (1921–1929)', in S. Cronin (ed.), *Reformers and Revolutionaries in Modern Iran: New Perspectives on the Iranian Left* (London: RoutledgeCurzon, 2004), pp. 147–64.

Baikov, A.A. 'Zadachi AN SSSR', *Vestnik Akademiia nauk* 1–2 (1944), pp. 24–30.

Balzer, H.D. 'The Engineering Profession', in Balzer (ed.), *Russia's Missing Middle Class: The Professions in Russian History* (Armonk, NY: M.E. Sharpe, 1995), pp 55–88.

Belikov, A.M. 'Transfert de l'industrie soviétique vers l'est (juin 1941–1942)', *Revue de l'histoire de la Deuxième Guerre mondiale* 43 (1961), pp. 35–50.

Bellamy, C. 'Brute Force and Genius: Stalin as War Leader', in J. Ryan and S. Grant (eds), *Revisioning Stalin and Stalinism: Contradictions and Complexities* (London: Bloomsbury Academic, 2021), chap. 4.

Berry, M.J. 'Science, Technology and Innovation', in M. McCauley (ed.), *Khrushchev and Khrushchevism* (Bloomington, IL: Indiana University Press, 1987), pp. 71–94.

Biriuzov, S. 'Predislovie', in M.N. Tukhachevsky, *Izbrannye proizvedeniia* (Moscow: Voenizdat 1964).

Brandenberger, D.L. 'Terribly Romantic, Terribly Progressive, or Terribly Tragic: Rehabilitating Ivan IV under I.V. Stalin', *Russian Review* 58:4 (1999), pp. 635–54.

— 'Stalin, the Leningrad Affair, and the Limits of Postwar Russocentrism', *Russian Review* 63:2 (April 2004), pp. 241–55.

— 'Stalin as Symbol: A Case Study of the Personality Cult and Its Construction', in S. Davies and J.R. Harris (eds), *Stalin: A New History* (Cambridge: Cambridge University Press, 2005), pp. 249–270.

— 'The Fate of Interwar Soviet Internationalism: A Case Study of the Editing of Stalin's 1938 *Short Course on the History of the ACP(b)*', *Revolutionary Russia* 29:1 (2016), pp. 1–23.

Brandenberger, D.L. and A.M. Dobrovsky. '"The People Need a Tsar": The Emergence of National Bolshevism as Stalinist Ideology, 1931–1941', *Europe-Asia Studies* 50:5 (July 1998), pp. 873–92.

Brandenberger, D., A. Amosova and N. Pivovarov. 'The Rise and Fall of a Crimean Party Boss: Nikolai Vasil'evich Solov'ev and the Leningrad Affair', *Europe-Asia Studies* 71:6 (July 2019), pp. 951–71.

Brody, R.J. 'Ideology and Political Mobilization: The Soviet Home Front during World War Two', *Carl Beck Papers in Russian and East European Studies* 1,104 (October 1994).

Brooks, J. '*Pravda* Goes to War', in R. Stites (ed.), *Culture and Entertainment in Wartime Russia* (Bloomington, IN: Indiana University Press, 1995), pp. 9–27.

Brüggemann, K. and A. Kasekamp. 'The Politics of History and the "War of Monuments" in Estonia', *Nationalities Papers* 36:3 (2008), pp. 425–48.

Budnitskii, O. 'The Intelligentsia Meets the Enemy: Educated Soviet Officers in Defeated Germany, 1945', trans. S. Rupp, *Kritika* 10:3 (summer 2009), pp. 629–82.

— 'Istoriia voiny s Napoleonom v sovetskoi propagande, 1941–1945', *Rossiiskaia istoriia* 6 (2012), pp. 157–69.

— 'The Great Patriotic War and Soviet Society: Defeatism, 1941–42', *Kritika* 15:4 (autumn 2014), pp. 747–97.

Burds, J. 'The Soviet War against "Fifth Columnists": The Case of Chechnya, 1942–4', *Journal of Contemporary History* 42:2 (April 2007), pp. 267–314.

Castillo, G. 'Peoples at an Exhibition: Soviet Architecture and the National Question', in T. Lahusen and E. Dobrenko (eds), *Socialist Realism without Shores* (Durham, NC: Duke University Press, 1997), pp. 91–119.

Chaqueri, C. 'Sultanzade: The Forgotten Revolutionary Theoretician of Iran – A Biographical Sketch', *Iranian Studies* 17:2/3 (spring–summer 1984), pp. 215–35.

Chase, W.J. 'Microhistory and Mass Repression: Politics, Personalities and Revenge in the Fall of Béla Kun', *Russian Review* 67:3 (2008), pp. 454–83.

Chuvikov, V. 'Uchenie Lenina–Stalina o voinakh spravedlivykh i nespravedlivykh', *Bol'shevik* 7–8 (April 1945), pp. 14–26.

Clark, K. 'Ehrenburg and Grossman: Two Cosmopolitan Jewish Writers Reflect on Nazi Germany at War', *Kritika* 10:3 (summer 2009), pp. 607–28.

— 'Shostakovich's Turn to the String Quartet and the Debates about Socialist Realism in Music', *Slavic Review* 72:3 (autumn 2013), pp. 573–89.

Dale, R. 'Rats and Resentment: The Demobilization of the Red Army in Postwar Leningrad, 1945–50', *Journal of Contemporary History* 45:1 (January 2010), pp. 113–33.

David-Fox, M. 'What is Cultural Revolution?', *Russian Review* 58:2 (April 1999), pp. 181–201.

— 'Multiple Modernities vs Neo-Traditionalism: On Recent Debates in Russian and Soviet History', *Jahrbücher für Geschichte Osteuropas* 54:4 (2006), pp. 535–55.

'Delo o tak nazyvaemoi "anti-sovetskoi trotskistskoi voennoi organizatsii v Krasnoi armii"', *Izvestiia TsK KPSS* 4 (1989), pp. 42–80.

'Deportatsiia Nemtsev (sentiabr' 1941–fevral' 1942 g.)', in *Deportatsiia Narodov SSSR (1930–1950-e gody)* O.I. Milov (comp.) (Moscow: Institut etnologii, 1995).

Di Biagio, A. 'Moscow, the Comintern and the War Scare', in S. Pons and A. Romano (eds), *Russia in the Age of Wars, 1914–1945* (Milan: Feltrinelli, 2000), pp. 83–102.

Dickinson, A. 'Quantifying Religious Oppression: Russian Orthodox Church Closures and Repression of Priests, 1917–1941', *Religion, State and Society* 28:4 (2000), pp. 327–35.

'Dokumenty russkoi istorii', *Istochnik* 2:15 (1995), pp. 99–144; pp. 112–15.

Dyker, D.A. 'Soviet Agriculture since Khrushchev: Decentralisation and Dirigisme', *IDS Bulletin* 13:4 (1982), pp. 29–35.

Edele, M. 'Soviet Veterans as an Entitlement Group, 1945–1955', *Slavic Review* 65:1 (spring 2006), pp. 111–37.

Epoletov, N.I. 'Iz opyta raboty kompartii po razvitiiu partizanskogo dvizheniia (1941–1944)', *Voprosy istorii KPSS* 5 (May 1987), pp. 99–109.

Erickson, J. 'Barbarossa June 1941: Who Attacked Whom?', *History Today* 51:7 (July 2001), pp. 11–17.

Estraikh, G. 'The Life, Death and Afterlife of the Jewish Anti-Fascist Committee', *East European Jewish Affairs* 48:2 (2018), pp. 139–48.

Fairbanks Jr, C.H. 'Clientelism and the Roots of the Post-Soviet Disorder', in R. Suny (ed.), *Transcaucasia, Nationalism and Social Change: Essays in the History of Armenia, Azerbaijan and Georgia*, rev. edn (Ann Arbor, MI: University of Michigan Press, 1996), pp. 341–76.

Filtzer, D. 'Standard of Living versus Quality of Life: Struggling with the Urban Environment in Russia during the Early Years of Post-War Reconstruction', in J. Fürst (ed.), *Late Stalinist Russia: Society between Reconstruction and Reinvention* (London: Routledge, 2006), pp. 81–102.

Firsov, F.I. 'Dimitrov, the Comintern and Stalinist Repression', in B. McLoughlin and K. McDermott (eds), *Stalin's Terror: High Politics and Mass Repression in the Soviet Union* (New York: Palgrave Macmillan, 2003), pp. 56–81.

Firsov, F.I. and I.S. Iazhborovskaia. 'Komintern i Kommunisticheskaia partiia Pol'shi', *Voprosy istorii KPSS* 12 (December 1988), pp. 20–35.

Fisher, E. 'Ot narodnogo fronta k obshchenatsional'nomu frontu', *KI* 8–9 (1942), pp. 26–30.

Fitzpatrick, S. 'Cultural Revolution Revisited', *Russian Review* 58:2 (April 1999), pp. 202–9.

Fletcher, W.C. 'The Soviet Bible Belt', in S.J. Linz (ed.), *The Impact of World War II on the Soviet Union* (Totowa, NJ: Rowman & Allanheld, 1985), pp. 91–106.

Förster, J. 'Das Unternehmen "Barbarossa" als Eroberungs- und Vernichtungs-Krieg', in Horst Boog et al. (eds), *Das deutsche Reich und der Zweite Weltkrieg*, 4 vols (Stuttgart: Deutsche Verlags-Anstalt, 1983), vol. 4, *Der Angriff auf die Sowjetunion*, pp. 413–50.

Friedberg, M. 'Literary Culture: "The New Soviet Man" in the Mirror of Literature', in D.N. Shalin (ed.), *Russian Culture at the Crossroads: Paradoxes of Postcommunist Consciousness* (New York: Routledge, 2018), pp. 239–58.

Gazarian, S. 'Eto ne dolzhno povtoritsa', *Zvezda* 2 (1989).

Gefter, M. 'Stalin umer vchera . . .', in A.A. Protashchik (ed.), *Inogo ne dano* (Moscow: Progress, 1988).

Gerovitch, S. 'Stalin's Rocket Designers' Leap into Space: The Technical Intelligentsia Faces the Thaw', *Osiris* 23:1 (2008), pp. 189–209.

Gordin, M.D. and K. Hall. 'Introduction: Intelligentsia Science inside and outside Russia', *Osiris* 23:1 (2008), pp. 1–19.

Gorelik, G. 'The Top-Secret Life of Lev Landau', *Scientific American* 277:2 (August 1997), pp. 72–7.

Gor'kov, Iu.A. and Iu.N. Semin. 'Konets global'noi lzhi. Operativnye plany zapadnykh pogranichnykh voennykh okrugov 1941 svidetel'svuiut – SSSR ne gotovilsiia k napadeniiu Germaniiu', *VIZh* 2 (March–April 1996), pp. 5–17, and 4 (July–August 1996), pp. 3–17.

Gorodetsky, G. 'Was Stalin Planning to Attack Hitler in June 1941?', *RUSI Journal* 131:2 (1986), pp. 69–72.

Graham, L.R. 'The Formation of Soviet Research Institutions: A Combination of Revolutionary Innovation and International Borrowing', in D.K. Rowney and G.E. Orchard (eds), *Russian and Slavic History* (Columbus, OH: Slavica, 1977), pp. 49–75.

Graziosi, A. 'Collectivisation, révoltes paysannes et politiques gouvernementales à travers les rapports du GPU d'Ukraine de février–mars 1930', *Cahiers du monde russe* 35:3 (1994), pp. 437–72.

Grichenko, T.A. and A.A. Stognii. 'Viktor Mikhailovich Grichenko i ego shkola', *Matematichni mashin i systemu* (2006) 4, pp. 3–14.

Gromov, V.E. et al. (eds). 'Vklad uchenykh v oborone strany (1941–1945 gg.)', in G.D. Komkov et al. (eds), *Akademiia nauk SSSR. Kratkii istoricheskii ocherk* (first edition), 2 vols (Moscow: Nauka, 1974).

Haber, M. 'Socialist Realist Science: Continuity of Knowledge about Rural Life in the Soviet Union, 1943–1958', doctoral thesis, UCLA, 2013.

Harris, J. 'The Origins of the Conflict between Malenkov and Zhdanov: 1939–1941', *Slavic Review* 35:2 (June 1976), pp. 287–303.

Harrison, M. 'N.A. Voznesensky (1 December 1903–30 September 1950): A Soviet Commander of the Economic Front', Warwick Economics Research Paper Series no. 242, University of Warwick, Department of Economics, 1983.

Hedeler, W. 'Ezhov's Scenario for the Great Terror and the Falsified Record of the Third Moscow Show Trial', in B. McLoughlin and K. McDermott (eds), *Stalin's Terror: High Politics and Mass Repression in the Soviet Union* (New York: Palgrave Macmillan, 2003), pp. 34–55.

Hellbeck, J. 'Working, Struggling, Becoming: Stalin-Era Autobiographies and Text', in I. Halfin (ed.), *Language and Revolution: Making Political Identities* (London: Frank Cass, 2002), pp. 135–60.

— '"The Diaries of Fritzes and the Letters of Gretchens": Personal Writings from the German–Soviet War and Their Readers', *Kritika* 10:3 (summer 2009), pp. 571–606.

Holloway, D. 'Stalin and Intelligence: Two Cases' (unpublished essay).

Holquist, P. '"Information Is the Alpha and Omega of Our Work": Bolshevik Surveillance in Its Pan-European Context', *Journal of Modern History* 69:3 (1997), pp. 415–50.

— 'Violent Russia: Deadly Marxism? Russia in the Epoch of Violence, 1905–1921', *Kritika* 4:3 (spring 2003), pp. 627–52.

Hunter, H. 'Successful Spatial Management', in S.J. Linz (ed.), *The Impact of World War II on the Soviet Union* (Totowa, NJ: Rowman & Allanheld, 1985), pp. 47–58.

'Iosifu Vissarionovichu Stalinu', *Vestnik Akademiia nauk* 1–2 (1944), pp. 20–1.

'Istoricheskie korni nemetskogo fashizma. Stat'ia akademika R.Iu. Vippera. Avgust, 1941', *Istoricheskii arkhiv* 4 (2000), pp. 187–204.

'Istoriia Velikoi Otechestvennoi voiny. Delo marshala G.I. Kulika (ianvar'–mart 1942 g.)', *Izvestiia TsK KPSS* 4 (August 1991), pp. 197–210.

Kangaspuro, M. and J. Lassila. 'From the Trauma of Stalinism to the Triumph of Stalingrad: the Toponymic Dispute over Volgograd', in J. Fedor et al. (eds), *War and Memory in Russia, Ukraine and Belarus* (Cham: Palgrave Macmillan, 2017), pp. 141–70.

Kapitsa, P.L., 'Ob organizatsii nauchnoi raboty v Institute fizicheskikh problem', *Vestnik Akademiia nauk* 6 (1943), pp. 75–89.

Kaplan, C. 'The Impact of World War II on the Party', in S.J. Linz (ed.), *The Impact of World War II on the Soviet Union* (Totowa, NJ: Rowman & Allanheld, 1985), pp. 157–88.

Kenez, P. 'Black and White: The War on Film', in R. Stites (ed.), *Culture and Entertainment in Wartime Russia* (Bloomington, IN: Indiana University Press, 1995), pp. 157–75.

Khanin, G.I. 'The 1950s: The Triumph of the Soviet Economy', *Europe-Asia Studies* 55:8 (June 2010), pp. 1,187–211.

Khavin, A.F. 'Razvitie tiazheloi promyshlennosti v tretei piatiletke (1938–iiun' 1941 gg.)', *Istoriia SSSR* 1 (1959), pp. 10–35.

Khlevniuk, O.V. 'The Objectives of the Great Terror, 1937–1938', in J. Cooper, M. Perrie and E.A. Rees (eds), *Soviet History, 1917–53: Essays in Honor of R.W. Davies* (New York: Palgrave Macmillan, 1995), pp. 158–76.

— 'The Reasons for the Great Terror: The Foreign-Political Aspect', in S. Pons and A. Romano (eds), *Russia in the Age of Wars, 1914–1945* (Milan: Feltrinelli, 2000), pp. 159–69.

— 'Stalin and the Generals: Reconstructing Trust during World War II', *Europe-Asia Studies* (October 2021), pp. 1–22.

Khrennikov, T. 'O muzyke i muzykal'noi kritike', *Oktiabr'* 4 (1948).

Khrulev, A.V. 'Stanovlenie strategicheskogo tyla v Velikoi Otechestvennoi voine', *VIZh* 6 (June 1961), pp. 64–86.

Kirilenko, G.V. 'Ekonomicheskoe protivoborstvo storon', in G.N. Sevost'ianov (ed.), *Voina i obshchestvo, 1941–1945*, 2 vols (Moscow: Nauka, 2004), vol. 1, pp. 333–59.

Kirschenbaum, L.A. ' "Our City, Our Hearths, Our Families": Local Loyalties and Private Life in Soviet World War II Propaganda', *Slavic Review* 59:4 (winter 2000), pp. 825–47.

Kirshin, Iu.Ia. 'Kontseptsiia mirovoi sotsialisticheskoi revoliutsii i sovetskaia voennaia doktrina', *Soviet Union/Union Soviétique* 18:1–3 (1991), pp. 80–99.

Kocho-Williams, A. 'The Soviet Diplomatic Corps and Stalin's Purges', *Slavonic and East European Review* 86:1 (2008), pp. 90–110.

Konasov, V.B. and A.V. Tereshchuk. 'Novyi podkhod k uchetu bezvozvratnykh poter' v gody Velikoi Otechestvennoi voiny', *Voprosy istorii* 6 (1990), pp.185–8.

'Korolev, Sergius Pavlovich', *Russkaia Vikipediia*.

Kozlov, B.I. 'Akademiia nauk SSSR v gody voiny. Urok istorii', *Vestnik RAN* 75:5 (2005), pp. 387–92.

Kruglov, A.I. 'O nekotorykh prichinakh bol'shoi poter' Sovetskikh Vooruzhennykh sil v pervom periode Velikoi Otechestvennoi voiny', in *Liudskie poteri SSSR v period Vtoroi mirovoi voiny. Sbornik statei* (Saint Petersburg: Izd-vo Russko-Baltiski informatsionnyi tsentr Blits, 1995), pp. 71–123; pp. 97–9.

Kulish, V.M. 'Sovetskaia istoriografiia Velikoi Otechestvennoi voiny', in Iu.N. Afanasev (ed.), *Sovetskaia istoriografiia* (Moscow: Rossiiskii gosudarstvennyi gumanitarnyi universitet, 1996), pp. 274–311.

Kumanev, G.A. 'Sovetskie zheleznodorozhniki v pervyi period Velikoi Otechestvennoi voiny (1941–1942)', *Istoriia SSSR* 1 (1959), pp. 36–52.

Kumanev, G.A. and L.M. Chuvakov. 'Sovetskii Soiuz i Lend-Liz, 1941–1945', in G.N. Sevost'ianov (ed.), *Voina i obshchestvo, 1941–1945*, 2 vols (Moscow: Nauka, 2004), vol. 1, pp. 60–87.

Kuromiya, H. 'Accounting for the Great Terror', *Jahrbücher für Geschichte Osteuropas* n.s. 53:1 (2005), pp. 86–101.

Kuzmin, N. 'Ob odnoi nevypolnennoi direktiva Glavkoma', *VIZh* (September 1962), pp. 49–56.

Kuznetsov, I.I. 'Stalin's Minister V.S. Abakumov 1908–54', *Journal of Slavic Military Studies* 12:4 (March 1999), pp. 149–65.

Lang, D.M. 'A Century of Russian Impact on Georgia', in W.S. Vucinich (ed.), *Russia and Asia: Essays on the Influence of Russia on the Asian Peoples* (Palo Alto, CA: Stanford University Press, 1972), pp. 219–47.

Lazitch, B. 'Stalin's Massacre of the Foreign Communist Leaders', in M.M. Drachkovitch and B. Lazitch (eds), *The Comintern: Historical Highlights. Essays, Recollections, Documents* (Palo Alto, CA: Stanford University Press, 1966), pp. 45–65.

Leonov, M. 'Lenin o voine i roli moral'nogo faktora v nei', *Agitator i propagandist Krasnoi armii* 6 (March 1945), pp. 19–32.

Leonova, L.S. 'Deiatel'nost' vyshei shkoly i Akademicheskikh uchrezhdenii v gody Velikoi Otechestvennoi voiny', *Novaia i noveishaia istoriia* 6 (November–December 2010), pp. 73–87.

Lewin, M. 'Fin de parti', in Lewin, *Le Siècle soviétique* (Paris: Fayard, 2003), pp. 174–80.

Liebich, A. and O. Myshlovska. 'Bandera: Memorialization and Commemoration', *Nationalities Papers* 42:5 (2014), pp. 750–70.

Livschiz, A. 'Pre-Revolutionary in Form, Soviet in Content? Wartime Educational Reforms and the Post War Quest for Normality', *History of Education* 35:4–5 (July–September, 2006), pp. 541–60.

Lysenko, T.D. 'O nekotorykh osnovnykh zadachakh sel'skokhozaistvennoi nauki', *Vestnik Akademiia nauk* 5–6 (1942), pp. 49–59.

Malysheva, E.M. 'Sovetskaia publitsistika i SMI v gody Velikoi Otechestvennoi voiny. Opyt aktualizatsii', in I.I. Gorlova et al. (eds), *Kulturnoe nasledie severnogo Kavkaza kak resurs mezhnatsional'nogo soglasiia. Sbornik nauchnykh statei* (Moscow-Krasnodar: Institut naslediia and Iuzhnyi filial, 2015).

Mamoulia, G. 'The First Cracks in the Imperial Base of the Post-War USSR: Georgia and the South Caucasus, 1946–1956', 6th Silk Road International Conference: 'Globalization and Security in Black and Caspian Seas Regions' (Tbilisi and Batumi, 27–29 May 2011), pp. 63–72.

Martin, T. 'The Origins of Soviet Ethnic Cleansing', *Journal of Modern History* 70:4 (December 1998), pp. 813–61.

Maslov, A.A. 'Forgiven by Stalin: Soviet Generals Who Returned from German Prisons in 1941–45 and Who Were Rehabilitated', *Journal of Slavic Military Studies* 12:2 (1999), pp. 173–219.

Mastny, V. 'The Cassandra in the Foreign Commissariat: Maxim Litvinov and the Cold War', *Foreign Affairs* 54:2 (1976), pp. 366–76.

'Materialy fevral'sko–martovskogo plenuma TsK VKP(b), 1937 goda', *Voprosy istorii* 11–12 (1995), pp. 3–26.

'Materialy plenuma TsK VKP(b) (1944)', in S.A. Mel'chin et al. (comp.), *Istoricheskii arkhiv* 1 (1992), pp. 61–5.

McLoughlin, B. 'Mass Operations of the NKVD, 1937–8: A Survey', in B. McLoughlin and K. McDermott (eds), *Stalin's Terror: High Politics and Mass Repression in the Soviet Union* (New York: Palgrave Macmillan, 2003), pp. 118–52.

Mel'tiukhov, M.I. 'Spory vokrug 1941 goda. Opyt kriticheskogo osmysleniia odnoi diskussii', *Otechestvennaia istoriia* 3 (1994), pp. 4–22.

Miasnikaia, A. 'Otechestvennaia voina i sovetskaia literatura', *KI* 7 (1942), pp. 68–75.

Miller. A. 'The Romanov Empire and the Russian Nation', in S. Berger and A. Miller (eds), *Nationalizing Empires* (Budapest: Central European University Press, 2015), pp. 309–68.

Mosely, P.E. 'Soviet Policy and Nationality Conflicts in East Central Europe', in Mosely, *The Kremlin and World Politics: Studies in Soviet Policy and Action* (New York: Vintage Books, 1960), pp. 221–46.

'Moskovskie chekhisty v oborone stolitsy, 1941–1944', in Iu.B. Smirnov and V.G. Ushakov (comps), *VIZh* 1 (1991), pp. 10–13.

Mukhin, M.Iu. 'Evoliutsiia sistemy upravleniia sovetskoi oboronnoi promyshlennost'iu v 1921–1941 godakh i smena prioritetov "oboronki"', in G.B. Nabatov et al. (comp.),

Velikaia Otechestvennaia voina. Voprosy istorii. Materialy mezhdunarodnoi nauchno-metodicheskoi konferentsii 18–20 aprelia 2000 g. k 55-letiu pobedy v Velikoi Otechestvennoi voine (Nizhny Novgorod: Nizhegorodskii gos. universitet, 2000).

— 'The Market for Labor in the 1930s: The Aircraft Industry', in M. Harrison (ed.), *Guns and Rubles: The Defense Industry in the Stalinist State* (New Haven, CT: Yale University Press, 2008), pp. 180–209.

'Muzhestvo protiv bezzakoniia. Dokumenty arkhiva Kominterna o bor'be za spasenie kommunistov-internationalistov ot stalinskikh repressii', *Problemy mira i sotsializma* 7 (1989), pp. 89–92.

Nadzhafov, D.G. 'The Beginning of the Cold War between East and West: The Aggravation of Ideological Confrontation', *Cold War History* 4:2 (January 2004), pp. 140–74.

Narinsky, M.M. 'I.V. Stalin i M. Thorez, 1944–1947. Novye materiali', *Novaia i noveishaia istoriia* 1 (1996), pp. 19–28.

Naveh, S. 'Mikhail Nikolayevich Tukhachevsky', in H. Shukman (ed.), *Stalin and His Generals* (London: Phoenix Press, 1997), pp. 255–74.

Nikonorova, T.N. 'Konstruiruia roskosh'. Bytovoe prostranstvo Sovetskoi nomenklatury, 1940–1952 gody', *Soviet and Post-Soviet Review* 43 (2016), pp. 219–42.

Novikov, V.N. 'Shefstvo Berii', in A. Antonov-Ovseenko et al. (eds), *Beriia. Konets kar'ery* (Moscow: Politizdat, 1991), pp. 237–55.

'O razvertyvanii partizanskogo dvizheniia. Telegramma sekretaria TsK KP (b) Belorussii, chlena Voennogo Soveta Zapadnogo fronta P.K. Ponomarenko I.V. Stalinu, 2 iiulia 1941', *Izvestiia TsK KPSS* 7 (1990), pp. 158–202.

Orlov, V. 'Prokofiev and the Myth of the Father of Nations: The Cantata *Zdravitsa*', *Journal of Musicology* 30:4 (autumn 2013), pp. 577–620.

Ostashko, T.H. 'Vlast' i intelligentsia. Dinamik vzaimootnoshenii na rubezhe 1920–1930-kh godov', *Otechestvennaia istoriia* 2 (1998), pp. 19–24.

'Partorg rotu N.L. Sheshenina I.V. Stalinu, ne pozdnee 22 avgusta, 1941'. *Izvestiia TsK KPSS* 9 (1990), pp. 193–215; pp. 204–6.

Pechatnov, V. 'Exercise in Frustration: Soviet Foreign Propaganda in the Early Cold War 1945–1947', *Cold War History* 1:2 (January 2001), pp. 1–27.

Petrov, N. and A. Roginsky. 'The "Polish Operation" of the NKVD, 1937–8', in B. McLoughlin and K. McDermott (eds), *Stalin's Terror: High Politics and Mass Repression in the Soviet Union* (New York: Palgrave Macmillan, 2003), pp. 153–72.

Petrov, I.I. 'Iz istorii partiinogo rukovodstva pogranichnymi voiskami (1941–1944 gg.)', *Voprosy istorii KPSS* 1 (January 1985), pp. 35–49.

Plokhy, S. 'The Call of Blood: Government Propaganda and Public Response to the Soviet Entry into World War II', *Cahiers du monde russe*, 53:2/3 (2012), pp. 293–319.

— 'When Stalin Lost His Head: World War II and Memory Wars in Contemporary Ukraine', in J. Fedor et al. (eds), *War and Memory in Russia, Ukraine and Belarus* (Cham: Palgrave Macmillan, 2017), pp. 171–88.

Polova, Z. 'Collaboration and Resistance in Western Ukraine (1941–1947)', doctoral thesis, Central European University, 2006.

Pons, S. 'Stalin, Togliatti, and the Origins of the Cold War in Europe', *Journal of Cold War Studies* 3:2 (spring 2001), pp. 3–27.

'Protokol no. 3, zasedaniia Komissii Politbiuro, TsK KPSS. "O tak nazyvaemom leningrad-skom dele"', *Izvestiia TsK KPSS* 2 (1989), pp. 124–37.

Putin, V. 'The Real Lessons of the 75th Anniversary of World War II', *The National Interest*, 18 June 2020; online at https://nationalinterest.org/feature/vladimir-putin-real-lessons-75th-anniversary-world-war-ii-162982 (accessed 25 November 2021).

Razin, E. 'Lenin o sushchnosti voiny', *Bol'shevik* 1 (January 1943), pp. 46–54.

Redlich, S. 'The Jewish Antifascist Committee in the Soviet Union', *Jewish Social Studies* 31:1 (January 1969), pp. 25–36.

— 'Jews in General Anders' Army in the Soviet Union, 1941–42', *Soviet Jewish Affairs* 1:2 (1971), pp. 90–8.

Rees, K.M. 'Recasting the Nation: Transforming the Heroes of the Soviet Union into Symbols of Kazakhstani Patriotism', *Nationalities Papers* 39:4 (2020), pp. 445–62.

Reese, R.R. 'The Red Army and the Great Purges', in J.A. Getty and R.T. Manning (eds), *Stalinist Terror: New Perspectives* (New York: Cambridge University Press, 1993), pp. 198–214.

— 'The Russian Orthodox Church and "Patriotic" Support for the Stalinist Regime during the Great Patriotic War', *War and Society* 35:2 (May 2014), pp. 131–53.

Rieber, A.J. 'Persistent Factors in Russian Foreign Policy: An Interpretive Essay', in H. Ragsdale (ed.), *Imperial Russian Foreign Policy* (Cambridge and Washington, DC: Cambridge University Press and Woodrow Wilson Center, 1993), pp. 315–59.

— 'Zhdanov in Finland', *Carl Beck Papers in Russian and East European Studies* 1,107 (February 1995).

— 'Stalin: Man of the Borderlands', *American Historical Review* 5 (December 2001), pp. 1,683–96.

— 'Civil Wars in the Soviet Union', *Kritika* 4:1 (2003), pp. 129–60.

— 'The Crack in the Plaster: Crisis in Romania and the Origins of the Cold War', *Journal of Modern History* 76 (March 2004), pp. 62–106.

— 'Stalin as Foreign Policy Maker: Avoiding War, 1927–1953', in S. Davies and J.R. Harris (eds), *Stalin: A New History* (Cambridge: Cambridge University Press, 2005), pp. 140–59.

— 'Popular Democracy: An Illusion?', in V. Tismaneanu (ed.), *Stalinism Revisited: The Establishment of Communist Regimes in East-Central Europe* (Budapest: Central European University Press, 2008), pp. 103–30.

— 'Nationalizing Imperial Armies: A Comparative and Transnational Study of Three Empires', in S. Berger and A. Miller (eds), *Nationalizing Empires* (Budapest: Central European University Press, 2015), pp. 595–605.

Rigby, T.H. 'Early Provincial Cliques and the Rise of Stalin', *Soviet Studies* 33:1 (January 1981), pp. 3–28.

Roberts, G. 'Litvinov's Lost Peace, 1941–1946', *Journal of Cold War Studies* 4:2 (spring 2002), pp. 23–54.

Roman'ko, O.V. 'Krymsko-Tatarskie formirovaniia. Dokumenty tret'ego reikha svidetel'svuiut', *VIZh* 3 (1991), pp. 89–95.

Romano, A. 'Permanent War Scare: Mobilization, Militarization and Peasant War', in S. Pons and A. Romano (eds), *Russia in the Age of Wars, 1914–1945* (Milan: Feltrinelli, 2000), pp. 103–20.

Rosefielde, S. 'Documented Homicides and Excess Deaths: New Insights into the Scale of Killing in the USSR during the 1930s', *Communist and Postcommunist Studies* 30:3 (September 1997), pp. 321–31.

Samuelson, L. 'Mikhail Tukhachevsky and War-Economic Planning: Reconsiderations on the Pre-War Soviet Military Build-up', *Journal of Slavic Military Studies* 9:4 (1996), pp. 804–47.

— 'Wartime Perspectives and Economic Planning: Tukhachevsky and the Military Industrial Complex', in S. Pons and A. Romano (eds), *Russia in the Age of Wars, 1914–1945* (Milan: Feltrinelli, 2000), pp. 187–214.

Sapir, J. 'The Economics of War in the Soviet Union During World War II', in I. Kershaw and M. Lewin (eds), *Stalinism and Nazism: Dictatorships in Comparison* (Cambridge: Cambridge University Press, 1997), pp. 208–36.

Sartorti, R. 'On the Making of Heroes, Heroines and Saints', in R. Stites (ed.), *Culture and Entertainment in Wartime Russia* (Bloomington, IN: Indiana University Press, 1995), pp. 176–93.

Schechter, B. '"The People's Instructions": Indigenizing the Great Patriotic War among "Non-Russians"', *Ab Imperio* 3 (2012), pp. 109–33.

Seniavskaia, E.S. 'Dukhovnyi oblik frontovogo pokoleniia. Istoriko-psikhologicheskii ocherk', *Vestnik Moskovskogo universiteta* 8:4 (1992), pp. 39–51.

Shapoval, Iu. 'The Ukrainian Years, 1894–1949', in W. Taubman et al. (eds), *Nikita Khrushchev* (New Haven, CT: Yale University Press, 2000), pp. 8–43.

Sharp, T. 'The Russian Annexation of the Koenigsberg Area, 1941–45', *Survey* 23:4 (1977), pp. 156–62.

Shaw, C.D. 'Making Ivan-Uzbek: War, Friendship of the Peoples, and the Creation of Soviet Uzbekistan, 1941–1945', doctoral thesis, University of California, Berkeley, 2015.

Shaw, D.J.B. and J.D. Oldfield. 'Soviet Geographers and the Great Patriotic War, 1941–1945', in L. Berg and A. Grigorev', *Journal of Historical Geography* 47 (January 2015), pp. 40–9.

Shkarovsky, M.V. 'Russkaia pravoslavnaia tserkov' v 1943–1957 godakh', *Voprosy istorii* 8 (1995), pp. 36–56.

Shlapentokh, V. and V. Bondartsova. 'Stalin in Russian Ideology and Public Opinion: Caught in a Conflict between Imperial and Liberal Elements', *Russian History* 36:2 (2009), pp. 302–25.

Shneer, D. 'Soviet Jewish Photographers Confront World War II and the Holocaust', in V.A. Kivelson and J. Neuberger (eds), *Picturing Russia: Explorations in Visual Culture* (New Haven, CT: Yale University Press, 2008), pp. 207–213.

Shtein, Z. 'Sud'ba diplomata. Shtrikhi k portretu Borisa Shteina', in N.V. Popov (comp.), *Arkhivy raskryvaiut tainy ... Mezhdunarodnye voprosy. Sobytiia i liudi* (Moscow: Gospolitizdat, 1991), pp. 286–306.

Shteppa, K.F. 'The "Lesser Evil" Formula', in C.E. Black (ed.), *Rewriting Russian History*, 2nd edn (New York: Vintage Books, 1962), pp. 107–19.

Siegelbaum, L.H. 'The "Flood" of 1945: Regimes and Repertoires of Migration in the Soviet Union at the War's End', *Social History* 42:1 (2017), pp. 52–72.

Simonov, N.S. '"Strengthen the Defence of the Land of the Soviets": The 1927 "War Alarm" and Its Consequences', *Europe-Asia Studies* 48:8 (1996), pp. 355–64.

Sobolev, D.A. 'Istoriia Samoletov 1919–1945', *Repressii v Sovetskoi aviapromyshlennosti* (Moscow: ROSSPEN, 1997).

Sokolov, B.V. 'Sootnoshenii poter' v liudakh i boevoi tekhnike na sovetsko-germanskom fronte v khode Velikoi Otechestvennoi voiny', *Voprosy istorii* 9 (1988), pp. 116–26.

Sokolov, V.V. 'Na postu zamestitelia Narkoma inostrannykh del SSSR (O zhizni i deiatel'nosti B.S. Stomoniakova)', *Novaia i noveishaia istoriia* 5 (1988), pp. 111–26.

— 'Posol SSSR F.T. Gusev v Londone v 1943–1947 godakh', *Novaia i noveishaia istoriia* 4 (2005), pp. 102–28.

Sontag, J.P. 'The Soviet War Scare of 1926–27', *Russian Review* 34:1 (January 1975), pp. 66–77.

Sosnovy, T. 'The Soviet Military Budget', *Foreign Affairs* 42:3 (April 1964), pp. 487–94.

Starinov, I.G. 'Podrivniki na kommunikatsiia agressora', *Voprosy istorii* 2 (1988), pp. 100–12.

Stefanovsky, G.A. 'Politicheskie organy armii i flota', *Voprosy istorii KPSS* 6 (1989), pp. 18–32.

Stehle, H.J. 'Sheptyts'kyi and the German Regime', in P.R. Magocsi (ed.), *Morality and Reality: The Life and Times of Andrei Sheptyts'kyi* (Edmonton: Canadian Institute of Ukrainian Studies, 1989), pp. 125–44.

Stepanov, R.A. 'Nel'zia igrat' tsiframi', *VIZh* 6 (1989), pp. 38–42.

Suvenirov, O.F. 'V searmeiskaia tragediia', *VIZh* 3 (1989), pp. 39–48.

— 'Represii v partorganizatsii RKKA v 1937–1938 gg', *Voprosy istorii KPSS* 6 (1990), pp. 37–49.

Swain, G. 'The Comintern and Southern Europe, 1938–43', in T. Judt (ed.), *Resistance and Revolution in Mediterranean Europe, 1939–1948* (London: Routledge, 1989), pp. 34–41.

Taborsky, E. 'Beneš and Stalin: Moscow, 1943 and 1945', *Journal of Central European Affairs* 13 (1953), pp. 154–81.

Tarle, E.V. 'Tevtonskie rytsari i ikh "nasledniki"', *Vestnik AN SSSR* 5–6 (1942), pp. 38–48.

Tayler, L. 'Le Parti Communiste Français and the French Resistance in the Second World War', in T. Judt (ed.), *Resistance and Revolution in Mediterranean Europe, 1939–1948* (London: Routledge, 1989), pp. 53–70.

Tazva, K. 'Poet-borets', in Tashliev, S. (ed.), *Ob estonskoi literature. Sbornik literaturno-kriticheskikh stat'ei* (Tallinn: Estonskoe gosudarstvennoe izd., 1956).

Thurston, R. 'The Stakhanovite Movement: The Background to the Great Terror in the Factories, 1935–1938', in J.A. Getty and R.T. Manning (eds), *Stalinist Terror: New Perspectives* (Cambridge: Cambridge University Press, 1993), pp. 142–62.

Toman, T.B. 'Partiia v pervye mesiatsy voiny', *Voprosy istorii KPSS* 7 (July 1991), pp. 36–49.

Tomoff, K. 'Uzbek Music's Separate Path: Interpreting "Anticosmopolitanism" in Stalinist Central Asia, 1949–52', *Russian Review* 63:2 (April 2004), pp. 212–40.

Trapāns, A. 'The Latvian Communist Party and the Purge of 1937', *Journal of Baltic Studies* 11:1 (1980), pp. 25–38.

Tromly, B. 'The Leningrad Affair and Soviet Patronage Politics, 1949–1950', *Europe-Asia Studies* 56:5 (July 2004), pp. 707–29.

Tucker R. 'On Revolutionary Mass-Movement Regimes', in Tucker, *The Soviet Political Mind: Studies in Stalinism and Post-Stalinist Change*, rev. edn (New York: Norton, 1972), pp. 3–19.

Uldricks, T.J. 'The Icebreaker Controversy: Did Stalin Plan to Attack Hitler?', *Slavic Review* 58:3 (autumn 1999), pp. 626–43.

Vasil'eva, O.Iu. 'Russkaia pravoslavnaia tserkov', 1927–1943', *Voprosy istorii* 4 (1994), pp. 35–46.

'Velikaia druzhba narodov SSSR', *Bol'shevik* 13 (13 July 1938), pp. 1–7.

Vinogradov, I. 'Zhizn' i smert' sovetskogo poniatiia "druzhba narodov"', *Cahiers du monde russe* 36:4 (December 1995), pp. 455–62.

Vlasov, I. 'O sovetskom patriotizme', *Propagandist i agitator Krasnoi armii* 5 (March 1945), pp. 14–20.

Volin, B. 'Velikii russkii narod', *Bol'shevik* 9 (1 May 1938), pp. 26–36.

Volkov, A.M. 'Kolkhoznoe krest'ianstvo SSSR v pervye poslevoennyi gody', *Voprosy istorii* 6 (1970), pp. 3–19.

Von Geldern, J. 'Radio Moscow: The Voice from the Center', in R. Stites (ed.), *Culture and Entertainment in Wartime Russia* (Bloomington, IN: Indiana University Press, 1995), pp. 44–61.

Walters, P. 'The Russian Orthodox Church and the Soviet State', *Annals of the American Academy of Political and Social Science* 483 (January 1986), pp. 135–45.

Weiner, A. 'Introduction: Landscaping the Human Garden', in Weiner, *Landscaping the Human Garden: Twentieth-Century Population Management in a Comparative Framework* (Palo Alto, CA: Stanford University Press, 2003), pp. 1–10.

Wheatcroft, S.G. 'The Soviet Famine of 1946–1947, the Weather and Human Agency in Historical Perspective', *Europe-Asia Studies* 64:6 (2012), pp. 987–1,005.

Wheeler, M. 'Pariahs to Partisans to Power: The Communist Party of Yugoslavia', in T. Judt (ed.), *Resistance and Revolution in Mediterranean Europe, 1939–1948* (London: Routledge, 1989), pp. 119–29.

Whitewood, P. 'Stalin's Purge of the Red Army and the Misperception of Security Threats', in J. Ryan and S. Grant (eds), *Revisioning Stalin and Stalinism: Contradictions and Complexities* (London: Bloomsbury Academic, 2021), pp. 40–50.

Wood, E.A. 'Performing Memory: Vladimir Putin and the Celebration of WWII in Russia', *Soviet and Post-Soviet Review* 38:2 (2011), pp. 172–200.

Yaresh, L. 'The Campaign of 1812', in C.E. Black (ed.), *Rewriting Russian History*, 2nd edn (New York: Vintage Books, 1962), pp. 268–75.

Yekelchyk, S. 'Stalinist Patriotism as Imperial Discourse: Reconciling the Ukrainian and Russian "Heroic Pasts", 1941–1945', *Kritika* 3:1 (2002), pp. 51–80.

Youngblood, D.J. 'A War Remembered: Soviet Films of the Great Patriotic War', *American Historical Review* 106:3 (June 2001), pp. 839–56.

'Za pravil'noe osveshchenie istorii kompartii Latvii', *Kommunist* 12 (1964), pp. 65–9.

Zezina, M. 'Crisis in the Union of Soviet Writers in the early 1950s', *Europe-Asia Studies* 46:4 (1996), pp. 649–61.

Zhukov, Iu.N. 'Bor'ba za vlast' v rukovodstve SSSR v 1945–1952 godakh', *Voprosy istorii* 1 (1995), pp. 23–39 and 2 (1995), 1–8.

INDEX